The Northern Ireland Troubles in Britain

Manchester University Press

The Northern Ireland Troubles in Britain

Impacts, engagements, legacies and memories

Edited by Graham Dawson, Jo Dover and Stephen Hopkins

Manchester University Press

Published by Manchester University Press
Altrincham Street, Manchester M1 7JA

www.manchesteruniversitypress.co.uk

British Library Cataloguing-in-Publication Data
A catalogue record for this book is available from the British Library

Library of Congress Cataloging-in-Publication Data applied for

ISBN 978 07190 9631 0 hardback
ISBN 978 07190 9632 7 paperback

First published 2017

Typeset in Sabon and Gill Sans by
Servis Filmsetting Ltd, Stockport, Cheshire
Printed in Great Britain by
Bell & Bain Ltd, Glasgow

Contents

Figures

Tables

Contributors

Notes on contributors

L. J. Armstrong is a postdoctoral researcher in the department of Design History and Theory at the University of Applied Arts, Vienna. She previously worked at the University of Brighton, where she taught on the BA Humanities programme, and as a researcher at the Victoria and Albert Museum and the Glasgow School of Art. She completed an AHRC funded PhD in 2013 at the University of Brighton and BA History (First Class) and MA Cultural History (Distinction) at the University of Manchester, where she first developed an interest in the subject of memory and commemoration in Ireland. Having grown up in Northern Ireland, she is interested in the live role history plays in contemporary Irish politics.

Ted Aubertin was born in Edinburgh in 1953 and joined the Parachute Regiment in 1971. Ted was invalided out in 1974 after being wounded on the border at Crossmaglen, Northern Ireland. After leaving the Army Ted went on to work in social work. Ted took early retirement and went to Combat Stress for treatment for post traumatic stress disorder (PTSD). Ted got involved with the Foundation for Peace in Warrington in 2004 and has since participated in dialogue work. Ted has spoken about his experiences at conferences in the UK and Ireland and passes on his experiences of trauma to others who are dealing with their own experiences.

Stephen Baker is a Lecturer in Film and Television Studies at the Ulster University and is the co-author of two books with Greg McLaughlin, *The Propaganda of Peace: The Role of Media and Culture in the*

Northern Ireland Peace Process (Intellect, 2010) and *The British Media and Bloody Sunday* (Intellect, 2015).

Geoffrey Bell was born in Belfast and educated at Magee College Londonderry/Derry, Trinity College Dublin and the University of Leeds. His books include *The Protestants of Ulster* (Pluto, 1976), *Troublesome Business, the Labour Party and Ireland* (Pluto, 1982), *The British in Ireland* (Pluto, 1984) and *Hesitant Comrades: The Irish Revolution and the British Labour Movement* (Pluto, 2016). He wrote the television documentaries *The Cause of Ireland* (Channel 4, 1983) and *Pack Up the Troubles* (Channel 4, 1991) He curated *Ireland: What Was That About?* (Eastside, Tower Museum, Londonderry/Derry, 2010). In the 1960s he was active in the civil rights movement in Northern Ireland; in the 1970s and 1980s he was active in Britain on Irish issues, which he wrote about in Michael Farrell (ed.), *Twenty Years On* (Brandon, 1988).

Jo Berry has been transforming her wound from losing her father, Sir Anthony Berry, in a terrorist attack, the bombing of the Grand Hotel in Brighton, on 12 October 1984. She has founded a charity, Building Bridges for Peace, which works to understand the roots of violence and to promote conflict prevention and conflict transformation. In 2000 she met Patrick Magee, who was responsible for planting the bomb and they have now shared platforms over one hundred times, speaking to the All-Party Parliamentary Group on Conflict Issues, Basque peace groups, Combatants for Peace, conferences in the Lebanon and Rwanda, and at prisons, schools and universities. Jo has been involved with the Tim Parry Johnathan Ball Foundation for Peace's peace and reconciliation programmes since 2000. She is chair of the International Network for Peace and a Fellow of the Institute for Democracy and Conflict Transformation at the University of Essex.

Annie Bowman is the daughter of Captain Barry Gritten of 321 EOD Unit, Royal Army Ordnance Corps. Her father was killed by a bomb in 1973 in Derry/Londonderry. The impact on Annie and her family has been long lasting. Annie became involved with the Tim Parry Johnathan Ball Foundation for Peace in 2003 and has been involved in leadership, storytelling, dialogue and advocacy work. Annie has participated in dialogue events in the UK, in Ireland and in South Africa, has spoken at a European Conference in Brussels and to Emergency Responders and has also spoken to Israeli and Palestinian families at a conference in Ireland.

Maude Casey was born in Luton to Irish parents and grew up in north London. She attended the University of Sussex, the Université d'Aix-Marseille and Goldsmiths College, University of London. Her novel *Over the Water* (The Women's Press, 1987) was short-listed for the Whitbread Award, the Fawcett Book Prize and the Carnegie Medal. She works in solidarity with those displaced by global war. As a member of the Remaking Picasso's Guernica collective (https://remakingpicassosguernica.wordpress.com/) she is committed to collaborative working practices. Her recent return to writing has led to shortlisting for the Bridport Short Story Prize.

Verity Combe is a Practice as Research PhD student in the department of Film, TV and Theatre at the University of Reading. She uses performance as a tool to identify with such issues as conflict, oppression, gender and empowerment. Her research explores artistry and identity in performance while considering audiences and their culturally formed value systems. In 2010 she completed an MA in Theatre and Performance at Queen Mary, University of London, where she researched the practice of Jo Berry and Patrick Magee and their work together in the wake of the Brighton Bomb. As a teenager she passed the British Army's officer selection process and became a successful recipient of the Army Undergraduate Bursary until waiving it to continue with her postgraduate research.

Graham Dawson is Professor of Historical Cultural Studies and Director of the Centre for Research in Memory, Narrative and Histories at the University of Brighton, England. He is author of *Soldier Heroes: British Adventure, Empire and the Imagining of Masculinities* (Routledge, 1994) and *Making Peace with the Past? Memory, Trauma and the Irish Troubles* (Manchester University Press, 2007), and co-editor of *The Politics of War Memory and Commemoration* (Routledge 2000, 2015), *Trauma and Life Stories* (Routledge, 1999, 2014) and *Contested Spaces: Sites, Representations and Histories of Conflict* (Palgrave Macmillan, 2007).

Paul Dixon is Professor in Politics and International Studies at Kingston University. He has taught at Queens University Belfast and the universities of Luton, Leeds and Ulster. He has published *Northern Ireland: The Politics of War and Peace* (Palgrave, 2nd edition 2008) and, with Eamonn O'Kane, *Northern Ireland since 1969* (Longman, 2011), and edited *The British Approach to Counterinsurgency: Hearts and Minds from Malaya to Afghanistan* (Palgrave, 2012). He has published widely on British policy (*British Journal of Politics and International Studies,*

Irish Political Studies, Contemporary Record), the Northern Ireland Peace Process (*Political Studies, Political Studies Quarterly, Journal of Peace Research, Political Quarterly*), conflict theory (*Nations and Nationalism, Democratization*), counterinsurgency (*Journal of Strategic Studies*) and the militarisation of British politics and society (*Berliner Debatte*).

Jo Dover currently works for a charity supporting the medical welfare needs of the armed forces community. Previously she spent fourteen years working for the Tim Parry Johnathan Ball Foundation for Peace and managed the 'Survivors for Peace' Programme working with people affected by conflict and terrorism, including combatants, and civilians bereaved, injured and witness to acts of terrorism and conflict anywhere in the world. Jo has been a member of various emergency planning inter-agency groups, including a UK government Expert Working Group, and has worked with European and International Networks for Victims of Terrorism, including a European Commission Radicalisation Awareness Network. In 2014, the University of Liverpool made Jo an Honorary Research Associate in the Sociology and Criminology Department in recognition of her work.

Aaron Edwards is a Senior Lecturer in Defence and International Affairs at the Royal Military Academy Sandhurst. His books include *Transforming the Peace Process in Northern Ireland: From Terrorism to Democratic Politics* (Irish Academic Press, 2008; edited with Stephen Bloomer), *A History of the Northern Ireland Labour Party: Democratic Socialism and Sectarianism* (Manchester University Press, 2009; 2011), *The Northern Ireland Conflict* (Oneworld, 2010; with Cillian McGrattan), *The Northern Ireland Troubles: Operation Banner, 1969–2007* (Osprey, 2011), *Defending the Realm? The Politics of Britain's Small Wars since 1945* (Manchester University Press, 2012; 2014) and *Mad Mitch's Tribal Law: Aden and the End of Empire* (Mainstream/Transworld Books, 2014; 2015). His latest book, *UVF: Behind the Mask*, will be published by Merrion Press in 2017.

Nadine Finch is an Honorary Research Fellow at the University of Bristol in the School of Policy Studies. She now works in the field of children's rights at a European Union level. Her publications include *Seeking Asylum Alone in the United Kingdom* (Harvard University Committee on Human Rights Studies, 2006), *Levelling the Playing Field* (UNICEF UK, 2010), *Judicial Implementation of Article 3 of the CRC in Europe* (UNICEF and the Office of the United Nations High Commissioner for

Human Rights Regional Office for Europe, 2012), *Always Migrants: Sometimes Children* (European Commission CONNECT Project, 2014) and *Proposal for a Revised National Referral Mechanism* (Anti-Trafficking Monitoring Group, 2014). Nadine was previously employed at the Greater London Council between 1984 and 1986 and the London Strategic Policy Unit (LSPU) between 1986 and 1987 to research and produce a briefing paper on policing the Irish community in London. Her research also appeared in *Policing London*, an LSPU publication. She subsequently worked as a human rights barrister between 1991 and 2015.

John Hill is Professor of Media at Royal Holloway, University of London. He has written widely on film and television in Britain and Ireland and is the co-author of *Cinema and Ireland* (Croom Helm, 1987) (with Luke Gibbons and Kevin Rockett) and the author of *Cinema and Northern Ireland* (British Film Institute, 2006). He is also the leader of an AHRC-funded research project (2013–16), 'The History of Forgotten Television Drama in the UK', and the editor of the forthcoming *Companion to British and Irish Cinema* (Blackwell).

Stephen Hopkins is Lecturer in Politics in the Department of Politics and International Relations at the University of Leicester. His book, *The Politics of Memoir and the Northern Ireland Conflict*, was published in 2013 by Liverpool University Press. He is also the author of several recent articles, including, 'The Chronicles of Long Kesh: Irish Republican Memoirs and the Contested Memory of the Hunger Strikes', in *Memory Studies* (Vol. 7, No. 4; 2014), and 'Sinn Féin, the Past and Political Strategy: The Provisional Irish Republican Movement and the Politics of "Reconciliation"' in *Irish Political Studies* (Vol. 30, No. 1; 2015).

K. Neil Jenkings is a Senior Research Associate at the School of Geography, Politics and Sociology, Newcastle University, UK. He has published widely on military identity, memory, memoirs and has investigated the military participation of cadets, reservists and regulars in the British Armed Forces. His research and writing also explores the production of textual and praxeological social action of various kinds, including military experiences and memories and their textual reproduction and consumption.

Lesley Lelourec is a Senior Lecturer and Pro-Vice Chancellor for International Relations at the University of Rennes 2, France. Her research focuses on British attitudes to Ireland, Northern Ireland and the Troubles, and her PhD thesis, entitled 'La perception anglaise de la question d'Irlande: enquête auprès de 39 habitants de Nottingham' (The English perception of the Irish Question: a study of 39 Nottingham residents) was completed in 2006. Her recent publications include 'Promoting mutual understanding and/or enriching the curriculum? The contribution of the Ireland in Schools forum to bringing Ireland into the English classroom' (*Irish Studies in Europe*, Vol. 4) and she has co-edited (with Grainne O'Keeffe-Vigneron) *Ireland and Victims: Confronting the Past, Forging the Future*, in the Re-imagining Ireland series (Peter Lang, 2012).

Greg McLaughlin is a Senior Lecturer in Media Studies at Ulster University. He is the author of *The War Correspondent* (Pluto, 2nd edition forthcoming) and has co-authored two books with Stephen Baker, *The Propaganda of Peace: The Role of Media and Culture in the Northern Ireland Peace Process* (Intellect, 2010) and *The British Media and Bloody Sunday* (Intellect, 2015).

Jenny McMahon joined the Women's Royal Army Corps (WRAC) in 1968 as a physical training instructor. In 1974 Jenny was injured in the M62 coach bomb; she sustained lower limb injuries and went on to develop PTSD. Following a year recovering from her physical injuries, Jenny continued to serve in the WRAC for a further twenty-two years. The last two years of her military service were spent as a physiotherapist at the Queen Elizabeth military hospital in Woolwich where she treated many other military personnel injured in the Troubles in Northern Ireland and England. She then worked at the MoD's Physiotherapy Department at Headley Court before retiring. She became involved with the Tim Parry Johnathan Ball Foundation for Peace in 2009 following her attendance at a memorial service for victims of the M62 coach bomb, thirty-five years after the event.

Tony Murray is Director of the Irish Studies Centre at London Metropolitan University. He is curator of the Archive of the Irish in Britain, comprising documents, audio and video recordings, books, photographs and ephemera cataloguing the history of the Irish in Britain from the late nineteenth century to the present. He curated the exhibition *When Did You Come Over? The History of the Irish in Britain* (2000) and co-produced a documentary film about elderly Irish people in London, *I Only Came Over for a Couple of Years …* (2005). He runs the annual Irish Writers in London Summer School and Irish in Britain

Seminar Series and researches literary and cultural representations of the Irish diaspora. His book, *London Irish Fictions: Narrative, Diaspora and Identity*, was published by Liverpool University Press in 2014.

John Newsinger is Professor of Modern History at Bath Spa University. He is the author of a number of books, including *Fenianism in Mid-Victorian Britain* (Pluto, 1994); *Dangerous Men: The SAS and Popular Culture* (Pluto, 1997); *Rebel City: Larkin, Connolly and the Dublin Labour Movement* (Merlin, 2003); *Orwell's Politics* (Palgrave, 1999); *The Blood Never Dried: A People's History of the British Empire* (Bookmarks, 2006); *Fighting Back: The American Working Class in the 1930s* (Bookmarks, 2012); and *Them and Us: Fighting the Class War 1910–1939* (Bookmarks, 2015). A revised and expanded edition of his book *British Counterinsurgency* was published in 2015.

Susan O'Halloran was born in London and was educated at Oxford and the London School of Economics. She was a further education lecturer, manager and policy advisor until 2009. She is currently researching ancient history at Birkbeck. Susan was active in the 1968 student protest movement, a founder member of the London Women's Liberation Workshop, and from 1975 an active member of Sinn Féin Britain until its absorption into the broader solidarity movement in the mid 1980s. Subsequently Susan contributed to discussion and organisation in Belfast and London as the peace process developed and she continues to engage with Sinn Féin's political agenda and other Irish issues.

Laura O'Reilly was awarded her MA Globalisation: Politics, Conflict and Human Rights in 2016. For her BA dissertation she researched the impact that historical counter-terrorism legislation, introduced following the Irish Republican Army's (IRA) Birmingham pub bombs in 1974, consequently had on the Irish community within the city. Having grown up in Birmingham, and being third-generation Irish, she is also interested in the recollections of her own family and, furthermore, the importance that oral history can play in conflict resolution.

Di Parkin was a community worker and a Left political activist from the late 1960s to the 1980s, when she was a member of Labour Women for Ireland and part of a delegation to Belfast and Armagh. She worked in the women's units of the Greater London and Ealing Councils, and then as a freelance consultant and researcher primarily on equal opportunities. As a writer and historian, she is author of *Sixty Years of Struggle* (Betteshanger Social Welfare Scheme, 2007), a history of the militant

Kent colliery, Betteshanger; and co-author of *100 Fishponds Rd. Life and Death in a Victorian Workhouse* (Tangent Books, 2015). She is now an active member of the Bristol Radical History Group.

Max Pettigrew is an Associate Tutor in the Department of Media and Communication at the University of Leicester. Previously, he has been a lecturer at Bath Spa University, Anglia Ruskin University and Cardiff University, where he was awarded his PhD in the School of Journalism, Media and Cultural Studies. His PhD research analysed a crucial period in Anglo-Irish history when the Northern Ireland conflict was shifting into the Northern Ireland peace process. The central focus concerned the broadcasting ban (1988–94) and how the British newspaper industry represented the British government in introducing and lifting this direct censorship. His research interests include the application of critical approaches to analyses of power, language, history and the mass media as well as newspaper representations of political violence and protest.

Aly Renwick joined the British Army at sixteen years of age in 1960. He purchased his discharge in 1968, after serving for a short time in Northern Ireland. He then helped organise the anti-Vietnam War protests, whose demonstrations he had attended while still a soldier. When British troops were ordered onto the streets of Northern Ireland in 1969, he helped establish the Irish Civil Rights Solidarity Campaign and later the Anti-Internment League. In late 1973 he was a founding member of the Troops Out Movement, becoming one of its national organisers over the next four years. In 1978 he helped found and run Information on Ireland. He has taken part in peace and reconciliation work in Britain and Ireland, has worked with Northern Ireland veterans who are suffering from PTSD and is now a member of Veterans For Peace UK.

Ann Rossiter is an immigrant Irish feminist activist and writer. Before retirement she taught Irish Studies at a number of academic institutions. Her book, *Ireland's Hidden Diaspora: The 'Abortion Trail' and the Making of a London-Irish Underground, 1980–2000* (IASC, 2009), based on her activism in the Irish Women's Abortion Support Group, was published in 2009. She is working on her second book, *Mad, Bad and Dangerous to Know, Reflections on Anglo-Irish Feminist Encounters during the Troubles*, which was also the subject of her doctoral thesis. She is currently a member of the London-based feminist performance art direction action group, Speaking of I.M.E.L.D.A. (Ireland Making England the Legal Destination for Abortion).

Rachel Woodward is Professor of Human Geography at the School of Geography, Politics and Sociology, Newcastle University, UK. Her research and writing explores militarism and its spatial and social consequences. This includes studies of the politics of military land use, the conversion of former military sites, the form and function of gender relations and masculinities within armed forces, military identities and the effects of military experience, and the mediation of personal and public military memories through print media and published autobiographical accounts.

Acknowledgements

The editors thank Lesley Lelourec and Gráinne O'Keeffe-Vigneron from *Le Centre d'Études Irlandaises* (the Irish Studies Centre) at the University of Rennes 2, France, who organised the conference 'Ireland and Victims: Recognition, Reparation, Reconciliation?' in September 2010, where our collaboration began; the University of Brighton for the small grant from the Research Network Fund which enabled us to develop our ideas, and for hosting our conference on 'The Northern Ireland Troubles in Britain: Impacts, Engagements, Legacies and Memories' under the auspices of the Centre for Research in Memory, Narrative and Histories in July 2012; the Tim Parry Johnathan Ball Foundation for Peace at Warrington for its a wealth of input into and support for the conference, and for the involvement in it of several participants from the Foundation's 'Survivors for Peace' programme; the University of Leicester for making possible a number of editorial meetings; and Manchester University Press for believing in the value of our project.

Abbreviations

AIL	Anti-Internment League
BBC	British Broadcasting Corporation
CDU	Campaign for Democracy in Ulster
CRC	Community Relations Council
DUP	Democratic Unionist Party
GFA	Good Friday Agreement
GLC	Greater London Council
GOC	General Officer Commanding
HMP	Her Majesty's Prison
IBRG	Irish in Britain Representation Group
ICRSC	Irish Civil Rights Solidarity Campaign
IED	improvised explosive device
IRA	Irish Republican Army
ITV	Independent Television
LCI	Labour Committee on Ireland
LIWC	London Irish Women's Centre
LP	Labour Party
LSPU	London Strategic Policy Unit
LWI	Labour Women for Ireland
MP	Member of Parliament
NCO	non-commissioned officer
NMA	National Memorial Arboretum
NUJ	National Union of Journalists
OP	observation post
PIRA	Provisional Irish Republican Army
PSNI	Police Service of Northern Ireland
PTA	Prevention of Terrorism Act
PTSD	post-traumatic stress disorder

RTÉ	Raidió Telefís Éireann
RUC	Royal Ulster Constabulary
RUC GC	Royal Ulster Constabulary (George Cross)
SF	Sinn Féin
TNA	The National Archives
TOM	Troops Out Movement
UDR	Ulster Defence Regiment
USC	Ulster Special Constabulary
USCA	Ulster Special Constabulary Association
UUP	Ulster Unionist Party
UWC	Ulster Workers' Council
WLM	Women's Liberation Movement

Introduction: The Northern Ireland Troubles in Britain: impacts, engagements, legacies and memories

Graham Dawson and Stephen Hopkins

This book addresses a paradox: that the Northern Ireland conflict, commonly known as 'the Troubles', has had profound and shaping impacts upon politics, culture and the lives of many thousands of people in Great Britain, producing lasting legacies that continue to resonate nearly half a century after the eruption of political violence in 1968–69; but that engagements with the conflict, and with its 'post-conflict' transformation, from within Britain have been limited, lacking, frequently problematic, often troubled, in ways that are not fully grasped or considered.

Some impacts of the conflict 'in and about Northern Ireland'[1] upon Britain may be signalled by some stark figures. The military deployment of British armed forces, known officially as Operation Banner, lasted thirty-eight years, from 14 August 1969 to 31 July 2007. One of the British Army's most senior officers during that period, General Sir Mike Jackson, has described it as 'one of the most important campaigns ever fought by the British Army and its fellow Services ... the longest to date [and] one of the very few waged on British soil'.[2] Over 250,000 Regular Army soldiers served in Northern Ireland during the campaign, with a peak deployment of 28,000 at the peak of the campaign during the summer of 1972.[3] A total of 1,441 members of the UK's armed forces died 'as a result of operations in Northern Ireland [NI] or ... Irish Terrorism ... outside of NI', of whom 874 were members of the Regular Army and other services (excluding regiments recruited from Northern Ireland); of these, 507 died due to 'Terrorist action' and 367 from other causes.[4] A further 6,307 military personnel were injured.[5] The British Army was responsible for killing 301 people during the conflict, of whom 158 were civilians, all but twenty of them Irish Catholics, and 104 were members of the Provisional Irish Republican Army (PIRA).[6] Between 1973 and 1997, the PIRA's bombing campaign in England resulted in over 500 recorded incidents in which 115 people were killed and 2,134 people were injured – often seriously – many of whom were civilians.[7] In total, nearly 17 per cent of all those who died in the conflict were from Great Britain, and 'many more have been affected including relatives, friends and colleagues of the dead and injured, witnesses of incidents, those who have been psychologically affected, and members of the emergency services'.[8] Further human costs of the conflict can be discerned in figures relating to the Prevention of Terrorism Acts (1974, 1978), which gave the British police emergency powers of arrest, detention and exclusion under which more than 55,000 people had been interviewed by the mid 1980s and 6,932 people were detained between 1974 and 1990.[9]

There has been relatively little systematic research to date addressing these impacts, or exploring the complex legacies and memories of the Northern Ireland Troubles in Great Britain. Initiatives in Britain to engage with them in the context of the Irish peace process have been piecemeal and fragmented. Whilst there is a widely expressed sense of relief that the violent conflict appears largely over, nonetheless, for both the political elites and the wider public, Northern Ireland, in both its historical and contemporary settings, remains viewed as 'a place apart', with a lack of salience for British politics, society and the wider culture more generally.[10] Indeed, according to Catterall and MacDougall, there has been 'considerable uncertainty in [British] electors' minds as to whether Northern Ireland was actually part of the United Kingdom'.[11]

This should not be viewed as altogether surprising, given that both during the Troubles and prior to them during the Stormont era of devolved government, British attitudes often reflected embarrassment, indifference and a deep-rooted desire to keep Northern Ireland at arm's length, to 'quarantine' the problems associated with the conflict (see the chapters by Dixon (3) and Hopkins (4) in this volume). Indeed, from 1921 until 1972, Northern Ireland was governed with minimal engagement from Westminster; as Bloomfield has argued, 'perversely, the United Kingdom Government was arguably less well-informed about developments in this patch of its own territory than it was about the more remote dominions and even many foreign countries'.[12] Northern Ireland was understood by many as 'an intrusion' in British politics, 'despite continued efforts on the part of successive Governments to keep it off the agenda'.[13] In keeping with the political elite, there is only patchy evidence that British public opinion was any more likely to engage with the problems of Northern Ireland and there has been little sign of willingness to undertake a process of critical self-reflection regarding the role of the British State (and its armed services) in the conflict (see the chapters by Newsinger (1) and Bell (5)).

This has been in sharp contrast to the position in Northern Ireland itself, where efforts to discuss the contested past have been a regular, and fundamental, aspect of the contemporary political discourse since the start of the peace process in 1993–94 and the Good Friday/Belfast Agreement of 1998. This has occurred in terms of UK government-sponsored endeavours, such as the Eames/Bradley Consultative Group on the Past (2009), or the Haass/O'Sullivan negotiations (2013). However, it has also been a significant part of civil society's engagement in shaping the historical narratives of the conflict. These wide-ranging debates and initiatives have encompassed collective memories, life-storytelling, commemorative practices, theatre and performance, oral history projects and myriad others. With respect to Northern Ireland itself, academic treatments of the social, political, cultural and psychological legacies of conflict have also proliferated in this period.[14] The state-sponsored attempts at 'dealing with the past' have tended to become highly politicised and partisan encounters, despite the best efforts to ensure that consultation is meaningful and broadly conceived. Despite the tentative, and thus far unimplemented, agreement signed at Stormont House in 2014, there is no settled consensus regarding how best to take this work forward in a spirit of post-conflict peace building.

Arguably, one of the reasons for this has been the tendency for the UK State implicitly or explicitly to deny its role and activities as a protagonist in the conflict. Consequently its status and function throughout has been characterised by ambiguity. Should it be interpreted as essentially an 'insider', the sovereign power in the territory, fighting a determined insurrection by 'terrorists'? Or was it instead really an 'outsider', keeping the peace between two antagonistic national-religious-ethnic communities, trying to act as a 'neutral arbiter' and 'honest broker', encouraging the 'moderate silent majority' who, it was hoped, would be willing to share power under a renewed devolved administration in Belfast? This ambivalence has suited the purposes of Westminster policy makers (from both major parties), who could portray their Northern Ireland policies in terms that represented a careful balancing act. However, it may be argued that this uncertainty has ultimately been damaging for British popular understanding of the conflict and, specifically, of the role in it of the British State. It has also led to confusion and disagreement within popular understandings in Great Britain regarding the nature of the 'peace process' in Northern Ireland. Has this involved an appeasement of terrorism, with Irish republicans now enjoying genuine power in the devolved government in Belfast? Does it represent a clear victory for the State, given that Northern Ireland remains part of the UK and the insurgency has been contained, or even defeated? Or might it represent a resolution of historical enmities, enabling a lasting reconciliation 'between the peoples of both islands', as envisaged in the Downing Street Declaration of 1993 (and perhaps symbolised by the Queen's handshake with the Deputy First Minister in the Northern Ireland Executive, former PIRA leader Martin McGuinness, in 2012)?[15]

Some civil society initiatives in Britain have engaged constructively with the legacies of the conflict and made some headway in terms of personal healing and reconciliation (see, for example, Lelourec's chapter 18 analysing the aftermath of the Warrington bomb of 1993). Arguably, however, they have done so despite the ambiguity and neglect at the heart of the British State's response, and at least in part because they have been able to circumnavigate the central problem of its political responsibility and accountability. It might be said that the conflict was 'intellectually interned' in Britain, with few among the political elite or the mass of the British public deciding to engage with either the historical context or the lived experience of the violent conflict.

For victims/survivors caught up in the violence, as well as the tens of thousands of British service personnel with direct experience of the conflict, this luxury of indifference was simply not available as an option (see the testimonies of Aubertin (chapter 2), McMahon (chapter 6), Bowman (chapter 19) and Berry (chapter 23) in this volume). For political activists motivated to intervene in the conflict, it was also true that Northern Ireland became a significant cause in British political life (see the chapters by Renwick (8), O'Halloran (9), Rossiter (11) and Parkin (12)); though this was always a minority view.

However, in the representation of Northern Ireland as an incomprehensible place (what Mary Hickman terms the 'othering' of Ireland[16]), official discourses arguably helped to promote a 'turning away' from the problem in the British population at large. Ex-Prime Minister Edward Heath lamented in 1985: 'I confess I have always found the Irish, all of them, extremely difficult to understand.'[17] On the Labour side, similar views were expressed by ex-Prime Minister Harold Wilson: 'any politician who wants to be involved with Ulster needs their head examining'.[18] This was aided by mainstream media reporting (see Baker and McLaughlin (chapter 13), Pettigrew (chapter 16)) which tended to replicate the lack of deep-seated engagement (with some honourable exceptions such as Peter Taylor's consistently ground-breaking documentaries), or actively reproduced anti-Irish racism (Finch (chapter 10), Casey (chapter 15)). Consistent opinion polls showing a majority in favour of British withdrawal are open to conflicting interpretations (see Bell (chapter 5), Dixon (chapter 3), Renwick (chapter 8)) and did not necessarily represent a principled anti-colonial or anti-imperialist political stance, but also reflected sentiments of indifference, embarrassment and unease at the ongoing violence.

By contrast, in the post-Agreement era there has been a mixture of relief that the conflict appears to be 'over', and also impatience with any groups in Northern Ireland who might be accused of 'dragging politics back into the past'. There are even some British politicians and officials from the New Labour era who have argued that the Northern Ireland peace process is a 'model for export'.[19] Although the Blair administration did prioritise policy towards Northern Ireland in a fashion that was not true for many of its predecessors, and has not been the case for its successors, nonetheless this has been accompanied by a misplaced confidence, even hubris. The peace process has sometimes been portrayed as a totemic and unique achievement, an incontrovertible example of a successful understanding of how to defuse an insurgency, or handle terrorist challenges. This simplistic approach has not been supported by very much genuine engagement with the ongoing legacies of the conflict, nor the continuing elements of instability and sectarianism that still characterise political relations in Northern Ireland. 'Bringing in the extremes' or 'talking to terrorists'[20] has become a mantra in British rhetoric, but it masks a vacuum in serious efforts to reflect critically upon the UK State's role in the conflict.

Switzer and Graham identify a type of 'memorial agnosticism' on behalf of the UK State.[21] This is not simply about a cultural and political amnesia with regard to the history of the British State's coercion and neglect in Northern Ireland (the Saville Inquiry into 'Bloody Sunday' and the apology of the Prime Minister David Cameron in its wake, suggest that there is some belated willingness to face up to the realities of at least some specific, and egregious, instances of British Army malfeasance). It is also about a range of unresolved (and sometimes unaddressed) issues that open up important questions concerning the wider relationship between the British people and their own State (and its understanding of its imperial history; see the chapters by Newsinger (1) and Armstrong (22)). This is one reason why the silences (and, latterly, some of the noise) that characterise British attitudes towards the legacies of conflict are of wider import. The present volume hopes to stimulate, through the prism of Northern Ireland, debate regarding the wider character of this relationship.

Central to any critical consideration of this matter must be the ideological strategies of the British State, deployed in what the then Prime Minister Edward Heath in 1972 famously referred to as the 'propaganda war',[22] to construct common sense understandings of the conflict and its history, to render the coercive and frequently illegal violence of British armed forces in Ireland effectively invisible within British popular narratives and to marginalise or discredit oppositional voices in Britain. Ideologically, the conflict was framed within official discourse as a problem exclusively of Irish violence. This was constructed either as inter-ethnic conflict between the 'two tribes' which required intervention by the peace-making British 'honest broker', or more insistently as irrational republican 'terrorism' by criminals which required the reassertion of law and order through police work and criminal justice supported by the military. This framing exerted hegemonic pressure on the ways in which the conflict could be talked about, represented and understood with legitimacy (whilst simultaneously reasserting the State as sole arbiter of the distinction between legitimate and illegitimate violence).

The efficacy of such framing stems partly from the deep historical roots of British popular memory, in which the deployment of Britain's armed forces is represented (as Baker and McLaughlin (chapter 13) argue in this volume), in the terms of a 'national narrative' and its versions of Britishness, as essentially benign, just and measured in response to threats by various kinds of evil-doers to British national interests, national security and 'our way of life'.[23] For many people in Britain, constructions of this kind made meaningful and affective sense in a context where bomb and gun attacks by the PIRA introduced violent death, fear and multiple disruptions to socio-economic activity and everyday life into the towns and cities of England from 1973 to 1997. The national consensus shaped by this hegemonic narrative was structured by a set of simple binary equivalences – British/Irish, benign/evil, law and order/ terrorism – that polarised the field of public discourse and debate, instituted demands for conformity and 'loyalty' and raised the risks of dissidence by demonising alternative voices and perspectives (see Hill's chapter 17).

While this kind of discursive construction is familiar in more recent times from President George W. Bush's so-called 'war on terror' following the 9/11 attacks on the USA, it has a longer genealogy in British (and 'Western') counter-insurgency strategies deployed in response to anti-colonial and anti-imperialist struggles of the twentieth century (including the Irish War of Independence 1919–21).[24] Continuities in personnel as well as in strategies and techniques link the British Army in 'Ulster' to its post-1945 campaigns in Malaya, Cyprus, Kenya and Aden (as Renwick (chapter 8) and Finch (chapter 10) argue in this volume). However, these continuities tended to be obscured in the British State's ideological management of its withdrawal from Empire, largely completed by 1970, which was the year when the Army's relations with Northern nationalists broke down in rioting, the Falls Road curfew and the first armed exchanges with both branches of the IRA. Whilst British popular imperialism began to wane during the 1960s, anti-imperialism – or even its less forthright meshing with liberal humanitarian opposition to 'what is being done in our name', of the kind that flourished in the Peace With Ireland Council of 1920[25] – never inspired a sizable popular mobilisation for British withdrawal from the North of Ireland.

The State's management of decolonisation, and its framing of the Northern Ireland conflict as an 'internal' matter and decidedly not an anti-colonial struggle, were further underpinned by systematic practices to hide from public knowledge the routine use of extra-judicial killing, torture and mass-incarceration of civilian populations in 1950s Malaya and Kenya.[26] These have included concealment of the very existence of State archives and documentation, revealed only in 2011 during a successful legal case brought by Kenyan former detainees against the British State, which has established the basis in international human rights legislation for further legal actions concerning crimes committed by British colonial authorities.[27] The investigation of systematic human rights abuses and their concealment by the State in the colonial era is throwing light upon and setting precedents for public scrutiny of these practices in relation to matters of truth and justice in Northern Ireland[28] (and, as Baker and McLaughlin argue in chapter 13, with respect to recent deployments in Afghanistan and Iraq as well).

This hegemonic instituting of a legitimatory national narrative, with its accompanying polarisations, coercions and silences, framed the Northern Ireland conflict in ways that secured broad popular tolerance for British military involvement and wider counter-insurgency measures undertaken by the State. Even so, the Troubles was never a popular war in the sense that, say, the Falklands expedition was, with its popular mobilisations of support and its celebrations of the Task Force and its 'victory', that framed the grieving for its loss of life. In contrast, the conduct of the Irish war, sustained over decades rather than days, generated unease and anxiety, criticism and resistance on an altogether larger scale.[29] In the early years of the deployment, as Paul Dixon argues in this volume (chapter 3) and elsewhere, it held out the prospect that a 'populist movement for withdrawal ... might emerge' in response to the first deaths of soldiers;[30] and as chapters in Part II of the book demonstrate, it met with serious, committed political opposition within Britain throughout the 1970s and 1980s, by the Troops Out Movement, elements within the Labour movement and the socialist Left, and a range of activist groups and campaigns motivated by anti-imperialist and/or feminist politics as well as concerns about human rights abuses. As chapters in Part III of the book make clear, dissenting voices and practices contesting the national narrative and policies of the State also materialised in the cultural sphere as writers (see Murray, chapter 14 and Casey, chapter 15), film-makers (Hill, chapter 17), broadcasters and journalists (Pettigrew, chapter 16) fought to keep open spaces where more nuanced and complex understandings, as well as directly oppositional narratives, could be produced and circulated. In a variety of ways, these counter-narratives were grounded on a defence of principles – justice and fairness, universal and inalienable human rights, democratic pluralism, national self-determination, solidarity with the oppressed – that were considered to be violated or placed in jeopardy as a result of the British State's conduct of the conflict.

While hegemonic discourse stemming from the State has had to shift, if ambivalently, to accommodate the new political landscape of the peace process (as discussed earlier), the wider field of public representations of the conflict in Britain – now a terrain of memory – has to a significant extent remained frozen in the polarised, antagonistic forms of wartime. This reproduction of conflict-era narratives, stances and emotions into the time after, commonly referred to as 'post-conflict' or 'transitional', is a central concern in wider debates about 'conflict resolution', 'peace building' and 'conflict transformation'.[31] Far from being over and done with – as many people in Britain think of the Irish Troubles since the 1998 Agreement and the destruction of PIRA's arsenal in 2005 – 'the past' continues to make its presence felt long afterwards, influencing and 'living on' into the time of peace. Indeed, the problem of 'the past' constitutes the terrain on which such efforts towards any future-oriented remaking of politics, social relations and cultural worlds damaged by political violence must work. 'Dealing with the past', as this issue has come to be known,[32] requires engagement with the legacies of conflict that take the form of unresolved questions of truth and justice; polarised understandings, feelings and identities of those involved and affected; and the 'memory wars' through which competing claims about the causes of, and responsibilities for, the conflict are expressed, clash and may enter into dialogue.[33]

According to Ashplant, Dawson and Roper, 'The politics of war memory and commemoration is precisely the struggle of different groups to give public articulation to, and hence gain recognition for, certain memories and the narratives within which they are structured.'[34] The history of any particular struggle, they suggest, may be traced through analysis of the relations between 'those memories which are publicly articulated, and … those which have been privatized, fragmented or repressed'.[35]

A key question for 'post-conflict' societies, then, is whether it is possible to create a public culture committed to engaging with the 'present past' in ways that enable the articulation, critical exploration and wider recognition of these privatised memories and silenced experiences. In Northern Ireland, over two decades since the paramilitary ceasefires that launched the peace process, considerable work has gone into building a more democratic, pluralist public culture open to the telling of – and listening to – narratives of the conflict across a diverse range of experiences, promoting historical reflection, dialogue and exchange about the past, and enabling unrecognised effects of the conflict to be acknowledged and addressed.[36] This has been a hugely difficult process, but nonetheless some progress may be discerned.

Great Britain, by contrast, could be described as a post-conflict society that does not recognise itself as such. Public lacunae continue to operate in ways that seal off from wider visibility and understanding the historical and current experiences of those groups and individuals most seriously affected by the Troubles. This volume addresses a number of these experiences, including those of the bereaved families of military personnel who died whilst serving in Northern Ireland – Dixon (chapter 3), Jenkings and Woodward (chapter 7), Bowman (chapter 19), Edwards (chapter 21); Irish communities, families and individuals subjected to anti-terrorist legislation, miscarriages of justice and associated anti-Irish racism – Finch (chapter 10), Murray (chapter 14), Casey (chapter 15), O'Reilly (chapter 20); the civilian victims, survivors and bereaved of IRA attacks in England – Lelourec (chapter 18), Berry (chapter 23), Combe (chapter 24); seriously injured and often traumatised ex-soldiers – Aubertin (chapter 2), McMahon (chapter 6); and republican and other political activists campaigning against British State policies in a hostile and dangerous environment – O'Halloran (chapter 9), Rossiter (chapter 11), Parkin (chapter 12). The conflict also touched many other lives in Britain, in ways that are only beginning to be noticed. For example, the Brighton-based dramatists Julie Everton and Josie Melia, researching the local impact of the IRA's attack on the Conservative Party conference in 1984 for their play, *The Bombing of the Grand Hotel* (2015), elicited dozens of stories existing in an almost entirely privatised sphere of experience, from workers in the emergency services, hotel staff, surgeons at the local hospital, the police, the co-ordinator of the local Irish club and local councillors.[37] Another largely invisible historical experience – and one regrettably reproduced by this volume – is that of Northern Irish Protestant and unionist migrants in Britain during the Troubles, often (mis)recognised as simply 'Irish' in host communities impervious to nuanced distinctions of culture, identity and politics, but with a marginal or problematical relationship to an 'Irish in Britain' community constructing itself as Catholic and nationalist.[38]

Despite – or because of – the tendency of the British State towards silence, amnesia and denial regarding its own role in the conflict and responsibility for the conflict's legacies, some important instances of active engagement with those legacies from grassroots organisations and groupings in Britain have emerged in the context of the peace process. These have very different motivations, as three examples demonstrate. The Tim Parry Johnathan Ball Foundation for Peace, launched in 1995 in response to the Warrington bombing two years earlier (as Lesley Lelourec explores in chapter 18 of this volume), established a permanent Peace Centre as the base for long-term undertakings in peace building. These included, from 2001, its Legacy Project 'to identify and support people in Britain who had been affected by the conflict in and around Northern Ireland' (subsequently widening its scope in the 'Survivors for Peace' programme);[39] research and advocacy that identified and challenged the absence of statutory support for British victims and survivors of the Troubles;[40] and an annual Peace Lecture which on 18 September 2013 brought Martin McGuinness, Sinn Féin's Deputy First Minister in the devolved Northern Ireland Executive, to speak in Warrington. The Foundation for Peace played an important role in the development of this present volume, by supporting the participation of several contributors – Aubertin (chapter 2), McMahon (chapter 6), Bowman (chapter 19) and Berry (chapter 23) – who have benefitted from its work. (Jo Berry's unique, important and sustained dialogue with Patrick Magee is explored in Verity Combe's chapter 24.)

In a contrasting case, *Ireland: What Was That About?* was a small-scale research project and exhibition produced in 2011 by Eastside Community Heritage, a community history organisation in East London. This reveals 'hidden memories and voices ... of two groups of people from Great Britain' – British soldiers and activists from the Troops Out Movement – involved in 'the recent political and military conflict in Northern Ireland', presented as a 'contested history [that] is also an attempt at mutual understanding and post-conflict reconciliation'.[41] The project produced a booklet and a permanent website, and culminated in a two-day event bringing together participants (and a group of East London school students) at the Warrington Peace Centre.

A further contrasting example is that of Justice 4 the 21, a justice campaign organised by families of the twenty-one people who died in the Birmingham pub bombings of 1974 (discussed by Finch, chapter 10, Casey, chapter 15 and O'Reilly, chapter 20 in this volume), for which the Birmingham Six were wrongfully convicted and eventually released on appeal, with no one subsequently held to account. Justice 4 the 21 engages in memorial activities to keep alive the memory of the victims and of the families' loss after more than forty years, but also campaigns for the cases to be reopened and fully investigated. As a result of the campaign, on 1 June 2016 the Birmingham and Solihull Coroner announced her decision to reopen the inquest into the deaths.[42]

Two further general points may be made about the 'post-conflict' unlocking and challenging of hegemonic public representations of the Northern Ireland Troubles in Britain, with their lacunae and silences, and the related opening-out of polarised narratives to more complex, nuanced and diverse (if also often contested) understandings. These observations may suggest productive ways of reading this book.

Firstly, silencing must be recognised as an active process that is repro-duced through modes of complicity and unwillingness to engage with voices that seek to 'break the silence', as well as by discouragement or suppression that deploys hostility, discrimination or intimidation to raise the bar of negative consequences.[43] It manifests in many differ-ent arenas, both private and public. Jo Berry, in her chapter 23 in this volume, recalls not being able to tell people about what had happened to her in losing her father in the Brighton bomb, because of responses that encouraged her to 'let go' of it. Similarly, Annie Bowman in her chapter 19 describes people in Britain physically turning away from her as if from a taboo when she begins to speak about the reasons for her recon-ciliation work in Ireland.

The public voicing of Irish republican perspectives, or views in any way supportive of them, continues to be a risky business in England today. Di Parkin's interviewees for her chapter 12, all Labour Party activ-ists promoting dialogue with Sinn Féin in the 1980s, prefer to remain anonymous in order to conceal their political work in the past from their employers. Anecdotally, these concerns – and counter-measures for what Marie Breen Smyth has termed identity management[44] are widespread, especially among those who have or seek public positions of respon-sibility and accountability. A vivid example of the way political sym-pathy for, or engagement with, Irish republicanism during the conflict continues to provide a basis for hostility and delegitimisation in British public culture can be seen in the attacks on Jeremy Corbyn during his successful campaign for the Labour Party leadership in 2015, and sub-sequently on Corbyn and his Shadow Chancellor, John McDonnell, for their 'links with the IRA' and refusal to single out republican violence for condemnation.[45] More thoughtful critics of Corbyn and McDonnell might point out that 'silencing' could also work in a different way here: they presented their position in 2015 as if, in the 1980s, they had simply been encouraging dialogue and a 'peace process' with Irish republican-ism *avant la lettre*. However, during the early and mid 1980s, Corbyn was unashamedly a supporter of Irish republicanism's right to 'resist' British 'oppression'.

What it takes to open up these histories in the face of such silenc-ings – whether by political activists challenging the dominant national narrative, or victims of violence speaking out about painful emotions, or ex-soldiers speaking out against active service (Aubertin, chapter 2; Renwick, chapter 8), or young people probing their own buried family history (O'Reilly, chapter 20) – should not be under-estimated and needs to be more thoroughly understood. This volume contributes to that understanding.

Secondly, the critique and challenging of dominant narratives of the conflict, and the unlocking of binary oppositions and polarisations, does not necessarily manifest in their renunciation and the produc-tion of entirely new, alternative representations. It also, perhaps more commonly, occurs through a reworking of existing positions to render them more complex, reflective and open to engagement with the posi-tions adopted by others, including opponents. Throughout this volume, writers deploying analysis, or polemic, or testimony, grapple with inher-ited positions and established understandings, revisiting and reassessing them in the light of the hindsight of twenty, thirty, forty or more years. In this sense, 'frozen' narratives, perhaps all too familiar to those who lived through this conflict, may be reproduced and reasserted in the pages of this book; but they do so in relation to memory-work and historical enquiry that interrogates the significance of meanings made in the past for the present moment, inviting a recasting of memory or the generating of new historical questions and interpretations.

Crucially, it is apparent that the various engagements with the histo-ries and memories of the Northern Ireland Troubles in Britain made by many of the contributors to this book intersect with their awareness of a political context that has changed substantially since 1994, let alone 1969. Most obviously, their engagements with the legacies of the Irish conflict – or Northern Irish conflict[46] – are filtered through concerns with the effects of subsequent war and conflict involving British armed forces, notably in Iraq and Afghanistan, with the Islamophobia and repres-sion produced by the 'war on terror' since 2001, and with attacks on British and other cities in the West by radical Islamist insurgents. These developments provoke renewed interest in their antecedents, as when Conservative MP David Davis criticises the strategy of the intelligence services in hindering the movements of suspected Islamist terrorists, due to 'long-established practices in the UK, dating back to the Troubles in

Northern Ireland';[47] when public commemoration of British war dead from recent conflicts stimulates reflection on its absence for those who died in the Troubles (Jenkings and Woodward, chapter 7), or generates new configurations of unionist memory through inclusion of the Ulster Special Constabulary at the National Memorial Arboretum (Armstrong, chapter 22); and when parallels are drawn between the climate of suspicion and fear engulfing Britain's Muslim communities today and the situation of Irish communities during the Troubles (Murray, chapter 14; Casey, chapter 15). The contribution of women's history to transnational feminisms and emerging interest in the history of social movements provide other political lenses through which to view resistance to the State in Britain during the Irish conflict (see Renwick, chapter 8; Rossiter, chapter 11).

This book breaks new ground in exploring the legacies of the Northern Ireland conflict in terms of individuals, political and social relationships, and communities and cultures in Britain. Holding together within a single framework the diverse experiences and understandings of the conflict in the lives of those who were engaged in the fighting, those who were bereaved, injured or otherwise directly harmed by it, and those who campaigned against it, the book investigates the ways in which people in Britain have lived with, responded to and engaged with (or *refused* to engage with) the conflict, in the context of contested political narratives produced by the State and its opponents.

Our intention is to establish a new field of enquiry, generating and setting an agenda for further research and debate. The book, then, has four main aims: to investigate the history of responses to, engagements with and memories of the Northern Irish conflict in Britain; to explore absences and weaknesses or silences in this history; to promote a wider academic and public debate in Britain concerning the significance of this history, and the lessons to be learned from the post-conflict efforts to 'deal with the past' in Northern Ireland; and to provoke reflection on the significance of opening up hitherto unexamined histories and memories of the Troubles, and the ways in which ongoing conflicts between competing understandings of the past might be addressed and negotiated. It does not claim to be a comprehensive or exhaustive study, and invites consideration of its own silences and absences.

The book consists of twenty-four chapters by authors working on a wide range of related themes from a diverse range of disciplinary perspectives – social, political and cultural history; politics; media, film and cultural studies; law; literature; performing arts; sociology; peace studies – that are more commonly kept separate in discipline-specific debates. Unusually, the book also includes the voices of political activists, writers and artists, as well as individuals personally affected by the Troubles, writing in forms of memoir, testimony, oral history and reflective essay, that enter into dialogue with analytical inquiry.

The chapters are organised in four thematic sections. Part I addresses perspectives associated with the British State (by no means an undifferentiated entity), and explores differences and tensions in outlook and understanding articulated across a range of political and military voices, from prime ministers to the families of British soldiers. Part II investigates anti-State activisms and traces a hidden history of organisations and campaigns – from the Troops Out Movement and Sinn Féin Britain to feminist groupings and the Labour movement – through the voices and analyses of former activists. Part III explores cultural representations of the Troubles in Britain, in readings of news reportage, imaginative fiction and film from the conflict era that analyse their textual construction and contestation of meaning, and reflect on the significance of these texts from vantage points within post-conflict culture. Part IV considers a range of questions relating to memory, peace building and 'dealing with the past' in Britain, and explores a number of ways in which those affected by the Northern Ireland conflict have worked to transform its painful and divided legacies, whilst reflecting on the difficulties and continuing contestations that are necessarily encountered in any such endeavour. More than twenty years since the ceasefires of 1994, and with the fiftieth anniversary of the civil rights marches that triggered the conflict due to fall in 2018, we believe this to be a timely initiative.

Notes

1 This phrase is used by the Healing Through Remembering organisation. See www.healingthroughremembering.org (Accessed 19 December 2015).
2 Foreword to Ministry of Defence, *Operation Banner: An Analysis of Military Operations in Northern Ireland*, Army Code No. 71842 (London: MoD, July 2006).
3 Ministry of Defence, *Operation Banner*, para 105.
4 Ministry of Defence, response to Freedom of Information request: 'FOI Smyth 02-01-2013-160507-018 correspondence dated: 29 December 2012'. Available at www.whatdotheyknow.com/request/operation_banner_soldiers_that_d (Accessed 20 December 2015).
5 G. Bell (ed.), *Ireland: What Was That About?* (London: Eastside Heritage Publications, 2010), no page numbers.
6 D. McKittrick, S. Kelters, B. Feeney, C. Thornton and D. McVea, *Lost Lives: The Stories of the Men, Women and Children Who Died as a Result of the Northern Ireland Troubles* (Edinburgh: Mainstream, 2007), p. 1561.

7 G. McGladdery, *The Provisional IRA in England: The Bombing Campaign 1973–1997* (Dublin: Irish Academic Press, 2006). See also *The Legacy: A Study of the Needs of GB Victims and Survivors of the Northern Ireland Troubles* (Warrington: Tim Parry Johnathan Ball Trust, 2003).

8 *The Legacy*, p. 1.

9 *Statewatch*, 2 (May/June 1991); and see Nadine Finch's chapter 10 in this volume.

10 See D. Murphy, *A Place Apart* (London: John Murray, 1978).

11 P. Catterall and S. McDougall, 'Introduction: Northern Ireland in British politics', in P. Catterall and S. McDougall (eds), *The Northern Ireland Question in British Politics* (Basingstoke: Macmillan, 1996), p. 1.

12 K. Bloomfield, *A Tragedy of Errors: The Government and Misgovernment of Northern Ireland* (Liverpool: Liverpool University Press, 2007), p. 13.

13 Catterall and McDougall, 'Introduction', p. 1.

14 See, for example, P. Shirlow and B. Murtagh. *Belfast: Segregation, Violence and the City* (London: Pluto, 2006); G. Dawson, *Making Peace with the Past? Memory, Trauma and the Irish Troubles* (Manchester: Manchester University Press, 2007); P. Lundy and M. McGovern, 'Truth, justice and dealing with the legacy of the past in Northern Ireland 1998–2008', *Ethnopolitics*, 7:1 (2008), 177–93; C. Switzer and S. McDowell, 'Redrawing cognitive maps of conflict: Lost spaces and forgetting in the centre of Belfast', *Memory Studies*, 2:3 (2009), 337–53; C. Hackett and B. Rolston, 'The burden of memory: Victims, storytelling and resistance in Northern Ireland', *Memory Studies*, 2:3 (2009), 355–76; K. Simpson, *Truth Recovery in Northern Ireland: Critically Interpreting the Past* (Manchester: Manchester University Press, 2009); E. M. Meehan and C. McGrattan (eds), *Everyday Life after the Irish Conflict: The Impact of Devolution and Cross-border Cooperation* (Manchester: Manchester University Press, 2012); C. McGrattan, *Memory, Politics and Identity: Haunted by History* (Basingstoke: Palgrave Macmillan, 2012).

15 'Queen and Martin McGuinness shake hands', BBC News (27 June 2012). Available at www.bbc.co.uk/news/uk-northern-ireland-18607911 (Accessed 21 December 2015). For the text of the Joint Declaration on Peace, 15 December 1993, see M. Cox, A. Guelke and F. Stephen (eds), *A Farewell to Arms? From 'Long War' to Long Peace in Northern Ireland* (Manchester: Manchester University Press, 2000), pp. 327–30.

16 M. Hickman, '"Binary opposites" or "unique neighbours"? The Irish in multi-ethnic Britain', *Political Quarterly*, 71:1 (2002), 50–8 (51).

17 Heath was speaking in the House of Commons debate on the Anglo-Irish Agreement (1985); see www.hansard.millbanksystems.com/commons/1985/27/nov/anglo-irish-agreement (Accessed 18 December 2015).

18 Cited in P. Dixon, *Northern Ireland: The Politics of War and Peace* (Basingstoke: Palgrave, 2001), p. 58.

19 See E. O'Kane, 'Learning from Northern Ireland? The uses and abuses of the Irish "model"', *British Journal of Politics and International Relations*, 12 (2010), 239–56.

20 This is the title of a recent book by Jonathan Powell, the Blair administration's key figure in the negotiation of the Agreement. See J. Powell, *Talking to Terrorists: How to End Armed Conflicts* (London: Bodley Head, 2014).

21 C. Switzer and B. Graham, '"From thorn to thorn": commemorating the Royal Ulster Constabulary in Northern Ireland', *Social and Cultural Geography*, 10:2 (2009), 153–71.

22 'It had to be remembered that we were in Northern Ireland fighting not only a military war but also a propaganda war.' Confidential Downing Street Minutes, 1 February 1972, in D. Mullan, *Eyewitness Bloody Sunday* (Dublin: Wolfhound, 1998), p. 270.

23 See A. Smith, *Myths and Memories of the Nation* (Oxford: Oxford University Press, 1999).

24 J. Newsinger, *British Counterinsurgency* (Basingstoke: Palgrave Macmillan, 2nd edn, 2015).

25 D. G. Boyce, *Englishmen and Irish Troubles: British Public Opinion and the Making of Irish Policy 1918–22* (London: Cape, 1972), pp. 61–102.

26 D. Anderson, *Histories of the Hanged: Britain's Dirty War in Kenya and the End of Empire* (London: Weidenfeld and Nicolson, 2005); I. Cobain, *Cruel Britannia: A Secret History of Torture* (London: Portobello, 2012).

27 I. Cobain, 'Mau Mau victims to receive £13.9m compensation', *Guardian* (6 June 2013), p. 10; I. Cobain, 'Historians criticise Foreign Office over hoard of secret files', *Guardian* (14 January 2014), p. 15.

28 See, for example, the case of Liam Holden, whose conviction for the murder of a soldier in Belfast in 1972 was quashed by the Court of Appeal in 2012 due to the use of torture: I. Cobain, 'Army "waterboarding victim" who spent 17 years in jail is cleared of murder', *Guardian* (21 June 2012). A judicial review in London in 2015 into allegations of atrocities committed in 1948 by the British Army in Malaya brought an intervention by Northern Ireland's Attorney General 'because of the precedent it will set for the official duty to investigate so-called legacy cases from the Troubles': O. Bowcott, 'My 11th birthday: The day that British soldiers shot my father', *Guardian* (22 April 2015), p. 12.

29 For a comparative analysis, see P. Dixon, 'Britain's "Vietnam syndrome"? Public opinion and British military intervention from Palestine to Yugoslavia', *Review of International Studies*, 26:1 (2000), 99–121.

30 Ibid., p. 109.

31 See, for example, J. P. Lederach, *Preparing for Peace: Conflict Transformation Across Cultures* (New York: Syracuse University Press, 1995); B. Hamber, *Transforming Societies after Political Violence* (New York: Springer, 2009).

32 B. Hamber, 'Dealing with painful memories and violent pasts. Towards a framework for contextual understanding', in B. Austin and M. Fischer (eds), *Transforming War-related Identities*. Berghof Handbook Dialogue Series No. 11 (Berlin: Berghof Foundation, forthcoming 2016). Available at: www.berghof-foundation.org/fileadmin/redaktion/Publications/Handbook/Dialogue_Chapters/dialogue11_hamber_lead.pdf (Accessed 16 December 2015).

33 Dawson, *Making Peace with the Past?*

34 T. G. Ashplant, G. Dawson and M. Roper, 'The politics of war memory and com-memoration: Contexts, structures and dynamics', in T. G. Ashplant, G. Dawson and M. Roper (eds), *The Politics of War Memory and Commemoration* (London: Routledge, 2000), pp. 3–85 (p. 16).

35 Ibid.

36 See, for example, C. McKimm, 'Narrative, imagination and a pluralist vision', in J. Magowan and N. Patterson (eds), *Hear and Now … and Then … Developments in Victims and Survivors Work* (Belfast: NIVT, 2001), pp. 95–103; and the work of Healing Through Remembering.

37 S. van Leeuwen (ed.), *The Brighton 'Grand Hotel' Bombing: History, Memory and Political Theatre*, Working Papers in Memory, Narrative and Histories, 2 (Brighton: Centre for Research in Memory, Narrative and Histories, 2016 forthcoming).

38 Historical research on this issue has only recently begun. See J. Devlin Trew, 'Negotiating identity and belonging: Migration narratives of Protestants from Northern Ireland', in *Immigrants and Minorities*, 25:1 (2007), 22–48; J. Devlin Trew, *Leaving the North: Migration and Memory, Northern Ireland, 1921–2011* (Liverpool: Liverpool University Press, 2013). These studies contribute to an emerging historical literature on the Irish in Britain during the Troubles; see, for example, S. Sorohan, *Irish London during the Troubles* (Dublin: Irish Academic Press, 2012); B. Hazley, 'Re/Negotiating "suspicion": Exploring the construction of self in Irish migrant's memories of the 1996 Manchester bomb', *Irish Studies Review* 21:3 (2013), 326–41.

39 J. Dover, J. M. Kabia and R. Aubrey, 'Dialogue in conflict transformation', in L. Lelourec and G. O'Keeffe-Vigneron (eds), *Ireland and Victims: Confronting the Past, Forging the Future* (Oxford: Peter Lang, 2012), pp. 117–36 (p. 118).

40 *The Legacy*.

41 See www.hidden-histories.org.uk/northern_ireland/index.html (Accessed 17 December 2015). See also Bell, *Ireland*.

42 www.justice4the21.co.uk (Accessed 9 June 2016). *Guardian* (2 June 2016), p. 11.

43 See S. Cohen, *States of Denial* (Cambridge: Polity, 2001); K. Schaffer and S. Smith (eds), *Human Rights and Narrated Lives* (Basingstoke: Palgrave Macmillan, 2004).

44 M. B. Smyth, *Truth Recovery and Justice after Conflict: Managing Violent Pasts* (Abingdon: Routledge, 2007), p. 37.

45 See www.telegraph.co.uk/news/politics/Jeremy_Corbyn/11924431/Revealed-Jeremy-Corbyn-and-John-McDonnells-close-IRA-links.html (Accessed 17 December 2015). See also 'Corbyn is criticised by victims' families', *Belfast Telegraph* (6 August 2015).

46 The question of terminology in respect of how to characterise the 'conflict' or 'war' in Northern Ireland (or the North of Ireland, or the Six Counties) is signifi-cant for all researchers in this field. The editors have not attempted to impose a uniform usage in this volume, and individual contributors have decided upon the specific terminology to be used in each chapter.

47 *Guardian* (28 February 2015), p. 1.

Part I

Perspectives from the British
State, politics and the military

1

'The truth, the whole truth…': some British political and military memoirs of the Troubles

John Newsinger

That the peace in Northern Ireland remained fragile twenty years after the IRA's cease-fire of 1994 was demonstrated in a number of ways on 30 April 2014. That day Prime Minister David Cameron entertained the eight Democratic Unionist MPs at 10 Downing Street, courting their support in case of a hung Parliament after the 2015 general election. By an astonishing coincidence, Sinn Féin's President, Gerry Adams, was arrested that very same day. Adams was subsequently released from police custody after being questioned for four days concerning the murder of Jean McConville and his alleged membership of the IRA. And this coincided quite nicely with the decision of the Secretary of State, Theresa Villiers, not to order an inquiry into the Ballymurphy shootings of 9–11 August 1971, the 'Belfast Bloody Sunday' as it is sometimes known, which saw ten civilians shot dead by members of the Parachute Regiment.[1] Among the dead were a Catholic priest, Father Hugh Mullan, and mother of eight Jean Connolly. The lack of British press and television coverage of this denial of justice to the families of these victims was in stark contrast to the British media's saturation coverage of Adams' arrest. And, of course, any increase in tension takes place in the context of deteriorating social and economic circumstances that potentially provide the ideal backdrop for a renewal of conflict. The Cameron government's apparent willingness to 'play the Orange card', as it has been described, raised real fears that peace would actually be put at risk for parliamentary advantage.[2]

In such circumstances, the need for continued attention to Northern Ireland affairs is obvious. One particularly fruitful area of academic study is the memoir literature that the years of conflict generated. There have been many memoirs written by British politicians from both the Conservative and Labour parties that discuss their involvement in

Northern Ireland affairs. Inevitably, these are self-serving to say the least, but nevertheless they are useful for the insight they provide into the way that these men and women justify the decisions they were a party to. They are a guide to the public attitudes adopted by the political class and to how these change over time according to circumstances. One interesting example of this is the way that attitudes towards Ian Paisley change in Labour politicians' memoirs from the hostility of the early years of the conflict to the sometimes positively friendly attitudes of the peace process period.

Another significant body of memoir literature is the military memoir. This genre was given a huge boost by the Falklands War, which seems to have expanded the audience for such books dramatically, a situation that still continues today. To a considerable extent military memoirs dealing with the war in Northern Ireland piggy-backed on this development; indeed, in many memoirs Northern Ireland is merely one campaign among many. Nevertheless, the military memoir literature is of considerable interest for what it reveals regarding how soldiers were 'conditioned', how they were prepared for war, and how inappropriate this preparation was for the situation in Northern Ireland. The popularity of soldiers' tales is, of course, an interesting cultural phenomenon in its own right.

The war

A number of preliminary points are worth making concerning the development, progress and conclusion of the conflict in Northern Ireland. First of all, it seems clear that the unionist response to the civil rights movement made some sort of IRA campaign inevitable. What was certainly not inevitable, however, was the character of that campaign, its protracted nature, the level of violence and the number of casualties on all sides. Indeed, a very strong case can be made that the thirty years' war in Northern Ireland was very much the result of Conservative policies in the province, together with the conduct of the British Army. Attempts to contain the conflict and undermine the increasing support for physical-force republicanism were effectively abandoned once the Conservatives took office in 1970. The unionists were given carte blanche to crush Catholic resistance, with the Army being used to prop up Orange rule. The consequences were disastrous. The Falls Road curfew (July 1970), the introduction of internment (August 1971), the Ballymurphy shootings, Bloody Sunday (January 1972) and a host of small-scale everyday episodes successfully alienated the Catholic population, providing the IRA with a wide-enough support base to sustain a protracted campaign.[3] According to Jonathan Powell, Tony Blair's chief of staff, Gerry Adams no less, had actually told Blair 'about how Bloody Sunday had turned his community definitively against the army. And he believed internment had helped create the modern IRA.'[4] Even with a more conciliatory approach to the Catholic community, there would have been an IRA campaign, but it would have been possible to contain it to something comparable to the dimensions of the 1950s IRA campaign, rather than its escalating in the way that it did.

The failure of a military solution led to recognition at Westminster of the need for a political settlement. The problem that successive British governments faced was how to conciliate the nationalist minority in the face of unionist intransigence. William Whitelaw's attempt at establishing a power-sharing executive in 1974 was overwhelmingly rejected by Protestants and, once Labour had taken power, was brought down by the Ulster Workers' Council (UWC) general strike. Harold Wilson's Labour government retreated from the attempt at a political settlement. Instead, the British moved away from a counter-insurgency response to the IRA and instead adopted an internal security approach, the cornerstones of which were police primacy and criminalisation. This new approach, which became increasingly sophisticated over time, was to successfully put the IRA on the defensive.

It is important to recognise that alongside the security forces' campaign against the IRA there was a parallel loyalist paramilitary murder campaign that between 1972 and 1976 was responsible for the deaths of at least 500 people, overwhelmingly Catholic civilians without any IRA affiliation, often killed after horrific torture. This continued at a lower level throughout the Troubles, although by 1992 and 1993 the loyalists were actually killing more people than was the IRA. The part that loyalist murder gangs played in wearing down the IRA and its supporters in the Catholic community is not given enough attention in most military histories of the conflict. The extent of the collusion between these gangs and elements within the security forces is still not fully known and probably never will be.[5]

Instead of building on the successes of the Labour government, the Thatcher government precipitated the hunger-strike crisis that gave the IRA a massive boost in terms of popular support within the Catholic community and abroad. While this episode certainly strengthened Thatcher's position at home, in Northern Ireland it gave the republicans renewed hope of success and arguably prolonged the conflict by a decade. The disastrous consequences of Thatcher's mishandling of the hunger strikes actually forced her hitherto hard-line pro-unionist government into seeking a political settlement. Continued security force

successes, together with the activities of the loyalist murder gangs, persuaded the republicans to take advantage of this. The road to the Good
Friday Agreement was opened up.

Soldiers' stories

The subject of military memoirs is one of considerable interest,
although serious academic discussion is still in its early stages. All that
space permits here is a look at what a number of memoirs tell us about
the part the military played in the alienation of the Catholic community
during the early years of the conflict. We shall look at three memoirs:
A. F. N. Clarke's *Contact*, first published in 1983 and recently reissued
in a new edition, Harry McCallion's *Killing Zone*, published in 1995
and Michael Asher's *Shoot to Kill*, published in 1990. All three writers
were former members of the Parachute Regiment. Memoir literature
is not a reliable source, inevitably self-centred, dependent on memory,
susceptible to falsehood and prone to exaggeration. Nevertheless,
these memoirs taken together do tell us something convincing about
the culture of the Paras and about their conduct in Northern Ireland.
These were 'shock' troops trained for bloody combat with other soldiers. Their capacity for unrestrained violence was a positive virtue,
something to be celebrated, part of their group culture. Serious questions are raised by these memoirs about the advisability of using troops
imbued with their particular ethos in operations involving interaction
with civilians.

A. F. N. Clarke's *Contact* is a justly acclaimed account by a junior
officer of two tours in Northern Ireland that was made into a very
powerful, award-winning BBC film. He emphasises the extent to which
the Paras were concerned about their 'reputation', the importance of
getting across to a hostile population the idea that 'we don't seem to
have hang-ups about using force of the most vicious kind whenever possible'. Indeed, he provides plenty of evidence to validate this reputation.
He writes of men 'praying for a contact … for the opportunity to shoot
at anything on the street, pump lead into any living thing and watch
the blood flow'. He saw men 'putting more powder into baton rounds
to give them more poke; some insert pins and broken razor blades into
the rubber rounds'. He even saw 'buckshee rounds' that had had 'the
heads filed down for a dum-dum effect'. The Paras had been trained 'to
the ultimate in death-dealing'. He writes of the arrival of a new squad
in the province: 'Death in the eyes. Blood-lust. Training paying off. Not
training. Conditioning. Twenty-five controlled thugs.'[6] There is a grim
inevitability about the Ballymurphy shootings and Bloody Sunday.

Harry McCallion's *Killing Zone* is primarily concerned with his time in the Special Air Service (SAS), but he also recounts his experiences as a Para. The regiment was, he observes, a 'hard place'. During training, or conditioning as Clarke terms it, he hesitated over finishing off a 'wounded terrorist' and was rewarded with a kick 'in the ribs so hard I was bruised for weeks'. The result of this conditioning was that many Paras 'would have made the SS [*SchutzStaffel*] look like boy scouts' and he was personally 'even more brutal than most'. Even allowing for exaggeration, this certainly helps to explain the alienation of the Catholic population and the rise of the IRA. One particular episode he describes superbly captures the part the military played in IRA recruitment: in August 1971 his battalion killed its first man outside the Springfield Road Royal Ulster Constabulary (RUC) station. A van had backfired and, mistaking the noise for gunfire, the duty sergeant fired two shots into the vehicle, killing the driver, Harry Thornton. This trigger-happy response provoked a riot. What was not known at the time, however, was that one of the Paras procured a piece of the dead man's skull 'and used it as an ash tray'.[7] If this had become public in the immediate aftermath of the incident, one suspects that the outbreak of rioting might well have assumed insurrectionary proportions. McCallion's 1995 revelation provoked no outcry, no outraged *Daily Mail* or *Daily Express* headlines condemning this barbarism. What, one is entitled to wonder, would be the response, even today, if an IRA memoir were to admit to a volunteer's having used a piece of a British soldier's skull as an ash tray?

The third memoir, Michael Asher's *Shoot to Kill*, is the most thoughtful and interesting. Since leaving the military, Asher has established a substantial reputation as an explorer and writer. He is the author of a number of novels, travel books, biographies and military histories. His book *The Regiment* is one of the best histories of the SAS and he also researched and wrote an important book, *The Real Bravo Two Zero*, on the Bravo Two Zero patrol during the Gulf War. This volume subjected the two bestselling accounts by the pseudonymous Andy McNab and Chris Ryan, *Bravo Two Zero* and *The One That Got Away*, respectively, to critical scrutiny and is of particular interest to anyone with an interest in military memoirs.[8] His own memoir provides yet another disturbing account of the culture of the Parachute Regiment.

The conditioning of new recruits certainly seems a more appropriate term than training. Everyone, Asher insists, is a potential killer. What the Paras did was take 'that capability and articulate it. They dressed it up in a maroon-red beret and gave it an identity.' The savagery present in every man was turned 'into something useful, something really destructive'. You spent eighteen years learning 'to contain the violence which boiled in your brain, and now the Paras opened the floodgates'. He brings out the problems this caused in Northern Ireland most effectively.

Asher remembers his comrades' response to the Bloody Sunday shootings when they heard the news on the radio: 'I am ashamed to say we cheered.' He writes:

> It never even occurred to us that there might be a moral issue. It occurred to us still less that opening fire was bad tactics. We had no preparation for the propaganda. We did not know or care that this action would bring about the downfall of the Stormont Parliament and turn world opinion staunchly against the British. We didn't know that it gave the advantage to the IRA. We were not trained or schooled in subtlety.

This last remark is something of an understatement. His account of how they entertained themselves off duty is of considerable interest. There were regular fights 'to determine the pecking order and who can boss who'. And somewhat more exotic were the 'grunge' contests where 'they tried to outdo each other in acts of gross obscenity, like eating shit and drinking urine'. This behaviour informed their interaction with the civilian population. Once again, it is worth quoting Asher at length:

> During house searches they vented their anger on their victims, smashing down doors and breaking up furniture, kicking and rifle-butting anyone who resisted, making lewd suggestions to the women of the house and threatening the children ... They battered a stray cat that wandered past the OP [observation post] and held up its mangled corpse to the children who came looking for it. Several of them boasted of dragging a mentally deficient girl into the OP and forcing her to perform oral sex.

This was how they had been trained or conditioned to behave. The animal inside them had been 'deliberately unchained, deliberately starved and made hungry to kill'. They 'had been brainwashed into believing that cruelty and aggression were the most desirable qualities' and turned into 'a hurricane of brutality ready to burst forth on anyone or anything that stood in our way'.

Even when a turn away from 'blunt force trauma' was policy, there were still problems convincing the Paras that this was compatible with their reputation. Asher joined the Paras' intelligence section and describes the problems that were encountered in getting the Paras to moderate their violence. He recounts one occasion when a young IRA volunteer had been killed planting a bomb that exploded prematurely. His father had no IRA sympathies and had not known his son was a member. It was decided to bring him in, show some sympathy and try to cultivate him as a source. The squad sent to pick him up could not take any of this intelligence nonsense seriously and when he arrived the man had not only been roughed up but was covered in blood from where the corporal had bitten his nose. Far from any contrition, this episode actually 'started a new fashion', so that for a while every prisoner brought in had to have their nose bitten.[9]

These testimonies are not republican propaganda but are the recollections of former soldiers. Even allowing for exaggeration and for the publishing industry's striving for sensationalism, they still certainly assist in our understanding of why the war in Northern Ireland developed in the way that it did.

Politicians' stories

Professional politicians are serial, some would say, pathological liars. The spectacle at the Leveson Inquiry (2011–12) into the culture and ethics of the British media, of a succession of senior politicians lying under oath about Rupert Murdoch's political influence ('Rupert who?'), was a salutary demonstration of this. Nevertheless, political memoirs do still provide a useful commentary on the war, on how the politicians want it to be understood, and the authors often unwittingly reveal more of themselves than they intend.

Here, we will focus on the memoirs of some Labour politicians. First of all, there is an interesting change in tone in memoirs over the period under scrutiny from the avuncular Jim Callaghan to the positively megalomaniacal Tony Blair. Whereas political leaders once claimed to be trying to improve the country, now they seem to feel obliged to claim to be saving it! Margaret Thatcher began this, but, if anything, Blair took it even further. John Major's memoirs, perhaps understandably, avoided this tendency towards the messianic. Certainly Callaghan could afford to be self-deprecating in a way that would not be considered appropriate by most contemporary politicians. In his still impressive account of the start of the Troubles, *A House Divided*, first published in 1973, Callaghan told a story that very much placed blame for the situation on Westminster neglect, from which he did not exempt himself. He describes how, on a visit to the Bogside, he was confronted by 'a small grey-haired man' who showed him an old photograph taken in 1954, when a much younger Callaghan had visited Derry investigating the unemployment situation. The man told him '"I was unemployed then and I have not had a day's work since". I shall never forget the reproach.' Even though Callaghan was very much on the right of the Labour Party, this is very definitely not the language of New Labour.

One interesting aspect of the memoirs of Labour ministers and prime ministers (at least before Blair) is their hostility to the unionists and their absolute loathing for Paisley and Paisleyism. Callaghan, for example, makes clear that as far as he was concerned the unionists were not just part of the problem, they *were* the problem. They resisted every attempt to remedy the Catholic community's legitimate grievances, and he recalls telling Terence O'Neill, the Ulster Unionist Party Prime Minister, that this would inevitably lead to increasing violence. While he considered the Burntollet[10] march of January 1969 'ill-advised', he is absolutely scathing about the conduct of the RUC in Derry at the end of the march. There was 'what appeared to be a major breakdown in discipline of a kind which would not have been tolerated in a British police force'. He describes Bernadette Devlin's maiden speech in the Commons as 'the most eloquent maiden speech I have ever heard'. There can be no doubt that Callaghan regarded the Catholics as having legitimate grievances and that it was unionist recalcitrance that was driving the province down the road to disaster.

The situation was to be dramatically worsened when the Conservatives took office in 1970 because they effectively handed security over to the Unionist government. A Labour government, he insists, would never have placed British troops 'under the authority of the Ulster Unionist government'. It was vital that the Army should not be seen as 'an arm of the Ulster Unionist Government'. Indeed, according to Callaghan, the Provisional IRA only gained an 'ascendancy' because 'insensitive political handling' alienated 'the majority of the Catholic population'. He is adamant that the government should have banned the Orange marches that summer and that the failure to do this 'led to the disastrous events of the next few days and opened the way for the Provisional IRA to pose, wrongly, as the only reliable defenders of the Catholic population'. It is hard to disagree with this assessment. Of course, this begs the question of whether Labour would have stood up to the unionists more successfully if they had been returned to office in 1970. Certainly, Labour hostility towards and distrust of the unionists made them very much aware of how they would make the situation worse if given the opportunity, whereas the incoming Conservatives regarded them as their friends and allies. According to Callaghan, the new Conservative Home Secretary, Reginald Maudling, made no attempt to consult with him regarding the situation he was inheriting. In fact, Maudling thought Northern Ireland a terrible place, not a bit like England, and was quite relieved to let the unionists sort their problems out themselves. Callaghan, it has to be said, presents a much too rosy appreciation of the situation while he was at the Home Office. He is very much mistaken in thinking that even at that stage war could have been avoided. An IRA campaign was inevitable, but what the Conservatives and their Unionist allies did was ensure that this campaign had enough popular support to sustain itself through years of conflict. Instead of a reprise of the 1950s campaign, the 1970s campaign was to inaugurate a conflict of a completely different kind.

Callaghan considers the Falls Road curfew of 3–5 July 1970, with its five civilian dead and widespread brutality, as an early indication of the disastrous impact of the lack of political oversight from London. As far as he was concerned, 'The adverse impact on the Catholic community was out of all proportion to the success of the army's haul.' The sheer scale of the operation was inappropriate and there should have been simultaneous searches in Protestant areas. As it was, the operation allowed the Provisional IRA to argue that 'the Army was the servant of the Ulster Unionist Government'. As for the introduction of internment, it was, at least in part, a substitute for 'the kind of political proposals that would have improved the prospects of Catholic cooperation', proposals that were not forthcoming 'because of their fear of adverse Protestant reaction'. And as Callaghan observes, internment 'could not be successful unless [Prime Minister] Lynch cooperated in the South and helped to seal escape routes'. So much was 'obvious to anyone who thought about the matter'. He was still taken by surprise by the ferocity of the response that internment produced. What is impressive is how much of Callaghan's 1973 critique is now conventional wisdom.[11]

Harold Wilson, the Labour Prime Minister during these years, was much more hostile to the unionists than even Callaghan. In his account of the 1964–70 Labour governments, while he praises O'Neill's efforts at reform, he describes him as hamstrung by 'his atavistic grass-roots supporters and many of his backbenchers, to say nothing of a black reactionary group in his Cabinet'. 'Black reactionaries' was not a phrase Wilson used lightly. The Ulster Unionists were beyond the pale as far as he was concerned, so backward were their politics. The start of the Troubles was 'the culmination of three centuries of atavistic intolerance' and 'nearly fifty years of unimaginative inertia and repression'.[12] In his memoir of his 1974–76 government, Wilson acknowledges that even the Conservatives had eventually recognised that the Catholic minority 'could not be asked to face another forty years of exclusion from power' and that a political initiative intended to satisfy their political aspirations offered the best hope of undermining support for the IRA. The Sunningdale Agreement and the power-sharing Executive were the result. The Wilson government actually presided over the downfall of the Executive, overthrown by the UWC general strike. As Wilson bitterly observed, 'the bully boys had won'.[13] One point worth making here is that both Wilson and Callaghan made clear in their memoirs that they supported the eventual reunification of Ireland.

The Secretary of State at the time of this setback was Merlyn Rees, the author of one of the most soporific of late twentieth-century British political memoirs. Looking back, Rees argues that the power-sharing Executive was always doomed because 'there was little support for Sunningdale in the majority community'. While he concedes that mistakes might well have been made in the handling of the strike, nevertheless, 'I feel strongly that there was, and is, no way of putting down an industrial/political dispute supported by a majority of the community'.[14] Others are not so sure. Willie Whitelaw, the Conservative architect of Sunningdale, even though Rees was 'a particular friend of mine', still felt that 'they gave in too early to the violence of the Protestant workers' and that the power-sharing Executive would 'have repaid a far more determined reaction from the Labour Government'.[15] He was not alone in appreciating the irony that it was a Labour government, 'traditionally most critical of the Ulster Protestants who gave in on this occasion to Protestant violence'. This view is broadly shared by future Labour Foreign Secretary David Owen, who puts the setback down to Rees's inexperience. In his opinion, the Northern Ireland Office should have gone to Bill Rodgers who, together with Home Secretary Roy Jenkins, would have been able to insist that 'these self-styled loyalists ... were faced down'.[16] Purely by coincidence, both Rodgers and Jenkins were to join him in establishing the breakaway Social Democrats. It has to be said that Roy Jenkins' memoirs do not inspire any confidence in his ability to stand up to the UWC. Indeed, he actually remarks that Wilson offered the Home Office responsibility for Northern Ireland in 1974, but he 'had the good sense to turn that down immediately'.[17]

With the road to a political settlement closed by the UWC victory, the Labour government turned to policies of police primacy and criminalisation as methods for containing the IRA. These were initiated under Rees, but the man most associated with them was Roy Mason. In his memoir, *Paying the Price*, Mason remembers telling Callaghan that he wanted constitutional change on 'the back burner' so that he could focus on security and unemployment. There was hardship in parts of Northern Ireland that had not been seen in his native Barnsley since the 1930s, and remedying this was an essential underpinning for success against the IRA. There was in Catholic areas 'a pool of misery on which the IRA could draw'. These were the areas 'where it found its recruits, its safe houses and its political support'. Mason is particularly scathing with regard to Ian Paisley, whose campaign for the restoration of Stormont seriously compromised the security effort. As far as he was concerned,

Paisley was 'a bully and a bigot ... who seldom touched on a political problem without making it worse'. Indeed, in his time, the 'most dangerous threat to Northern Ireland' came from the Paisleyites. He had nothing but 'contempt' for the man, complaining that even though he knew that 'I had been harassing the IRA with as much vigour as was legally acceptable in a liberal democracy', it was never enough. The belief in the Catholic community that harassment had gone beyond the acceptable was to help bring down the Labour government in a vote of confidence. To his credit, Mason acknowledges Social Democratic and Labour Party leader Gerry Fitt's speech in the Commons announcing that he would not support the government as 'a tour de force'. Fitt was angry over 'the decision to increase the number of Ulster seats' and 'was equally bitter about the Bennett report [from 1979; this investigated interrogation techniques and complaints by those detained], which he claimed revealed that men had been "ill-treated" in the holding centres'. Mason is virtually alone in acknowledging the part played by the 'ill-treatment' of suspects in the downfall of Callaghan's government, although he did deny the validity of the allegations themselves.[18]

The Thatcher government's disastrous handling of the hunger strikes, with the consequent dramatic increase in support for the IRA, led to renewed attempts at conciliating the Catholic population and engaging with the Dublin government. This inevitably necessitated confrontation with the Paisleyites. Thatcher herself was completely out of sympathy with such initiatives and effectively repudiates them in her memoirs.[19] The irony of the Thatcher government's, no less, beginning the road to the peace process, the Good Friday Agreement and the still astonishing sharing of power between the Paisleyite Democratic Unionists and Sinn Féin, is something to savour. While it was to be the Blair government that brought the conflict to an end, it is worth noting that there is every likelihood that if the Major government had had a large enough parliamentary majority it would have been able to reach a settlement. This was not to be, and in May 1997 Tony Blair took office.

In his memoirs, *Outside In*, Peter Hain somewhat embarrassingly quotes his senior officials and various commentators telling him that he, Peter Hain, was the man who brought peace to Northern Ireland. He quotes someone telling him that 'you were the man who did it, Peter. You came as an outsider and brought a whole new strategy. You had the balls to front them all up and to keep going. Without you it wouldn't have happened.'[20] This rather pathetic effort at getting some recognition for his work in Northern Ireland becomes a bit more understandable when one turns to Tony Blair's memoirs, where his various Secretaries of State get at best a few sentences' mention so as not to obscure the fact that *he* was the man who brought peace to Northern Ireland. According to Hain, he insisted on being present at every meeting Blair had with Sinn Féin, something you would never know from Blair's account.

On the first page of the chapter on Northern Ireland in his memoirs, Blair points out that even Winston Churchill had despaired of solving the Northern Ireland problem. Given the nature of the problem, he generously concedes that Churchill 'can be forgiven his ... defeatism'. He could do it, though. After this somewhat unpromising introduction, the rest of the chapter continues in much the same vein, with Blair trying to qualify his 'Messiah complex' with an uncomfortable jokiness. The only real exception to this is his account of how he, the grandson of a Donegal Orange Grandmaster, came to marry Cherie, a Catholic, which is very well done. He remembers his grandmother, in the grip of Alzheimer's, grabbing his arm and telling him never to marry a Catholic. Everything had been stripped away from her, with only 'the residue of sectarian aversion' left. One example of his jokiness will suffice: the Drumcree negotiations (the dispute centred upon an Orange parade outside Portadown, which caused significant violence in 1997 and 1998). We are told that the Garvaghy Road residents were 'the unreasonable of the unreasonable of the unreasonable'. In fact, they were 'in the premier league of unreasonableness, they left every other faction, in every other dispute, gasping in their wake'. One of their leaders, Breandan MacCionnaith, according to Blair, 'took unreasonableness to an art form'. He was 'completely and totally nodless', conceding nothing, not even acknowledging pleasantries, so that Blair claims that in the end he found it amusing to start a proposal and then pause so that the man could say 'no' before he had even said what it was. Singling out the Garvaghy Road residents in this way is, it has to be said, distasteful, even cowardly. He does extend this jokiness to himself, however, humorously deprecating his 'Messiah complex': he pokes fun at himself for the occasion when he famously told the press that 'Today is not a day for soundbites. But I feel the hand of history on my shoulder.'

The division between Protestant and Catholic is, for Blair, a historical anachronism. The province was divided by 'the sheer, unadulterated vastness of the hatred' and defined by a 'barbaric atavism'. He gives an interesting example of the sheer contrariness of the people: Sinn Féin had invited a Palestinian delegation to visit and Palestinian flags were flying throughout republican areas. In response, Israeli flags went up in unionist areas. There is a dimension to this episode that Blair misses, that he is completely blind to. In the republican areas, they were championing the oppressed, while in the unionist they were championing the oppressor. If he had not been blind to this distinction he would have been disqualified from his later role as the positively Orwellian Middle East Peace envoy, always calling for war! And, of course, Blair, unlike either Wilson or Callaghan, actually supported the Union.[21]

At the end of exhaustive negotiations, Blair considered the measure of his success. On 8 May 2007, he was at Stormont for the inauguration of the new Executive. It was as if 'we were in a dream … sworn enemies were sitting together exchanging pleasantries as if the previous decades had never happened'. There was a protest taking place at the gates. It was 'about Iraq. When I saw it, I felt that Northern Ireland had just rejoined the rest of the world.' For Blair, Northern Ireland is of special importance because here he can actually claim a historic success. The problem for him is that the demonstrators protesting about Iraq were to be proved right. His memoir is part of his effort to prevent this becoming his epitaph.[22]

Conclusion

Soldiers' memoirs come in two varieties: the celebrity memoir and the 'get it off my chest' memoir. The celebrity memoir is concerned to strike a pose and establish or sustain a reputation. The various memoirs of Andy McNab are in this category. More common is the 'get it off my chest' memoir, although it has to be insisted that there need be nothing apologetic about this category. It is more concerned with the soldier's unit, with the typicality of the author's experience of conflict, what they share with other soldiers, rather than with what supposedly marks them out. They do not have to endorse the conduct they describe, merely tell it like it was. These memoirs are the tales of men being acted upon, dealing with circumstances outside their control. The three soldiers' memoirs considered here fall into this category. Even allowing for exaggeration, whether at the publisher's insistence or merely straining after impact, they nevertheless tell a story that is absolutely congruent with the IRA's success in winning a degree of popular support and sympathy among the Catholic population in Northern Ireland. Winning 'hearts and minds' was not in the average Para's lexicon. From this point of view they are valuable testimonies to what went wrong in the early 1970s.

Politicians' (and generals') memoirs are much more concerned with the notion of 'legacy', with trying to influence how the writer will be regarded by 'history'. This inevitably calls their reliability into question way beyond the routine concerns of faulty memory, old-fashioned dishonesty and the partial understanding or even the misunderstanding of events. Callaghan's 1973 memoir, for example, is very successful in establishing his acute understanding of what went wrong once the

Conservatives took office in 1970, but less convincing in establishing that he would have been more successful had Labour won the general election that year. Nevertheless, his memoir is immensely valuable for showing how early in the conflict the security disasters of 1970–72 were publicly acknowledged. What is also of considerable interest is the loathing of Paisley and Paisleyism that Labour memoirs exhibit up until the Blair years. Even right-wing Labour politicians such as Callaghan and Mason still had sympathy for the 'underdog' that was very deliberately banished by New Labour. There were Labour memoirs, such as Roy Jenkins', that showed scant concern for the 'underdog', scarcely even a token lip-service. Blair's memoirs, however, are pretty much unique. He is very self-consciously a 'celebrity', a world statesman. It is not just his self-importance, but the peculiar way that it is informed by a positively messianic tone. This has the unfortunate effect of reducing crises and conflicts to a walk-on role in the Tony Blair story. Northern Ireland's importance derives not so much from the conflict and the effect it had on the lives of those living there, as from the amount of attention that Blair devoted to solving it. Clearly, memoir literature is an important area of study. The special interest of the literature regarding the Northern Ireland conflict derives from the conflict's protracted nature, the level of violence that it involved and the complex political manoeuvring involved in reaching a settlement. What the memoirs examined here reveal is the contribution that the soldiers made to intensifying the conflict, while the politicians' tales are concerned to demonstrate their part in trying to bring it to an end. The politicians inevitably tend to assign blame elsewhere and to earn whatever plaudits they can for themselves. Their various contributions are part of the struggle over the parentage of the fragile peace in Northern Ireland.

Notes

1 *Belfast Telegraph* (30 April 2014).
2 N. Watt, 'No 10 woos Ulster MPs in case of hung parliament', *Guardian* (9 May 2014).
3 See J. Newsinger, *British Counterinsurgency: From Palestine to Northern Ireland* (Basingstoke: Palgrave, 2002), pp. 158–70.
4 J. Powell, *Great Hatred, Little Room: Making Peace in Northern Ireland* (London: Bodley Head, 2008), p. 46.
5 See M. Punch, *State Violence, Collusion and the Troubles: Counter-Insurgency, Government Deviance and Northern Ireland* (London: Pluto, 2012) and A. Cadwallader, *Lethal Allies: British Collusion in Ireland* (Dublin: Mercier, 2013).

6 A. F. N. Clarke, *Contact* (London: Secker, 1983), pp. 42–3, 53.

7 H. McCallion, *Killing Zone* (London: Bloomsbury, 1995), pp. 28, 29, 30, 32.

8 See M. Asher's, *The Regiment* (London: Viking, 2007) and *The Real Bravo Two Zero* (London: Cassell, 2002). Also A. McNab, *Bravo Two Zero* (London: Bantam, 1993) and C. Ryan, *The One That Got Away* (London: Century, 1995).

9 M. Asher, *Shoot to Kill* (London: Phoenix, 2003), pp. 65, 120, 151.

10 This march from Belfast to Derry was organised by the student-led People's Democracy movement, rather than the Northern Ireland Civil Rights Association.

11 J. Callaghan, *A House Divided* (London: Collins, 1973), pp. 10, 12, 14, 48, 84–5, 146, 164–5.

12 H. Wilson, *The Labour Government 1964–1970* (London: Weidenfeld and Nicolson, 1971), p. 349.

13 H. Wilson, *Final Term: The Labour Government 1974–1976* (London: Weidenfeld and Nicolson, 1979), pp. 71, 78.

14 M. Rees, *Northern Ireland: A Personal Perspective* (London: Methuen, 1985), pp. 43, 90.

15 W. Whitelaw, *The Whitelaw Memoirs* (London: Aurum, 1989), pp. 121–2.

16 D. Owen, *Time to Declare* (London: Michael Joseph, 1991), pp. 222–3.

17 R. Jenkins, *A Life at the Centre* (London: Macmillan, 1991), p. 371.

18 R. Mason, *Paying the Price* (London: Robert Hale, 1999), pp. 161, 173, 174, 193, 218, 224. H.C. Bennett QC, *Report of the Committee of Enquiry into Police Interrogation Procedures in Northern Ireland* (London: HMSO, 1979), Cmnd 7497.

19 See J. Newsinger, 'Thatcher, Northern Ireland and the "Downing Street Years"', *Irish Studies Review*, 2 (1994).

20 P. Hain, *Outside In* (London: Biteback, 2012), p. 273.

21 J. Powell provides a useful account of Blair's efforts to convince the Unionists that he was himself a unionist. See Powell, *Great Hatred*. pp. 9–13.

22 T. Blair, *A Journey* (London: Arrow, 2010), pp. 152, 154, 155, 156, 158, 160–1, 187–8, 199. For Blair as a Thatcherite see also N. Fairclough, *New Labour, New Language?* (London: Routledge, 2000), and my 'True crime stories: Some New Labour memoirs', *International Socialism*, 129 (2009).

2

'I got shot through the head with an Armalite round'[1]

Ted Aubertin

I was a soldier serving with the Parachute Regiment in the early seventies. My first experience of the 'Troubles', as people called it, was after Bloody Sunday in January 1972. I was sitting in the depot having lunch as a recruit in Aldershot when the officers' mess was blown up, and the roof shook and everything else, and that was the first time I'd had any experience in England of any 'Troubles' or anything else like it. I think when I first was injured, I thought of myself as a victim. I consider myself a survivor; that's how I perceive myself today.

I served with 1 Para in Northern Ireland for Operation Motorman, which was the first real tour I did out there. Basically we were running around trying to round up what was then thought of as the 'troublemakers'. I don't think that was a particularly successful operation in any way, shape or form. Our understanding of Northern Ireland and the Troubles, as far as I'm concerned anyway, was zilch. We weren't given an awful lot of information, you weren't expected to think and you weren't really expected to get a grip of what it was about. We were supposed to be what they called 'aid to the civil authorities', which meant we were supposed to be doing a kind of policing role, or helping and supporting the police, to maintain the democratic process. And, it was a very simplistic thing. I was a very young man at the time, I was probably about nineteen years of age, and we were very, very confused, we didn't know what was going on half of the time. When I was in Belfast, we were running around areas, and the only reason we knew which the area was, was by the flags that were flying or signs that were up which said 'FTQ', which stood for something to the Queen, and the other one said 'FTP', and that stood for something else to the Pope. So you knew by looking at the wall which area you were in. In those days you didn't have the demarcations which later came about, where they had republican areas, unionist areas and it was all marked off much more clearly. You had the 'peace wall' and all that sort of business going up, but that was in the early days. So that was really my first experience out there.

It was quite a shock to me to say the least, because I hadn't expected anything like that, and it was like walking down any English street, and here I was, walking around the streets of Belfast carrying an SLR (self-loading rifle) in my hand. To me Belfast was part of Great Britain, part of the United Kingdom, part of this country, and they drank the same tea we drank, they had the same sort of football teams and so on and so forth. So it was a very, very weird experience. I actually remember asking a lot of the time, 'what the hell are we doing here, and why are we doing this?' And then being told that we were the aid to the civil authorities, and that's why we had to be there. I knew in the back of my mind even then that this didn't seem right, not to be on British soil carrying weapons around, when I had joined the British Army with the intention, as most young men had done, to see a bit of adventure, to travel. I expected to end up somewhere like Germany or some other foreign clime, but not in Northern Ireland. So that was my first real introduction.

I suppose my first journey into peace and reconciliation started on 16 March 1974. That's when I was on the border with a group of soldiers on patrol, where we got ambushed by the IRA, and they opened fire on us. It was the day before St Patrick's Day, and I felt this was part of their celebration for that in some ways. Two friends were killed in the same patrol, and I was very badly wounded. I got shot through the head with an Armalite round, through the cheek, the jaw, the shoulder and the leg. I wasn't actually expected to live. And the next thing I can honestly remember was waking up in hospital, thinking I'd been out for a drink, because I had this splitting headache, but I couldn't move and I couldn't see, and I thought that I was in Aldershot.

So gradually I recovered from that, which was quite amazing, and then I was invalided out of the service as 80 per cent disabled. In those days there was no such thing as post-traumatic stress disorder (PTSD), there was no recognition that if you had been to too many incidents, or you'd had too many experiences, that that was going to have an effect on you, which would affect you throughout your life and indeed may not necessarily show up till later on.

I went through a period of complete denial. I tried talking to people in England about the experience of Northern Ireland, with my friends that I had gone to school with and other people I knew, and nobody in this country really had a clue about what was going on out there, that it was in a sense a war.

At that stage I was obviously full of resentment and anger at what had happened to me, because I had hoped to make the Army my career, and as such, I was very negative in some ways. I turned that round and I ended up getting myself a job in social work, after having several operations. Life became normal again, except for the fact that I wouldn't talk about all the things that had happened to me. When I was asked how I had got the scars, I would say I was in a car crash. Now that to me was the way I thought I was coping with it, and for many, many years after that I did quite well. I've had a fairly good career in social work, I got married, the usual sort of run-of-the-mill stuff. But throughout that period I also started having flashbacks and nightmares and other irrational behaviours which I couldn't really explain. I'd lose my temper for no apparent reason. When I actually looked back at when I had lost my temper, I couldn't work out why. I'd be frightened of something that you wouldn't normally be frightened of. That is PTSD, although I wasn't aware of it at the time.

It's a bit like if you take the 'fight and flight' angle. For a normal human being, in the primitive part of the brain, you are set up so that if a danger approaches, you either go and fight that situation to protect yourself, or you run away, one of those two things happen. It pumps adrenalin around the system, it gets you ready for action, basically. It's like a switch that goes on. Then afterwards your body returns to normal and everything goes back to the way it should be as a normal human being, the anxiety level drops. With somebody that suffers from PTSD, if you take 100 per cent, instead of it going back down to zero again because of a stress situation, it stays at 50, or 40, or 30 per cent. So you've got far less ability in some ways to cope with a stressful situation than a normal human being would have. You can get the same thing with a civilian; it's not just a military situation. So I had that to contend with, which I hid quite well. Because I'd been involved in social work, I actually did counselling, I was helping families who needed support, and I was looking at other people all the time and not looking at myself.

Perhaps thirty-five years later, I had a mental breakdown. I went to see my general practitioner, who sent me to see a psychiatrist who I did sessions with once a week for about three or four months, and he couldn't work out what was wrong with me. We talked about my family, we talked about all sorts of things. Then he realised that this must have had something to do with my service in the Army, even though it was such a long time ago. I got sent off to a charity called Combat Stress. When I arrived there, within the space of a couple of hours, I sat in the TV lounge/smoking room, and realised that I was reacting in exactly the same way as half of the people that were sitting in those rooms, and these were people that had PTSD. They were all ex-soldiers that were still reacting like that. I then went to see the psychiatrist, who indeed diagnosed me with the illness and suggested that I come along for treatment to try and help the condition, which was a great help to me. I had accepted I had a problem. I started doing the various therapies, and it's helped me a great deal. But there was still this thing in the back of my mind, when I would sit and talk to other soldiers there, I could walk out of one room and into another room and sit down and join a group of soldiers, and it was as if they had just come back in off patrol from Northern Ireland, or from Iraq or from wherever it was that they'd been. They were still caught in the past, they were still trapped in that reaction to a situation, or that memory of it. They hadn't actually moved forward. I partly realised in myself that I hadn't moved forward, I hadn't done anything to facilitate my understanding of what had happened to me back in '74.

Jo Dover from the Warrington Peace Centre came along to give a talk to the soldiers about Northern Ireland at Combat Stress, and I realised that this was a way of me helping myself to reach some kind of understanding of what that had all been about in Northern Ireland, and to reach some kind of peace with myself. So, as a result of that, I became involved in the programmes that were being run at the Peace Centre. I went up to Warrington and attended quite a few of their programmes there. During that period I met people that were from Northern Ireland, I met people from both communities that had been affected by the conflict. I began to gain some kind of understanding as to what had happened. I had a desire to help, a desire to try and put something back into the communities there, because I felt, from my own perspective, that not a lot had changed, and I felt that there was a need to change. If what happened out there was going to mean anything, then I felt that there was a need for people to make progress. In order to change the situation, you have to understand it and I had this great desire to understand what people thought about the situation.

I'll just give you some little examples. A few years ago I spent Remembrance Sunday on a mountain in Southern Ireland with a group of people, one who was PSNI (Police Service of Northern Ireland), one who was ex-RUC (Royal Ulster Constabulary), one who was ex-UVF (Ulster Volunteer Force), one who was ex-IRA (Irish Republican Army) and myself, and we had our own little five-minute silence remembering the people that we had all lost. I had a poppy and they had Irish wreaths which symbolised the Cross. I put down a small object there which said 'Peace Peace Peace'. That was one of the things that stuck in my mind, because this group of people were all intent on trying to find some kind of solution to the problems that had affected all of us.

Another part of my personal journey was when I was introduced by the Peace Centre to the Glencree Centre for Peace and Reconciliation in Southern Ireland. During one of their programmes, we were sitting round as a group, and if you wanted to talk, you had to pick up a stone on the table, which was the 'peace stone'. When I saw that stone and we were using that stone, I remembered that I had my own stone at home. When I came back from Northern Ireland the first time, I'd picked up a stone off the pavement, thinking I might return it to the person that had given it to me, but never did. I put it in my pocket and I carried that back with me, and I still had that stone at home. It felt like the reverse of the stone of peace. So I decided that my stone needed to go back. On one of my trips over there, I took that stone and I returned it to a Belfast graveyard, and I took a photograph of it, which was a kind of symbolic closure of some of the experiences that I had had. It was very much a personal journey for me because I wanted to help myself. During the process of that journey, and having come from a social work background, I realised that I wanted to try and help other people within the community. It's not an intellectual journey, and I wouldn't describe it as a political journey, it's very much a personal journey that I'm sharing. I feel that one of the things that's missing sometimes from books and philosophies is the personal, the individual view of the people. I feel there's a great difference, and this is not meant in any disrespect, between people that have been affected by or experienced the situation, and those that write books about it with statistics or have an intellectual or a philosophical understanding of a situation. I felt that very much, that I could offer my own personal experience to help.

Note

1 This chapter originates in a talk presented at 'The Northern Ireland Troubles in Britain: Impacts, Engagements, Legacies and Memories' conference at Brighton, 11–13 July 2012. The talk and answers to questions were recorded, transcribed and amalgamated to form this written text.

3

'A real stirring in the nation': military families, British public opinion and withdrawal from Northern Ireland

Paul Dixon

On 6 February 1971, Gunner Curtis became the first 'British' soldier to be killed in action in Northern Ireland for almost fifty years. His mother-in-law said, 'My daughter believes the troops should be pulled out and the mobs left to fight it out amongst themselves.' On 24 September 1971 the *Daily Mail* published an opinion poll that suggested that a 59 per cent majority of British public opinion favoured the withdrawal of British troops from Northern Ireland.[1] After March 1972, when the Conservative government suspended the Stormont Parliament, both major British parties, although formally committed to a bipartisan approach to devolved power sharing, became increasingly sympathetic to Irish unity and withdrawal. This chapter will argue that this sympathy for withdrawal was predominantly motivated by a 'populist' desire to avoid the deaths of British soldiers regardless of the consequences for Northern Ireland. Leading British politicians, both publicly and privately, did contemplate withdrawal from Northern Ireland. Initially this was most likely to be achieved through Irish unity, but once unionist power had been demonstrated – by the Ulster Workers' Council (UWC) strike of 1974 – an independent Ulster was the most obvious route to British extrication.

Political wavering on Northern Ireland's constitutional future and semi-public consideration of withdrawal created severe tensions in political–military relations. The dominant perspective in the Army on Northern Ireland, shared by some on the 'hard right' of British politics (most prominently Enoch Powell), emphasised the importance of political will and determination in defeating an insurgency. From this perspective the politicians' 'low profile' approach to security, negotiations with the IRA, release of detainees and flexibility on the constitutional future of Northern Ireland encouraged republican violence, resulting in unnecessary and higher casualties among British troops. The 'weakness' of this approach also encouraged the mobilisation of loyalist paramilitaries, threatening the military with an unsustainable 'war on two fronts'.

The 'Bring Back the Boys from Ulster Campaign' (BBU) was launched by the parents of a soldier serving in Northern Ireland in May 1973 and reflected 'a real stirring' in the British nation for withdrawal. The launch of this populist campaign among army relatives coincided with the halving of recruitment to the Army. The BBU campaign reflected the strain on the British Army and the war-weariness of the British public which was reflected in the desire of some British politicians to withdraw from Northern Ireland. The crisis of the Army during this period is the context in which some on the 'hard right' of British politics, in the Conservative Party, the military and the intelligence agencies, employed 'dirty tricks' against both Labour and Conservative politicians.

Britain's 'Palestine syndrome' and Northern Ireland

Britain's 'Palestine syndrome' refers to the perception among the political elite that the deaths of British soldiers in Palestine had outraged domestic public opinion and accelerated British withdrawal during the period 1946–48 when the State of Israel was founded. In response to the deaths of British soldiers there was anti-Jewish rioting in Britain and a demand both for repression of Zionist insurgents and for withdrawal.[2] Britain's 'Palestine syndrome' was not part of popular consciousness in the way the 'Vietnam syndrome' was in the US, but it set a precedent, demonstrating the possibility that the loss of British troops could result in an 'unstoppable' popular backlash among domestic public opinion. There was 'little sign' of a public reaction to Malaya, Kenya and Cyprus, but the fear of it impacted on British policy in Cyprus, Aden and Northern Ireland after 1969.[3]

The bipartisan approach of the British political parties towards Northern Ireland was designed to limit inter-party conflict. An absence of party conflict would reduce the likelihood that a wider debate would be stimulated among the media and public leading to disillusion and calls for withdrawal.[4] In Northern Ireland the Provisional IRA consciously tried to mimic the success of 'national liberation movements' against 'British imperialism' and sought to kill as many as were killed in Aden in order to force the withdrawal of troops.[5] From March 1973 to March 1976 the PIRA launched its most intensive period of bombing in England. This was designed to generate pressure for withdrawal from 'indifferent' British political and public opinion.[6] Withdrawal might be brought about through 'sickening the Brits' with indiscriminate attacks on pubs

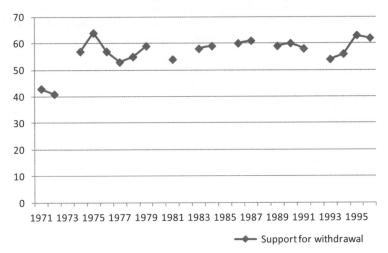

(Gallup Political Index 1971-81, British Social Attitudes Survey 1983-96)

Figure 3.1 The support of Great British public opinion for withdrawal from Northern Ireland, 1971–2001.

and civilians, galvanising anti-Irish, chauvinist sentiment. Alternatively, a more targeted campaign on 'military targets' might 'win over' the British public to a more 'principled' pro-Irish nationalist position.

British public opinion has generally shown little interest in the conflict, but simultaneously has displayed strong feelings on the issue.[7] On 24 September 1971 an NOP poll for the *Daily Mail* suggested that a majority 59 per cent of British public opinion supported withdrawal from Northern Ireland. After 1974, opinion polls suggested consistent British support for withdrawal (Figure 3.1). Yet a 1978 survey concluded, 'British public opinion appears to endorse a "tough" Ulster policy for its own sake, regardless of the consequences, good, bad or nil.'[8] Opinion polls suggested that the British public tended to believe that the IRA were 'terrorists'; thought that suspects weren't handled roughly enough; supported internment; and didn't think the Army was to blame for the 'Bloody Sunday' shootings.

Bipartisanship and the growing demand for withdrawal, 1971–73

There is contemporaneous evidence, both public and private, of the British government's ambivalence over the Union and a rhetorical shift away from power sharing within Northern Ireland and towards

Irish unity – if only as a way of extricating Britain from the conflict.[9] This raised hopes among republicans of victory and corresponding fears among loyalists that, regardless of the public assurances, 'perfidious Albion' would sell out the Union. The meeting between the British and Irish prime ministers in September 1971 to discuss the conflict in the North indicated that the Conservative government was no longer treating the issue as a solely internal, UK matter. Subsequently, in his Guildhall speech to the City of London, British Prime Minister Edward Heath declared as legitimate the nationalists' aspiration for Irish unity by democratic and constitutional means. If the majority in Northern Ireland wanted Irish unity, Heath argued that no British government would stand in the way.

In November 1971 the Labour leader and former Prime Minister, Harold Wilson, supported Irish unity by consent in his fifteen-point plan. Privately, senior Labour politicians began to discuss British withdrawal under the code-name 'Algeria' – because they feared that public discussion of withdrawal would worsen the violence in Northern Ireland. They increasingly saw the conflict as a 'colonial' problem from which they should withdraw, rather than an internal 'British' problem.[10] The Conservative government's response to Labour's Irish unity plans was not hostile and there were public reports of an emerging bipartisan consensus in favour of Irish unity.[11] In March 1972 Wilson, having previously refused to meet the IRA, reversed his position and met them in Dublin. This paved the way for direct talks between the Conservative government and the IRA in June 1972.

The concerns of leading Labour and Conservative politicians were reflected in private Cabinet discussions and the public shift of bipartisanship towards a greater sympathy towards the goal of Irish unity. On 10 September 1971, Heath told Brian Faulkner, the Northern Irish Prime Minister, that British public opinion was not going to tolerate the deployment of the Army in Northern Ireland unless there were talks among politicians on how to deal with the conflict.[12] As early as October 1971, the Defence Secretary, Lord Carrington, was reported to have spoken 'frankly' to four Northern Irish ministers, warning them of growing withdrawal opinion in Britain and that this was being prevented by the bipartisan approach at Westminster.[13] On 7 October Heath told Faulkner that the British public was losing patience and the government could not support Faulkner unless public opinion was behind it.[14] After Bloody Sunday (January 1972), ministers in the Conservative Cabinet expressed their concerns about the rise of 'troops out' sentiment in Britain; yet, to threaten withdrawal might lead to greater bloodshed in Northern Ireland.[15] Heath argued that British public opinion was becoming restive amid 'a growing feeling that they could not go on indefinitely doing a horrible job with no sign of an improvement'.[16] The British political elite was reluctant to publicly express its anxiety that the deaths of British troops could precipitate an unstoppable movement for withdrawal, for fear that this would encourage IRA attacks. Douglas Hurd, head of Heath's political office 1968–74, expressed these anxieties through fiction,[17] but there are also ongoing claims that in private Conservative ministers favoured withdrawal and Irish unity. This alarmed the Irish government.[18]

British politicians, from both major parties, attempted to shore up the centre ground by threatening the people of Northern Ireland, particularly unionists, with the 'consequences' of rejecting Britain's power-sharing approach.[19] Increasingly the British Army were coming into conflict with loyalist paramilitaries as well as republicans and the Army were portrayed as 'pig in the middle'.[20] Harold Wilson warned Heath that the moment of truth was being reached in Northern Ireland, there was a limit to what the British people could stand in a situation that was becoming 'increasingly un-British'. The British people would not stand for the deployment of British troops in a cross-fire situation. James Callaghan 'clarified' a speech by Wilson in which he appeared to call for withdrawal from Northern Ireland, saying that it did not imply any threat of British withdrawal but merely recognised the feelings of those British who said, 'let them get on with it'.[21]

The Labour front bench was officially committed to Northern Ireland's constitutional guarantee (which promised that constitutional change would occur only with the consent of a majority in Northern Ireland), but its rhetoric contradicted this commitment; it suggested that if British plans to establish a power-sharing Executive at Stormont failed to produce a solution, then Labour would consider advocating withdrawal. Wilson told Westminster that there would be the possibility of 'an agonising reappraisal over the whole field of the Great Britain–Northern Ireland relationship' if the people of Northern Ireland rejected 'the main principles' of the White Paper.[22] Stan Orme, a Labour spokesperson on Northern Ireland, claimed that there was a 'real stirring in the nation' and that momentum for withdrawal was growing.[23] Wilson told his Huyton constituency that 'there is a growing feeling in this country, a feeling which could rapidly become irresistible, that we cannot ask the forces to continue to provide a temporary military holding operation'.[24] After Labour won the February 1974 general election, Roy Mason, Minister of Defence (and later Secretary of State for Northern Ireland), delivered a speech which heightened fears of a possible British pull-out by speaking of mounting pressure for withdrawal 'because of the large number of troops in Northern Ireland and the large number of families and children that were being affected'.[25]

The 'Bring Back the Boys from Ulster' campaign

The BBU campaign (1973–74) was particularly problematic for the British State because it drew its support from army families who could affect recruitment levels and put pressure on rules of engagement. Some argue that the influence of military families has increased during the late twentieth and early twenty-first century.[26] During the twentieth century the British Army was increasingly a married army, so not only parents but also wives and husbands were a growing constituency of influence. In 1871 only 1.5 per cent of the Army's rank-and-file soldiers aged twenty to twenty-four were married, as compared to 23.03 per cent in the general population. By 1971 this situation had been transformed, with one-third of British male soldiers having wives and/or children. By 1979 two-thirds of male soldiers were married: 'It was a slow process by which the British Army accepted the necessity not only of allowing soldiers to marry, but of providing soldiers' wives with decent living conditions and soldiers with pay adequate to support a family.'[27] Military families were a strong influence on serving soldiers and on their decision to re-enlist in the Army. The Grigg Committee (1958) had concluded that 'there seems to be little doubt that parents are the paramount influence in a young man's decision whether or not to join the forces on a regular engagement'.[28] With the increase in married soldiers, this influence was likely to extend to their partners. Military families also provide a disproportionate number of new recruits to the military, so it was important to the military to keep this constituency happy.[29]

The BBU campaign was launched in May 1973, but there had already been concerns about how military families were reacting to the conflict.[30] In December 1972 twenty-eight soldiers suddenly wanted to buy themselves out of the 2nd Battalion the Parachute Regiment after its fifth tour to Ulster within three years was announced. Fifteen (nine of whom were married) of the twenty-eight specifically mentioned Northern Ireland as a reason for leaving. On 12 May 1973 *The Times* announced that the 2nd Battalion, strongly criticised by republicans, was to be rested after its tour ended in July 1973. The defence correspondent of *The Times*, Henry Stanhope, attributed this to the pressure from army wives, who 'had a point'.[31] The Army was overstretched and front-line infantry units were doing one tour in Ulster every eighteen months, which meant that a married infantryman could expect to see his wife on about half the days in the year.[32]

On 5 May 1973 Sergeant-Major William Vines was killed in South Armagh by an IRA landmine detonated by command wire from across the border. Corporal Terence Williams and Trooper John Gibbons of the Parachute Regiment were among reinforcements sent to the area near Crossmaglen when they apparently triggered a second booby-trap device.[33] In Reading, England, Margaret 'Peggy' Chaston heard a news flash over the radio announcing the deaths of the three soldiers. Her son, Paul, was serving as a cook in Northern Ireland, although when there was a shortage of manpower he did take part in foot patrols. Peggy Chaston and her husband, Neville, a corporation worker and former soldier, decided to set up a campaign for the withdrawal of British troops. They placed an advertisement in the *Sunday Times*:

> 'The Mother of a Soldier serving in Northern Ireland would like to contact the Parents and Wives of other soldiers with the aim of forming a Petition for the withdrawal of Troops from Ireland. Please contact Reading [xxxxxx].'

The advertisement was an 'abysmal failure', with only two phone calls received.

On 15 May the *Daily Mirror* published an article on the campaign. Peggy Chaston told the *Mirror*: 'The boys have been caught between two bigoted sides. Yet people have become bored with what happens to soldiers in Ulster.... It's time the wives and mums were heard.'[34] The Chastons followed up on the *Mirror* article by placing an ad in its personal column on 17 May 1973. It was a great success. Two hundred and twelve people rang on the day the ad was placed. Neville Chaston recalled: 'All who rang were for the Campaign, all wished to help and virtually [all] were involved with a relative serving in Ulster or had served or had been notified that he would be going in the near future.'[35] A petition was drawn up calling for the immediate withdrawal of troops from Northern Ireland. Within a week 3,586 signatures had been received; two days later the total had climbed to 6,393. The aim was to secure 20,000 signatures for the petition, one for each soldier serving in Northern Ireland. By 10 June the campaign had received at least 600 letters. It was estimated that 75 per cent of these were from relatives of serving soldiers.[36] By 21 June, when the BBU's first petition was handed in to 10 Downing Street, 42,535 signatures had been collected, largely by the relatives of serving soldiers. The second petition, in October 1973, raised a total of 99,711 signatures. The third petition, containing the grand total of 119,939 signatures, was handed in to 10 Downing Street in May 1974. This represented a remarkable success for the campaign and was achieved with minimal publicity, little finance and no formal organisation.

The BBU campaign was populist and resolutely 'non-political'. This was partly because 'people had little or no faith in them [politicians]'. Neither did they approach 'influential' people: 'They are not necessary. The Hammer of Public opinion is sufficient.'[37] The Chastons were not political activists and their desire for the 'boys to be brought home' could be more accurately described as reflecting a British rather than Irish nationalism. Neville Chaston described the thinking behind the establishment of the campaign. The Army had been deployed in aid of the civil power and 'Most people thought that the riots and hooliganism would be quelled in very short order.' But when the violence continued the soldiers found themselves caught in the middle, unable to fight back. The wives and mothers saw the conflict on the television continue as the generals claimed that violence was being contained and the politicians called for patience. The generals started to talk as if the conflict might continue for decades. The 'establishment' requested that the media give less prominence to Ulster. The British people were 'disgusted' at the complete lack of agreement among the politicians in Ulster and Britain. Good ideas were doomed by the intransigence of Ulster politicians. The British Army's hands were tied by a 'myriad of Rules and Regulations', which meant they were unlikely to defeat the IRA. Wives and mothers became nervous wrecks and many soldiers came home in a highly nervous state and at the point of battle exhaustion.[38]

There is plenty of evidence in the BBU campaign of anti-Irish prejudice. The Chastons showed little concern for the impact of withdrawal on the Irish.[39] Robert Chesshyre of the *Observer* reviewed the 600 letters received by the Chastons. He wrote that they displayed 'a vicious anger against the Irish coupled with a bewilderment about what British soldiers are doing in someone else's conflict'. He cited this extract as typical of a mother's letter:

> I say withdraw the boys and let the rest fight it out between themselves. The really decent families could come here, we found houses for the Asians … If I lose my son and his children lose their father for a sick people like the Irish who fight each other under the cloak of religion, I shall always believe they are not worth dying for.[40]

Another mother similarly argued,

> I felt sorry for the Irish people to begin with, but now they disgust me, they are cowards … I would not buy anything that comes from Ireland, north

and south, I would starve first.... I am sick of hearing about a blood bath if the troops come out, what is it now? A slow drawn-out bloodbath.... [L]et the Army do its job and fight or bring them out.[41]

Some parents expressed sympathy for Irish unity, but their primary interest was the safety of their sons.

The Second World War's 'conventional warfare' – between uniformed armies – dominated the perception of these military families. The conflict in Northern Ireland, by contrast, was unconventional; uniformed British soldiers patrolled and were attacked and sniped at by an unseen enemy, as well as enduring the hostility of men, women and children in the local population. They were fighting with their hands tied behind their backs in an impossible situation. Some had joined the Army to avoid the dole queues or to learn a trade. One mother wrote: 'My Son joined the Army to serve his Country, not to be spat on and pelted with stones by Women and Children.'[42] Mrs Q and her husband had signed the papers to allow their sixteen-and-a-half-year-old son to join the Army but later regretted it: 'We fully realised that in the event of war he would be called to go, but the troubles in Ireland are quite different. It isn't a fair battle these boys are fighting – it's waiting to be murdered.'[43] The mother of one dead British soldier explained:

My son was shot by a sniper's bullet he didn't stand a chance, they dont know who thier fighting or what thier fighting for. he had a fine career in the army as a PTI [physical training instructor] ... he leaves a wife and boy of 3½ years. Please dont get me wrong, as I know he was a soldier and was trained to defend his country but not this humiliation these lads have to go thro, its heartbreak for familys to see their loved one treated like this, but yu see its the same the world over no one cares until it happens to thier familys. (Original spelling and grammar)[44]

On 24 May 1973 Henry Stanhope of *The Times* noted the 'resilience' of the security forces, but by 7 June he argued that the Army, army families and the soldiers themselves were 'losing heart' at playing policemen in Ulster, and if power sharing failed they would favour withdrawal.[45] Within two months of Peggy Chaston starting her campaign, Christopher Walker of *The Times* described her as 'A housewife [who] shakes the politicians': 'Whatever the outcome of her campaign, Mrs Chaston has demonstrated one thing: given determination and the right mood of public opinion, a housewife can start a movement capable of worrying the most skilful of politicians.'[46] The BBU campaign fizzled out in autumn 1974 for lack of support – paradoxically perhaps – just as the likelihood of withdrawal appeared to be increasing.

Military–political antagonism and Northern Ireland

From the perspective of British counter-insurgency theory and those on the 'hard right' of British politics the wavering support of British politicians for the Union undermined 'political will', encouraged IRA and loyalist violence and cost the lives of British soldiers. This wavering was exemplified by the 'softly, softly' approach to security, introduction of 'Special Category' status for IRA prisoners, conciliation of nationalists, negotiations with the IRA and release of detainees.[47]

The Conservative and Labour governments' more political approach towards Northern Ireland met with considerable resistance from the British Army. The Army watched 'helplessly, as its hard-earned military success was washed away and the Catholic areas, as one officer commented bitterly, "were handed back to the Provisionals on a plate"'.[48] The government's 'appeasement' of the PIRA was provoking a growing 'loyalist backlash', putting 'the Army in an unenviable and probably impossible position'.[49] There was strong loyalist opposition to the British government's power-sharing experiment because they believed it would drive unionists into a united Ireland. This created problems for Ulsterisation, because unionists were reluctant to join a force that appeared to be implementing a policy to which they were strongly opposed.[50] The military wanted fewer restrictions on the use of force, while the politicians believed this would inhibit a political solution. The General Officer Commanding (GOC), General Sir Harry Tuzo, wanted 'the concept of minimum and reasonable force, as it is presently interpreted' to be temporarily suspended, the rules of engagement changed, special courts and an act of indemnity for the security forces passed.[51] Army officers were 'convinced that the Army had a better understanding of what was going on and they rated the Government as being politically naïve.[52]

The launch of the BBU campaign in May 1973 came at an awkward time for the British government and Army. The most violent year of the conflict was 1972, during which 108 British soldiers died. The period June 1972 to May 1973 marks the high point of Army deaths during the conflict and coincided with the high point of violence during the Troubles.[53] The IRA's bombing campaign in England began in March 1973. In Northern Ireland, local and assembly elections in May and June 1973 resulted in a poor showing for more 'moderate' candidates and this led to pessimism about the prospects of political agreement.

In 1973 the Army experienced a recruitment crisis, which was related to its role in Northern Ireland. Recruiting figures plummeted (Table 3.1). The armed forces in 1973–74 recruited only 60 per cent of their required

Table 3.1 British Army recruitment figures and deaths, 1969–76

Year	Army recruitment	Year	Army deaths	Army wounded or injured	Locally recruited forces: RUC/ UDR deaths
1969–70	21,411	1970	0	620	2
1970–71	24,337	1971	44	381	16
1971–72	31,298	1972	108	542	43
1972–73	26,484	1973	59	525	21
1973–74	15,310	1974	44	453	22
1974–75	22,041	1975	15	151	18
1975–76	27,238	1976	14	242	40

Sources: Dixon, 'Britain's "Vietnam syndrome"?', p. 111; McKittrick et al., *Lost Lives*, p. 1473; Sidney Elliott and W. D. Flackes, *Northern Ireland: A Political Directory 1968–99* (Belfast: Blackstaff Press,1999), p. 684.

numbers, and this was largely as a result of the shortfall in recruitment to the Army. Lord Carrington, Minister of Defence, commented in June 1973: 'Northern Ireland has had some effect, not among serving soldiers so much, but parents who may have discouraged their sons from going into the Service.'[54] The *Guardian* reported that 'Whitehall top brass' were meeting to consider how to counter the 'Bring the troops home' movement.[55]

Containing the withdrawal movement

The political and military elites used several techniques to contain the influence of the withdrawal movement. The bipartisan approach of the British political parties was essentially preserved and during the mid to late 1970s Ulsterisation was implemented, putting the locally recruited Ulster Defence Regiment (UDR) and RUC in the front line as far as possible and reducing the exposure of the British Army.[56] The proportion of deaths suffered by the locally recruited security forces rose, and in 1975 there were more deaths from among the RUC/UDR than the British Army (see Table 3.1).[57]

The Army responded to the challenge from army relatives with a programme of reform to deal with the disaffection of army wives.[58] The Army also put pressure on military families to stop their political activity, partly by threatening serving soldiers with the consequences of their family's activities.[59] 'Dirty tricks' also appear to have been used against the Chastons, as they had to deal with allegations that they were aiding the IRA, endangering British troops and seeking to manufacture a campaign to secure their son's safety (he had been withdrawn from Northern Ireland after death threats). Some newspapers refused to take advertisements for the BBU campaign and the Chastons claimed that a 'D' notice had been used against reporting of their campaign.

Although the BBU campaign collapsed in autumn 1974, Prime Minister Harold Wilson, and many of those close to him, continued to support withdrawal and seriously explored this option. However, the power of loyalism, demonstrated by the UWC strike, meant that independence for Northern Ireland, rather than a united Ireland, appeared to be the British government's easiest route to extrication from the conflict. The withdrawal option was rejected within government on the grounds that it would lead to an escalation of violence and a brutal civil war, leaving a destabilised Ireland in its wake.[60] Tension between the military and the Labour government persisted. The GOC, General Sir Frank King, publicly opposed Labour's 'ceasefire' with the IRA in 1975–76 and the release of detainees, arguing that it gave the IRA a chance to regroup when the Army was within a couple of months of defeating them.[61] The GOC's public attack reflected the private views of leading officers in the Army that the government's policy was promoting the aims of the IRA. There were substantiated allegations of 'dirty tricks' conducted by the Army against the Labour government.[62]

Conclusion

This chapter has challenged a number of assumptions about the history of the recent conflict in Northern Ireland. First, the IRA's 'armed struggle' was not 'irrational' and did have some prospect of 'success'. Britain's retreat from Empire appeared to demonstrate that violence could precipitate withdrawal. British public, party and elite opinion (most particularly that of Harold Wilson) did demonstrate sympathy for withdrawal and either Irish unity or, later, Ulster independence. The IRA's 'success', however, was most likely to result in what Sinn Féin's President Ruairí Ó Brádaigh feared: a more intense civil war – which he described as a 'Congo' situation – and no united Ireland.[63] Consequently, it was 'a tragedy beyond words' that the IRA continued their 'armed struggle' when the British did not have 'any selfish, strategic or economic interest' in Northern Ireland. The principal force preventing a united Ireland was not the British politicians but the opposition of unionists.

The British Conservative and Labour governments of the early to mid 1970s did react to the ongoing conflict and Irish unity was supported by the Labour Party (although it did not become official party policy until 1981), but it also had a remarkable level of sympathy among the Conservatives too (even under Margaret Thatcher this option was not ruled out).[64] The extent of this support for withdrawal was concealed from the public, if not very well, behind a bipartisan approach, because politicians feared that openly debating withdrawal would lead to increased violence in Northern Ireland.

The BBU campaign illustrated the anti-Irish chauvinism that was a powerful motor behind British support for withdrawal and that, arguably, continues to motivate scepticism about military intervention. The BBU campaign also illustrated the potential influence of military families on the British Army's operations and capabilities, which dates from at least the period of Britain's withdrawal from Palestine and up to the recent conflicts in Iraq and Afghanistan. In the UK and elsewhere, military families can influence whether armies fight and under what rules of engagement. The National Audit Office's report on *Recruitment and Retention in the Armed Forces* (2006) did find that the war in Iraq, scandals at Deepcut Barracks and allegations about the treatment of Iraqi prisoners were impacting on the parents and gatekeepers of potential recruits.[65]

The crisis of the British State over Northern Ireland during the early to mid 1970s suggests that there was a real danger that the disaffection of British public opinion, combined with the violence in Northern Ireland, could have led to a point where the British State could no longer have contained the conflict, leading to all-out civil war and perhaps threatening British and Irish democracy. This provides important evidence to support Colin Wallace's allegations about the use of 'dirty tricks' against Labour and Conservative politicians because the 'hard right', Enoch Powell and some leading figures in the military, believed that the bipartisan approach undermined efforts to defeat the IRA and cost the Army in deaths and casualties.

The crisis of British policy during the 1970s is also relevant to the decision of the Conservative government not to become too aggressively involved in the war in the former Yugoslavia in the 1990s. There were persistent majorities for British withdrawal from Northern Ireland from the mid 1970s, even though Northern Ireland is part of the UK, with a majority of the population tending to identify as British. The British deployed up to 21,800 soldiers in Northern Ireland in July 1972 plus 8,500 members of the UDR and about 4,200 members of the RUC (approaching 35,000 in all) for a population of just 1.5 million. This explains why the politicians and military with experience of Northern Ireland were sceptical about military intervention in Yugoslavia.[66]

Notes

1 I am grateful to Stephen Hopkins for feedback on this chapter. I am solely responsible, however, for its content. This chapter will use 'British' to refer to the inhabitants of England, Wales and Scotland. This should not be taken to mean that there are no British people in Northern Ireland.

2 P. Dixon, 'Britain's "Vietnam syndrome"? Public opinion and British military intervention from Palestine to Yugoslavia', *Review of International Studies*, 26:1, January (2000).

3 J. Darwin, *The End of Empire* (Oxford: Blackwell, 1991); S. Carruthers, *Winning Hearts and Minds: British Governments, The Media and Colonial Counter-Insurgency 1944–1960* (London: Leicester University Press, 1995).

4 P. Dixon, '"A house divided cannot stand": Britain, bipartisanship and Northern Ireland', *Contemporary Record*, 9:1 (1995); J. Callaghan, *A House Divided* (London: Collins, 1973), p. 179.

5 M. Maguire, *To Take Arms* (London: Macmillan, 1973), p. 74; Dixon, 'Britain's "Vietnam syndrome"'. G. McGladdery, *The Provisional IRA in England* (Dublin: Irish Academic Press, 2006).

6 McGladdery, *The Provisional IRA*, p. 59.

7 B. Hayes and I. McAllister, 'British and Irish public opinion towards the Northern Irish problem', *Irish Political Studies*, 11:1 (1996), p. 67.

8 R. Rose et al., *Is There a Concurring Majority about Northern Ireland?* (Glasgow: University of Strathclyde, 1977), p. 27; Hayes and McAllister, 'British and Irish public opinion'.

9 P. Bew, P. Gibbon and H. Patterson, *The State in Northern Ireland 1921–1972* (Manchester: Manchester University Press, 1979); P. Dixon, '"A tragedy beyond words": interpretations of British government policy and the Northern Ireland peace process', in A. Edwards and S. Bloomer (eds), *Transforming the Peace Process in Northern Ireland: From Terrorism to Democratic Politics* (Dublin: Irish Academic Press, 2008), pp. 114–18; T. Hennessey, *The Evolution of the Troubles 1970–1972* (Dublin: Irish Academic Press, 2007), Chapter 6.

10 J. Haines, *The Politics of Power* (London: Coronet, 1977).

11 *Guardian* (29 November 1971); *The Economist* (11 December 1971); E. Heath, *The Course of My Life* (London: Hodder and Stoughton, 1988), pp. 432, 436.

12 Hennessey, *Evolution*, p. 186.

13 The National Archives (TNA) PREM 15/472 Letter A. W. Stephens to 'Peter' 4 October 1971.

14 Hennessey, *Evolution*, p. 197.

15 TNA 'Confidential Annex' CM(72) 5th Conclusions, Minute 3, 3 February 1972.

16 TNA Minutes of Meeting held at 10 Downing Street, 4 February 1972, paragraphs 9, 10 and 42.

17 Dixon, 'Britain's "Vietnam syndrome"'.

18 *New Statesman* (21 July 1972); *Irish Times* (26 September 1972); *Irish Times* (7 October 1972).

19 *The Times* (24 March 1973); *House of Commons Debates*, vol. 846, col. 57, 13 November 1972.

20 D. Hamill, *Pig in the Middle: The Army in Northern Ireland 1969–85* (London: Methuen, 1986).

21 *The Times* (4 December 1972). Wilson had been speaking to a Labour club in his Huyton constituency on 2 December.

22 *House of Commons Debates*, vol. 853, col. 1538, 29 March 1973; *Guardian* (17 May 1973). The White Paper ('Northern Ireland Constitutional proposals') was issued in March 1973 and envisaged the election by proportional representation of a new Northern Ireland Assembly, and a power-sharing cross-community Executive.

23 *Guardian* (18 June 1973).

24 *New Statesman* (29 June 1973).

25 *Irish Times* (25 April 1974).

26 E. Luttwak, 'Where are the great powers? At home with the kids', *Foreign Affairs* (July/August 1994); R. Fox, 'The dot com generation won't fight', *New Statesman* (5 June 2000); Dixon, 'Britain's "Vietnam Syndrome"', pp. 118–19.

27 C. Enloe, *Does Khaki Become You?* (London: Pluto, 1983), p. 58.

28 Brigadier Sir John Smith, MP in *Hansard*, House of Commons Debates, 24 November 1958, Vol. 596, cols 53–159.

29 Enloe, *Does Khaki Become You?* pp. 49, 77.

30 *Evening News* (3 April 1973).

31 *Guardian* (7 December 1972); *The Times* (7 December 1972); *The Times* (12 May 1973); Henry Stanhope, *The Soldiers: An Anatomy of the British Army* (London: Hamish Hamilton, 1979), p. 146.

32 C. Ryder, *The Ulster Defence Regiment* (London: Mandarin, 1992), pp. 62–3; *The Times* (31 March 1974); P. J. Dietz and J. F. Stone, 'The British All-Volunteer Army', *Armed Forces and Society*, 1:2 (1975), 186.

33 D. McKittrick et al., *Lost Lives* (Edinburgh: Mainstream, 1999), pp. 353–4.

34 *Daily Mirror* (15 May 1973).

35 N. Chaston, 'An account', 7, in the Chaston Papers (CP), Imperial War Museum, London.

36 *Observer* (10 June 1973).

37 Letter, Chastons to D. Davenport, *The Times* (16 June 1973).

38 Chaston, 'An account', 2–3, CP.

39 Interview with N. Chaston, 12 July 1994; *Sunday Independent* (3 June 1973).

40 *Observer* (10 June 1973).

41 Letter, Mrs PG to P. Chaston, 17 May 1973, CP.

42 Mrs ML to P. Chaston 17 May 1973, CP.

43 Mrs Q to Chastons, 14 March 1974, CP.

44 Mrs GCV to Mr P n.d. (May 1973?), CP.

45 *The Times* (7 June 1973).

46 *The Times* (2 July 1973); *Irish Times* (21 June 1973).

47 *Daily Telegraph* (3 June 1974); *News Letter* (20 June 1974); Paul Dixon, 'Counter-insurgency strategy and the crisis of the British state', in P. Rich and R. Stubbs (eds), *Counter Insurgent States* (London: Macmillan, 1997).

48 M. Dillon, *Twenty Years of Terror: The IRA's War against the British* (London: Bantam, 1996).

49 Hamill, *Pig in the Middle*, p. 110; see also M. Carver, *Out of Step*, pp. 424–5, 423.

50 Ryder, *The Ulster Defence Regiment*, pp. 52.53.

51 H. Bennett, 'From direct rule to motorman: Adjusting British military strategy for Northern Ireland in 1972', *Studies in Conflict and Terrorism*, 33 (2010), 516.

52 Hamill, *Pig in the Middle*, 106–7; *The Spectator* (17 August 1974).

53 M. McKeown, *de Mortius* (Dublin: Irish Information Partnership, 1985), p. 7.

54 *The Times* (20 June 1973); see also *The Times* (15 June 1973); *The Times* (16 August 1973); Dietz and Stone, 'The British All-Volunteer Army', pp. 171, 189 fn. 29, 186.

55 *Guardian* (26 June 1973).

56 *House of Commons Debates*, vol. 871, col. 1466, 4 April 1974.

57 P. Dixon, *Northern Ireland: The Politics of War and Peace* (Basingstoke: Palgrave, 2nd edn, 2008), pp. 159–65.

58 A. Beevor, *Inside the British Army* (London: Corgi, 1993), p. xiii; Stanhope, *The Soldiers*, p. 147.

59 See Enloe, *Does Khaki Become You?*, pp. xxix, 52.

60 B. Donoughue, *The Heat of the Kitchen* (London: Politico's, 2003), p. 137; B. Donoughue, *Downing Street Diary* (London: Jonathan Cape, 2005), pp. 124, 129, 253, 386–7, 506, 562, 619.

61 *The Times* (14 April 1975).

62 P. Foot, *Who Framed Colin Wallace?* (London: Pan, 1989).

63 *Irish Times* (30 September 1974).

64 TNA, Cabinet Conclusions (81) 26th Conclusions, 2 July 1981 Confidential.

65 Luttwak, 'Where are the great powers?', p. 24; Fox, 'The dot-com generation won't fight'; P. Dixon (ed.), *The British Approach to Counterinsurgency: From Malaya and Northern Ireland to Iraq and Afghanistan* (Basingstoke: Palgrave, 2012), pp. 118–19.

66 Dixon, 'Britain's "Vietnam Syndrome"'.

4

The memoir writing of the Wilson and Callaghan governments: the Labour Party and constitutional policy in Northern Ireland

Stephen Hopkins

> It is impossible to imagine a successful British policy in Northern Ireland, or at least one whose success could begin to be judged for at least a generation.[1]

The purpose of this chapter is to analyse the memoir writing of senior Labour Party (LP) politicians who were closely engaged in developing and implementing government policy towards Northern Ireland during the administrations of Harold Wilson (1964–70 and 1974–76) and James Callaghan (1976–79). Studying the memoirs of these leading policy makers can furnish researchers with an understanding of the lived experience of individuals attempting to deal on a day-to-day basis with the intricacies of policy in a context (after 1970) of regular, and sometimes intense, political violence. It is important, in this view, to complement or supplement the careful interpretation of the archival sources (which are largely available for the 1960s and 1970s) with personal reflections about the governance of Northern Ireland.[2] Of course, this methodological approach does not suggest that these sources are without drawbacks and limitations. However, even with 'all the distortions to which this type of personal historiography is prey, the potential for honesty, accuracy and insight remains'.[3] Even when some of these memoirists are tempted to retrospectively vindicate their own decisions, perhaps at the expense of a more rounded, balanced judgement, or when they attempt to exculpate themselves and protect or enhance their reputations for posterity, nonetheless the critical reader can determine a good deal from the 'deliberate gap in the narrative: the momentous elision, the leap in the story'.[4]

The argument presented here is that the significant degree of continuity in the Labour governments' constitutional policy towards Northern

Ireland is not always reflected in the memoir writing of the key protagonists. Those who were closely involved in the efforts to forge a lasting,
peaceful settlement of the conflict in the 1970s tended to see those
attempts frustrated. The prevailing tone of their memoirs is weariness
and sadness at the lack of progress, often accompanied by an effort to
salvage their own reputations. On the other hand, as John Newsinger's
chapter 1 in this volume demonstrates, the memoir writing of recent
New Labour figures is marked by a tendency to self-congratulation; the
apparent success of the 'peace process', both in terms of the initial negotiation of the 1998 Good Friday/Belfast Agreement, and its culmination
with devolution to a power-sharing Executive at Stormont in 2007,
has tempted many individuals to associate themselves with this longed-
for development. As so often with memoir, these reflections are Janus
headed; they look backwards, helping to shape the historical narrative,
but they are also contemporary interventions in the political debate at
the time of publication. The next section provides an overview of the
evolution of LP policy towards Northern Ireland during the course
of the Wilson and Callaghan administrations, before turning attention
to the detail of the memoir writing relating to the 1970s.

The evolution of Labour Party policy during the early Troubles: 'Raising false hope and fuelling exaggerated fears'?[5]

Despite a common view that the British LP has historically been
sympathetic to Irish nationalist concerns and objectives, in fact the
LP in government was responsible for a significant strengthening of
the British State's commitment towards Northern Ireland, with the
passing of the 1949 Ireland Act. The Attlee government's legislation cemented the position of Northern Ireland within the United
Kingdom by giving the unionist-dominated Stormont Parliament an
effective veto regarding any potential constitutional change. Although
a small number on the left wing of the LP defied the government
whip, the prevailing view was that a 'firm line in favour of partition'
was justified, given the Dublin government's stance of neutrality in
the Second World War and its decision in the aftermath to declare
a Republic and leave the British Commonwealth.[6] The legislation,
from first to third reading, was pushed through in 'just over a week',
and subsequently the pressure on Westminster governments to take a
genuine interest in the affairs of Northern Ireland receded.[7] So much
so that when the Wilson government was elected in 1964, 'it was unen-
cumbered by anything that could properly be described as a Northern
Ireland policy'.[8]

In truth, Northern Ireland was not considered as a significant issue by the vast bulk of LP members, voters or leaders. There may have been some inchoate sympathy for Irish unity as an objective, but this rarely formed a deep-rooted commitment or the basis of a policy priority. As Aaron Edwards put it, 'rather than being ideologically wedded to the nationalist goal of Irish unity, it could be argued that the party's Northern Ireland policy has actually been characterised by an ambivalent non-interventionist approach'.[9] Although some of those who were anti-partition had organised themselves as the 'Friends of Ireland' in the 1940s,[10] and a small but active group (the Campaign for Democracy in Ulster[11]) had tried to highlight abuses of power under the Stormont system in the mid 1960s, in general terms the LP had supported this policy of 'non-intervention', whereby unionist administrations had effectively been given a free hand in the governance of the province, within the overall budgetary limits established in Whitehall.

In the period 1964–68, while Wilson's government did register the growing demands for meaningful reform of the Stormont system, the policy remained one of offering support, sometimes tacit and sometimes more explicit, to Prime Minister O'Neill's Ulster Unionist Party (UUP) administration, 'believing, as it did, that O'Neill was moving in the right direction'.[12] Some of Wilson's rhetoric might have led Protestant unionists to fear (and, by contrast, Catholics to hope) that a Labour government would take a more robust line in support of the civil rights movement's agenda. However, 'in office he [Wilson] showed a surprising readiness to accept O'Neill's claims to be engaged in a courageous attempt to reconstruct the north's political system'.[13] This was an early indication that what Labour politicians said about Northern Ireland in opposition (and, for that matter, during their retirement), and what Labour governments tended to think was practicable in government were often quite distinct; in the words of Sir Oliver Wright (Wilson's private secretary), 'when you are actually sitting at the Cabinet table in Number 10 the world looks very different, and the world *is* very different'.[14]

Thus, when the rioting in Northern Ireland became particularly intense in August 1969, the Westminster government was ill-prepared, and not predisposed to intervene *politically*, even if there was some recognition that the deployment of British troops would inevitably require a more focused concentration upon the politics of Belfast and Derry.[15] Arguably, it was precisely this recognition that made some government figures (including the Defence Secretary, Dennis Healey) nervous about the operation, and unwilling to countenance a longer-term intervention. According to a recent critical study of James Callaghan's journey to Downing Street, the then Home Secretary had no interest 'at all' in Northern Ireland prior to taking up the post.[16] Callaghan's biographer makes the point that he had made a fleeting visit to Northern Ireland as part of an LP delegation in 1954, but 'he did not dwell on Irish matters thereafter'.[17] Yet, it was Callaghan who effectively pushed through the decision to deploy troops and who utilised the issue to rebuild his political reputation (both within the LP and in terms of wider public opinion, after his resignation as Chancellor).

Rhetoric and reality in policy making

According to one largely unsympathetic critic, Callaghan's record of involvement in Northern Ireland saw him enjoy his 'only unambiguous moment as a reformer'.[18] Callaghan himself clearly viewed the Northern Ireland crisis as an opportunity; he described the situation in August 1969 as 'a most enviable position for any politician to be in': the Prime Minister and Cabinet were on holiday (or, in the case of Healey, in hospital), and Callaghan enjoyed real authority.[19] Within the Home Office, 'we all felt we were doing something vital to save lives and restore peace. Certainly, in simple, human terms it was the most meaningful experience of my political life.' Of course, this was written before Callaghan became Prime Minister in 1976, but it is still instructive that he saw the crisis largely in terms of his own political prospects. It is interesting to speculate regarding the reasons why Wilson seemed content to permit his Home Secretary to dominate this issue after August 1969, but there is no doubt that Callaghan took advantage of this opening to build a power base around the issue. It is not clear the extent to which, from the beginning, Callaghan viewed the commitment of British troops as prefiguring a longer-term operation, but it is clear that, without an obvious 'exit strategy', Northern Ireland offered 'neither limitations of scope nor authority', and Callaghan was determined to be 'front and centre' as *the* key decision maker in the Cabinet.[20]

Callaghan made a 'triumphant' or even 'quasi-royal' visit to Belfast and Derry in late August, in which he played an almost prime-ministerial role.[21] Although he met with the Stormont Cabinet, it was his impromptu address to the Catholic population in the barricaded Bogside in Derry that remains vivid. Callaghan reported later that his 'short-term aim was to try to restore a sense of self-confidence in the Ulster Unionist Cabinet, which appeared to be sunk in apathy, and to calm the fears of the Catholic community without awakening those of the Protestants'.[22] He was disparaging about the communications failures of the UUP government; by contrast, Callaghan congratulated himself in the following terms: 'I appeared to be talking with confidence, certainty and firmness. I tried to convey a sense of the authority of Westminster, that I knew what had to be done and would see that it was done.'[23]

Even if Callaghan might be forgiven for such self-promotion at the time, there can surely be no excuse for it in retrospective autobiographical judgement. Yet, Callaghan is hailed by Kevin Morgan as giving the air of a 'major-league performer showing the parish-pump locals how to run their affairs'; in particular, he 'appeared as little less than a great deliverer to supporters of civil rights'. Perhaps the apogee of this hagiographic apologia, and a fine example of a fundamental misunderstanding of the political position in Northern Ireland, is Morgan's claim that 'the disappearance of the B Specials was especially acclaimed *on all sides*'.[24] Such a hubristic tone, from both Callaghan and his biographer, seems entirely misplaced. This is especially the case when we consider that Callaghan's *A House Divided* was published in 1973, when it was clear that Northern Ireland 'was no longer a success story as far as anyone was concerned'.[25]

Subsequently, there has been some debate regarding whether the Labour government might have introduced 'direct rule' from Westminster immediately. However, Neumann argues that the government's strategic objective was to 're-insulate' politics in Great Britain from Northern Ireland, by encouraging a 'reformed *status quo ante*'.[26] Another well-placed memoirist, Ken Bloomfield (who acted as O'Neill's private secretary), argued that 'the Wilson Cabinet also demonstrated at that time the lack of real knowledge and "feel" for Northern Ireland which arose from decades of detachment'.[27] Nevertheless, Bloomfield went on to display the nuanced character of this judgement, acknowledging that 'the delay in the introduction of direct rule following military intervention had some calamitous consequences', one of which was the imposition of 'intolerable pressures' on the UUP (and the further growth of Paisleyism), as well as the 'potential confusion of responsibility' between the Belfast and London administrations.[28] Although Wilson had occasionally sounded as if he was willing to contemplate a 'more aggressive' policy towards O'Neill (and his successor as Stormont Prime Minister, James Chichester-Clark), in fact 'this does not appear to have been more than a rhetorical commitment'.[29]

The Labour government was keen to *support* a joint programme of reform with Stormont, including communiqués which gave the British Army's GOC an important degree of control over the use of the RUC and the Ulster Special Constabulary in combating rioting; which set up the Scarman and Hunt reports (into the civil disturbances of 1969, and the future of policing, respectively); and which sought to tackle some of the core grievances (such as the allocation of public housing) of the civil rights movement.[30] It was hoped that this programme would both restore stability on the streets and lead to a significant shift in the character of government in Northern Ireland. However, the UK government conceived its function as a *supervisory* role, and 'in the ten months between the deployment of troops [and the June 1970 general election], the strategy was to monitor and implement joint reforms which, it was hoped, would bolster the Stormont administration and satisfy the demands of the civil rights movement'.[31] From the perspective of the Stormont government, however, this position was still experienced as a 'humiliation', with the government of Northern Ireland reduced to the status of a 'client regime'.[32]

As Dixon has argued, there were 'strong incentives' towards continuity in British policy towards Northern Ireland, and when the Conservative government of Edward Heath replaced the Labour administration in June 1970, constitutional policy continued to be founded upon the twin pillars of majority consent for any putative change in Northern Ireland's status and an essentially bipartisan approach amongst the parties at Westminster.[33] Of course, an effective consensus regarding the key elements of fundamental British policy is emphatically not the same thing as a specific agreement concerning *all* aspects of that policy, and it is particularly important here to identify the gap between a party's public rhetoric and its core positions. Dixon has been particularly concerned to expose the differences between what a party does and the way that it acts, at the front and back of the political stage. One way of attempting to uncover these differences is a careful reading of what some of the key policy makers have to say about their efforts to reconcile their personal preferences with the inevitable constraints of office.

Harold Wilson, in his memoir *Final Term* (1979), recognised that his espousal, while in opposition in November 1971, of a fifteen-point plan for a united Ireland had been unrealistic.[34] Still, it is instructive that Wilson in opposition, and in his memoir writing, appeared to struggle with his personal desire to promote Irish unity, on the one hand, and his recognition, on the other hand, that such a policy, particularly if pursued unilaterally by a UK government, would in fact cause destabilisation and, in all probability, an upsurge in violence. Among key figures in the government, such as Senior Policy Advisor Bernard Donoughue, there was undoubtedly a desire to extricate the administration from Northern Ireland; for Donoughue, this was a matter of an emotional identification with the Catholic minority, and an interpretation of the conflict that saw the problem through an anti-colonial prism. Wilson, according to Donoughue, shared similar 'radical instincts' towards Ireland, and 'nurtured the same ambition to make progress [in Northern Ireland] which had tempted and misled several previous British Prime Ministers.'[35] It is interesting that much later, in his memoirs, Donoughue recognised that this one-sided approach had been a miscalculation of the realities of political power in Northern Ireland: without the majority of Protestants supporting any putative settlement, little could be achieved, 'something often ignored by Labour's instinctive pro-republicanism'.[36] Even if there was no publicly acknowledged plan to actively promote British withdrawal in 1974–76, nonetheless Wilson's previous flirtation with this possibility meant that unionists were bound to be 'deeply suspicious' of the LP's intentions in government, fearing that they 'might seek to abandon the region'.[37] The IRA's ceasefire in 1975, and dialogue between the British government and senior republicans, only served to exacerbate this sense of impending betrayal.[38]

In a more nuanced fashion than Wilson, Callaghan also pronounced in favour of a united Ireland, once the LP was in opposition. In his 1973 book on the subject he argued that this should be the objective of British policy, but only as part of a 'freely negotiated voluntary agreement [between the main parties representing unionism and nationalism]'.[39] Of course, when Callaghan became Prime Minister in 1976, this judgement had not been forgotten by either side in Northern Ireland, although Callaghan himself seemed not to remember it! Indeed, in November 1975, Donoughue reported that Callaghan was one of a group of Cabinet ministers who, faced with a range of policy papers, 'all said "do nothing". Just sit and wait. No new initiatives.'[40] However, the memory of his earlier stance must, yet again, have increased the wariness with which unionists approached his administration, and the disappointment felt by constitutional nationalists, once it became clear that the government would not be actively attempting to put this long-term policy prescription into effect.

Later on, after Callaghan had left Downing Street, he once again espoused a somewhat similar policy initiative: the UK government should declare itself ready to continue 'to fulfil to the limit its responsibilities for the maintenance of law and order for a predetermined, fixed number of years'. At the end of this period, the UK State would offer continued British citizenship to those who desired it (in a scheme for dual citizenship), but then would 'withdraw from the Province at which time it would become an independent state'.[41] Writing in his memoir in 1987, Callaghan argued that this speech (delivered in the Commons in July 1981, at the height of the republican hunger strike) 'still represents my view', although he did recognise it as a 'desperate remedy'. He went on to argue 'that nothing should be done to hamper any future new initiative by a British government to find a better solution'; but, if no such initiative or solution was forthcoming, then 'the time will come when Britain and Northern Ireland must begin to think the unthinkable'.[42] What Callaghan did not acknowledge, in either his 1973 or 1987 books, is that this kind of off-the-cuff policy speculation undermined the prospects of the incumbent administration either to make progress towards inter-party negotiation in favour of a power-sharing devolved government or, indeed, simply to stabilise the often fraught situation under 'direct rule'. It also encouraged extremist elements amongst both the republican and loyalist movements to believe that the UK government (and the LP in particular) was 'malleable'; this policy ambivalence was a key factor in the ongoing political instability and the failure of the British counter-insurgency strategy to demonstrate the necessary determination during the critical early years of the conflict.[43]

Geoffrey Bell recognised that after the change of government in 1970 'it was correct to assess the differences between the two parties as minimal'.[44] He went on to criticise the pursuit of bipartisanship as 'timid and conservative [...] almost an end in itself', but Wilson's subsequent intervention was greeted, especially from an Irish nationalist and republican perspective, as 'a rare crack in the wall of all-party unanimity'. In fact, Wilson's schema for a constitutional commission involving the UK, Republic of Ireland and Northern Ireland governments, with a united Ireland as its predetermined end goal, was a classic 'solo run'. Despite his high-profile position as leader of the opposition, and the authority he could bring to this policy debate, Wilson's intervention did not fundamentally alter either the continuing relevance of bipartisanship in practice or the LP's cautious strategic position. Indeed, the LP annual conference in 1972 remitted a motion calling for a declaration in support of the principle of a united Ireland, and instead effectively reaffirmed the centrality of majority consent. Of course, considerable damage had nonetheless been done in terms of unionist confidence in any future Labour government's commitment to this cardinal principle.[45]

Bipartisanship and continuity: the politics of retrospective judgement

In terms of bipartisanship, Callaghan had enjoyed what he termed 'unstinting support' as Home Secretary from his opposite number, Quintin Hogg.[46] Indeed, 'at times Hogg's support was unequivocal': after a three-day visit to Northern Ireland in October 1969, Hogg 'told a news conference, "I'm backing Callaghan for all I'm worth", and added that "the Unionists are mistaken if they think they would get a better deal from me"'.[47] However, whilst a bipartisan approach characterised the essential policy positions of the main parties at Westminster, nevertheless this was not always how the key protagonists either experienced or interpreted the issue. It has been argued that Callaghan, as Shadow Home Secretary from June 1970 until November 1971, was considerably less charitable to his successor, Reginald Maudling, than Hogg had been with him.[48] Although Callaghan recognised in his memoirs that Maudling had been 'thrown in at the deep end' on becoming Home Secretary, he was explicitly critical of his supposed *laissez-faire* approach, and particularly his unwillingness to consult with Callaghan or draw upon his experience. He stated that 'I used to take him [Hogg] fully into my confidence', and this was 'in marked contrast to Reginald Maudling's attitude when our roles were reversed'. At various junctures in his writing, and especially with respect to the Conservatives' support for the Stormont government's introduction of internment in August 1971, Callaghan accused Maudling of seeming to be 'more of an observer than actively in charge of events'.[49] Whatever one makes of this critique, Callaghan is at pains to point out that Labour remained essentially supportive of UK government policy during 1970–74.

One can speculate about the extent to which, had the LP won the election and continued in office after 1970, policy would have deviated significantly from the Conservatives' line of march. Paul Deveney is sceptical, but is also forthright about the fortune that Callaghan enjoyed in terms of his capacity to use the issue of Northern Ireland to build his standing in the party, and also in the wider milieu of political opinion. Had Callaghan continued as Home Secretary, following similar policy lines, then 'all the benefits that Northern Ireland provided to his political rehabilitation, the image of him as a decisive leader and champion of civil rights, would have unravelled'.[50] Looking back on this period after his elevation to the Lords, Callaghan was willing to acknowledge that he did not, in fact, have a great depth of understanding of the dynamics of the Troubles, but this is certainly not the impression he gave in *A House Divided*. From the perspective of memoir writing, it is also interesting to note that a number of senior civil servants were troubled by both the tone and content of Callaghan's publication: Philip Allen (recently retired from the Home Office), and Burke Trend (the Cabinet Secretary) were both sceptical regarding the project, and concerned that such a volume could easily destabilise an already difficult situation for the Conservative government. Unlike previous ministerial memoirs, Callaghan's book would be a direct intervention in a policy arena that not only was still very sensitive, but in which delicate inter-party negotiations (concerning the potential creation of a power-sharing Executive) were likely to be ongoing.[51] There is evidence that officials were worried that Callaghan might breach the Official Secrets Act, and although he observed the protocol by sending his draft manuscript to the Cabinet Office, Callaghan seemed happy enough to adopt a 'tone of disparagement' towards a number of officials and politicians in Belfast who were still grappling with the problem.[52] Neil Cairncross (Deputy Under-secretary at the Home Office), despite being personally praised for his work on Northern Ireland in the book, was nevertheless hostile to its publication, on the grounds that it disclosed information that should remain sealed until 'close to the end of the century', that it was conspicuously unfair to Maudling and that it would jeopardise Callaghan's prospects of being considered 'neutral' should he ever again be a major player in Northern Ireland's affairs.[53]

When Callaghan became Prime Minister in 1976, one could have been forgiven for expecting Northern Ireland to be a policy arena of genuine significance for his government. Given that he had devoted himself to publishing a detailed analysis of the 'dilemma of Northern Ireland', it seemed reasonable to expect that he might have accorded the problem the same kind of priority that Tony Blair subsequently did in the 1990s and 2000s. Of course, the structural constraints, in particular the attitude of the republican movement, make the two periods quite distinct. In fact, he largely allowed his Secretaries of State for Northern Ireland, Merlyn Rees (1974–76) and Roy Mason (1976–79) to dominate policy making, and according to Bernard Donoughue (who headed the policy unit at No. 10), he wanted to keep the matter 'as quiet as possible'.[54] For O'Leary, both Wilson and Callaghan acted as if they were 'in office but not in power, devoting little but frustrated attention to the region'.[55] According to Deveney, Callaghan 'had no intention of ever revisiting that issue as an insider': this was partly because he 'was too astute a politician to ever allow himself to be dragged back into a battle that he had essentially won'.[56] Callaghan's ghost writer, the journalist John Clare, was later highly critical of the purpose of *A House Divided*, which he felt was designed to keep alive in the public mind Callaghan's 'successes' in Northern Ireland, rather than forming any authentic effort to grapple with the province's myriad problems. The timing of the publication was also noteworthy; Callaghan was determined that the book should appear in autumn 1973, despite the misgivings of civil servants, because to delay might mean that the hoped-for benefits of being in the limelight as a self-declared authority on Northern Ireland would not accrue *before* the general election (which was expected in the near future).

Both Merlyn Rees and Roy Mason have written memoirs of their experiences as Secretary of State for Northern Ireland, and it is instructive to compare them with each other and with Callaghan's volume. Like Mo Mowlam in the New Labour era, for Rees, Northern Ireland was *the* central experience of his ministerial career, and he devoted his memoir to his 'personal perspective' of the conflict, even though Callaghan promoted him to Home Secretary soon after he became Prime Minister.[57] Rees's book is unusual amongst ministerial memoirs, in that the focus was upon his experiences of what most observers would consider a significantly less powerful Cabinet position. Even after he had left Belfast, Rees reflected that 'I could not shake off my thoughts about it, even though working there had not been easy [...] My experience there had left me with an abiding interest in Ireland and I would never have that sense of involvement in any other job.'[58] Rees's memoir is a detailed, almost day-by-day account of the fluctuations of dealing with policy in the province, but unlike his mentor, Callaghan, one does gain the impression that he was wholly committed to the search for progress in Northern Ireland, and felt a genuine affinity with its oft-maligned people. Paradoxically, perhaps, Rees has been judged as 'indecisive', and constantly deferred his policy decisions until they had been endorsed by Callaghan.[59]

By contrast, Roy Mason was despairing of the prospects for a constitutional settlement, and his period in office is often regarded as concentrating upon law and order (and also socio-economic issues), almost to the exclusion of political initiatives. However, although Mason and Rees were 'remarkably different in personality and profile', this has sometimes been confused with an authentic, fundamental difference in strategy, for which the evidence is significantly less clear cut.[60] Rees was heavily criticised by many Irish nationalists and unsympathetic commentators, not to mention some within the LP governing elite, for not doing more to 'face down' the loyalist UWC strike in May 1974, which paved the way for the collapse of the power-sharing Executive and the reintroduction of direct rule (which was to last until 1999).[61] However, as Rees argued in his memoir, it was certainly not unreasonable to believe that the Executive had already lost majority support among unionists, and whether or not the UK government had instructed the Army to take a far more robust line against intimidation by loyalists, the experiment was very unlikely to endure.[62] Even a critic of Rees's alleged lack of conviction has recognised that 'Sunningdale need not have died in May 1974, even if it may have had an inevitable later rendezvous with a coroner.'[63] Rees proceeded to support the holding of another election to a Constitutional Convention in 1975, but the results confirmed that there was little popular appetite to support a renewed effort to create a devolved power-sharing administration at Stormont. Having demonstrated as much, Rees left office with a valedictory minute for Callaghan, in which he argued for the continuation of the present policy: 'positive and fair direct rule for an indefinite period until a form of devolved government could be achieved which was acceptable to both parts of the community'. This should be accompanied by a security policy that stressed 'the rule of law applied by the police, with the support, as necessary, of the army'.[64]

During Mason's tenure for the rest of the Callaghan years, this emphasis upon security policy, based on police primacy, criminalisation and normalisation, did indeed trump constitutional initiatives, but this did not mark a genuine break in policy continuity. One of the pertinent differences between Rees and Mason, however, is the fashion in which they reflect on their time in Belfast: in Mason's case, even though he published his memoir twenty years after he had left Northern Ireland, nonetheless he still appeared to be deeply affected. He acknowledged that the ordeal had left 'lasting scars' that had 'cast a shadow over his life', and his preface deals with the sense of threat he continued to feel, believing himself to still be a target for assassination.[65] Unlike Rees, although Mason could appreciate the 'tranquil beauty' of the Antrim hills, this was recognised only in order to contrast the landscape with the people living there, who were consumed with hatred and murderous intent. In his book, Mason revelled in his reputation as a security-obsessed hardliner, and he recalled his insistence that there could be no compromise in the battle of wills between a democratic government and a terrorist organisation (he was described by Martin McGuinness as having 'beat the shit' out of the IRA). In this context, it is interesting that Mason inadvertently caused significant difficulties for Rees when, in 1974 as Defence Secretary, Mason had 'ruffled the dovecot' (in Rees's phrase) when he had argued in a speech that the pressure was increasing in Great Britain to set a date for British withdrawal. Wilson was forced to clarify that British policy had not changed in its essentials, after concern was expressed in Dublin. But, once again, the LP's ambivalent statements caused a huge furore in Northern Ireland itself, with unionists deeply anxious about the signals such comments appeared to send. Mason realised that his 'foolish comments' had complicated life for the incumbent Secretary of State, whilst Rees confined himself to the pithy observation, 'I was left wondering why the speech had been made in the first place.'[66]

Conclusion

A close reading of the memoir writing of some of the key LP protagonists of the 1960s and 1970s can help researchers to understand and interpret the evolution of policy towards Northern Ireland. Although there were many important elements of continuity in this period, none-theless the LP's rhetorical stance could often be in tension with the fundamental aspects of its position. This was particularly the case when the party was in opposition, and both Wilson and Callaghan risked destabilising the political life of Northern Ireland with sometimes careless, or perhaps populist, attempts to react to the prevailing lack of empathy in British public opinion towards the problem. The contrast between Callaghan's apparent intense interest in the affairs of Northern Ireland from 1968–73, and his relative neglect both before and after this era is instructive, and reading *A House Divided* alongside *Time and Chance* provides a clear illustration of the deep-rooted ambivalence at the heart of Labour's treatment of the issue.

Much of this memoir writing conveys the 'great disappointment' that the LP in government did not (or could not) do more to promote a radical departure in constitutional policy.[67] This might be interpreted by some leftist critics as further confirmation that the LP in government has often been willing to ditch its radical instincts, in favour of a cautious and hidebound approach. However, this chapter has argued that Northern Ireland was a policy arena that was too sensitive and dangerous to be pressed into service as part of the regular left–right 'debate' within the LP. As Aveyard has correctly argued, despite the *contemplation* of radical policy departures by many of the leading protagonists, ultimately the key principle had to remain majority consent within Northern Ireland and the continuing but elusive search for parallel majorities in favour of power sharing. In the meantime, 'direct rule' was the inevitable result: 'while this could be criticised as no strategy at all, the quite reasonable counter-argument is that any strategy beyond the above principle [trying to foster majority consent for power-sharing] was useless'.[68] In spite of the misgivings of some leading personalities in the government, in the absence of a willingness to resurrect a version of Sunningdale, British constitutional policy needed to be 'tactical, contingent and pragmatic'.[69]

Notes

1 B. Pimlott, *New Statesman* (13 November 1987). See also, B. Pimlott, *Frustrate Their Knavish Tricks: Writings on Biography, History and Politics* (London: Harper Collins, 1995), p. 202. This judgement, made in the aftermath of the Enniskillen Remembrance Day bombing illustrates the degree of despair that was prevalent during this period.

2 For good examples of the careful study of the relevant archives, see T. Hennessey, *Northern Ireland: The Origins of the Troubles* (Dublin: Irish Academic Press,

2005) and T. Hennessey, *The Evolution of the Troubles, 1970–72* (Dublin: Irish Academic Press, 2007).

3 G. Egerton, 'The anatomy of political memoir: Findings and conclusion', in G. Egerton (ed.), *Political Memoir: Essays on the Politics of Memory* (London: Frank Cass, 1994); p. 348. See also S. Hopkins, *The Politics of Memoir and the Northern Ireland Conflict* (Liverpool: Liverpool University Press, 2013), pp. 1–16.

4 R. Foster, *Telling Tales and Making It Up in Ireland* (London: Penguin, 2002), p. 1.

5 P. Bew and P. Dixon, 'Labour party policy and Northern Ireland', in B. Barton and P. Roche (eds), *The Northern Ireland Question: Perspectives and Policies* (Aldershot: Avebury, 1994), p. 163.

6 P. Bew and H. Patterson, *The British State and the Ulster Crisis* (London: Verso, 1985), p. 9. See also G. Bell, *Troublesome Business: The Labour Party and the Irish Question* (London: Pluto, 1982), pp. 86–99.

7 Bell, *Troublesome Business*, p. 96.

8 Bew and Patterson, *The British State*, p. 10.

9 A. Edwards, 'Interpreting New Labour's political discourse on the peace process', in K. Hayward and C. O'Donnell (eds), *Political Discourse and Conflict Resolution: Debating Peace in Northern Ireland* (Abingdon: Routledge, 2011), p. 46.

10 See B. Purdie, 'The Friends of Ireland: British Labour and Irish nationalism, 1945–49', in T. Gallagher and J. O'Connell (eds), *Contemporary Irish Studies* (Manchester: Manchester University Press, 1983).

11 See P. Rose, *How the Troubles Came to Northern Ireland* (Basingstoke: Macmillan, 2000). Bell (*Troublesome Business*, pp. 102–4) commented that the CDU 'gained impressive support, at least on paper … Yet apart from producing some hard-hitting and informative propaganda, the CDU achieved little. It had no discernible effect on the Labour government.'

12 Bew and Dixon, 'Labour Party policy', p. 153. See also P. Rose, 'Labour, Northern Ireland and the decision to send in the troops', in P. Catterall and S. MacDougall (eds), *The Northern Ireland Question in British Politics* (Basingstoke: Macmillan, 1996), pp. 95–9.

13 Bew and Patterson, *The British State*, p. 11.

14 Sir Oliver Wright, cited in Rose, 'Labour, Northern Ireland', p. 92.

15 Neumann has argued that there were three significant factors in what he terms the British 'avoidance of responsibility': the ignorance among British policy makers with regard to Northern Ireland; the historical belief that British intervention would 'cause more harm than good'; and the fear of a Protestant unionist backlash if 'their' Parliament was removed. See P. Neumann, *Britain's Long War: British Strategy in the Northern Ireland Conflict, 1969–98* (Basingstoke: Palgrave Macmillan, 2004), pp. 43–4.

16 P. Deveney, *Callaghan's Journey to Downing Street* (Basingstoke: Palgrave Macmillan, 2010), p. 124.

17 K. Morgan, *Callaghan: A Life* (Oxford: Oxford University Press, 1997), pp. 113–14.

18 B. O'Leary, 'Northern Ireland', in A. Seldon and K. Hickson (eds), *New Labour, Old Labour: The Wilson and Callaghan Governments, 1974–79* (London: Routledge, 2004), p. 241.

19 J. Callaghan, *A House Divided: The Dilemma of Northern Ireland* (London: Collins, 1973), p. 70.

20 Deveney, *Callaghan's Journey*, pp. 125–7.

21 Ibid., p. 131. Bew and Patterson, *The British State*, p. 22.

22 Callaghan, *A House Divided*, p. 70.

23 Ibid., p. 71.

24 Morgan, *Callaghan*, pp. 349, 351. Emphasis added.

25 This is the view of Anthony Howard, then editor of the *New Statesman*, cited in Deveney, *Callaghan's Journey*, p. 167.

26 Neumann, *Britain's Long War*, pp. 44–5.

27 K. Bloomfield, *A Tragedy of Errors: The Government and Misgovernment of Northern Ireland* (Liverpool: Liverpool University Press, 2007), p. 20. See also K. Bloomfield, *Stormont in Crisis: A Memoir* (Belfast: Blackstaff, 1994), pp. 116–18.

28 Bloomfield, *A Tragedy*, pp. 20–1.

29 Bew and Patterson, *The British State*, p. 20. See also H. Patterson, *Ireland since 1939: The Persistence of Conflict* (Dublin: Penguin Ireland, 2006), p. 213.

30 For a detailed study of relations between the British Army, the police and the often fraught relationship between the Westminster government and Stormont with regard to security policy, see A. Edwards, '"A whipping boy if ever there was one"? The British Army and the politics of civil–military relations in Northern Ireland, 1969–79', *Contemporary British History*, 28:2 (2014), 166–89.

31 M. Cunningham, *British Government Policy in Northern Ireland, 1969–2000* (Manchester: Manchester University Press, 2001), p. 6.

32 Bloomfield, *Stormont in Crisis*, p. 118. See also Patterson, *Ireland since 1939*, p. 214.

33 P. Dixon, 'British policy towards Northern Ireland 1969–2000: Continuity, tactical adjustment and consistent "inconsistencies"', *British Journal of Politics and International Relations*, 3:3 (2001), 342.

34 H. Wilson, *Final Term: The Labour Government, 1974–76* (London: Michael Joseph, 1979), p. 70. Tom Hennessey (*The Evolution*, p. 200) has shown that the Irish government reacted with interest to Wilson's kite-flying; it was 'keen to exploit any openings that might push the British towards Irish unity by breaking the bipartisan approach to the North at Westminster'.

35 B. Donoughue, *Prime Minister: The Conduct of Policy under Harold Wilson and James Callaghan* (London: Jonathan Cape, 1987), p. 128. In his published diaries of the 1974–79 period, Donoughue also reflects the concern, in the wake of the UWC strike, that a long-term policy was required; in effect, this meant the 'unmentionable' prospect of British withdrawal, and a Cabinet committee was tasked with considering this dramatic possibility (Bernard Donoughue, *Downing Street Diary* [London: Jonathan Cape, 2005], pp. 124, 127).

36 B. Donoughue, *The Heat of the Kitchen* (London: Politico's, 2003), p. 365.

37 S. Aveyard, 'The "English disease" is to look for a "solution to the Irish problem":

British constitutional policy in Northern Ireland after Sunningdale 1974–1976',
Contemporary British History, 26:4 (2012), 530.

38 See T. Craig, 'From backdoors and back lanes to backchannels: Reappraising
British talks with the Provisional IRA, 1970–1974', *Contemporary British
History*, 26:1 (2012), 97–117.

39 Callaghan, *A House Divided*, p. 187.

40 Donoughue, *Downing Street Diary*, p. 562.

41 J. Callaghan, *Time and Chance* (London: Collins, 1987), p. 500.

42 Ibid., pp. 500–1.

43 See P. Dixon, *Northern Ireland: The Politics of War and Peace* (Basingstoke:
Palgrave, 2001), p. 120.

44 Bell, *Troublesome Business*, p. 113.

45 Aveyard, 'The "English disease"', p. 544.

46 Callaghan, *A House Divided*, p. 64. See also Bell, *Troublesome Business*, p. 113.

47 Deveney, *Callaghan's Journey*, p. 149.

48 Ibid., p. 135.

49 Callaghan, *A House Divided*, pp. 64, 145, 146.

50 Deveney, *Callaghan's Journey*, p. 151.

51 Ibid., pp. 157–75.

52 Cited in ibid., p. 160.

53 Ibid., p. 159.

54 Cited in ibid., p. 155. Aveyard concurs, arguing that 'Callaghan showed little
interest in renewing discussion of Northern Ireland's constitutional future' ('The
"English disease"', p. 544).

55 O'Leary, 'Northern Ireland', p. 242.

56 Deveney, *Callaghan's Journey*, 160.

57 For fuller details on the memoir-writing of secretaries of state, see Hopkins, *The
Politics of Memoir*, pp. 133–58.

58 M. Rees, *Northern Ireland: A Personal Perspective* (London: Methuen, 1985),
pp. 316–17.

59 Deveney, *Callaghan's Journey*, p. 167.

60 O'Leary, 'Northern Ireland', p. 243.

61 See, for example, Donoughue (*Prime Minister*, p. 130), who argued that the
'capitulation to the [UWC] strike was suspiciously and unnecessarily quick'. For
a nationalist critique, see A. Currie, *All Hell will Break Loose* (Dublin: O'Brien,
2004), p. 267.

62 Rees, *Northern Ireland*, pp. 85–90. See also Hopkins, *The Politics of Memoir*,
pp. 127–32.

63 O'Leary, 'Northern Ireland', p. 256.

64 Rees, *Northern Ireland*, p. 317.

65 R. Mason, *Paying the Price* (London: Robert Hale, 1999), p. 10.

66 Ibid., p. 125; Rees, *Northern Ireland*, pp. 60–1.

67 Donoughue, *Prime Minister*, p. 137.

68 Aveyard, 'The "English disease"', p. 545.

69 Ibid., p. 545.

5

British questions

Geoffrey Bell

> It is no longer the Irish question, it is the British question. (Kevin McNamara, Parliamentary Labour Party Spokesperson on Northern Ireland, 1991)[1]

In the spring of 1991, I interviewed several leading British politicians on their understanding of the historical and contemporary nature of the British–Irish conflict. All had recent experience of Northern Ireland. One was an MP who, as a soldier, had served in Northern Ireland; the rest had been or were either UK government ministers in Northern Ireland or party spokespeople on the issue. The three British political parties in Parliament were represented. These interviews were for an hour-long television documentary, *Pack Up the Troubles*,[2] which was broadcast later that year on Channel 4 and for which I did most of the interviews and wrote the commentary. This was the first and only documentary to appear on British television which directly argued for British political and military withdrawal from Northern Ireland. It included a public opinion poll, conducted by MORI.

The poll showed general support in Britain for such a withdrawal, with 23 per cent favouring immediate withdrawal and 38 per cent for withdrawal within a pre-set time period of between one and four years. Only 31 per cent said the troops should remain indefinitely. Perhaps more surprisingly, 37 per cent said that the British Army had made no difference to the situation in Northern Ireland, and 36 per cent said they had made the situation worse; only 17 per cent said they had been helpful. Other results of the polls will follow.

The film was specifically pitched to Channel 4 and commissioned by it as one that would reflect the views of the opinion poll, which, while not yet conducted at this early stage, was, as both the film-makers and Channel 4 knew, likely to favour a 'troops out' sentiment, for such was the track record of such polls. All of the interviewees were also told that the film would be informed by the poll. At a deeper level the film argued that both contemporarily and historically Ireland had a British problem. The film sought to suggest what this was, but the poll also reflected this general sentiment: 68 per cent said successive governments had not done enough to resolve the conflict, with 23 per cent saying they had. This result in particular is interesting in that it suggests that a 'troops out' sentiment was not, as is often assumed, inspired by a view that the Irish were a hopeless case and all Britain should do was just wash its hands of them; rather the majority opinion was that Britain had responsibilities that its politicians had not and were not facing up to.

The majority of voices in the film were British: the politicians themselves, journalists, academics and relatives of British soldiers killed or severely injured while serving in Northern Ireland and a relative of one of the Birmingham Six. It is fair to say that the non-politicians sought to identity the British problem; the politicians, for the most part, rather illustrated it. Two Irish politicians were also interviewed – Seamus Mallon of the Social Democratic and Labour Party and Ian Paisley of the Democratic Unionist Party – but the focus of these interviews was their assessment of the knowledge that their British counterparts had of the political situation in Northern Ireland and the value of their contribution to resolving it. In other words, while the documentary was about the Troubles, more particularly it was concerned with British perceptions of and solutions to these, past and present.

As is the way of such matters, only a small fraction of these interviews ever made it to screen; however, I later lodged both the footage and the transcripts of the interviews with the Linen Hall Library, Belfast. Most of the interviews were quite lengthy, up to an hour, which allowed them to become discussions rather than instant sound bites. The exception was an interview with the then Secretary of State for Northern Ireland, Peter Brooke, which was conducted too late to be transcribed and was quite short. As far as I am aware, the transcripts of all the other interviews have not been used in any subsequent research or publication. Yet they do provide an instructive insight into the attitudes of members of the British political establishment towards Ireland, the Irish and the conflict then taking place in Northern Ireland and elsewhere, including in Britain. What follows looks at these attitudes, and the opinions and comprehensions expressed within them. It is a snapshot, taken at a particular time, but of an important group of British protagonists in the conflict in which a wider panorama can be detected. The nature of this will also be examined here, as will its relevance to what was to follow when peace broke out.

First, it is useful to summarise the context. The year 1991 was ten years after the republican hunger strikes and seven years before the Good Friday Agreement (GFA). John Major had succeeded Margaret Thatcher as British Prime Minister the year before and on 9 November 1990 Peter Brooke, the Secretary of State for Northern Ireland, had declared in a speech in London that Britain had 'no selfish strategic or economic interest' in Northern Ireland. Although British politicians had expressed such sentiments before, the timing of this announcement seemed to mark a move away from what some saw as the intransigent 'No, No, No' attitude of the Thatcher approach to the conflict.

Interestingly, we now know that Brooke's speech was shown in confidence to the Provisional IRA in advance.[3] In 1991 Brooke was to initiate the Brooke/Mayhew talks in an attempt to find a basis for a long-term settlement to the conflict,[4] and although these came to nothing, they can now be seen as something of a forerunner for the GFA talks.[5] Sinn Féin (SF) was excluded from the Brooke/Mayhew process.

Brooke's LP Shadow Secretary of State in 1991 was Kevin McNamara, who had a long track record of support for the civil rights movement in Northern Ireland. His appointment was the culmination of a political process within Labour which had seen the party move towards a more pro-Irish unity position, which began with the party conference endorsing 'unity between the two parts of Ireland' at its 1981 conference.[6] McNamara had played a significant part in the debate leading up to that decision, describing Northern Ireland as 'an imperial relic', and saying 'I don't believe Britain should be there'.[7] In 1991 a by-election for Belfast City Council saw a victory for SF, as a result of which it became the second-largest political party on the council. This reflected its political growth and Irish republicanism's growing emphasis on politics. And, back in England, after years of campaigning, the Birmingham Six were released (see O'Reilly's chapter 20 in this volume), an injustice finally overturned. That other injustices, particularly in Northern Ireland itself, were perceived to be continuing was suggested in the opinion poll when 55 per cent said they were very or fairly concerned about the human rights situation there; 29 per cent were not. Again, this suggested a public worry about government policy, rather than an anti-Irish sentiment which would blame the Irish for their own woes.

More generally, 1991 was a moment of straws in the wind, of new attitudes emerging and, especially within British political elites, of some movement away from an adherence to old certainties. At times, the interviews testify to this more questioning approach. There was, for example, an acceptance from some that Britain's traditional Irish policy merited criticism and had consequences for the present. Lord Gowrie, Conservative

Minister of State in Northern Ireland from 1981 to 1983, said, 'I feel that Britain is a very old and stable democracy and it is rather disgraceful that Britain can't get this [Northern Ireland] sorted out.' Gowrie's immediate boss, James Prior, Secretary of State for Northern Ireland in the Thatcher government said, 'I think we've treated the Irish so badly in the nineteenth century and in earlier ones as well, that they really suspect every move we make.' Indeed, he suggested that even in recent history the British government had got things wrong, saying, 'I don't think there was any-thing like the understanding in London about the impact of the hunger strike', and even more candidly, of Margaret Thatcher, 'I don't think she understood the Irish or the Irish problem at all'. In a similar vein, an LP spokesperson on Northern Ireland, Stuart Bell, was quite prepared to criticise his side. Speaking of Roy Mason's period as Secretary of State for Northern Ireland (1976–79), he said this was 'a continuation of the Tory government policy ... a very firm pro-Unionist, anti-IRA line ... I don't think it was a sensible, constructive policy'. Another LP spokesperson, Peter Archer (Shadow Secretary of State for Northern Ireland from 1983 to 1987), referred back to historic responsibilities when speaking of the period of 1912–21:

> Until that time the English attitude to Ireland had been 'Well, we want Ireland to remain in the Commonwealth' – they saw Ireland to some extent as a colony, I suppose, and they like to see it was red on the map ... Once the government got the idea, 'Well perhaps we can solve it by dividing Ireland' – they had to contend with the English unionists, they had to contend with the Protestant majority in the North, and they had to contend with the Army which wasn't by any means necessarily committed to carrying out the orders of the civilian government – and the settlement which eventuated was one which quite deliberately engineered a Northern Ireland enclave, which was designed to contain a permanent Protestant majority; so that wasn't an unintended consequence, it was done on purpose.

Bringing the narrative more up to date, Lord Gowrie even praised what had been, up until then, in the eyes of the British establishment, the most obdurate manifestation of Irish fanaticism: 'I have to say that I do respect now, and did at the time, the integrity of the position of the hunger strikers ... it's a brave thing to try to starve yourself to death, and indeed to do so successfully. It's a horrible thing to do. It needs a great deal of determination and conviction to do it. So, one has to pay tribute to that integrity.'

Taking all these views together we could almost say that here was the British political establishment, or at least important sections of it, accepting responsibility for the mess that Northern Ireland was in: citing

nineteenth-century misrule, the sectarian nature of the partition settlement, the repression of the Roy Mason years and the ignorance of the
Thatcher years. Of course all or some of those interviewed may have had
their own agenda. Most obviously James Prior did not share the right-
wing politics of his boss; indeed his posting to Northern Ireland was, he
claimed in his interview, a consequence of this. He said, 'I think it was
convenient for Mrs Thatcher to get me out of the way by sending me
to what some people termed as Siberia actually ...This was regarded
as being a way of getting rid of a troublesome person, without actually
dismissing them from the government. So I was sent to Northern Ireland
to get me out of the way.'

Historically there is nothing particularly innovative in British politicians' admitting that their collective policies in the past left something
to be desired. There is, for example, the case of Joseph Chamberlain, the
Liberal MP who broke with Gladstone and split the Liberal Party over
Gladstone's support for Home Rule, thus denying its implementation.
For these actions Chamberlain earned the antipathy of Irish nationalists
then and since. Yet even he could say that 'I am sorry to say it has been
only too often the case in Irish affairs that we have attempted to redress
grievances after too long a delay, and we have had to pay an increasing penalty every day that we have postponed our necessary action.'[8]
However, this acknowledgement did not moderate Chamberlain's
unionism, and certainly, despite the evidence that some of the British
protagonists in the conflict were becoming more self-critical of their
own collective history when *Pack Up the Troubles* was produced, such
unionism was still alive and well in the British polity in 1991. Here is
what Lord Colnbrook, or Humphrey Atkins that was, Secretary of State
for Northern Ireland from 1979 to 1981, said:

> This is part of the United Kingdom, which has got a lot of people who want
> to detach it from the United Kingdom, but the majority want to stay there
> and it is our job to protect them as far as we can. It is part of the United
> Kingdom. For heaven's sake two of my cousins live there. It is just as much
> a part of the United Kingdom as Devonshire is, where my daughter lives ...
> and if there's a group of people who say we want to detach you and take
> you away and make you part of a foreign country, and the majority, includ-
> ing my cousins, don't want to, then it's my business to try and defend them.

This is a traditional unionist view, and states with some passion that
the job of the British is to support unionism. Another traditional view,
this time associated with the British military establishment, came from
Michael Mates, a Tory MP who was an ex-soldier, who had served five
tours of duty in Northern Ireland. He was to become a Conservative

junior minister for Northern Ireland in 1992–93. When asked what the 'Irish Problem' was, he said, 'Terrorism – it is being promoted by a minority with many interests other than getting the British out of Ireland. There's a lot of crime involved, there's a lot of protection involved, but the terrorism is there and it is very mildly supported by very few people.'

This final point was a contention which was hardly supported by the deployment of 300,000 British troops during the lifetime of the Troubles, but the general argument here, that essentially Northern Ireland was a security problem, was a common view. Stuart Bell, despite his criticism of Roy Mason's policies, also reduced the problem to one of law and order; that is, British law and Irish disorder. He said, 'I don't think the [British] troops are part of the problem. I think the problem is the IRA and the counter-reaction from the loyalist paramilitaries, and that's the problem. It is a security problem. It is a problem of those who believe that death resolves a political issue … other people's deaths [and] their own; holding life very cheap.'

So it is a security problem, not a political problem, and the problem is with the Irish and, he seems to suggest, the Irish allegiance to death as a political tool. This latter argument is, of course, one the English have frequently used over the centuries: that the problem is and always has been Irish propensity to violence. Even Peter Archer, who came across as the most open minded of all those interviewed, also referred to this. On the one hand, he judged that historically Irish recourse to violence was, if not justified, at least understandable because when the Irish 'simply addressed reasoned arguments to the English nobody listened, and they felt that until they were violent, nothing seemed to happen'. On the other hand:

> I think going a long way back in Ireland there is something which arises almost as the embodiment of the tragedy at the heart of the godhead. The feeling that the whole universe, as St Paul said, 'groaneth and travaileth', and that there is no way of having an effect without an element of violence and tragedy. And it doesn't only mean inflicting violence on other people. It means being prepared to suffer violence. It is the theology of the cross and I think there is a feeling in Ireland that violence, suffering violence had merits in itself, in a way the Protestant English never understood.

One of the consequences of the view suggested here, namely that the Irish have some sort of cultural attachment to violence, is that this can excuse or underplay violence against them, especially if that comes from your own side. And this in turn allows Archer, and of course many others, to avoid their own side's responsibility for their lawlessness, even if accepting that they at times misbehave. He said:

I don't think that any government in London ever actually said, 'Let's see
how tyrannical we can be in Northern Ireland. Let's see how many people
we can torture. Let's see how many we can shoot on sight.' I don't think it
was ever like that. I think it was largely a leaden-footed reaction to a very
difficult problem ... Yes I think the British government, successive British
governments have made mistakes, partly because they weren't quite sure
what to do when they got the judgement wrong, partly because they tended
to get a bit over-emotional. They lost their tempers.

There may indeed be something in what Archer is saying here, but
spot the difference: the Irish are culturally sympathetic to violence;
the English just lose their tempers. Similarly when I interviewed Lord
Holme, the spokesperson on Ireland for the Liberal Democrats in 1991,
he described Bloody Sunday as 'an inappropriate use of force'.

While these views minimise British violence, others go further and refuse
to acknowledge any British or unionist responsibility for the political and
historical situation which produced it. For example, when I asked Atkins
'What do you understand as the reason for the violence?', his superficial
reply not only avoided causality, but made clear where his sympathies lay:

The IRA, who are responsible for most of it. I'm afraid that some of the
other violence, from the so-called loyalists, is what you might call comple-
mentary violence. Because, if the IRA go around murdering a lot of people
who are unionists, then there are some elements among the unionists that
think it is right to go round murdering a lot of people who are republican.
But I think it is reactive, that.

Leaving aside that loyalist violence in the 1960s predated that from the
nationalist community, what has some significance here is that while
Atkins is not justifying loyalist violence, he comes close to it. He came
even closer when he discussed both previous violence and the potential
for any future such violence:

If at any time in the future the British government was so foolish as to say,
'Look, we've had enough of all this, I think the best course for people living
in Northern Ireland is to become part of the Republic', then the threat of
violence [from the unionists], the war which was apparent in the early part
of the century and which led to the establishment of Northern Ireland as a
separate entity, that would be there again. They'd fight – that is the lesson
and that is what happened before, as you know ... Carson and all those
people were importing arms.... They were ready to fight, and I think they
would be again today. That's the lesson.

Or, as Randolph Churchill famously put it a hundred years before,
'Ulster will fight and Ulster will be right'. These were words later judged
by one eminent historian as an invitation to Ulster Protestants to start

a civil war.[9] But again, when the words or actions of British politicians threaten or even deliver mayhem, somehow it is never their fault. For example, here is Atkins on the hunger strike of 1981:

> Ten people died and that was, I think, very sad. I don't think we could have prevented that. We tried, goodness knows we tried hard. But it was a question of trying to get into the head of the hunger strikers that we were not actually going to give in to their demand ... We tried to make it clear to them that if they went on and refused food they would die. But that we were not going to give in.

Does 'we could not have prevented' the deaths and 'tried hard' to prevent them, square with 'we were not going to give in'? This comes back again to the avoidance of responsibility. When asked about possible British withdrawal, Labour's Kevin McNamara had this to say:

> If one is saying let us withdraw British troops tomorrow, or in five years' time, what we do know is that there have been 40,000 people through the Ulster Defence Regiment [UDR] who didn't join the UDR to support the concept of a united Ireland.

Indeed they did not: they joined for the 'defence' of 'Ulster', and with that terminology the UDR soon came to be made up overwhelmingly of loyal Ulster Protestants. So, when the question 'Who set up and trained the UDR in the first place?' was put to McNamara, his reply was:

> That's quite beyond the argument. I mean one can [ask] which came first, the chicken or the egg. With the greatest respect they are there and they are part of the equation just as much as the British Army, just as much as the IRA. Whether I like them being there or not doesn't enter the matter at all. They are there. Who was responsible in that sense doesn't really matter.

We now know that as early as 1975 the British authorities, including the leadership of both of the main political parties, knew that the UDR was a huge problem, having been told in private by the Army that it was 'heavily infiltrated by extreme Protestants and that in a crisis situation they could not be relied on to be loyal' to the UK government.[10] So surely it did matter where the origins of this problem lay, and who was responsible for it. McNamara's reluctance to address this issue may just have had something to do with the fact that it was a Labour government that set up the UDR in the first place. So did a future Labour government have a responsibility to try to solve the UDR problem? Not at all, apparently:

> So you would *not* be in favour of disbanding and disarming the UDR if you came into power?

I never said that.
Well would you be *in* favour?
I never said that either.

This may be an example of the usual equivocation to which politicians are prone, but alternatively or additionally, it could be an example of the equally customary British refusal to admit to their Irish mistakes, and their reluctance to fix them. The latter explanation becomes more persuasive when McNamara was asked to comment on the Labour government's 1974 Prevention of Terrorism Act (PTA), passed following the Birmingham pub bombings by the IRA in 1974. It was described as 'draconian' by Labour Home Secretary Roy Jenkins when he introduced it in the House of Commons, and it was later described by one prominent solicitor as 'a significant and devastating encroachment on the rights and freedom of the citizen in the UK'.[11] This had a particular effect on the Irish community in Britain and Irish people travelling to Britain. For McNamara:

> The Prevention of Terrorism Act is seen as an instrument of harassment ... [But] I mean I can remember when the PTA was introduced, it was introduced specifically and directly to protect Irish men and women in this country, who, following the enormous and terrible outrage of Birmingham were subject to persecution, to abuse on the factory floors, to the windows of their homes split open.

McNamara himself was subject to window smashing, but that does not disguise the fact that to say that the purpose of the PTA was to defend the Irish community is something of a rewriting of history. More generally, however, the dominant sentiment of British politicians of all varieties is to have no truck with history at all and instead call on all concerned to forget about the past. Indeed, to do otherwise appears to constitute an Irish original sin. For Lord Gowrie, 'People are fighting an old quarrel and an old issue, and have been doing so for far too long.' Or there is Michael Mates:

> The least useful part of the discussion about the Northern Ireland situation or the Irish situation in general or the British/Irish one has been because everybody tries to analyse it with what went wrong in the past. I don't believe that that is anything that gets us one width further.

And Humphrey Atkins, when I asked him about the Conservative support for the 1912 unionist rebellion, said:

> You are asking me to judge my predecessors aren't you? My successors are going to judge me. I am not prepared to say what should have been done before I was born, for heaven's sake.

A couple of observations can be made about such attitudes. The first is almost too obvious and is the mantra of historians: that to understand the present you have to explore the past. That is why *Pack Up the Troubles* devoted some time to explaining the events in Ireland from 1912 to 1921 which led to the establishment of Northern Ireland, because without that knowledge an understanding of Northern Ireland in 1991 was bound to be flawed. Second, in this case it can also be suggested that those who dismiss the relevance of the past are in danger of failing to learn its lessons; they are prone to relive it by repeating the old mistakes motivated by old attitudes. The example of the hunger strike is a case in point. In 1917 another famous Irish prisoner, Thomas Ashe, died while on hunger strike, insisting that his crimes were political. His funeral produced what one of Ireland's great modern historians, F. S. L. Lyons, called 'a political demonstration unexampled since the [1916] rising'.[13] Similarly, the death of hunger striker Bobby Sands, on Atkins' watch, produced the largest funeral procession in Ireland since partition. Even from his own point of view, Sir Humphrey should have read some history and realised that invoking a rerun of Ashe was not the wisest thing he could have done.

The British sentiments already discussed – the pro-unionism, accusations of Ireland's addiction to violence, everything is the fault of the Irish, Britain had never bad intent towards Ireland and unionist/loyalist violence is excusable – all have historical precedents. For instance, traditional British unionism insisted that, whether or not the Irish wanted to rule themselves, the greater good of the UK as a whole could not allow that. Professor A. V. Dicey, whose book *England's Case Against Home Rule,* was the bible for those opposing Gladstone's plans for Irish Home Rule, puts it as follows:

> Home Rule is no doubt primarily a scheme for the government of Ireland, but it is also much more than this: it is a plan for revolutionising the constitution of the whole United Kingdom. There is no unfairness therefore, in insisting that the proposed change must not take place if it be adverse to the interests of Great Britain. This is merely to assert that the welfare of thirty million citizens must, if a conflict of interest arise, be preferred to the interests of five million citizens.

Here is a 1990s version from Labour's Stuart Bell:

> If you look at Wales and Scotland, England, none of us have the right to opt out of the United Kingdom. Only the Northern Irish people have the right, given from 1922, to opt out. They have the right if they feel in their majority that they ought to be part of the South then they are entitled to be a part of the South. That is the view today, as it was in 1922. That cannot be right.

No state in the entire world that I am aware of, says that a part of the state can go off somewhere else if it feels like it. This is an extraordinary situation that has built in a tremendous insecurity within the unionist community.

Summing up the ideological inheritance is Sir Humphrey Atkins in this same old, familiar mixture of imperial certainty and patronising colonialism:

We are the United Kingdom. We are [made up] of Great Britain and Northern Ireland, and this is an entity, which has been the case for a very long while. The Irish are an industrious people. They work very hard and they do a lot of things extremely well. They used to build marvellous ships in the war; and furthermore they're great soldiers. What I really mean is that we are one people, with different roots.

The attitudes of British politicians towards the Irish conflict, explored in these interviews, were also at work in a controversy surrounding their use in our documentary film, *Pack Up the Troubles*.[14] This centred on the intervention of the leadership of the LP, specifically the office of the then leader, Neil Kinnock. They had seen a preview tape of the documentary and were disturbed by a passage in the film in which we highlighted a difference between two Labour Shadow Northern Ireland Secretaries of State, Archer and McNamara. The issue was talks with SF. Archer had said, 'I was never prepared knowingly to have talks with terrorists. I was prepared in certain circumstances to have discussions with people who said we may approve of the terrorists, and I think that is a very important distinction.' These words were illustrated in the film by a cutting from a newspaper of Archer having talks with SF councillors over minor social issues and of Neil Kinnock being aware of these discussions. McNamara, however, was much more hard line, saying that until the IRA's armed struggle was unequivocally ended he would not talk, even with SF, because 'They are apologists for military activity'. Now, of course if that attitude had been adopted by Tony Blair (who accepted that a ceasefire, as opposed to a declaration ending the IRA campaign, was sufficient for official talks to begin), or indeed by Gerry Adams (in that the British government was an apologist for the military activity of Britain's armed forces), then guns and bombs would still be going off in Ireland. It is also the case that our opinion poll showed support for all-inclusive talks. When respondents were asked if they would support these, 78 per cent said they would. Even when SF was specifically mentioned, 51 per cent said they should be included, with 31 per cent saying they should not.

Despite the public's apparently endorsing Archer's general approach, his account of his talks riled the then Labour leadership. They contacted Channel 4, and said that because of that passage in the film they would seek an injunction to stop it being shown. They said we lied over Archer having discussions with SF members, even though Archer defended this in the film, and they disputed the newspaper report of Kinnock's approval of the meeting. All lies they said. We pointed out that we had Archer on film testifying to all of this, and they were sent the unedited interview and relevant press cuttings. Through Channel 4 as an intermediary we suggested that they talk with Archer. They said Archer was 'out of the country' and still insisted it was all fabrication and that Channel 4 must withdraw the entire film. Channel 4 declined this invitation. The following day, which was the day of the broadcast, Labour came back to Channel 4 and said they would now only insist on the removal of the offending passage. Again, an injunction was threatened and again Channel 4 resisted. Eventually, two hours before broadcast the threats ceased. The documentary went ahead as scheduled and received good reviews; SF's *An Phoblacht* and *The Times* were particularly complimentary.

What is instructive here is the issue that had the LP running to lawyers: it did not want it broadcast that it had once had even minor discussions with SF. The irony was that this attitude underlined what the documentary was trying to say about the chief features of Ireland's British problem in 1991. First, British politicians had a caution bordering on timidity when it came to trying to resolve the conflict. Second, if in doubt, too many tended too easily to lapse into an espousal of traditional policies and attitudes from colonialism to censorship. And third, the British public, as evident in our opinion poll, was way ahead of the politicians in seeking a more radical approach to Northern Ireland. Indeed the poll respondents' recommendations actually went further than did the GFA: only 31 per cent wanted Northern Ireland to remain in the UK, with 25 per cent favouring an independent Northern Ireland and the same percentage favouring Irish unity. In other words, while the majority of British public opinion did not share an agreed vision of the future for Ireland – and they were not alone in that – it did agree that the unionist status quo was past its sell-by date.

Eventually, at least as far as an inclusive dialogue was concerned, the public won out, with ceasefires proving sufficient to allow official talks to proceed. It is beyond the scope of this analysis to speculate how and why this occurred,[15] just as it is too soon to assess the permanence of the current settlement, but one suggestion can be made. While the emergence of the GFA is often popularly explained in Britain as the Irish coming to their senses, the opinions and attitudes quoted above suggest that many in the British political elite in 1991 had some way to go before they were able to embrace the empathy needed from peace participants. Yet, some of the views also reported here, specifically from Archer and Gowrie, did show an ability to go beyond British tribal thinking, and perhaps these were examples of the starting point for what was to follow. However, Ian Paisley told *Pack Up the Troubles* that Secretaries of State for Northern Ireland 'have not only institutionalised our problems but exacerbated the situation'. Now, no one, least of all Paisley himself, would suggest that the Irish themselves have always been beacons of reasonableness and tolerance, but on the basis of the extracts produced above this is one judgement of the Reverend Doctor which it is not easy to disprove.

Notes

1 Interview by author, the *Pack Up the Troubles* transcripts, April 1991 (also titled *Why Don't They Just Get Out?*), MSS, Linen Hall Library, Belfast (no reference number). The author also holds copies of these which may be consulted on request. Unless otherwise stated all direct quotations that follow are from these transcripts. The following are the pages in question. Peter Archer: pp.1–31; Lord Holme: pp. 33–50; Michael Mates: pp. 51–78; Kevin McNamara: pp. 79–130; Lord Prior: 131–54; Lord Colnbrook (Humphrey Atkins): pp. 155–79; Stuart Bell: 180–99; Ian Paisley: pp. 200–13; Lord Gowrie: pp. 257–77.

2 *Pack Up the Troubles*, directed by Lin Solomon and Cahal McLaughlin, Northside Productions for Channel 4, 1991.

3 D. de Breadún, *The Far Side of Revenge* (Cork: The Collins Press, 2001), p. 6.

4 For more details see D. Bloomfield, *Political Dialogue in Northern Ireland: The Brooke Initiative, 1989–92* (Basingstoke: Macmillan, 1998).

5 For more details see P. Arthur, *Special Relationships* (Belfast: Blackstaff Press, 2000).

6 G. Bell, *Troublesome Business* (London: Pluto Press, 1982), p. 146.

7 Ibid., p. 143.

8 J. Chamberlain, *Home Rule and the Irish Question. A Collection of Speeches Delivered between 1881 and 1887* (London: National Radical Union, 1887), p. 5.

9 J. C. Beckett, *The Making of Modern Ireland* (London: Faber and Faber, 1966), p. 400.

10 This was reported in a meeting between PM James Callaghan, Northern Ireland Secretary Merlyn Rees, Conservative leader Margaret Thatcher and Shadow Secretary Airey Neave. See National Archives CJ4/1443, Conservative Policy on Northern Ireland, Report from Prime Minister's Office, 10 September 1975.

11 Peter Hall, 'The Prevention of Terrorism Acts', in Anthony Jennings (ed.), *Justice Under Fire* (London: Pluto Press, 1990), pp. 144–5.

12 F. S. L. Lyons, *Ireland Since the Famine* (London: Fontana, 1971), p. 387.

13 A.V. Dicey, *England's Case Against Home Rule* (London: John Murray, 1886), p. 7.
14 The following is based on the memory of the author, which has been checked by others involved in the film.
15 See, for example, Arthur, *Special Relationship*.

6

'The coach never arrived back at its destination'[1]

Jenny McMahon

In 1968 I decided to join the Women's Royal Army Corps, initially for six years – that was the original idea. I trained as a physical training instructor, and had postings in the UK, Germany and Benbecula. Towards the end of 1973 I was posted to Catterick Garrison in West Yorkshire and was there for about six months. It was February 1974, when I had been invited to a friend's christening in Bury, but the only way I was going to get there was via coach. The trains were on strike, I couldn't drive and didn't have a car. I'm not keen on travelling by coach as I suffer from motion sickness. But that was the only way I was going to get there, and I was determined to go and spend the weekend with my friends, and attend the christening.

I had a lovely weekend. Sunday evening 3 February, my friend dropped me off to catch the coach which was leaving Oldham at 11.30 p.m. My friends lived in Bury but the coach was leaving Oldham to return to Catterick Garrison. The coach never arrived back at its destination. When I got on the bus, there weren't many spare seats left, I was one of the last people to get on. As I was walking up the aisle of the middle of the bus, the lads at the back were whistling and shouting and saying, 'Come on love, come and sit with us'. I was younger then – remember, this was 1974. I was heading to the back of the bus when I saw a seat on the left-hand side, and decided to sit here. I settled down for the return journey and remember looking at the clock at the front of the coach about a quarter to twelve, midnight, and I must have dozed off.

The next thing I remember was a horrendous noise which woke me up. I could feel my legs being tangled up. It was so quick and so sudden, I couldn't really work out what was happening. I must have been knocked out, because when I came round I was lying in the middle of the motorway, on the M62. I soon realised where I was and thought, 'I'm going to get run over, I'm a goner'. I had fallen through the bottom of the bus and was dragged along the motorway. I could feel my legs, my legs were burning, and they felt as if they were on fire. I was sprawled out on my back, I couldn't feel my left arm, at first I thought I'd lost my left arm. I couldn't understand what was happening. Then I could hear a lot of noise and commotion about fifty yards down the motorway, and I could see what I can only describe as half a bus.

I started shouting, and screaming, 'Somebody come and help me', and two young lads came and put their coats over me. It was very cold, early February. My legs were in intense pain and covered in blood. It didn't seem that long after when the police came, and I asked 'What's happened?' And they said, 'Well we think it's a bomb', but I just couldn't comprehend that. Although obviously something had happened because of the devastation to the bus.

I was taken to Batley General Hospital, and one of the policemen came with me in the ambulance. I was initially at Batley, then transferred to the Cambridge Military Hospital, Aldershot which was closer to my home and easier for my family to visit. I had multiple injuries to my legs, lacerations, open wounds, fractures, blast injuries and flash burns, which required several stitches and a skin graft on the right ankle. My hair and eyebrows were singed, but fortunately I had no facial injuries.

I spent nearly two months in hospital. Some of my wounds were slow to heal, due to infections. My natural instinct was to try and get back to normality and get fit again. I was young, I was fit, I was active, I played all sorts of sports, I played tennis, and I was in the Army Gymnastic Display Team. I was determined to get back to doing the activities I enjoyed, although at one stage I had my doubts, as I had a lot of pain in my right foot walking and in weight-bearing activities and thought I was going to be a cripple. During my recovery I never received any physiotherapy, rehab or counselling. It didn't happen in those days, it's what I call DIY, 'Do It Yourself'. So that's what I try to encourage other people to do. It took me a long time to get on another bus or coach, and to this day I never go to the back. Eventually I did make a good recovery, it took nearly a year, and although I did go back to work, I couldn't initially do the job that I had been trained to do. But I soldiered on as you do when serving in the Armed Forces. My family, friends and colleagues were very supportive during and after the recovery process.

I managed to get fit, stayed in the Army and continued my role as a physical training instructor and achieved the rank of sergeant. A few years later I had the opportunity of training as a remedial gymnast. I had always been interested in medical conditions and I am a caring person by nature. It was a two-year, full-time course and I was fortunate to train whilst still serving. As a remedial gymnast I specialised in exercise therapy and rehabilitation. Once qualified I was posted to the Joint Services Medical Rehabilitation Unit at RAF Chessington, where I worked on the gym floor and was involved in exercise therapy and rehabilitation of other service men and women, many who had also sustained injuries from IRA bomb blasts, gunshot wounds and terrorist attacks. I spent two years at Chessington, and found it personally very rewarding. It was quite hilarious at times with some of the camaraderie that went on, as you can imagine, mainly service men and very few women.

In 1985 I had the opportunity of converting over to physiotherapy, and successfully completed the conversion course and was posted to the Queen Elizabeth Military Hospital in Woolwich. Again I was involved in the rehabilitation, treatment, of servicemen and women, many having been injured in the Northern Ireland atrocities, others who were in the UK. I always felt that I could relate to these individuals with my own personal experience.

I completed twenty-two years in the Army, which I didn't anticipate when I first joined; I was just going to do six and then come out, but once I'd opted to do the remedial gymnast training, you were committed to a certain number of years, and then from there you have to make a decision, 'do I come out or do I continue serving?' So I continued serving.

I came out of the Army in 1990 and went to work for a company in London as a physiotherapist, and was involved in setting up a new health and fitness centre. I was well qualified, with lots of experience. I completed six years there and was ready to move on. I was commuting daily into London on the trains. There were several incidents with bombs going off, bomb hoaxes, strikes with the railways, and the trains were often delayed for various reasons. It got to the point where I didn't feel safe travelling by train, so I decided to look for another job nearer home.

I successfully applied for and accepted the role of physiotherapist at the Defence Medical Rehabilitation Centre at Headley Court. I think my military background helped to secure the job. I commenced my new role in 1996, and completed thirteen years. I was heavily involved in the physiotherapy treatment of our young lads and lasses who were returning from Iraq and Afghanistan with horrendous injuries. Many had lost limbs due to improvised explosive devices, others had sustained gross traumatic injuries and deformities from rocket-propelled grenades, gun shot wounds and road bombs. They were not simple injuries, but were very complex and complicated, including multiple wounds and fractures, severe abdominal and buttock flesh wounds, neurological disorders and brain injuries.

I have never been in a war and I have never trained to go to war, but I do feel from my own personal experience that I could relate to the guys and the lasses that were coming back from these battle zones, regarding the personal emotions and physical, mental and psychological issues that you have to live with. It was over twenty years later I realised that I actually experienced PTSD, but didn't know it at the time. In the mid nineties, whilst I was working at Headley Court, one of the psychologists gave a lecture on PTSD and I was sitting listening and thinking, 'Yes I've been there, I've seen that, I've done that, and I've experienced that.' But somewhere along the line I came out of it, I don't know where and I don't know when. I do know it was an honour and a privilege to help other survivors who had been injured in other conflicts. It has been a very rewarding job and, looking back now, helped me in coming to terms with my own personal experience of terrorist activity. Twelve people were killed in the M62 bomb explosion including a family with two young children. All were sitting at the back of the coach. I have always felt I had a very lucky escape.

Note

1 This chapter originates in a talk presented at 'The Northern Ireland Troubles in Britain: Impacts, Engagements, Legacies and Memories' conference at Brighton, 11–13 July 2012. The talk and answers to questions were recorded, transcribed and amalgamated to form this written text.

7

Serving in troubled times: British military personnel's memories and accounts of service in Northern Ireland

K. Neil Jenkings and Rachel Woodward

What are the legacies and memories of the Troubles for those 300,000 military personnel, many serving multiple tours of duty, who were deployed in Northern Ireland with the British Armed Forces? It is possibly too early to say this definitively; archives of personal letters and accounts are often only created on the emergence of artefacts (correspondence, diaries and medical records etc.) after the death of participants and spouses. Oral histories may be collected, and collections created, by individuals and institutions where the will and resources exist to do so, but these are frequently fragmentary and unsystematic. However, what is clear from the evidence we have is that the Troubles presented – and continue to present – a difficult story for many personnel. Deployed initially to assist with civil protection in the summer of 1969, and operational throughout the 1970s and 1980s as the violence in the province ebbed and flowed, the personnel were gradually withdrawn as the peace process gained traction, and only a small contingent remain. The Northern Ireland deployment, Operation Banner, contrasts with the drama of the 1982 Falklands campaign and the geopolitical significance of the Cold War deployments in Germany. Whilst the landscapes of military occupation and deployment in the province are slowly being reconfigured, so too are the memories of those who saw active service in the province where, in 1972, on average one soldier died every three days, and between 14 August 1969 and 31 July 2007, 1,441 UK Armed Forces personnel died: 722 as a result of direct action and 719 due to other causes.[1]

This chapter draws on conversations with former military personnel about their military pasts in Northern Ireland, and on the autobiographical accounts of personnel about deployment to the province, in order to explore how the memory work that these people have undertaken in the present provides a narrative about the Troubles which seeks to accommodate the experiences of their younger selves. One of the findings of the wider research, especially notable in our investigation of the production of published military memoirs, is the collaborative nature of the production of such personal accounts.[2] However, this is not to deny the individual nature of those experiences. In the words of one interviewee, 'you sign up, don't you, knowing that you possibly or potentially go over to places. But as a young eighteen, nineteen-year-old lad, you don't expect to get dropped straight into it.'[3] That experience, of being inserted as a trained but very young soldier into a conflict which has been subject to a host of changing and conflicting narratives following its 'conclusion', sits at the heart of this chapter.

Framing the experience of individual soldiers in Northern Ireland during the Troubles, we suggest that the armed forces constituted a third community alongside those broadly identified as Catholic (nationalist or republican) or Protestant (unionist or loyalist). Accounts of the Troubles necessarily need to take this third community into account, given the 300,000 personnel deployed and the long time period over which these deployments took place. It has been stated that much of the media coverage in the UK can be best described as pro-UK 'propaganda',[4] heavily biased towards the Army, yet by definition such accounts failed to represent the reality of the individual British soldier's experience of the Troubles. What are needed are accounts that do not prioritise a reading of that third community as a depersonalised and undifferentiated mass, representing the soldier as an unnamed and anonymous individual, available as the repository of a heroising or demonising metanarrative.[5] Instead we are keen here to explore this issue of legacy and memory as an individual and personal experience. As Hockey observes in his ethnography of soldiers undertaken during participant observation with a British Army unit which deployed to Northern Ireland:

> [T]he private soldier, like all social actors, is not a passive unreflecting puppet responding to the remote dictates of an external 'objective' and reified culture. On the contrary, the cultural elements such as self-images, maxims, modes of conduct constitute a language used ... to construct and account for [private soldiers'] own social world.[6]

One set of materials we use to explore the Troubles and its legacies are taken from a research project which, although not focused specifically on Northern Ireland, raised questions about its legacy most forcefully. The project focused on representations of the soldier[7] in print media and in soldiers' own personal photographic collections, and it is the latter data sources which we use here.[8] We collected data to inform an exploration of the ways in which soldiers construct and articulate their military identities.[9] Our data comprises the transcripts of one-to-one interviews structured around discussion of up to ten personal photographs chosen by the interviewee to represent their military life. In the data we use here, all our interviewees were former, rather than serving, personnel at the time of the interview.

During these interviews, the Troubles emerged incidentally and reflexively, and our interviewees collectively provided very varied accounts of their deployment to Northern Ireland. The stories discussed here should not be taken as representative of the entire range of possible experiences for British armed forces personnel across the period of the Troubles.[10] However, these stories are indicative of assertions of individual participation and presence in an armed force whose role in the Northern Ireland conflict as a third community participating in the Troubles is rapidly becoming obscured as regiments such as the Ulster Defence Regiment get amalgamated out of existence, as the media (and public) switch their focus to foreign wars and as a result of the general 'moving on' process that the 'peace process' has facilitated. Furthermore, they are illustrative of the personal traumas and triumphs, and the friendships and relations of enmity, which are often left out of discussions of the experience of soldiering in Northern Ireland. Following Butler's exposition of the positions of precarity, vulnerability and non-value into which some subjects, but not others, are cast, we consider there to be a responsibility towards 'a critical reflection on those exclusionary norms by which fields of recognisability are constituted', fields invoked when 'we mourn for some lives by responding with coldness to the loss of others'.[11] The jeering crowds around dying teenage soldiers or 'sectarian others' are indeed chilling in their lack of empathy, astounding soldiers fresh from Great Britain where they had usually grown up without knowing, or caring, about the religious and political orientations of their neighbours. However, they were often quick to be normalised to, and scarred by, the 'standards' prevailing during the Troubles. The Troubles were a time of 'civil war' that deteriorated into an unglamorous policing operation under the scrutiny of an often critical media and indifferent population. Unlike in Iraq and Afghanistan, the deaths of soldiers had to compete with 'innocent civilian' deaths of the Ulster and mainland British citizens. Even the deaths of terrorists were seen as murders and as martyrdom by one community or the other, whereas the role of the Army and their deaths were less easily heroicised, especially those of soldiers from outside the province. The Troubles are often viewed as something vaguely embarrassing that the majority of the British public would rather forget. The British public rallied around its returning troops from Iraq and Afghanistan, even though these deployments were not overwhelmingly popular nor without their detractors. However, Help for Heroes and the phenomenon of (Royal) Wootton Bassett were not a response seen by soldiers in relation to service in Northern Ireland, beyond initial deployment and welcome by the Catholic population, perhaps.

As a counter to these 'exclusionary norms', we also draw on military memoirs, the autobiographical accounts by individuals of military participation, which provide our second source of data here.[12] As the autobiographical accounts of soldiers show, authors are adamant about the grievability of the lives that are lost, in ways that are suggestive of a sense that their experiences as soldiers had become obscured and the sacrifices of their fellow soldiers were unacknowledged and unremembered. This lack of acknowledgement has been only partially, and relatively recently, redressed with the Ulster Grove at the National Memorial Arboretum at Lichfield (see chapter 22 by Armstrong in this volume). These accounts also reflect directly on the lasting consequences of military participation for post-military lives. Our research on memoirs explored the range of accounts published from 1980 onwards about service with British armed forces in a range of conflicts.

The conflict in Northern Ireland did not produce anything like the volume of memoirs prompted by the Falklands conflict in 1982; the relatively small body of autobiographical accounts reflects both the nature of the Northern Ireland conflict as a long drawn-out series of deployments rather than a distinctive, time-limited campaign, and also the unease which the civilian reading public has felt about the activities and deployments of the armed forces as a third community in a place which was, and is, part of the United Kingdom. There are two notable features of the Northern Ireland memoirs, however. The first is that they include accounts by two women personnel – when the body of over 220 military memoirs published between 1980 and the present includes only six by women personnel. Both these books – Sarah Ford's *One Up*[13] and Jackie George's *She Who Dared*[14] – are about enlisted women serving on attachment to an intelligence detachment, so their roles and experiences, and their published books, are unusual for women personnel.[15] The second point follows from this, which is that the majority of the books about service in Northern Ireland are about service with or on attachment to the Special Forces, reflecting publishers' expectations about the market niche for these narratives. The exception here is Clarke's *Contact*.[16] There is also a wider body of books which mention Northern Ireland deployments in passing, with the narrative focusing on another conflict (and we do not dwell on these here). Beyond this, the sub-set of Northern Ireland memoirs follow broader patterns within the genre as a whole, with a mixture of career autobiography,[17] vindication and recovery narratives[18] and action-adventure stories.[19]

We have, then, two sources of autobiographical data on which we draw – interview narratives around photographs, and published memoirs. In the remainder of this chapter we sketch out some of the key themes which emerge from both and which speak to the idea of a third community whose members' participation requires memory work in the present to contain and account for the effects of that experience and to establish the 'field of recognisability' for these people.

Youth and experience

The youth of soldiers when they were first deployed to Northern Ireland is notable. Although soldiers had to be aged eighteen on deployment (the British armed forces at that time recruited from the age of sixteen, and at age seventeen personnel could be deployed outside the UK), as Clarke notes of his troop, '[t]he oldest soldier is twenty and at twenty-five I am considered an old man'.[20] So, whilst the individuals deployed were led by more experienced non-commissioned officers (NCOs) and officers, were legally adult and had successfully passed through their basic military training, they were still teenagers, most of them not much older than eighteen. Looking at a photograph (Figure 7.1) of two armed soldiers patrolling in a residential area, its owner reflected:

> I went straight to my first unit, and probably the biggest experience of my life, at the tender age of eighteen, nineteen year old [They were] ... very young lads on an operational tour. Every time we went out, we were open for attack, bombings. We went to Northern Ireland at that time when it was marching season, so we had the riots that grew with the various marching bands. A bit of an eye-opener for a young eighteen, nineteen year old lad. Scary at times, no doubt about it.

Once conscription through National Service ended in 1960, all those serving with the British Army were volunteers.[21] As one interviewee remarked as he looked at a photograph (Figure 7.2) of his detachment of soldiers posed holding their rifles in formal style in front of high metal gates, concrete walls and barbed wire, with the sign 'HMP MAZE' indicating the location:

> That's the Maze tour in '85, that's the last tour I did ... That is the troop that went over, and everyone got the choice, do you want to go, or do you not want to go? They were asking for volunteers, and every one of them is

Figure 7.1 Soldiers of the Royal Electrical and Mechanical Engineers on foot patrol in Ardoyne, Belfast, 1982.

Figure 7.2 Maze Prison Royal Artillery Detachment, 1985.

a volunteer. Very few of these guys had been before ... all the senior ranks and full screws had been, but the gunners, there were about four who had been before.

He was asked why the soldiers in his detachment volunteered for active duties in Northern Ireland.

Probably, yeah just to get some experience. A lot of them had come straight from – this guy here and that one there, they were only turned eighteen, they had come from a junior leaders' regiment.

During the period of the Troubles, with the exception of the drama of the Falklands War in 1982, the British armed forces were not active in other theatres of operations beyond deployments to bases in Germany and Cyprus. Serving in Northern Ireland was therefore the closest that trained personnel could get to using their training on active service, honing their skills and getting military experience. Willingness to volunteer is not surprising for those trained in 'teeth arms' occupations. For others, deployment on patrols was more of a shock. For the interviewee looking at his photograph (Figure 7.3) of two soldiers patrolling in a residential area, the physical reality of patrolling was unexpected:

I joined as a vehicle mechanic, and I thought, yeah it will be no problem, I'll be in the workshop ... spannering away. I got to [X] Regiment, and they goes, 'ah we are going to Northern Ireland'. And said, 'you'll be going out

Figure 7.3 Londonderry Queen's Dragoon Guards foot patrol, 1973–74.

on the streets, we are short of bodies'. They always say you are a soldier first, a mechanic second in the army. So there I am, trained as a vehicle mechanic, or garage mechanic whatever you want to call it, civilian equivalent, patrolling the streets with a brick [four-man group], attending riots, stopping cars and checking their identities. Searching cars, house searches, cordons, even personal search[es], you could stop anybody in the street and search them, and arresting people as well.

As he reflected, it was the biggest experience of his life thus far.

Security and danger

Deployed personnel, on any operation, have to learn to read a new landscape. What is notable in the recollections of personnel deployed to Northern Ireland is the ways in which they encountered landscapes as simultaneously familiar and unfamiliar; Clarke's *Contact* is notable for the extent to which he structures a record of his experience around the familiar/unfamiliar landscapes he encounters as his company moves through its period of deployment. As part of the UK, with Belfast sharing an economic history in common with many great urban industrial centres in Britain, and with a great proportion of enlisted personnel originating in similar cities in Strathclyde, Tyneside, West Yorkshire, Lancashire and Merseyside, the landscapes they encountered of working-class housing and heavy industrial activity were very familiar. Differences were notable, however. The physical, visible marking out of the sectarian divide across the streets and areas of Belfast through the painting of kerbstones, lamp-posts and the gable ends of houses was specific to Northern Ireland. Learning to read the signs of territorial demarcation was necessary to the safety of personnel.

Memories of deployments to Northern Ireland, and the calibrations of safety and danger in the spaces of deployment, were invoked most frequently through photographs of units on active patrol, whether taken by a colleague or (as often happened) more formally by a unit or press photographer. Photographs which ostensibly appear to have nothing to do with active operations also do this work, and in discussing these – a picture of the interior of a sanger (observation post), for example, or of an individual during pre-deployment training – stories would emerge. A photograph shown to us by a musician, a Band of the Irish Guards member, gave an insight as our interviewee talked of the ways in which she and her regimental bandmates had to negotiate their mobilities across the province. Band personnel were seen as legitimate targets for IRA forces during the Troubles, with eleven members of the Royal Marines Band killed in Deal, Kent in September 1989;[22] the deaths of four soldiers of the Blues and Royals and seven Bandsmen of the Royal Green Jackets in Hyde Park in London in July 1982;[23] and an attempted bombing of Bandsmen of the Blues and Royals in St Albans, Hertfordshire in November 1991 (in which a premature explosion killed the suspected bombers rather than their targets).[24] Our interviewee discussed the Troubles through her photograph, taken from a newspaper, of band members in their red dress uniforms milling about before a performance in Dublin to celebrate the Queen's birthday.

> Yeah, we were in Dublin actually, and we'd done a job with – well, that is the other cutting that goes with it, 'Irish and British Army Band Strike up a Chord'. We did a concert together with the Irish Army Band, which caused a bit of hoohah with the IRA. So it was quite – it was not stressful for us, but there was a lot of security around, and it caused a bit of a stir and there was a few demonstrations outside of the Irish Army Barracks where I was playing in Dublin. [...] You know, we had a big audience, but it was [about] Northern Ireland and the IRA weren't happy about us being there, and we actually went on up to finish our tour in Northern Ireland, and we were going to travel from Dublin up to Belfast, and we had to go back to Holyhead on a freight ferry, and then wait for a bus … and go from Holyhead up to Stranraer and then from Stranraer to Belfast. Just to avoid any terrorist activity.

Whilst this is not a dramatic account of involvement in the Troubles, it illustrates well the ways in which the security situation affected all armed forces personnel, whatever their profession or engagement in Northern Ireland.

Negotiating around places of security and danger in landscapes which in appearance could often seem so familiar entailed negotiating around the individuals (republicans and loyalists) against whom deployed personnel engaged in active operations, and a civilian populace encountered in more mundane security operations. Places which were ostensibly more dangerous because of the higher levels of threat from paramilitaries or hostility from local civilians could be much simpler places to be. As a respondent explained whilst discussing a photograph of himself manning a roadblock and checkpoint:

> I much preferred Londonderry because, Londonderry you knew where you stood, they just hated your guts, it was that simple. In South Armagh in Keady, they were a bit two-faced about it, you know, you would walk past, they'd shake your hand, and say "how are you doing?" "Fine," blah, and then they would stab you in the back, where[as] there [in Londonderry] you knew exactly where you stood, you know they hated you.

This simultaneous proximity to and distance from people, in landscapes which are familiar and unfamiliar, is unsettling. Collins, in his account of Special Forces operations in the province, explores this unease with the familiarity he feels with people he is intimate with because his job demands it.

> Sometimes I feel I know these people like I know my own friends. Their houses, their families, their mates, their pubs, their routes to work. But I have never even spoken to them. And there is no way we could ever be friends.[25]

It is Sarah Ford's ability to blend into a landscape peopled with others not so different from herself which (alongside her military training, of course) enables this young Navy rating to be deployed with Special Forces on intelligence work in the province. Wearing jeans, letting her roots grow out a bit and carrying a pack of nappies, she describes close surveillance of a particular target on a housing estate of a type familiar across Britain. She walks past the house, having observed her target enter the front gate, timing with precision her movement through the space of this suburban back street and the moment when she will casually glance at the house and garden and observe whether the suspect is, as suspected, engaged in explosive-related activities in his garden. When she does so, after all her efforts, she sees that he is engaged in that most prosaic and familiar of suburban masculine domestic pursuits, the fixing of the family barbecue.[26]

Horsfall, Special Air Service trooper, reflects further on the difficulties of this unsettling normality of much of the province and the empathy for its residents that could ensue for the soldiers deployed on active service there:

> I had to come to terms with the knowledge that Northern Ireland was not all war zone; it was an integral part of the United Kingdom and most people were perfectly ordinary, just trying to get on with their everyday lives. My previous tours had been to bad trouble spots, right in the centre of enemy territory. This was the real Ireland: rolling green hills, slow, meandering rivers that ran into huge lakes, pubs full of people having a beer, and familiar shops.[27]

This sort of empathy gives some insight into the strains and stresses experienced by individuals who were trained personnel deployed specifically as tools for the pursuit of state-legitimated violence, but with a very real sense of identification with the people they were asked to target. Relating a particular incident whilst he was undertaking covert surveillance, Collins describes the stress this caused:

> The car remains there for fifteen minutes and for fifteen minutes I agonise. Of course, I don't get a command over the radio to shoot. No-one wants

responsibility for a shot like this. The other sniper isn't the sort of guy who would work on his own initiative. Should I? I lie on my hillside weighing up the problem. If he's a civilian he might have a wife and family. That would be a terrible mistake.[28]

This sense of identification takes different forms. For one ex-soldier, looking at a photograph taken by a unit photographer of members of the respondent's platoon running across a piece of rough open field with a housing estate in the background, this identification was prompted by discussion of this familiar/unfamiliar landscape and the capabilities of 'the enemy':

> It might sound a silly thing to say, but they were very good at what they did. They were. If you went over there with the impression they were just a bunch of thick Paddys, you would come back in a box. They were very, very good at what they did. You had a certain amount of grudging respect for the way – because they would plan it, and if they couldn't get you one day, they would come back the next and see if they could get you the next day – they would watch you and see how you worked.

Just as British Army personnel are taught to do, of course. For some, the question of identification was direct and obvious. As others have noted,[29] ultimately, respondents reflected on the sobering thought that, for those from places elsewhere in Britain, similar to Northern Ireland in economic history and opportunity, there was a certain sense of identification with those they were deployed against:

> I said this to an officer once, I said, you know something, because I read up a lot on the Troubles, and the causes of it, and I have always said that if I had been born in 1956, which is when I was born, if I had been born a Catholic and I had been born in North Belfast, I would have probably been on the other side – it is just the way it goes.

Similarly, for Collins, 'I know enough Irish history to suspect that, if I'd been born a Roman Catholic here, I'd possibly be one of them.'[30] However, for many soldiers their disgust with the terrorist atrocities was such it would allow no such 'identification', on principle.

Trauma and memory

This third community of British armed forces personnel shared the traumas of republican and loyalist communities and paramilitary forces. In our interviews with former soldiers, and in our reading of the memoirs of deployment to Northern Ireland, traumatic events are inescapable. As we have noted, the vast majority of regular personnel deployed were young, many barely out of their teens. Devereaux describes how, as a young member of the Parachute Regiment at Warrenpoint, where an IRA roadside double-bombing in 1979 killed eighteen British soldiers:

> Everywhere I looked I could make out bits of body: the remains of a torso high up in a tree to the right; forward of me, on the estuary's beach, intestines and what looked like half a head, the face side.[31]

A feature of our interviews was the ways in which individuals with Northern Ireland experience negotiated their recollections of (and often their wish not to recollect) traumas, engaging in what we have termed elsewhere 'memory work', as a way of describing an active labour in the present to find a way to deal with events in the past.[32] The individual mentioned above, who chose to discuss his time in Northern Ireland with reference to the photograph of the interior of a sanger rather than any image showing an individual or an identifiable place, explained his decision with reference to a couple of particularly traumatic incidents, noting as he did the lack of support available to help process his memories of the incident. For this individual, the event was compounded by the fact that he knew one of the individuals killed in the incident, and Devereaux also notes how the dead of Warrenpoint included six people with whom he had trained (one of whom was a close friend).

Hockey, in his ethnography of enlisted soldiers, which included a tour of Northern Ireland during the period of his research (informed also by Hockey's prior experience as a soldier), identifies two salient features of the deployment. One was the way in which personnel ultimately 'perceived all operational activities primarily in terms of how much they were likely to be physically threatened [and killed] doing them'.[33] The other was the cohesion effect of fatalities; 'the first two deaths the company suffered at the hands of PIRA reinforced mutual identification and solidarity amongst all members'.[34] One of the photographs an interviewee shared with us showed how identification with the bonded group operated into the present, as part of an ongoing process of accommodating and explaining how personnel negotiate the aftermath of violence and their participation in it. The photograph showed a man in blazer and tie, distinctively moustachioed, laughing to camera alongside a woman similarly smartly dressed.

> Trooper [X] as he was then, he looks like a Mexican ... that's a regimental reunion ... whether it's right or wrong but he was credited with a kill in Northern Ireland ... well this is what I was thinking, ... because you see there, having a rare old time, he is technically a killer you know ... Just, my

missus knew that he had done that, that he had shot somebody it's, but it's your situation that you are in, you know, you are, it's a family you are ... as a regiment so especially at squadron level everybody basically knew everybody, they knew the wife, the kids.

So, whilst he would distance himself from associating with someone who, under normal circumstances, had taken another's life, in the context of deployment to Northern Ireland, this was acceptable. As he also indicated, this normalisation extended to individuals such as the ex-Trooper's being accepted not only as part of the regimental family but also as someone welcomed by the personal family. Lethal force could, therefore, be justified and accommodated.

Our interviewees and their photographs enabled access to the ways in which former personnel engaged with their experiences in the Troubles. Interviews, though, can be very transitory events, and valuable as they were for informing us about ideas of identity and military participation, it is the memory work conducted through the writing and publication of the memoir which provides, for some, a more satisfactory way of dealing with the experience of trauma. It is a feature of the Northern Ireland memoirs that they can be read as attempts to negotiate – and even overcome – the effects of deployment-induced trauma. A good example is Jack Williams' preface to his memoir, *The Rigger* (about a signals operative attached to Special Forces), where he describes the change his tour induced, which led to a breakdown, his leaving the Army and the collapse of his marriage:

> I, like many another squaddie, left Northern Ireland a bitter and angry man. The experience had changed me forever. I can never return to the person I was. I don't want to. The comradeship, the stress, the long hours and never being able to relax anywhere, anytime, was a normal day ... Everybody is affected in one way or another by their tour over there, including the wives. It can sometimes take years for the infestation to appear. Then a mental breakdown occurs – the soldier diving for cover every time he hears a loud bang. The wife who cannot stop peering through the curtains every time a car stops outside. One way or another it affects you. It changes your mental attitude to life.[35]

Clarke notes a similar transformation in *Contact*:

> I really was quite a nice guy until I came out here. Now the frustrations are building and the inner violence seethes below the surface waiting for an opportunity to escape. Looking at this pathetic woman, I am not thinking about the broken home or deprived background. I am thinking 'I wonder what she is like between the sheets?' Swear at me, lady, and I'll crack you so hard your teeth will fall out.[36]

He records not only the degeneration of his own mental health but also that of others:

> An NCO in Flax Street Mill [in Belfast] went into the vehicle park and blew his brains out with a pistol. One of my soldiers was posted to a desk job when he was found to be talking to himself in an OP. He had cocked his rifle and was waiting to shoot anyone who walked down the street.[37]

Devereaux, responding to a combination of tedium and stress which led to behaviour which landed him in military detention for twenty-eight days, reflects how he:

> thought that my mum and dad and brothers did not understand what I was about. How could they know what it was like over there? I had nothing in common with them anymore … It was as if the 'Troubles' … had taken over me. I had to address these problems and put them right at the earliest possible opportunity.[38]

For Barry Donnan, his Northern Ireland posting was the last straw. In *Fighting Back*, a vindication and recovery narrative, the Troubles just exacerbated his own problems. Deployed to Northern Ireland and clearly unwell:

> I didn't have a clue, mind you who did? I was a soldier taking part in a conflict that I knew fuck all about, me and half the British Army. Who was the enemy? We didn't know most of the time. I had two enemies: the first was me and the second was the Army.[39]

Our most difficult interview was with a man who was clearly in the process of working through the traumas and memories from his Northern Ireland deployment ('it was fucking mental over there'), which were compounded by a self-perception in the present that this had been just one of multiple brutalising experiences in the British Army. For this angry man, a newspaper cutting of the funeral on 19 March 1988 of two soldiers who had been caught up in a republican funeral and killed by paramilitaries was his cue for explaining how this incident had affected him personally.

> So he left our troop on a six-month secondment, he was a full corporal. So there was the funeral and we were sitting in the bar, and suddenly a news-flash, and you have seen it yourself I imagine, 'cause it sticks in my mind every time I look at this. And this white Passat, pulls up to a funeral procession, and they were like a pack of vultures on them. It just choked me up. What had happened, he had just arrived, this guy. [Another Royal Signals corporal] was showing him the ropes, apparently this guy was a bit of a jack the lad, and thought he would take a short cut through the republican area so he could get back and catch his flight. They turned straight into a republican

funeral, the republicans ruled the area, they knew which car was who, and who was who. You didn't have a chance ... And you seen what happened, they dragged them out the car, stripped them naked and shot them dead ... I remember sitting in the bar with the lads and seeing his face on the telly, and then you see this car, and you see this dead body in the street. I remember, I was quite upset ... I remember them bringing him back, and the regiment was in shock. We had a service for him and the lads were saying 'The bastards'. It just fuelled the hatred and tension in Northern Ireland more.

Dewey, writing about PTSD and conflict, argues that 'the burden of killing and the traumatic loss of their most beloved comrades – continue to trouble men much more over the course of their lives than do the traditional symptoms of PTSD, including those related to fear'.[40] He observes that 'as I have watched vets over the last two decades, I have seen that those who hold onto the hate and who cannot begin to feel mercy for their former enemy, continue to reject the real help they need to recover. The hate keeps the war alive forever.'[41] For some of the soldiers who served during the Troubles it has been a long, long war indeed.

Conclusion

We started by saying that the Troubles still presented a difficult story for many soldiers who served in Northern Ireland. Many were very young on their first tours, inserted into a conflict which they knew little about and in an environment that, as part of the UK, often looked like home, and yet was dangerously different. The Troubles have been subject to a host of changing and conflicting narratives following its 'conclusion', and the definitive account has yet to be written. If such an account is to be achieved, or even attempted, it must include the experiences of the armed forces, the third community, and not in the form of 'official' military accounts. What are necessary are the stories of individual soldiers and their colleagues, friends and families. Published accounts of their experiences are slowly emerging in the form of memoirs and edited collections and there are newspaper and photographic collections that cover the period. What are still missing are archives of letters and related correspondence which were written during the events. Unlike in today's digital age, with easy access to telecommunications, during much of the Troubles the blue British Forces letter was still the main form of communication with home. These letters may provide a resource which facilitates a better and more inclusive understanding of the Troubles and their individual experiences, not just for the military historians, but for the soldiers themselves, facilitating their own understanding of the Troubles and their role in it. Eventually, even the public may come to reappraise the role of the soldier in the ever-emerging 'meaning' of the Troubles.

Notes

1 See K. Wharton, *A Long Long War* (Solihull: Helicon & Co., 2008), p. 38.
2 K. N. Jenkings and R. Woodward, 'Practices of authorial collaboration: the collaborative production of the military memoir', *Cultural Studies – Critical Methodologies*, 14:4 (2014), 338–50. See also K. N. Jenkings and R. Woodward, 'Communicating war through the contemporary British military memoir: The censorships of genre, state, and self', *Journal of War & Culture Studies*, 7:1 (2014), 5–17.
3 All the quotations unless otherwise indicated are taken from interviews with former personnel conducted as part of the 'Negotiating identity' project (see note 8).
4 L. Curtis, *Ireland the Propaganda War* (London: Pluto Press, 1984).
5 R. Woodward, T. Winter and K. N. Jenkings, 'Heroic anxieties: The figure of the British solider in contemporary print media', *Journal of War and Culture Studies* 2:2 (2009), 211–23.
6 J. Hockey, *Squaddies: Portrait of a Subculture* (Exeter: University of Exeter Press, 1986), p. 85.
7 We use the term 'soldier' throughout, as a synonym for men and women who serve in the British Army, the Royal Air Force and the Royal Navy (which includes the Royal Marines), except where explicit force identity is relevant to the narrative.
8 'Negotiating identity and representation in the mediated Armed Forces', January 2006–June 2007, ESRC, RES-000-23-0992.
9 See R. Woodward, T. Winter and K. N. Jenkings, '"I used to keep a camera in my top left-hand pocket": British soldiers, their photographs and the performance of geopolitical power', in F. MacDonald, K. Dodds and R. Hughes (eds), *Observant States: Geopolitics and Visuality* (London: Routledge, 2010), pp. 143–66; K. N. Jenkings and R. Woodward, 'Negotiating identity: Representation and self-representation of the soldier in photographs and memoirs', in C. Gunz and T. F. Schneider (eds), *Wahrheitsmaschinen: Der Einfluss technischer Innovationen auf die Darstellung und das Bild des Krieges in den Medien un Künsten* (Göttingen: V&R Unipress, 2010), pp. 159–74; R. Woodward and K. N. Jenkings, 'Military identities in the situated accounts of British military personnel', *Sociology*, 45:2 (2011), 252–68; R. Woodward, K. N. Jenkings and T. Winter, 'Negotiating military identities: British soldiers, memory and the use of personal photographs', in K. Hall and K. Jones (eds), *Constructions of Conflict: Transmitting Memories of the Past in European Historiography, Culture and Media* (Bern: Peter Lang, 2011), pp. 53–71; R. Woodward and K. N. Jenkings, 'Soldiers' photographic representations of participation in armed conflict', in S. Gibson and S. Mollan (eds), *Representations of Peace and Conflict* (London: Palgrave Macmillan, 2012), pp. 105–19.
10 Wharton, *A Long Long War*.

11 J. Butler, *Frames of War: When is Life Grievable?* (London: Verso, 2009), p. 36.

12 'The social production of the contemporary British military memoir', April 2009–April 2011, ESRC, RES-062-23-1493.

13 S. Ford, *One Up* (London: Harper Collins, 1997).

14 J. George, *She Who Dared* (Barnsley: Leo Cooper, 1999).

15 Both author names are pseudonyms. Jackie George's memoir, published in 1999. was initially withdrawn from sale by the publisher following MoD concerns about the exposure it gave to specific incidents involving British personnel. Despite the efforts of the publisher to reclaim copies which had already been sold, the book remains in circulation, though not in print.

16 A. F. N. Clarke, *Contact* (London: Secker & Warburg, 1983).

17 General Sir M. Jackson, *Soldier: The Autobiography* (London: Bantam Press, 2007).

18 B. Donnan, *Fighting Back* (Edinburgh: Mainstream, 1999).

19 A. McNab, *Immediate Action* (London: Transworld, 1995).

20 Clarke, *Contact*, p. 24.

21 We recognise that this bald statement obscures a more complex picture about patterns of British Army recruitment in the late 1970s and early 1980s, when economic collapse in some areas of the UK, particularly in former heavy industrial areas, prompted the enlistment of thousands who in a more prosperous economic climate would have had a wider range of employment opportunities. Although an all-volunteer force, there have always been questions about the extent to which military participation is truly voluntary.

22 See D. McKittrick et al., *Lost Lives* (Edinburgh: Mainstream Publishing Co., 2007), pp. 1179–80.

23 See ibid. pp. 908–10.

24 See ibid. pp. 1259–60.

25 F. Collins, *Baptism of Fire* (London: Transworld, 1997), p. 225.

26 Ford, *One Up*.

27 R. Horsfall, *Fighting Scared* (London: Cassell, 2002), p. 144.

28 Collins, *Baptism of Fire*, p. 235.

29 See A. Renwick, *Hidden Wounds*, London: Barbed Wire, 1999), p. 62.

30 Collins, *Baptism of Fire*, p. 237.

31 S. Devereaux, *Terminal Velocity* (London: Smith Gryphon, 1997), p. 43.

32 Woodward et al., 'Negotiating military identities'.

33 Hockey, *Squaddies*, p. 105.

34 Ibid., p. 99.

35 J. Williams, *The Rigger* (Barnsley: Pen and Sword, 2001), pp. vii–viii.

36 Clarke, *Contact*, p. 33.

37 Ibid., p. 42.

38 Devereaux, *Terminal Velocity*, p. 55.

39 Donnan, *Fighting Back*, p. 158.

40 L. Dewey, *War and Redemption: Treatment and Recovery in Combat Related Post Traumatic Stress Disorder* (Aldershot: Ashgate, 2006), p. 97.

41 Ibid., p. 206.

Part II
Anti-state activisms

8

Something in the air:
the rise of the Troops Out Movement

Aly Renwick

In the weeks before British troops were sent out onto the streets of Derry in 1969, the number one hit in the record charts was 'Something in the Air', by Thunderclap Newman. This song, which suggested that it was time to 'Call out the instigators … because the revolution's here', was to ring out over the barricades in West Belfast and at the student sit-ins and workers' struggles in Britain. The civil rights movement in Northern Ireland had taken its inspiration from the 1960s worldwide upsurge of student and worker revolts in general and the struggle for black civil rights in America in particular. In Britain there were student radicalism, industrial unrest and many protests against the American war in Vietnam.

It was a connection to the Vietnam War that led me to take a part in these events. In 1960, at sixteen years of age, I had joined the British Army as a boy soldier. After three years at an Army Apprentice School, I had served with the Royal Engineers in West Germany and then for short periods in Cyprus and Kenya. In 1966 I was serving with 34 Field Squadron, based at Tidworth Barracks in England, when we were told that we had to fly out to the Far East to help deal with problems in Brunei. In early October, we arrived in Singapore to acclimatise for a week, but after a few days there we were all called to a meeting and told we would now be going to north-east Thailand to complete the building of a military airfield there.

A few days later we flew out to the partially built airstrip, next to the Thai village of Loeng Nok Tha, which was about twenty-five miles from the border with Laos. This was during a crucial phase of the Vietnam War, and about fifty miles south of our airfield lay the town of Ubon, with its Royal Thai Air Force Base, from which the US 8th Tactical Fighter Wing sometimes flew over us on combat missions in their F-4

Phantom jets to strike targets in North Vietnam or on the Ho Chi Minh Trail in Laos.

Officially, Britain was playing no part in the Vietnam War, although Harold Wilson, the British Labour Prime Minister, had come under strong pressure from the United States to send British troops directly into this conflict. While he stood firm against this, it was thought that Britain could be helping the US in other, undeclared ways. Our close approximation to the conflict disturbed some of us and we began to question if our airfield was being built to 'further Thai economic development' as we had been told. We could see no sign of this and we began to suspect that it must be for reasons to do with the Vietnam War.

Forty-six years later, at the National Army Museum in Chelsea the airfield was mentioned in a lunchtime lecture about Britain and the Vietnam War: 'The new airbase was clearly designed to be used by fighter jets and heavy bombers and most probably was used in covert US attacks into Laos.'[1] This was what I and a few others had suspected and feared at the time, because, after nearly seven months, the runways had been built of concrete to a standard that jet aircraft could use and we were then pulled out at the end of April 1967, leaving the completed, but deserted, airfield.

After we returned to Tidworth, I started to travel to London to take part in the anti-Vietnam War demonstrations. Eventually, this brought me to the attention of the Special Investigations Branch (SIB) of the Military Police and my commanding officer told me that the SIB's reports said there was a possibility that I would try to make contact with enemy forces in conflict situations – and this suggested, therefore, that I could no longer be trusted. Shortly afterwards, in late 1968, I bought myself out of the Army, just after I had spent two months serving in a then passive Northern Ireland.

During my time in the Army I had changed from fairly conservative beliefs to ones a great deal more radical. These views had come from things I had seen and experienced in the Army, but also from a growing awareness of the state of the world and its peoples. So, now a civvy, I travelled to London to live and work because I wanted to help organise the then increasingly militant protests against the Vietnam War. I recognised that, although my story was somewhat unusual, I was in fact no different from the thousands of other people I now met on anti-war demonstrations, whose ideas and perceptions had been changed and sharpened by living through the 'decade of revolution' as the Sixties was sometimes called.

In 1965, a year before my trip to Thailand with the British Army, four members of the Labour Party in London, all of Irish descent,[2] joined forces with Paul Rose, a young Labour MP, to form the Campaign for Democracy in Ulster (CDU; see Hopkins, chapter 4 in this volume). The organisation worked to support the emergent civil rights movement in Northern Ireland and adopted three basic aims:

> To secure by the establishment of a Royal Commission a full and impartial inquiry into the administration of Government in Northern Ireland, with particular reference to allegations of discrimination on religious or political grounds in the fields of housing and employment and into the continued existence of the Special Powers Act.
>
> To bring electoral law in Northern Ireland at all levels into line with the rest of the UK, and to examine electoral boundaries with a view to providing fair representation for all sections of the community.
>
> To amend the Race Relations Act to include discrimination on religious grounds and to press for its operation throughout the whole of the UK, including Northern Ireland.[3]

The CDU's first public meeting, in the House of Commons, was chaired by Lord Brockway and was attended by a third of the sixty MPs who had sponsored the CDU. This was an impressive start, but the organisation had difficulties both in raising the issues in Parliament and in getting those in power to listen. Paul Rose, the Labour MP for Blackley, near Manchester, was English, but his interest in Northern Ireland had been raised through his contact with Irish constituents. He then decided to see for himself and visited Northern Ireland to look into the issues of discrimination and inequality. Later, Rose, in his book *Backbencher's Dilemma*, wrote about the problems they had in attempting to raise these questions in the House of Commons:

> Our main problem was to penetrate the blank wall of incomprehension and ignorance about Ulster. Members who knew about Saigon or Salisbury seemed to know nothing of Stormont. Others were worried at the delicate problem of religious controversy in their own constituencies ... The fact was there was a parliamentary convention, erected in holy writ by Speaker after Speaker, that prevented us raising matters of real substance on the floor of the House without being ruled out of order.[4]

Paul Rose also noted that: 'To the average Englishman, Irishmen are good entertainers and sportsmen and literary figures, but they are often regarded patronisingly where politics is concerned.'[5] While the CDU had achieved a measure of support from MPs, those in power at Westminster mainly ignored it. In *Backbencher's Dilemma*, Rose looked at why Labour kept resorting to supporting the status quo in Northern Ireland:

The sectarian bitterness in Northern Ireland is not seen as a legacy of past British policies but as evidence that Irishmen of whatever persuasion are congenitally unreasonable and should be left to knock hell out of one another.... The paucity of initiatives, with the sole exception of the abortive attempt at power-sharing, reflects the fear of getting too involved. The truth, however, is that Ireland suffers from an English problem.[6]

The CDU also had problems trying to build itself outside of the House of Commons, as Paddy Byrne noted in an internal document: 'No mass movement has developed and there is no indication that one will.'[7] Although the founders had wanted the CDU to be seen as a British organisation, Byrne also stated about their most likely supporters, the British Left, that they were 'Far too concerned to save socialism from extinction than to bother about Ulster, about which the mass of British people know little, care less.'[8] By the late 1960s a more militant civil rights movement had emerged in Northern Ireland, and in 1969 the Irish Civil Rights Solidarity Campaign (ICRSC) was formed in Britain to support it.

Towards the end of the 1960s, under the title of *Land Operations*, the British Army rationalised its secret tactical manuals into a series of volumes. Volume III, called *Counter-Revolutionary Operations*, was produced in August 1969 and drew together all the Army had learned in its series of small wars during the run-down of Empire.[9] British troops had already been ordered to make ready for possible duty in Northern Ireland and on Thursday, 14 August 1969, soldiers of the 1st Battalion, the Prince of Wales' Own, were sent out onto the streets of Derry. In late 1971, as the struggle in Ireland escalated into conflict, internment without trial was introduced, and, to protest against it, the Anti-Internment League (AIL) emerged – first in Northern Ireland and then in Britain. While many British radicals helped to form and support the ICRSC and AIL, many of their members and most of their leaders and speakers, like Bernadette Devlin MP, were Irish.

In early 1972, after British Army paratroopers had shot dead thirteen protesters on 'Bloody Sunday', there were angry reactions across the world. The Irish in Britain were prominent in the protests and marches that flooded onto the streets, including a 20,000-strong demonstration in London, organised by the AIL. Police refused permission for thirteen coffins to be carried into Downing Street and clashes broke out when mounted police charged into the crowd. A number of people were injured and 122 demonstrators were arrested. Early the next morning three members of the AIL central committee, John Gray, John Flavin and Michael O'Kane, were arrested at their homes and charged with 'conspiring to contravene the Public Order Act of 1936'.[10]

Two ex-members of the Beatles, both from Liverpool and with an Irish grandparent, protested in their own ways. In August 1971, John Lennon and Yoko Ono had joined an anti-internment march through London, Lennon displaying a *Red Mole* newspaper with its headline: 'For the IRA – Against British Imperialism', emblazoned across the front page.[11] After the killings in Derry in 1972, Lennon wrote 'Sunday Bloody Sunday' and 'The Luck of the Irish'.[12] That same year, Paul McCartney wrote 'Give Ireland Back to the Irish'. The record was banned by the BBC, but still made it to number sixteen in the British charts. It was number one in Ireland and Spain.[13]

The British Army were also facing problems, both in recruiting and holding on to their existing soldiers, as was pointed out in the Troops Out Movement's first bulletin, *Tom-Tom*, produced in early 1974:

> By December 31st 1973, the official casualty lists admitted that 205 British soldiers had been killed in Northern Ireland. This was already 24 more than in Aden and almost as many as in Borneo and Cyprus together … Little wonder, then, that recruitment and re-enlistment (the main source of NCOs) are running at the lowest level since National Service ended.[14]

British domestic opposition to the war was rising and Peggy Chaston, the mother of a serving soldier, started a national petition calling for 'our boys to be brought home' (see Dixon, chapter 3 in this volume).[15]

The statement of a soldier who had fled to Sweden to escape serving in Northern Ireland was printed in *Peace News*: 'I came to Sweden for asylum because of Northern Ireland. I do not think that what is happening there is very good. As I see it, there must be a simpler way of ending the fight without more people being killed. So I have left rather than fight in something I think is wrong.'[16] Years later, Harold Wilson's then press secretary, Joe Haines, told how Labour's leaders had secretly considered a radical change of their policy on Northern Ireland at this time (discussed by Hopkins, chapter 4 in this volume):

> There were times … especially in the Opposition years from 1970 to 1974, when I believed that the next Labour Government would take its courage to Parliament and announce that an orderly, but irrevocable, withdrawal was to take place. Courage it would certainly have needed, for withdrawal … was as unmentionable in Whitehall and Westminster as devaluation had been … (even when we did mention it privately, in the irresponsibility of Opposition, we only did so under the code-name of 'Algeria').[17]

Ironically, by the middle of 1973, there had been a downturn of work on Northern Ireland by the radical groups, who were concentrating on the industrial struggles in Britain which were to bring about the three-day week, a miners' strike and the end of the Heath Conservative government in early 1974.

I had been a member the ICRSC and was still a member of the AIL, which was now moribund. So, in August 1973, I became part of a small group of anti-imperialist activists who began to meet regularly in west London to plan the forming of a new organisation, one which would be keyed into the increasing dissent about the aggressive use of British troops in Northern Ireland, and also, like the anti-Vietnam War movement in the US, the concern about their mounting casualties. We decided to call the new organisation the Troops Out Movement (TOM) and we adopted 'Troops Out Now', based on 'Self-determination for the Irish People as a whole' as our two demands (Figure 8.1). Unlike the ICRSC and the AIL, which had mainly shown the Irish face of protest, we wanted the TOM's focus to be that of British people protesting about the use of their own troops in Ireland.

The organisation's first bulletin, *Tom-Tom*, stated that: 'The Troops Out Movement was formed in West London in September 1973 by a group of trade unionists, housewives, students and ex-soldiers.'[18] We knew there was a long and honourable tradition in Britain of opposition to the occupation of Ireland. This went back as far as the English Civil War (1642–51), when the Levellers had produced a document about Oliver Cromwell's proposed invasion of Ireland which asked: 'Whether those who pretend for freedom (as the English now) shall not make themselves altogether inexcusable in entrenching upon others' freedoms, and whether it be not the character of a true patriot to endeavor the just freedom of all men as well as his own?'[19] When some Leveller soldiers mutinied, rather than go with Cromwell's Army to Ireland, they were arrested and three were executed at Burford church in Oxfordshire.[20]

The first leaflet produced by the TOM connected the role of the British Army in Northern Ireland to the succession of colonial wars since the end of the Second World War, during the run-down of Empire:

> Since 1945 the British Army has taken part in 35 'little wars': Malaya, Kenya, Cyprus and Aden are just a few. The overwhelming majority of these operations were struggles by the peoples of British colonies for the right to rule their countries by themselves. The British press and mass media were used to mislead the people of this country about the exact nature of the role of the Army during these actions, often portraying the troops as a kind of peacekeeping force. A look at the casualty figures for any of these operations makes nonsense of this conception. In Kenya during the 'Emergency' the total white deaths, civilian and military, were less than 100, while more

Figure 8.1 'Ireland: Troops Out Now!' The poster appeared A2 size in the centre pages of the *Troops Out* magazine, Summer 1976. The artist, Jack Clafferty, was a founder member of the TOM.

than 11,500 African 'terrorists' were killed during operations by the British security forces.

The Troops Out Movement ... say that as the actions of the British Army are carried out in the name of the British people, it is time we took a stand against their presence in Ireland.[21]

The TOM's first major public meeting was held in Fulham Town Hall on 24 October 1973. We hoped to attract about a hundred people and increase our membership locally. Our expectations were exceeded and the *West London Observer* gave the meeting a big write-up:

A new freedom movement was born in Fulham this week. A movement dedicated to the withdrawal of troops from Ulster. Three hundred people or more packed Fulham Town Hall to give their support to the birth of the Troops Out Movement, which aims to rid Ulster of the British Army. ... For the first public meeting of the Troops Out Movement it represented a considerable coup in terms of 'name speakers' – Eamonn McCann, Jack Dromey NCCL [National Council for Civil Liberties], Labour MP James Wellbeloved, CND [Campaign for Nuclear Disarmament] campaigner Pat Arrowsmith, trade unionist Jim Kemp, and an unknown British soldier who has just returned from Ulster.[22]

It was obvious that the TOM meeting had struck a chord and others shared our views. We thought then that the organisation would rapidly expand and, aided by a December demonstration, when 1,000 people marched from Shepherds Bush Green to a rally in Hammersmith Town Hall, it did so. By the end of the year new TOM branches had already been formed in Manchester, Coventry, Birmingham and in north and south London.

A couple of years before TOM's inception, a former Belfast Army commander, Brigadier Frank Kitson, had published a book, *Low Intensity Operations*,[23] which had provoked debate about the possible use of troops against strikes or other workers' protests in Britain. The book was widely quoted, causing concern not only on the far Left, but also among sections of the broader Labour movement. Army training had become increasingly political throughout this period, as Terry, an army deserter on the run, told *Time Out* magazine:

We've all been through riot training as part of our normal training – it was a bit of fun at the time. One half of us pretended to be Irish or the miners – or whoever was on strike at the time – and the other half would just charge into them. We'd think, 'Today we'll really get those strikers or those Irish,' we really thought like that.[24]

While always focusing on the situation in Ireland, the TOM sought ways to link the struggle there to that of workers in Britain. In May 1974, TOM organised a conference in London on 'The British Army in Ireland and Its Projected Role in Britain'.[25] This was a great success with a capacity audience of over 700 people, and many more being turned away at the door. The event consolidated the TOM, helping to build a network of branches in England, Scotland and Wales. Peter Hain, reporting in the Young Liberals' paper, welcomed its 'important' focus on 'the immediate threat to political liberties in Britain posed by the British Army ... [T]he Conference went into a detailed analysis of the army's role in Northern Ireland, showing how the Irish Crisis is being used as a living laboratory for "counter subversive" activity in all "western democracies".'[26]

At the end of May 1974, the London *Evening Standard* carried the headline on its front page: 'Ulster: Back-bencher makes a startling claim – "Half Labour MPs want to pull out"'.[27] A few days later the *Daily Mirror*, which then claimed 'Europe's biggest daily sale', announced on its front page that: 'Britain must now face the most sombre option of all – to pull out the troops and abandon sovereignty.'[28] In July 1974 the Secretary of State for Northern Ireland presented to Parliament the government's latest White Paper on Northern Ireland. We set to work and, following the original's format and layout, published the TOM's 'Alternative White Paper on Ireland'. Eleven thousand copies were distributed and sold, or given out as complimentary copies to MPs and others whom we sought to influence.[29]

In May 1975, the TOM held another national conference on 'The British Labour Movement and Ireland'.[30] It took place with a minority Labour government in power and the month after our TV screens had been filled with pictures of the last US forces leaving Vietnam – by helicopter from the roof of the American embassy in Saigon. Organised on a delegate basis, this conference was also a resounding success, as the *Irish Post* reported in August of that year:

> During the past year or so the Troops Out Movement has represented the most forceful opposition in Britain to current policy in Northern Ireland. TOM is almost an entirely British organisation [... that] now claims to have over 1,200 members – in addition to an affiliated membership of more than 10,000. ... It draws much of its strength from the trade union movement and from the Labour Party. At its conference in London last May, 326 trade union branches were represented.[31]

With its anti-imperialist demands, the TOM brought together radical groups and individuals who instigated branch activity in local areas.

This established a TOM presence on the streets, which strengthened the organisation's national standing. While continually asserting the central demand for the withdrawal of the troops, the TOM frequently initiated actions on other issues thrown up by the conflict and often worked closely with other Irish protest, or support, groups and campaigns. Regularly we supported each other's actions and sometimes there was a degree of dual membership between organisations.

In February 1976, nine Labour MPs – Andrew Bennett, Sydney Bidwell, Maureen Colquhoun, Martin Flannery, Tom Litterick, Eddie Loyden, Joan Maynard, Ron Thomas and Stan Thorne – proposed and campaigned for a new policy on Ireland. They stated that: 'What the Government has done, and continues to do, is to underwrite the perpetuation of the Northern Ireland state as it was set up in 1921' and that this 'offers no solution'. They then proposed an alternative policy:

> First: Northern Ireland must again be placed in an all-Irish context … Constitutional changes have to begin to be made, which involve the people of Ireland, and of Britain. Unionists can no longer have exclusive rights in deciding the future of Ulster.
> Second: There must be a clear declaration by Britain that it aims to withdraw from Ireland, politically and militarily, within a limited period of time … negotiations and actions must go side by side … These are the fundamentals of a new policy on Ireland. … The government of Britain has positive instruments to hand if it will only use them. The ultimate solution, as it has been with other nations divided by a colonising power, lies with the people themselves. But for us the only solution lies in going to the root of the problem, which is here in Britain: in our unwillingness to actually get out![32]

The TOM worked with Labour MPs like these – and many others – who had the courage to stand against Westminster convention, break with bipartisanship and point out the abnormal situation in Northern Ireland. In order to bring all those who supported withdrawal together, TOM started to organise protests and demonstrations with others, like the British Peace Committee, Young Liberals and Connolly Association. Many of these supported 'withdrawal' but not nessessarly 'out now'. In conjunction with them we worked out formulations, like 'Immediately implement a policy of withdrawal', that all of us could march behind, but still keep our separate demands.

In April 1976 the eminent British historian A. J. P. Taylor was interviewed on Irish radio and casually answered a few questions about Northern Ireland. His pro-withdrawal remarks led to an outraged response in the British press. Afterwards, I interviewed him for the TOM paper, *Troops Out*. He said:

> If before the First World War the Home Rule Bill had been carried, in my opinion the unity of Ireland would have continued. After all Ireland has always been a united country. ... The British have always been the root cause of the troubles in Ireland for the past 400 years ... I think the policy of any British government should be withdrawal ... I think the presence of the British Army in Ireland prolongs the period of conflict and uncertainty ... the role of the Army inevitably encourages the growth of extremism on both sides.[33]

At the end of my interview with him, Taylor pointed out to me the real problem that had still to be faced in Ireland:

> The implication that the only cause of conflict in Northern Ireland is the IRA – isn't true. The immediate cause of the troubles in Northern Ireland was not nationalist agitation, but Protestant extremism. It provoked a nationalist response in return – the practical resentment of Roman Catholics against the way in which they are treated in Northern Ireland as an inferior part of the community.[34]

The 1975 TOM conference had won support for a mass delegation to Ireland, which occurred one year later in September 1976. The sixty-strong Labour Delegation to Ireland visited Dublin, Crossmaglen and Belfast. Thirteen Labour MPs and many trade union branches, constituency Labour parties, student unions and other working-class organisations sponsored it across Britain and Ireland. Shocked by what they saw and heard, the delegates passed on their views and experiences at feedback meetings. Many of the sponsors and delegates continued to support the TOM and other progressive campaigns on Northern Ireland. These included Ken Livingstone, then a Labour councillor in Lambeth and later a Labour MP and Mayor of London, Ernie Roberts, then the Assistant General Secretary of the Amalgamated Union of Engineering Workers and later a Labour MP, and Jonathan Hammond, who later became the president of the National Union of Journalists.

In the decades that followed, the TOM organised regular yearly visits to Northern Ireland that built lasting links with those subjected to daily contact with British troops. Throughout those years, against the background of the war – a bombing campaign in Britain, attacks on our demonstrations by the far Right, state harassment and state agents sent to infiltrate TOM – we sought to keep the withdrawal of British troops at the forefront of local and national politics. We campaigned against plastic bullets, no-jury courts and the H-Blocks and for free speech

Figure 8.2 'Northern Ireland. Break the Wall of Silence'. This cartoon appeared in the *Troops Out* magazine in May 1980 (vol. 3, no. 7, p. 5). Artist unknown.

and prisoners' rights (Figure 8.2). Local meetings, leafleting, petitions and pickets of Army recruitment offices strengthened the roots of the organisation. As well as national demonstrations in London and other big cities, local marches were held in Barnsley and Mansfield, the home constituencies of Northern Ireland Secretaries Roy Mason and Don Concannon.

During the time of conflict in Northern Ireland, opinion polls consistently showed a majority of British people wanting to see the withdrawal of their troops.[35] In 1984, for example, a report on British Social Attitudes, published by the independent academic institute Social and Community Planning Research, found 58 per cent in favour of the 'reunification of Ireland' and a majority wanting withdrawal of troops 'from the north'.[36] While people were willing to express this view in private, most were not willing to support it in public. It is difficult now for anyone to realise how hard it was then to explain the nationalist case, criticise the government or even suggest that talks should take place. Anyone who did so was liable to be identified and vilified in the media, and Ken Livingstone, who spoke out over many years, was constantly denigrated in the right-wing papers.[37] The TOM, by openly campaigning for a British withdrawal, helped keep this issue in the minds of the public and many people expressed a wish to see a united Ireland.[38]

Taking its inspiration and methods from the anti-Vietnam War protests and mobilising anti-imperialist opposition to the UK government's use of military force, the TOM can be compared to the Stop the War Coalition of today. They both organised as broadly based movements, with an affiliation of local and national groups and individuals; undermined the propaganda of the UK government and military; showed concern for the welfare of individual soldiers and provided a platform for dissident military personnel; and encouraged and drew out dissident opinion by building and highlighting the widespread opposition to war and the lack of peace talks.

The TOM, by keeping the demand for the withdrawal of British troops from Northern Ireland in people's minds, contributed towards bringing peace. The conflict, however, ended as a stalemate and all the sides had to compromise in order to reach agreement and bring peace. The peace process that emerged did, to some degree, address the issues of discrimination and inequality – and helped to create the conditions where republicans, and anyone else, can campaign peacefully for their aims. The power-sharing arrangement also ensures there can be no return to exclusive unionist rule. British soldiers, nevertheless, are still garrisoned in Northern Ireland and the peace process – although it could still provide a peaceful pathway towards these aims – has not as yet helped to end partition, or bring nearer a united Ireland.

The TOM, therefore, still continues, campaigning for the withdrawal of troops and for an end to British rule in Ireland.[39] The movement was started by people who were born around the end of the Second World War and who spent their formative years in the Sixties. I entered that decade respecting and trusting the establishment. I then questioned them, laughed at them, opposed their wars and wanted to see them replaced. I wasn't alone, however, because there were so many others. That is the real reason why this era is so often derided by our present ruling politicians and their friends. The Sixties is sometimes described as the era of drugs, sex and rock 'n' roll, but it also spawned a layer of political activists who in radical politics found a vision more addictive than drugs, more passionate than sex and more potent than rock 'n' roll. Those were heady times, when there was 'something in the air'.

The ethos of that decade was individual freedom, the collective responsibility of us all as human beings and the fight for a just and progressive society and world. We were inspired by the black civil rights struggle in America and the worldwide opposition to the US war in Vietnam. Back home, waves of student revolts, workers' industrial struggles and issues like racial equality, anti-imperialism, radical feminism and gay rights further fuelled us. During the Sixties a parallel movement, inspired by the same world events, had emerged in Northern Ireland – spearheading a struggle against the undemocratic and oppressive state there. Many Sixties activists here then turned to Ireland's British problem as a focus for their political work, and in late 1973 a number of them came together to found and build the Troops Out Movement, whose full history is yet to be written.[40]

Notes

1 R. Fleming, 'A jungle too far: Britain and the Vietnam War', lecture delivered at the National Army Museum, London, 6 December 2012. Recording available at www.nam.ac.uk/whats-on/lunchtime-lectures/video-archive/jungle-too-far-britain-vietnam-war (Accessed 18 November 2014). See also A. Renwick, *Britain and the Vietnam War*, at Veterans For Peace UK website, http://veterans-forpeace.org.uk/2014/britain-and-vietnam-war/, posted 26 May 2014 (Accessed 20 November 2014).
2 Bill O'Shaughnessy (Streatham Labour Party), Michael Melly (Putney Labour Party), Oliver Donohue (Hammersmith Labour Party) and Paddy Byrne (Croydon Labour Party). Byrne originally came from Dublin, Donohue from Portlaoise and Melly from Sligo.
3 B. Purdie, *Politics in the Streets* (Belfast: Blackstaff Press, 1990), p. 108.
4 P. Rose, *Backbencher's Dilemma* (London: Frederick Muller, 1981), p. 179. Saigon (Vietnam) and Salisbury (Rhodesia/Zimbabwe) were conflict areas at this time.
5 Rose, *Backbencher's Dilemma*, p. 179.
6 Ibid., pp. 179–80.
7 Purdie, *Politics in the Streets*, p. 119.
8 Ibid., p. 119.
9 *Land Operations. Volume III – Counter Revolutionary Operations* (No place of publication [London?]: Ministry of Defence, 29 August 1969). It was revised in 1971 and 1973 and at regular intervals afterwards.
10 *Anti-Internment News* (Bulletin of the Anti-Internment League), 2 (no date [February 1972?]).
11 A. Renwick, *Oliver's Army: A History of British Soldiers in Ireland and Other Colonial Conflicts* (Troops Out Movement website, 2004), Chapter 8, 'Back Home' section, www.troopsoutmovement.com/oliversarmychap8.htm (Accessed 4 November 2014).
12 For details of the songs see: www.beatlesbible.com/people/john-lennon/songs/sunday-bloody-sunday/; www.beatlesbible.com/people/john-lennon/songs/the-luck-of-the-irish/ (Accessed 3 November 2014).

13 *The British Media and Ireland* (London: Information On Ireland, 1979), pamphlet, p. 34; Renwick, *Oliver's Army*, chapter 8, 'Back Home' section.

14 *Tom-Tom*, Bulletin of the Troops Out Movement. This first bulletin of the TOM was produced in March 1974. Three *Tom-Toms* were produced, but none were dated or numbered. All three editions are in the TOM archives.

15 'Bring the Boys Home?' *This Week*, Thames TV, first broadcast 21 June 1973. Documentary about Peggy Chaston and her petition to withdraw the British troops from Northern Ireland.

16 Statement by Lance Corporal Kevin Cadwallader, Royal Engineers, in *Peace News* (8 June 1973).

17 J. Haines, *The Politics of Power* (London: revised edition, Coronet, 1977), p. 114.

18 *Tom-Tom*, first bulletin of the TOM, produced in March 1974.

19 H. N. Brailsford, *The Levellers and the English Revolution*. Spokesman University Paperback No. 14 (Nottingham: Spokesman Books, 1976), pp. 501–6.

20 Ibid., pp. 511–22. See also, Aly Renwick, *Agitators in the New Model Army*, at Veterans For Peace UK: http://veteransforpeace.org.uk/2014/agitators/, posted 25 March 2014 (Accessed 20 November 2014).

21 Troops Out Movement, first leaflet, titled 'Ireland: Troops Out Now', produced in October 1973.

22 *West London Observer* (2 November 1973).

23 F. Kitson, *Low Intensity Operations: Subversion, Insurgency and Peacekeeping* (London: Faber and Faber, 1971).

24 *Time Out* (7–13 April 1972).

25 Held on 11 May 1974 at the Collegiate Theatre, London WC1. In the TOM archives (see note 40) there are posters, other publicity material and reports, including one from the conference organising committee.

26 Peter Hain, in *Liberator* (July 1974). Hain later joined the Labour Party and in 2005 he became the Secretary of State for Northern Ireland.

27 *Evening Standard* (30 May 1974).

28 *Daily Mirror* (3 June 1974).

29 Published as an A4, 24-page pamphlet by the Literature Committee of the TOM. The first draft was written by Bob Purdie; a committee of TOM members then refined it to the version printed. There was a 5,000 first print run, followed by a 6,000 reprint. Copy in the TOM archives.

30 Held on Saturday, 24 May 1975 at the Collegiate Theatre, London WC1. In the TOM archives there are posters, other publicity material, the conference programme and reports.

31 *Irish Post* (30 August 1975).

32 The British Peace Committee produced the full statement as a leaflet (17 February 1976).

33 Interview with A. J. P. Taylor, *Troops Out* (Summer 1976), pp. 2–3. Following on from the three *Tom-Tom* bulletins, this was the first issue of the TOM paper and was followed by a second issue dated Winter 1976. After that, starting in 1977, *Troops Out* became an A4-size, 12-page magazine and came out monthly.

34 Ibid.
35 These ranged from 50 to 64%. Opinion polls finding majorities in favour of British withdrawal include: MORI, September 1971, 59%; Gallup, December 1975, 64%; Gallup, February 1977, 53%; Gallup, September 1978, 55%; Weekend World, November 1980, 50%; Marplan, April 1981, 58%; MORI, May 1984, 53%; MORI, January 1987, 61%; MORI, March 1988, 50%; Harris, December 1989, 51%. These poll results are not a comprehensive list, but are a selection from those collected by TOM members. TOM's full collected list was used in Aly Renwick's *Oliver's Army*, chapter 12, 'Public Opinion' section, available on the TOM website: www.troopsoutmovement.com.
36 *Sunday Times* (27 May 1984).
37 L. Curtis, *Ireland: The Propaganda War* (London: Pluto Press, 1984), pp. 207–12.
38 See also the phone poll carried out by the radio station LBC. Almost 9,000 people telephoned to vote and the *Irish Post* reported that: 'Fewer than two in every ten Londoners believe that Northern Ireland should remain in the United Kingdom. ... Almost three in every four people in London think that the North should become part of the Republic, but fewer than one in four think that Northern Ireland should become an independent state.' *Irish Post* (7 April 1984).
39 See Troops Out Movement website: www.troopsoutmovement.com.
40 A TOM archive is held by the Irish in Britain Archive at the London Metropolitan University:http://metranet.londonmet.ac.uk/irishstudiescentre/archive-of-the-irish -in-britain/collections/special-collections.cfm. Aly Renwick has a private TOM archive, which he holds in London. On the TOM website is his *Oliver's Army: A History of British Soldiers in Ireland and Other Colonial Conflicts*.

9

Memories of Sinn Féin Britain, 1975–85

Susan O'Halloran

Then and now

In March 2014 the Queen hosted a State banquet at Windsor for the President of Ireland, attended by Martin McGuinness, Sinn Féin's Deputy First Minister of Northern Ireland, who later joined the celebrations from a VIP box in the Royal Albert Hall. In May a Sinn Féin candidate topped the European polls in both Dublin and Northern Ireland. Sinn Féin councillors took more votes than any other party in the Northern local elections, and in the South Sinn Féin took control of Dublin. It is hard for young people now to comprehend how extraordinary these events would have seemed from the perspective of 1975, when I joined Sinn Féin in London. Things were very different then. The respect and legitimacy now accorded to the Sinn Féin elected representatives, both in Britain and in Ireland, contrasts unimaginably with their outlaw status forty years ago, in the days of the Provos.

In 1976 the British government launched its Northern Ireland counter-insurgency strategy, centred on 'criminalisation':[1] when captured and convicted, republicans would no longer be treated as political prisoners, but as ordinary violent criminals, their actions called mindless, irrational and evil. No political legitimacy was allowed to the resistance to British rule, no publicity permitted to its spokespeople. This led to years of republican prisoner and community struggle, starting with the blanket protest and culminating in the 1981 hunger strike. Now, there is instant global news, there is social media. In the 1980s it was difficult for the republican viewpoint to get any expression at all in the public news media (a difficulty formalised in 1988 by the extraordinary broadcasting ban on any republican voice from Ireland).[2] We in Sinn Féin Britain took it upon ourselves to be the political voice of the republican movement working for Sinn Féin in London.

This chapter is a memoir of the years 1975–85. I have tried to give a flavour of what it was like to be an activist then, the atmosphere on the London streets, in the capital of the occupying power, and to reflect on some of the changes that have taken place since then.

Oxford graduate to Sinn Féin activist

In 1968 the Civil Rights movement erupted in Belfast, led by the eloquent Queens University student Bernadette Devlin. This struggle so close to home opened my eyes. I simply had known nothing about that parallel universe, a brutal sectarian secret in British democracy. I too was a 1968 student and socialist, engaged with the burning political and human rights issues of the day, convincing us that popular action could change the world: black American civil rights, South African anti-apartheid, Vietnam, France in May '68, the Prague Spring. I was politicised by these global events, as were so many of my contemporaries.

But these were also the years of violent loyalist and British reaction to the civil rights protests in Northern Ireland: the Royal Ulster Constabulary (RUC) and loyalist attacks on the civil rights marches in 1968 and 1969, the Battle of the Bogside and arrival of the British Army, internment in 1971, the emergence of the Provisional Irish Republican Army (IRA) to defend its areas, Bloody Sunday in Derry in 1972. I took part in the London protests, public meetings and demonstrations and I joined the Troops Out Movement (TOM). However, like many radical young women of the time I was not comfortable in the male-dominated and doctrinaire varieties of socialist organisation available to us as activists, and I found my political home in the early 1970s in the nascent Women's Liberation Movement; thus much of my energy devoted to the Northern Ireland issue was through activities organised by women's groups.

In the early 1970s there was a bombing campaign in Britain, with many attacks in London. English prisons began to fill up with Irish republican prisoners. I was living in London in 1974 when the Birmingham pub bombs exploded. It was a shocking and stark event and the government response was swift. The Prevention of Terrorism Act (PTA) was rushed through Parliament, making it very difficult for the Irish in Britain to show any solidarity with those demanding their rights in Northern Ireland without crossing a line into illegality,[3] or at the very least arousing suspicion and distrust, an experience that would be recognised by members of the Muslim community today.

Most British opinion was united in implacable hostility, condemnation and incomprehension of this bombing and shared an indifference to and ignorance of what lay behind it. Its political illegitimacy was in no doubt. I reacted differently: I responded not as a progressive UK politico to another global struggle against injustice, but as second-generation Irish with family roots in the West of Ireland, and an implicit understanding of and empathy with Irish resistance. These were my people and I wanted to give them their voice, which in every way was silenced. In 1975 I set off to the Six Counties to explore for myself the situation that had led to this.

The Women's Movement was my main political milieu in 1974, so my first trip to the Six Counties (during the IRA's 1975 ceasefire) was for the feminist magazine *Spare Rib*. I went with the contacts and addresses of women in Belfast, Derry and Armagh to write an article on women in the nationalist communities.[4] I was both shocked and impressed at what I saw: shocked by the Army occupation on the streets, the watch towers, the burning of the Catholic areas by their loyalist neighbours, the feeling of being in a secret world under siege. I was impressed at the political engagement and solidarity of working-class nationalist communities. I stayed with families and talked mainly with women, teenagers and children. I was struck by their lack of sectarianism – they wanted equality and justice, to get rid of sectarianism.[5] When I came back I sought out Sinn Féin in the area of London where I lived.

Sinn Féin in Kilburn

Sinn Féin was organised in Britain as an integral part of Sinn Féin in Ireland, with local branches in the Irish areas of British cities, a seat on the central committee in Dublin and delegate voting rights at the annual conference. Members with a position (including me, with the misleadingly grand title of 'Sinn Féin London representative for international contacts') attended frequent meetings in Dublin and later in Belfast and we were well briefed on developing political strategy and policy. The criminalisation policy in 1976 meant an increasing need for Sinn Féin to become a strong political organ of protest and publicity in the Six Counties of Northern Ireland. Thus the political struggle shifted more and more towards the prisoners' demand for political status.

The party in Britain followed the same priorities. Our central *raison d'être* was repudiating criminalisation. In Britain this meant supporting the republican prisoners in jail and on trial in England, and their relatives, by collecting money and maintaining contact with them, distributing republican literature, organising protests as one element within the broader TOM and promoting the republican demand for the end of partition and of unionist domination as the root cause of the conflict.

Indeed my first activity when I joined Sinn Féin was the nightly picket outside the Ladbroke Grove home of Roy Jenkins (then Labour Home Secretary) in support of the hunger striker Frank Stagg. Convicted in 1973,[6] Stagg demanded repatriation, political status and an end to solitary confinement. For the full seventy-one days of his hunger strike (from December 1975 to his death in February in Wakefield Prison), we straggling bunch of about twenty marched with placards in the snow and ice of that winter around that pretty London square, shouting out 'Roy Jenkins you are a murderer!'

During a later protest against prison conditions by the Irish republican prisoners in Wormwood Scrubs we held regular Sunday pickets in the street right outside. The prisoners hung banners through the bars: we saw their arms waving, we waved back and we shouted back and forth with encouragement and messages from the outside, they from the inside.

Urban agitators, ordinary lives

There were only about fifteen to twenty of us active members in Kilburn, maybe another hinterland of twenty more.[7] Most were young men and a few women in their twenties and early thirties, a few older republicans, nearly all first-generation immigrants from the South of Ireland, and a few from the North, who had come here for work and found themselves in the building trade or on the buses, often single, with social lives centred on the pubs of Kilburn and Cricklewood. I was unusual in being second-generation Irish: people like me tended to join TOM, the women's Armagh Prison solidarity groups or the many Left groups of those years, including a strand within the Labour Party.[8] I had chosen to join Sinn Féin because I wanted the political point of view and experience of the people I had met in Belfast, Derry and Armagh to be heard and be given the respect it deserved. Quite simply, I was on their side.

Our activities were in the main very local. Ours was a dedicated, politically serious and intense little network, albeit a modest and somewhat ramshackle one. But remember, those were the days of low-tech agitation, no e-mails, no mobiles, no internet, Facebook or Twitter. Our only contact with the North was by phone or visits. We met monthly to plan our activities in a hired hall in Kilburn High Road. We held frequent marches from Cricklewood to Kilburn, ending with a mini rally in Kilburn Square. There was little community participation in these marches – quiet watching or stopping for a chat, but no hostility, and often with more police than marchers.

We sold Sinn Féin's *Republican News* (posted to us from Belfast in weekly bundles) in the many local pubs on Friday and Saturday nights. This was really the only source of news and republican opinion available in England. We collected money to support prisoners' relatives and counted it up in my flat at the end of the weekend, putting it into little plastic bank bags. On Monday morning I would cart it in a pushchair to Barclays in Kilburn High Road and deposit it in my own bank account (being the only one with a bank account – most Irish workers then were paid in cash, or cheques that publicans cashed for them). Then I sent a weekly cheque off to Sinn Féin in Belfast. This seemed natural at the time but oddly rash now, and innocent.

In fact a lot of what we did can now be seen as having a funny side. For example, here is another example of our up-front visibility, or maybe simply our insouciant youth. An Irish community organisation produced a directory of the Irish in Britain in the early 1980s. Provisional Sinn Féin was listed, with my name as the London contact and my home number. It didn't strike me as a problem until my mum answered the phone one day, to hear 'Hello, Teheran here. This is the Children of God, Hezbollah, on the line.' I did re-direct that one to the Belfast office, being reluctant to generate any more police interest in us. My family had already had experience of being held under the PTA, stopped with our small children at Fishguard on a holiday trip to Ireland. An unmarked Special Branch car parked regularly on our road: we knew by name 'our' Special Branch man, who would even nod to us as we came out. Our post was opened and resealed before we got it (reported to us by the nice second-generation Irish postman who happened to live next door).

Looking back, I think that the London Irish who supported us, with money and by buying the paper, and with really never a word against us, were glad that someone was affirming what many of them privately felt but were very afraid to openly express: that what was happening in the North was wrong, and that the fight back was justified. As an indication of this, when police came to our basement flat early one morning in September 1976, when I was pregnant with our first child, and took me and my husband off to Paddington Green police station for general questioning about our political activities, our Irish landlord, who lived upstairs in the same house with his wife and young family, was simply helpful and sympathetic when we got home, rather than kicking us out for bringing potential trouble to him. If asked privately and very discreetly, the big Irish building contractors and the dance hall owners gave us large sums of cash to fund our larger initiatives. One of these was a delegation to London of one hundred relatives of the hunger strikers in 1981, after the election as a Westminster MP by the people of Fermanagh and South Tyrone and subsequent death of Bobby Sands, to lobby embassies and the government, hold a press conference and speak at a reception we held at the Camden Irish Centre, which attracted a wide section of London's Irish community.

Hunger strike

During the hunger strike of 1981, on every evening throughout that summer we held a vigil in Kilburn Square as the ten men died between May and September. We kept the mock coffin in our hallway – bizarrely, as this was a shared lobby with our downstairs neighbours (a new flat now), a kindly middle-aged Irish couple who did not mind.

Sometimes we ventured into Central London for joint events with solidarity groups like TOM. We held a demo outside the US Embassy after Bobby Sands died, appealing to the US to intercede in the hunger strike. Another time we trundled into Westminster, all piled into an Irish subcontractor's lorry, parked up in Whitehall, as you could then, and picketed all day right outside 10 Downing Street. These were the days before the 1991 IRA mortar attack on Downing Street led to its closure behind gates.

Once during the hunger strike we turned up at the Hampstead home of Michael Foot, the Labour Party leader, protesting about Labour's failure to challenge the Conservative government's intransigence towards the hunger strikers.[9] He came out into his front garden and spoke to us over the gate. I felt rather sorry for him being all alone with only a couple of policemen (again, we see how different security is today) and harangued on all sides, and I admired his decency in coming out to talk to us. But the key point here is that we were taking to task Michael Foot – arguably the most radical left-wing leader the Labour Party has had, yet he was not willing to engage politically with the progressive republican movement in Northern Ireland. Even though he was a socialist and internationalist, Michael Foot exemplified the difficulty of generations of British politicians to see through Irish eyes. Ireland and its relationship with Britain remained a political blind spot.

Another incident vividly illustrates the curious context of the times: on the one hand, we were visibly up-front, and completely unabashed by how transgressive our activities were perceived to be in London at the time, while on the other hand, in our daily lives we were actually politically and socially extremely isolated, marginalised and vulnerable. For example, I personally lost contact with many political friends who seemed to think I had 'joined the IRA'. When my arrest and brief detention under the PTA appeared as a short item in a local Dublin newspaper, my relatives there were both mystified and mortified. We uneasily negotiated our ordinary lives and our politics within our London streets, under the eyes of the police and a wary population.[10] One day in spring 1981, I was at home washing nappies (Terry nappy days) when the phone rang. It was the Belfast Sinn Féin office saying that a CNN team wanted an urgent interview. Bobby Sands was not expected to live much longer. They were on their way to my flat now.

I was on my own with the children. I said, 'Oh, OK then, I suppose so', thinking, disloyally, 'Bad timing'. Half an hour later, a CNN van rolled up our Kilburn side street. They needed an outside broadcast and started to unload the van to set up their lights and cameras outside on the pavement. My reaction was revealing in its horror: 'No way, I live here, I have neighbours, they can't see me standing out there being interviewed!' So they reluctantly set up in my little back yard, after I had removed the washing line. I changed my T-shirt and brushed my hair, and they filmed the interview showing my upper half only, the children sitting on the ground, one hanging onto each ankle, while I reiterated the reasons for the hunger strike and the determination of the prisoners.

After the hunger strike

The hunger strike was a kind of watershed for us, as it was in another way for the political process that subsequently unfolded in Belfast, leading to the transforming of Sinn Féin strategy in the 1980s and 1990s: contesting elections in Ireland North and South whilst continuing the armed struggle (both the 'armalite and the ballot box'[11]).

But for us it was a bleak watershed. We felt deflated and defeated, even heartbroken by what we saw as the sheer wall of British inhumanity, the indifference of the British citizenry to the drama unfolding so close to home.

More positively, chinks began to appear in Britain's criminalisation policy and a political agenda began to emerge, albeit slowly. In 1982 Labour members of TOM invited Gerry Adams, the leading Sinn Féin figure in Northern Ireland,[12] to speak in London. This would have been the first Irish republican voice to be directly heard in London in many years – if he had been allowed to come. As it was, Adams was banned from entering Britain, but in February 1983 Ken Livingstone, Labour's Leader of the Greater London Council, held a high-profile meeting with Adams in Belfast. In June Adams was elected as Westminster MP for West Belfast, and in July he was able to visit London and express his views in the media and to politicians. The Labour Party MP Tony Benn met him, and in a reference in his *Diaries*, dated 26 July 1983, Tony Benn writes: 'Gerry Adams said there was an ongoing attempt to develop a dialogue as a basis for peace.' Benn comments: 'I thought this should be seen as a mission for peace. People are beginning to realize that whatever the attitude towards Northern Ireland, the present policy is one of absolute bankruptcy.'[13]

Sinn Féin in Northern Ireland had been winning elections and political channels began to be created.[14] In this changing situation, in 1985 the organisation in Britain was dissolved into the broader solidarity movement, after a prolonged consultation. This decision was not universally popular amongst members in Britain, but it was clear that once Sinn Féin began to be acknowledged, even if only discreetly, as a political player that had to be engaged with in order to resolve the conflict, our *raison d'être*, loudly and provocatively promoting their political claim, was unhelpful. A more persuasive and discreet approach was needed.

Sinn Féin supporters in London continued to prioritise their work for the IRA prisoners in British jails. Alongside this, some of us took on the task of arranging formal and informal meetings in London with individual politicians and journalists to enable further personal exposure of republicans from Northern Ireland, with a view to widening support from mainstream British voices and popular opinion. I continued facilitating these constructive contacts in the changing context of the 1980s and 1990s, leading up to the Good Friday Agreement of 1998.

How did it all end?

As I write this in 2014, Sinn Féin is in government in Northern Ireland, has elected representatives across Ireland north and south, five MPs and an office at Westminster. Adams and McGuinness are invited around the world to speak about conflict resolution and the experiences and lessons of what is still an ongoing process of peace and reconciliation within Northern Ireland. At home they are faced with the painful, volatile legacy of the conflict in people's lives, every bit as challenging as that of South Africa. At the same time they have taken on the strategically complex task of constructing an all-Ireland political presence and a plausible narrative of how and why the country could be re-united with support north and south.

I am proud of our steadfast belief in the political motivation, progressive politics and integrity of the leaders and protagonists of the republican movement in those early days of the conflict. We played our own modest part in giving the republican cause a voice in London in those years when other channels were stifled and suppressed. On a personal level I feel vindicated by the principled and empathetic way Sinn Féin's leaders have taken the process forward, trying to take the unionists along with them, and I am still 'on their side' in their current political path, just as I was in 1975. However, I know that reunification is no simple answer to the contemporary problems of Ireland north and south, in the same rocking boat as the rest of Europe in 2014. But then, in 1975, I was not a Sinn Féin supporter as a nationalist either, but as a protagonist for people living under injustice and inequality in their own country. This was the core driver of Sinn Féin's aim of ending the partition of Ireland, and still is. So, for me, although the challenges are different and my role is tangential, there is continuity from 1975 to 2014.

Notes

1 Part of the Ulsterisation strategy to pacify Northern Ireland. Responsibility for security went from British Army units to the Ulster Defence Regiment (UDR) and the local police force, the Royal Ulster Constabulary (RUC). Political prisoner status, known as Special Category Status, was removed from those convicted of offences connected with the Troubles.

2 See Pettigrew, chapter 16 in this volume.

3 See Finch, chapter 10 in this volume.

4 M. McKay, 'Living with the army in your front garden', *Spare Rib*, 43 (February 1976), 9–14. Mary McKay was my pseudonym.

5 In response to my article, some feminists commented in the *Spare Rib* letters page that supporting a nationalist and militaristic struggle led mainly by men was not the place of a feminist or socialist. I replied it was not anti-feminist for working-class women and girls in Catholic communities to take part with the men and boys of their families fighting the violence of the British State in their streets. While I shared the critics' contempt for masculine politics of violence and heroics, I thought they overlooked the fact that the main force which Catholic women had to face daily was the machismo and arrogance of British soldiers. For discussion of these debates, see Rossiter, Chapter 11 in this volume.

6 In 1973 Frank Stagg was sentenced for ten years for being the commanding officer of an IRA unit planning bombing attacks in Coventry. In March 1974 he and other IRA prisoners in Britain embarked on a hunger strike during which the hunger strikers were forcibly fed, leading to the death of Michael Gaughan. The other hunger strikers were granted repatriation to Ireland, but Stagg was not, and was subsequently held in solitary confinement. He refused to do prison work and in March 1974 he started another hunger strike in Long Lartin prison, which lasted thirty-four days until some concessions in the prison were granted. He was transferred to Wakefield Prison in 1975 and was again made to do prison work. In December he embarked on a hunger strike, demanding repatriation to Ireland during the 1975 truce.

7   Similar numbers worked in other Irish areas of London and other English cities.
8   See chapters in this volume by Renwick (chapter 8), Rossiter (chapter 11) and Parkin (chapter 12).
9   Conservative Prime Minister Margaret Thatcher was adamant that no change would be made to the prison regime as long as the hunger strike continued. She said that there was no question of conceding Special Category Status for republican prisoners, because she insisted that crime is crime, it is not political. The Labour Party supported this stance. It was a Labour government that removed Special Category Status in 1976.
10 Irish people in Britain were generally suspected by the British population, media and police of tacit sympathy with the IRA, at the very least, and, at worst, of failing to report on suspicious activities in their communities or providing safe houses. See Murray (chapter 14) and O'Reilly (chapter 20) in this volume.
11 'Who can really believe that we can win this war by the ballot box? But ... with a ballot box in one hand and an armalite in the other we can take power in Ireland,' Danny Morrison, Sinn Féin Director of Publicity, speaking at the 1981 Sinn Féin *Ard Fheis* (annual conference).
12 At this stage Gerry Adams, although the leading political figure in Sinn Féin in the Six Counties, was Sinn Féin Vice-President, while the President was still the more traditional republican Ruari O'Bradaigh based in Dublin. In June 1983 Adams was elected as abstentionist Westminster MP for West Belfast, and was elected as Sinn Féin President in November 1983.
13 T. Benn, *The End of an Era: Diaries 1980-90* (London: Hutchinson, 1992), p. 308.
14 Behind the scenes Sinn Féin had been working on a conflict resolution strategy, published in *Scenario for Peace* (1987; available at www.sinnfein.ie/contents/15210), which called for dialogue on the political situation in Northern Ireland. This was followed in 1988 by the first meeting between the SDLP leader John Hume and Gerry Adams, and in 1990, by the re-opening of the British government's contacts with Sinn Féin. In 1992 the Sinn Féin *Ard Fheis* adopted a revised document, *Towards a Lasting Peace in Ireland* (1994; available at www.sinnfein.ie/contents/15212), which refined the principles of unity by consent and an end to the British support for the unionist veto on any change. The basis for the Good Friday Agreement was being laid, even while the armed conflict continued.

10

Policing the Irish community in Britain

Nadine Finch

In his seminal work looking at the Irish community in Britain, Paddy Hillyard argued in 1993 that 'a suspect community has been constructed against a background of anti-Irish racism [and that] the community has suffered widespread violation of their human rights and civil liberties. As a consequence, the United Kingdom's reputation throughout the world for upholding human rights and civil liberties has been constantly compromised.'[1] He focuses on the use of the Prevention of Terrorism Act (PTA) 1974 and its effect on the Irish community, and I refer to the consequences of this particular piece of legislation in this chapter. But I also look at the totality of the means used to 'police' the Irish community during the 1970s and 1980s, which went much further than changes to the criminal law. These included the manner in which intelligence was gathered by the police and security forces and the development of new methods to control incidents which threatened, or were thought to threaten, public order. Most crucially, the State also relied on the negative public opinion encouraged by much of the media to demonise the legitimate attempts by members of the Irish community to give voice to concerns about the political and economic situation in the North of Ireland and the resulting widespread violation of human rights and civil liberties.

Throughout the 1970s and 1980s and into the 1990s merely being Irish was sufficient to trigger suspicion. For example, a Mr Loftus, a former president of the Irish Travel Agents Association, reported that prior to the 1987 Conservative Party conference in Blackpool he had been contacted by Bob Waters Travel, a tour operator specialising in Blackpool holidays. He was asked for the addresses for six members of two different families and told that the Blackpool police wanted their details and that they were checking all Irish people going there.[2]

Similarly, a spokesperson for the Blackpool District of the Union of Communication Workers said that Special Branch questioned Post Office workers about their Irish connections and general political beliefs and asked them about their political views and the views of their colleagues.[3] Such actions had the effect of discouraging many members of the Irish community from articulating their political views and increased their fear that they might be falsely accused of crimes that they had not committed or be subject to the same human rights abuses being experienced by their friends and relations in the North of Ireland.

The manner in which the Irish community was policed during the 1970s and 1980s was an extension, but also an escalation, of methods used in Ireland and other colonial settings in the past. From the perspective of 2015, it can be seen that a similar response to events in the Middle East has led to some authorities viewing the totality of the Muslim community as potential terrorists. But in the early 1980s the effect was far more domestic. Methods used against the Irish community were subsequently deployed to confront, amongst others, the black community, the miners, other trade unionists and a range of activists campaigning about the proliferation of nuclear weapons, threats to the environment and women's and gay rights. Targeted policing was a very powerful method for silencing protest about human rights abuses and rendering the Irish uniformly 'suspect' in the eyes of their neighbours and work colleagues. However, the decision by the government then in power to use methods developed in the North of Ireland to respond to protests by these other groups had unintended consequences. These groups began to understand that the Irish community had been targeted because they were prepared to take a stand against a wide range of abuses of their civil liberties and human rights and saw themselves as 'a risen people'.

This chapter is based on research which I conducted between 1984 and 1986 when I was employed as a policy officer working on race and policing issues at the Greater London Council (GLC)[4] and between 1986 and 1987 when I was employed by the London Strategic Policy Unit (LSPU)[5] as a researcher looking at the policing of the Irish community.[6] I have also been assisted by my own recollections of the 1980s, when I was variously a member of the London Labour Party Executive and the Labour Party's National Women's Committee and chair of the Labour Committee on Ireland (LCI).[7] In addition, I draw on my experiences during the 1984–85 miners' strike and the establishment of Labour Party Black Sections. This also informed my views of the manner in which the Irish community and others who expressed their opposition to government policy were treated.

The Prevention of Terrorism Act

The Prevention of Terrorism (Temporary Provisions) Act 1974[8] became law on 29 November 1974, shortly after the Birmingham pub bombings. Its powers were extensive and did not conform to the human rights safeguards contained in comparable criminal legislation in force at that time. For example, the Act permitted the police to detain an individual without charge for up to forty-eight hours and without any contact with members of his or her family, friends, a lawyer or a court. It also provided the police with the power to detain a person for a further five days with limited access to legal advice if this was approved by the Secretary of State for the Home Department. Section 3 enabled the Secretary of State for the Home Department to exclude British citizens from entering Great Britain but did not prevent them from living in the North of Ireland. In addition, Section 8 enabled the authorities to examine any passenger arriving in or leaving Great Britain or the North of Ireland.

The PTA was said to be an essential tool in the fight against terrorism, but in fact the numbers of individuals actually charged with any offence connected with Irish terrorism were very small. For example, in 1980, 537 individuals were detained under the PTA but only twelve were charged with any offence under the Act. This trend continued and, in 1983, 191 were detained and only sixteen were charged.[9]

The Act was subsequently amended in 1976[10] to add a new Section 11, which made it an offence not to provide information which may be of material assistance to the police in relation to acts of terrorism or the conviction of any terrorist. It was the police who set the parameters for the scope of this information, and detainees, who were not provided with legal advice, were often not clear of the purpose or scope of this obligation. For example, in 1987 Marian Stewart, the wife of an ex-prisoner from the North of Ireland, was detained and told that if she did not co-operate her children would be taken from her and put in care, including a child who suffered from cerebral palsy.[11]

As Viscount Colville reported in 1986, there was 'a widespread feeling that both port procedures and detentions are often "fishing trips" to gather information rather than an exercise directed at people who might themselves be terrorists'.[12] Section 8 of the PTA also provided police, immigration and customs and excise officers with the power to 'examine' passengers arriving in or leaving Britain or the North of Ireland to ascertain whether they were involved in Irish terrorism. This operated under a National Ports Scheme at 147 seaports and airports. In the period up to 30 September 1987, 6,610 people were detained for over an hour under this provision. Statistics relating to the use of

Section 8 were not published alongside data for detentions under other provisions of the PTA, but these statistics did appear in the HM Chief Inspector of Constabulary's Annual Reports. For example, his 1985 report noted that in that year alone 55,328 individuals were examined for under an hour.[13]

Many people did not wish to disclose that they had been detained or what they had been asked, but newspaper reports of individual incidents in the 1980s indicate that those with a history of speaking out about abuses of human rights and civil rights were targeted and/or asked questions on the basis of their general political profile. For example, Sheena Clarke, a local Sheffield councillor who was also a member of the LCI, was detained at Manchester Airport in 1985 on her return from a housing conference in Belfast. She was questioned about her opinions on events in Ireland, whether she had been on Irish demonstrations, what she thought of Labour Party policy on Ireland and whether she had been on Campaign for Nuclear Disarmament demonstrations.[14]

The Irish in Britain Representation Group (IBRG)[15] believed that the PTA was used to divide the Irish community from the mainstream British community and isolate it. It also viewed the Act as an attempt at political policing aimed at hearts and minds at an ideological level to intimidate and silence any political debate or opposition to British security policy in Ireland.[16] This view was supported by the experiences of activists at this time. For example, in 1979 two Irish women, Ann Boyle and Maire O'Hare, were detained for five days after arriving in London to address a socialist feminist conference. They reported that they were not questioned about anything specific.[17] Bernadette McAliskey, previously an MP, was stopped on her way to a speaking tour in England and many members of the British Labour movement were stopped and questioned when travelling on delegations to the North of Ireland.[18]

Miscarriages of justice

In 1974 there were a number of high-profile arrests of members of the Irish community in Britain. In 1974 Hugh Callaghan, Patrick Hill, Gerry Hunter, Richard McIlkenny, Billy Power and Johnny Walker (subsequently known as the Birmingham Six), who were part of the Irish community in Birmingham, were arrested and subsequently convicted on 16 August 1975 of the murders of the twenty-one people who died in the Birmingham pub bombings.[19] They were sentenced to life imprisonment and remained in prison until their convictions were quashed by the Court of Appeal on 14 March 1991. Four of them had made false confessions during the first three days after their arrests after being severely beaten. The fact that four of them were arrested on their way to Ireland and that they had acquaintances who were involved with Irish republicanism also appeared to influence both the prosecution and the jury. By 3 December 1974 the police had also arrested more than forty people in London in connection with the bomb explosions in two pubs in Guildford on 5 October 1974.[20] Most of them were from the Irish community in Kilburn. Subsequently three of them, Patrick Armstrong, Paul Hill and Gerard Conlon, together with an English woman, Carole Armstrong (the Guildford Four), were charged with the murder of the four people killed in Guildford. They were convicted and sentenced to life imprisonment, despite the existence of strong alibi evidence. However, it was later accepted that their convictions amounted to a miscarriage of justice, as Patrick Armstrong's alleged confession had been fabricated by police officers investigating the case.[21] They were released on 19 October 1989. On 3 December 1974 the police also arrested Gerard Conlon's father, Giuseppe Conlon, when he was visiting London in order to seek assistance for his son. His sister-in-law, Anne Maguire, her husband, Paddy, her sons, Vincent and Patrick, her brother, Sean Smyth, who had been living at her house, and a friend, Patrick O'Neill, who had merely called in to see them, were also arrested. The Maguire Seven, as they became known, were charged with possessing nitroglycerine for use by the IRA and convicted in March 1976. Their convictions were not quashed until 1991. At the time of their arrests, Vincent was 16 and Patrick 13 years old.[22]

Faulty tests undertaken by forensic scientists played a crucial role in the convictions of the Birmingham Six,[23] the Maguire Seven[24] and Judith Ward.[25] For example, in the cases of Judith Ward and the Birmingham Six, Frank Skuse, a scientist at the Home Office Forensic Laboratory in Chorlton, Lancashire, asserted that traces of nitroglycerine found on their hands meant that they had been in contact with explosives. In fact it subsequently emerged that these traces could equally have arisen from contact with floor polish, soap, playing cards and a wide range of domestic products. The so-called Greiss Test, which had been used, was discredited in a Granada TV programme in 1985,[26] and subsequently in the Court of Appeal when the Birmingham Six's convictions were quashed. Shortly after the TV programme was broadcast Frank Skuse took early retirement, allegedly forced out for 'limited efficiency'.[27]

In the nearly two decades following their convictions few, except for Chris Mullin, Robert Kee and some members of the Irish community, asserted that these convictions were unsafe.[28] Therefore, they remained a warning that no one in the Irish community in Britain could be confident that they would not also become a victim of further miscarriage of justice by being Irish and being in the wrong place at the wrong time. The convictions of the Birmingham Six were particularly significant for anyone who was politically active. This was because, although they were not members of Sinn Féin or the IRA, three of them had travelled with Sinn Féin members to an annual Wolfe Tone republican commemoration in Dublin in June 1974 and four of them mixed within their local community with known republicans.[29]

Anti-Irish racism

In addition to the State's use of the PTA, the British media played a significant part in isolating and criminalising the Irish community even when there were no charges or convictions. On 29 October 1982 the *Evening Standard* carried a Jak cartoon depicting an imaginary poster for a film which said 'Showing Now – The Ultimate in Psychopathic Horror – THE IRISH'.[30] The Irish in Britain Representation Group and the Ethnic Minority Unit at the GLC led protests about the anti-Irish racism implicit in the cartoon.[31] But the Press Council rejected complaints made by the GLC and upheld a complaint from the *Evening Standard* that the withdrawal of advertising in its paper by the GLC 'was a blatant attempt by a local authority to use the power of its purse to influence the contents of a newspaper and coerce the editor'. The Commission for Racial Equality also withdrew an initial request that the Attorney General should prosecute the *Evening Standard*.[32] Similar cartoons reflected a one-dimensional view of the Irish, and Michael Cummings, who worked for the *Express*, claimed that he had 'cartoonist's licence' for giving expression to the British view that the Irish were 'extremely violent, bloody minded, always fighting, drinking enormous amounts, getting roaring drunk'.[33]

Some articles in the press also appeared to stereotype members of the Irish community. Such articles could have a very adverse affect on an Irish individual's employment prospects. For example, Dr Maire O'Shea lost her job after being arrested under the PTA in 1985. Prior to her arrest she had been a consultant psychiatrist at the Stratford Road Day Centre in Birmingham.[34] Other articles suggested that those in the wider Irish community were indirectly implicated in acts of terrorism or, at the very least, were not willing to assist the police to find those who were responsible for such acts. For example, the *Guardian* commented, after an IRA bomb exploded at Harrods on 17 December 1983, that 'those held had been under surveillance since the bombing in which five people died and 91 were injured. They are suspected IRA sympathisers who, although not directly involved, might be able to give information leading to the terrorist.'[35]

The broadcasting ban

The election of the republican hunger striker Bobby Sands to the British Parliament in 1981 was the start of a move by Sinn Féin to use both the 'armalite and the ballot box' in its campaign for a United Ireland.[36] Alex Maskey was elected to Belfast City Council in a by-election in 1983 and in May 1985 fifty-nine Sinn Féin councillors were elected to district councils in the North of Ireland.[37] Later that same year some of these councillors began regular speaking tours in Britain, where they made contact with both the Irish and the wider British communities. For example, women councillors attended NALGO (National and Local Government Officers' Association) and other trade union conferences in that and following years.[38] This was an important addition to the meetings organised by LCI at Labour Party conferences from 1983 onwards at which Gerry Adams and other prominent Sinn Féin members spoke. These meetings were an opportunity to counter some of the false perceptions engendered by the anti-Irish racism prevalent in some parts of the media and opened up useful dialogues on abuses of civil, political and human rights in the North of Ireland.

In a move to attempt to close down this debate, the government imposed a broadcasting ban.[39] Between 19 October 1988 and 16 September 1994 the BBC and commercial radio and television stations were prohibited from transmitting the voices of any Sinn Féin representative, including those who had been democratically elected, or any representative of a number of named paramilitary groups. As Scarlett McGuire, one of the journalists who unsuccessfully challenged the ban in the High Court, later said, 'the case is not just about journalists and their ability to report Northern Ireland properly. It is about people not being able to understand what is happening there because it has not been reported properly.'[40]

High-profile policing

Special Branch had played a central role in relation to the policing of the Irish community in Britain since it was formally set up in 1883 as the Special Irish Branch, in response to a Fenian bombing campaign in London.[41] In the 1980s intelligence collected under the PTA by the National Ports Scheme was sent to Special Branch and stored on its own Metropolitan C Department computer,[42] which had a 'free text retrieval' facility, allowing for extensive cross-referencing and searches.[43] Special Branch also had the ability to access other official data banks[44] at will and was not obliged to make a record when it retrieved any information from these sources.

In addition Special Branch co-operated with the Post Office's Special Investigation Unit, which intercepted targeted mail, opened it using lasers and chemical treatments, copied it and returned it for delivery by the next post.[45] It also benefitted from the development of System X telephone exchanges, which meant that computer software enabled officers to listen in to individual calls and lines without the need for taps to be physically attached to an actual line.[46] By the end of 1986, 239 authorised phone taps, some of which covered complete organisations, were also in place.[47] The identity of these organisations was not disclosed in the Interception of Communications Commissioner's *Annual Report* but, given the interest in events in the North of Ireland at that time, it can be presumed that some of these organisations were within the Irish community. The blanket nature of these phone taps caused widespread concern and Lord Justice Lloyd, who was the first Interception of Communications Commissioner to be appointed under the Interception of Communications Act 1985,[48] said that the inclusion of the home telephone numbers of officials of the organisations under surveillance within the scope of a general warrant was an abuse of their civil liberties.[49]

At the same time, Special Branch was monitoring a wide range of newspapers, magazines and other publicly available material. This was complemented by information gleaned from local police officers and neighbourhood watch schemes and by attendance at public meetings.[50] All of this was in keeping with the theories developed by Major General Sir Frank Kitson, a foremost military theoretician. He had previously served in Kenya during the Mau Mau uprising and also in Malaya and Cyprus and was stationed in the North of Ireland between 1970 and 1972. It was his view that in the preparatory stage of any counter-insurgency campaign it was necessary to create a comprehensive profile of the characteristics and movements of any community with the potential for insurrection. He believed that this was best done by establishing an effective system of intelligence designed to obtain a large volume of low-grade information.[51] Kitson is credited with developing the first psyops[52] unit in the North of Ireland and was the brigadier in charge of the 1st Battalion of the Parachute Regiment, who were responsible for the killing of thirteen civilians on Bloody Sunday, 30 January 1972, although he was not present on the day. His ideas and methodology were subsequently adopted by police forces in the North of Ireland and England.[53]

One of Special Branch's core roles was also to assess potential sources of disorder and to acquaint itself with all potentially subversive individuals and groups. The official definition of subversion at this time was 'activities ... which threaten the safety or well-being of the state and which are intended to undermine or overthrow parliamentary democracy by political, industrial or violent means'.[54] The inclusion of the word 'political' in this definition placed the Irish in Britain at particular risk of surveillance, given the arguments being raised about the gerrymandering of constituencies in the North of Ireland and the calls for a united Ireland.

The militarisation of policing

The Irish community in Britain were also further intimidated by the images they saw in newspapers and on television of the manner in which nationalist communities in the North of Ireland were being 'policed'. They may also have witnessed the police in London using the snatch-squad tactics used by soldiers in the North of Ireland against trade union pickets outside Grunwicks Film Processing Laboratories in 1977,[55] as the factory in question was in Neasden, an area with a high number of Irish residents. At the very least they would have seen confrontations between trade unionists and the police on television, as these were reported on a daily basis. Riot shields also made their first appearance in London on 13 August 1977, when they were used in Lewisham.[56] During the 1980s, senior police officers also travelled to Ulster for courses in riot control run by the Royal Ulster Constabulary.[57]

However, few of these tactics were used in response to marches organised in London by the Troops Out Movement and other organisations to commemorate Bloody Sunday or the 1981 hunger strikes or to support calls for a united Ireland.[58] This was partly because these marches were relatively small and well stewarded. Instead, the police relied on the force of numbers and the fact that demonstrators were also having to contend with the additional hostility of violent and aggressive anti-Irish groups which would attend to harass and threaten them. Marches were also either restricted to areas such as Kilburn, which had a high number of Irish inhabitants who were mainly already supportive, or were designed by the police to finish in areas such as the old 'bull ring' near Waterloo, which placed demonstrators at risk of attack from those such as the National Front who would wait to ambush them as the demonstration broke up.

Plastic bullets in Britain

Nevertheless, when in July 1981 the then Home Secretary, William Whitelaw, authorised British police forces to acquire plastic bullets as an aid in riot control,[59] and when in 1982, 5,000 were issued, many members of the Irish community in Britain did feel intimidated.[60] They were well aware of the possible consequences of the use of plastic bullets and knew that their name was deceptive, as these bullets were solid PVC cylinders, which were four inches long and travelled at a speed of between 130 and 170 miles an hour. In the North of Ireland they had been used indiscriminately in situations of public unrest, and by July 1981, for every 4,000 plastic bullets used by the security forces, there had been one death. In total seventeen civilians, including three children between the ages of 10 and 16, were killed and many others suffered serious injury. People were blinded, suffered from brain damage and skull, jaw, cheekbone and arm fractures (as well as leg fractures), despite the fact that regulations for their use indicated that they should be aimed only at an individual's lower limbs.[61] At the time they were said to be the most dangerous 'less lethal' riot control weapon in service in national security forces anywhere in the world,[62] and those injured and killed included women, children playing or going about their day-to-day activities and a woman who thought that she was safe in her own home.[63] Therefore there would appear to be no basis in fact for the assertion by Sir John Hermon, then Chief Constable of the Royal Ulster Constabulary, that 'plastic bullets are used only against rioters who are themselves determined to kill, wound or cause destruction'.[64]

Plastic bullets were subsequently deployed for the first time in England on Broadwater Farm Estate in Tottenham on 7 October 1985. This estate is in the London Borough of Haringey, which also has a large Irish community. Their deployment here led to a consultative conference held on 28 November 1987 at the Haringey Irish Centre expressing concern about their use in the North of Ireland and in Tottenham.[65]

Strip searching

In November 1982 the new Governor of Armagh Women's Prison in the North of Ireland instigated a regime whereby women prisoners were strip searched before and after every court appearance, home or hospital visit or inter-prison journey.[66] This occurred at a time when the H-Block hunger strikes and the election of Bobby Sands as an MP for Fermanagh and South Tyrone in April 1981 had alerted the international community to the widespread abuses of civil and political rights which were occurring in the North of Ireland. There was a perception by the prisoners and their families and communities that the introduction of strip searching at this time was an attempt to further criminalise them in the eyes of the media and wider world.

A number of campaigns in support of the women in Armagh Prison were initiated and speaking tours were organised in Britain.[67] Many women in the Irish community in Britain were involved in these tours. Concern in the Irish community in Britain was also exacerbated by the cases of Martina Anderson and Ella O'Dwyer, two Irish republican prisoners detained in England. They were strip searched 381 and 388 times, respectively, whilst on remand in HMP Brixton Prison and serving their sentences at HMP Durham Prison between 1 July 1985 and 30 September 1986.[68] This was despite the fact that they were held in Category A high-security wings with an array of other security measures. Furthermore, during their trial at the Old Bailey they were strip searched on average three times a day.[69]

On 25 February 1985, Home Office Minister David Mellor told Parliament that 'general provisions on searching are contained in rule 39 of the Prison Rules and rule 43 of both the Youth Custody Centre Rules 1983 and the Detention Centre Rules 1983. These rules make it clear that prisoners (including remand prisoners) are to be searched on reception into a prison department and subsequently as the governor thinks fit.'[70] However, this did not allay concerns about this practice and the manner in which the searches were carried out.[71] For example, in 1987 Amnesty International concluded that 'strip-searching constitutes ill-treatment when carried out with the deliberate intention of humiliating or degrading prisoners. Furthermore, the organisation considers that the practice of strip-searching, given its nature, is open to abuse.'[72] The Prison Officers Association said that it shared the increasing and genuine concern about the human rights implications of this procedure.[73] The Police Sub-Committee of the London Strategic Policy Committee also accepted two reports which were critical of this practice.[74] On 5 December 1987 the LSPU held a conference on strip searching which was attended by around 300 delegates from local authorities, trade unions, women's groups, Irish community and campaign groups as well as journalists and researchers.[75] The conference condemned strip searching as a breach of human rights.

The fact that Irish women in prison were being strip searched and also suffering anti-Irish racism from other prisoners[76] further intimidated the Irish community in Britain. However, it was also an issue which brought the community into close contact with other communities and attracted sympathy for and developed better understanding of the civil and political conditions in the North of Ireland. The breadth of the delegates at the LSPU conference was just one example of this. They included peace activists, women from many ethnic-minority communities, women who were leaders of local councils and leading trade unionists.[77] They found common ground in opposition to a serious abuse of women's bodily integrity which was being used to intimidate and threaten those with particular political views.

Conclusion

Single-issue campaigns, such as those against strip searching and the use of plastic bullets in the North of Ireland, were able to make alliances with women's groups and groups concerned with civil liberties and the prevailing racist attitudes towards black and ethnic minority communities as oppressive public-order practices started to affect these wider groups. The surveillance and demonisation of the Irish community also echoed the increasing experience of trade unionists and those arguing for the democratisation of local services, the Labour Party and national government. This led to these wider groups gaining a greater understanding of the tactics being used against them and to an increasing interest in the human rights and civil liberties abuses suffered by the Irish community.

It also led to a number of very positive and long-lasting alliances being made by a whole range of single-issue and community groups adversely affected by the policies of successive governments from 1979 to 1990 and beyond. The fact that in the early and mid 1980s the GLC and LSPU were highlighting the experiences of many of these groups and publishing cutting-edge research about their needs and situations was also very important, as it gave publicity and also credibility to many of their concerns and needs. In particular, the funding provided by the GLC to Irish women, the Irish Book Fair, Irish youth seeking employment and older Irish individuals wishing to return to Ireland had the effect of highlighting the similarities between the Irish community and other communities and enabled the Irish community to have the courage to assert its culture and achievements, which rendered it far from 'suspect'.

Notes

1 P. Hillyard, *Suspect Community: People's Experience of the Prevention of Terrorism Acts in Britain* (London: Pluto Press, 1993), p. 273.
2 *Guardian* (22 September 1987).
3 *Irish Post* (26 September 1987).

4 The Greater London Council (GLC) was abolished by the Conservative government on 31 March 1986. Two of the reasons for its unpopularity with the government were its financial support for Irish community groups and the dialogue which it developed with Sinn Féin.

5 This was funded by nine London boroughs between 1986 and 1988.

6 For example, LSPU Police Monitoring and Research Group, *Policing the Irish Community*, Briefing Paper No. 5 (London: London Strategic Policy Unit, 1988); and LSPU Police Monitoring and Research Group, *Policing London: Collected Reports of the LSPU Police Monitoring and Research Group, No. 2* (London: London Strategic Policy Unit, December 1987).

7 The LCI was formed in the late 1970s by Labour Party members and trade unionists who believed that Labour Party policy needed to recognise the human rights and civil liberties abuses taking place in the North of Ireland and that there was a legitimate political argument for the unification of Ireland, which was based on the right to national self-determination. See also Parkin, chapter 12 in this volume.

8 *The Prevention of Terrorism (Temporary Provisions) Act* 1974 Chapter 56 (London: HM Stationery Office, 1974). Available at: http://cain.ulst.ac.uk/hmso/pta1974.htm (Accessed 2 June 2015).

9 Home Office statistics, published on a quarterly basis throughout this period and quoted in LSPU Police Monitoring and Research Group, *Policing London*, p. 53.

10 The Prevention of Terrorism (Temporary Provisions) Act 1976.

11 *An Phoblacht/Republican News* (13 August 1987).

12 Viscount Colville of Culross QC, *Report on the Operation in 1986 of the Prevention of Terrorism (Interim Provisions) Act 1984* (London: 1986). Available at: www.schedule7.org.uk/wp-content/uploads/2014/01/2_REPORT_Colville_fixedsmallpdf.com_.pdf (Accessed 12 June 2015). Viscount Colville was a judge and a hereditary member of the House of Lords who was appointed by the Home Secretary as the Independent Reviewer of Terrorism Legislation between 1986 and 1992, and reported back to Parliament on an annual basis.

13 *HM Chief Inspector of Constabulary's Annual Report* (London: HM Stationery Office,1985).

14 *Leeds Other Paper* (28 June 1985). For a further example, see the *Irish Post* (31 October 1987).

15 The IBRG was set up in 1981 to foster a positive identity for the Irish in Britain and to give effective representation to the Irish community at national and local level.

16 IBRG submission to the Colville Review, July 1987, unpublished. Available in the LSPU archive.

17 T. Gifford, *Where's the Justice? A Manifesto of Law Reform* (London: Penguin Special, 1986), p. 107.

18 M. O'Shea, 'Policing Irish women in Britain', in C. Dunhill (ed.), *The Boys in Blue: Women's Challenge to the Police* (London: Virago Press, 1989), p. 266. On delegations from Britain to the North of Ireland, see Parkin, chapter 12 in this volume.

19　See chapter 20 by O'Reilly in this volume.

20　R. Kee, *Trial and Error: The Maguires, the Guildford Pub Bombings and British Justice* (London: Hamish Hamilton, 1986), p. 49.

21　T. Kirby, 'Guildford Four plot dismissed: An inquiry into one of Britain's worst miscarriages of justice makes many criticisms but rejects the idea of an official cover-up', *Independent* (1 July 1994).

22　Kee, *Trial and Error*, pp. 272, 96.

23　C. Mullin, *Error of Judgment: The Truth about the Birmingham Bombings* (London: Chatto and Windus, 1986), pp. 165–71.

24　Kee, *Trial and Error*, pp. 236–9.

25　J. Ward, *Ambushed: My Story* (London: Ebury Press, 1993), pp. 35, 162, 166. Judith Ward was arrested on 18 February 1974 and charged with conspiracy to cause an explosion on the M62 motorway which killed twelve people on a British Army coach. While she was on remand, psychiatric reports, which were not disclosed to her defence team, the judge or the jury, indicated that she was suffering from an acute psychotic depression and was unfit to plead. She was convicted and spent the next eighteen years in prison before being released on appeal.

26　LSPU Police Monitoring and Research Group, *Policing the Irish Community*, p. 55.

27　*Guardian* (10 December 1987).

28　Mullin, *Error of Judgment*; Kee, *Trial and Error.*

29　Mullin, *Error of Judgement*, pp. 14–16.

30　L. Curtis, *Nothing but the Same Old Story: The Roots of Anti-Irish Racism* (London: Information on Ireland, 1985), p. 84. JAK, otherwise known as Raymond Jackson, drew cartoons for the *Evening Standard* from 1952 to 1997.

31　Ibid., pp. 84–5.

32　Ibid. See also T. P. Coogan, *Wherever Green is Worn: The Story of the Irish Diaspora* (London: Arrow, 2000).

33　Interview with Michael Cummings, *Irish Times* (29 May 1982). See also Casey, chapter 15 in this volume.

34　'PTA protest grows', *New Labour and Ireland*, 7 (May/June 1985), p. 7.

35　*Guardian* (22 December 1983). For another example, see *Daily Mail* (16 February 1987).

36　R. English, *Armed Struggle: The History of the IRA* (London: Pan, 2004), pp. 224–5.

37　'Unionist outrage: Attempt to exclude republican councillors', *New Labour and Ireland*, 8 (July/August/Sept 1985), p. 4.

38　See chapters by Parkin (12) and Rossiter (11) in this volume.

39　See Pettigrew's chapter 16 in this volume.

40　*Glasgow Herald* (27 May 1989).

41　T. Bunyan, *The History and Practice of the Political Police in Britain* (London: Quartet Books, 1983), p. 104.

42　Police Monitoring and Research Group, *Policing the Irish Community*, p. 42.

43　BSSRS Technology of Political Control Group with RAMPET, *TechnoCop: New Police Technologies* (London: Free Association Books, 1985), p. 33.

44 Such as those held by the Inland Revenue, Customs and Excise, the Immigration Service and the Department of Social Security.

45 LSPU Police Monitoring and Research Group, *Policing the Irish Community*, p. 41.

46 BSSRS Technology of Political Control Group, *TechnoCop*, pp. 99, 104–5.

47 *Annual Report of the Interception of Communications Commissioner* (London: Office of the Interception of Communications Commissioner, 1986). The Commissioner was appointed by the Prime Minister under S8(7) of the Interception of Communications Act 1985 and the *Annual Report* was placed before Parliament. This is recorded in *Hansard*: House of Lords Debate 26 March 1987, Vol. 486 col. 351–2WA. However, at that time you could only access the report if you had access to parliamentary records. I have presumed that an MP gave LSPU a copy but I no longer have access to this. Privacy International previously posted these reports on its website but in May 2015 they were no longer available there.

48 The Act was a response to the decision in the European Court of Human Rights in *Malone* v *UK* (1084) C 56. The Act permitted the interception of telephone and other telecommunication processes.

49 LSPU Police Monitoring and Research Group, *Policing the Irish Community*, p. 42.

50 Bunyan, *The History and Practice of the Political Police*, pp. 135–8.

51 F. Kitson, *Low Intensity Operations: Subversion, Insurgency and Peacekeeping* (London: Faber and Faber, 1971).

52 Psychological operations are designed to convey selected information and indicators to audiences to influence their emotions, motives, objective reasoning and ultimately the behaviour of governments, organisations, groups and individuals. This may include the dissemination of disinformation.

53 BSSRS Technology of Political Control Group, *TechnoCop*, pp. 104–5.

54 Special Branch Guidelines, Home Office, 1984. Unpublished document, available at: www.statewatch.org.news/2004/mar/special-branch-1984.htm (Accessed 20 May 2015).

55 Between 1976 and 1978 mainly female East African Asian workers at Grunwicks were in dispute with their employers. They received widespread trade union support and the police made 550 arrests during this period.

56 The National Front had organised a march from New Cross to Lewisham and this led to the organisation of a large counter-demonstration by an alliance of anti-fascists.

57 *Daily Mail* (15 July 1981).

58 See Renwick, chapter 8 in this volume.

59 LSPU Police Monitoring and Research Group, *Policing the Irish Community*, p. 14.

60 Haringey Irish Consultative Conference, *The Irish in Haringey: An Assessment of Need and a Programme for Action* (London: Haringey Council, 1987), p. 37.

61 LSPU Police Monitoring and Research Group, *Policing the Irish Community*, pp. 10–18.

62 J. Rosenhead, 'Plastic bullets – a reasonable force?', *New Scientist* (17 October 1985), 26–7 (p. 26).

63 LSPU Police Monitoring and Research Group, *Policing the Irish Community*, pp. 12–13.

64 *Sunday Times* (12 December 1982).

65 Haringey Irish Consultative Conference, *The Irish in Haringey*, p. 37.

66 LSPU Police Monitoring and Research Group, *Policing the Irish Community*, p. 26.

67 See chapters by Rossiter (11) and Parkin (12) in this volume.

68 LSPU Police Monitoring and Research Group, *Policing the Irish Community*, p. 25.

69 LSPU Police Monitoring and Research Group, *Policing London*, p. 64.

70 D. Mellor, Written Answer to Parliamentary Question, *Hansard*, House of Commons, 25 February 1985, Vol. 74 cols 32–3W.

71 Irish Prisoners Appeal, *Strip-Searching: End it Now*, pamphlet, 1986.

72 *Amnesty International Annual Report* (London: Amnesty International, 1987), p. 327.

73 Prison Officers Association, *Strip Searching, The Fact and The Fiction*, pamphlet, 1987. See also *Daily Mirror* (5 February 1987).

74 London Strategic Policy Unit, *Policing London*, pp. 63–7, 68–9.

75 N. Hutchinson, C. Keatinge, J. Kelly and S. Spurway, *Working Together to End Strip Searching: Report of a Conference 5 December 1987* (London: London Strategic Policy Unit, 1988), p. 5.

76 Women's Equality Group, *Breaking the Silence: Women's Imprisonment* (London: London Strategic Policy Unit, undated [1985?]).

77 Hutchinson et al., *Working Together to End Strip Searching*. The report contains a summary of the presentations made by delegates across this range.

11

'Not our cup of tea': Irish and British feminist encounters in London during the Troubles

Ann Rossiter

Women were central to the numerous protest organisations that sprang up in Britain throughout the thirty years of the Troubles. From the Civil Rights Committees set up in Birmingham, London, Manchester and elsewhere in the late 1960s, to the Anti-Interment League, Troops Out, People's Democracy, the Prisoners Aid Committee, the Irish in Britain Representation Group and many others, frequently they were the gel that held these organisations together, mainly as foot soldiers, occasionally as leaders. Although this changed over time, initially many were not politically engaged with feminist politics – some, indeed, may have been hostile to the feminist movement's philosophy and practice, feeling that personally they did not need it, or viewing it as a 'bourgeois deviation' from nationalist and class struggles. But for those who believed that the notion of 'civil rights' had to include women's legal and human rights ('there can be no liberation without women's liberation' was a popular slogan of the times), there was nothing for it but to set up their own groups where gender equality and women's empowerment were taken for granted, rather than being the source of incessant ideological battles.

The rise of the feminist movement in Britain, Ireland, the USA and elsewhere in its first phase at the turn of the twentieth century coincided with the rise of Ireland's movement for national independence. Equally, the second wave of feminism, or 'the Women's Liberation Movement' as it came to be called, again coincided with the rise of the nationalist movement in Northern Ireland in the late 1960s and early 1970s related to the suppression of the civil rights movement. However, despite these coincidences, a shared ideal of self-determination and a criss-crossing of membership, the two movements have sat uneasily in each other's company.

During the second wave, feminists across the globe argued that nation-alist movements rely on and reproduce patriarchy through traditional gender constructs, typically seeing women as mothers, as reproducers of the nation in a biological and cultural sense.[1] The right of a woman to define her sexuality is constrained, her reproductive rights proscribed, her sexual freedom heavily restrained and, as a mother, her right to work outside the home blocked through law, religion or custom. All of these were features of the southern Irish State forged by the forces of Irish nationalism following the War of Independence and the partitioning of the island in 1922, thus providing a negative precedent.

Since its inception, the southern State has purveyed the imagery of the passive, unquestioning and selfless 'Mother Ireland' and of Mary, the untainted Virgin Mother of Christ, as role models for women, despite female participation at all levels of the national struggle, including mili-tary combat.[2] Numerous battles have had to be fought over contracep-tion, divorce, homosexuality and censorship. A battle royal is still being fought over the right to abortion, virtually unobtainable not only in the southern State, but also in Northern Ireland.[3] It is hardly surprising, therefore, that many Irish feminists at home and 'across the water' in Britain concluded that any self-respecting feminist would choose to join the autonomous Women's Liberation Movement (WLM) and give the nationalist movement a wide berth.

However, members of the three groups to be discussed in this chapter, the Women on Ireland Collective (1973–74), the Women and Ireland Group (1976–80) and the London Armagh Co-ordinating Group (1980–87), all London based, were amongst those organisations that worked with and supported women who were not consciously feminist in the working-class republican communities in Northern Ireland, focusing on their struggles against the inequities of the Northern Ireland State, but not directly against the patriarchal order. All three defined the relationship of the Northern Irish State with Britain as an imperial one, the struggle against it as anti-imperialist and undifferentiated from others in Malaya (now Malaysia), Cyprus, Kenya or Aden (now South Yemen). The groups were non-hierarchical as well as being autonomous. Although they collaborated at times with a number of different organisations like Troops Out, they were not directly associated with any, other than the British WLM, and in particular its socialist-feminist strand. As was com-monplace in the WLM at the time, groups were informal, being a loose coalition of like-minded people focusing on an agreed agenda.

Loyalist and unionist women were not the focus of attention of any of the three groups because of their failure to tackle the prevailing structures of power in the sectarian State and its security apparatuses. In general, group members supported the Provisional Republican Movement's aspiration for the unification of the island, arguing that the Northern Irish State as it stood was 'not fit for purpose' in the level of its discrimination against the non-unionist population. How this could be achieved was another matter, and there were some differences of opinion over the scale and the boundaries of military action.

The account of the three groups that follows is based on a larger study[4] involving thirty in-depth interviews and a number of lengthy e-mail correspondences with authors, journalists and former activists that I conducted mainly in the late 1990s and early 2000s. These were augmented by considerable research on relevant historical and contemporary literature, including a small collection of material produced by the groups and, lastly, by my own membership in all three. To the best of my knowledge, this is the only detailed account published on feminist activism on the Irish National Question in Britain.

The Women on Ireland Collective, 1973–74

The small group of founder members of the Women on Ireland Collective were all from the Republic of Ireland. Few, if any, had a family background in the politics of the Irish National Question (the unresolved issues relating to the pursuit of nationhood). Like many Irish immigrants in Britain at the time, they were deeply influenced by events in Northern Ireland as the Troubles unfolded. In the midst of the fog of war the burden being shouldered by working-class women in republican areas was deeply troubling and the formation of the group was in part a response to this, but also part of a desire to take up feminist issues.

The actions of republican working-class women organised in street protests and committees – in response to the effects of internment, house burnings, house searches by the Army and RUC (ostensibly in pursuit of Provisional Irish Republican Army [PIRA] men, ammunition and bomb-making equipment), the ripping apart of houses and brutalisation of the occupants, the theft and destruction of property, imposition of frequent curfews, the massive use of live ammunition, rubber bullets and CS gas on rioters and the local population generally – has been well documented by several who participated,[5] and also by journalists,[6] writers and academics.[7] With so many of their menfolk detained or interned, women's lives changed dramatically. As the writer and feminist activist, Margaret Ward, has written: 'They were suddenly on their own, forced to cope, to become social security claimants in their own right, organizing family care around prison visits and taking part in political protests.'[8]

The Collective's work in its single year of existence was concentrated on promoting an understanding in the British WLM of the lives and political activism of women in working-class republican neighbourhoods. This was because the conflict was marginalised – or likely dismissed out of hand – by the WLM, despite Northern Ireland's being part of the United Kingdom. Fact-finding visits were made by Collective members and republican women were invited to address feminist gatherings throughout Britain. Although the WLM magazine *Spare Rib* gave intermittent coverage to their lives, as did *Outwrite Women's Newspaper*, in general WLM magazines, journals and newsletters tended to dodge the subject. Ireland was seen as too alien, the conflict too violent, too bound up with nationalism and religion, and too much a man's war, thus ensuring that there was no sustained debate. All in all, it was, as the English phrase has it, 'not our cup of tea', despite similarities with other such conflicts in many parts of the globe which were viewed more sympathetically and designated 'anti-imperialist struggles'.

A persistent argument permeating the critique of working-class republican women's activism, and frequently its dismissal in Northern Ireland itself and further afield, was the view that it was not feminist in nature. Lynda Edgerton, a leading member of the Northern Ireland Women's Rights Movement, a key organisation in the autonomous women's movement, confirms this position in arguing in a widely distributed essay published in London that republican women's efforts were 'directed almost wholly to civil rights rather than to women's issues' and, as such, were communal and familial rather than feminist.[9] Margaret Ward and Joanna McMinn, both from the Northern Irish feminist movement, argued in a more nuanced fashion:

> The sheer diversity of women's involvement in the community, coupled with a growing feminist movement [in Northern Ireland], meant that women were gaining recognition as political actors within the community. Not everyone was happy about it and certainly very few were prepared to accept the legitimacy of feminism, but it was obvious that women were not going to go away, or to retreat back into the home.[10]

If the Collective's work on publicising the plight of republican women in their communities in Northern Ireland through public meetings, organising conferences or fund-raising events to finance visits presented a problem for many British feminists, the issue of giving support to female prisoners' struggles proved even more difficult. The problem lay in the fact that the majority of female prisoners were incarcerated on charges of involvement in paramilitary activity. This became apparent when the Collective organised a forty-eight-hour symbolic hunger strike outside Brixton Prison in South London between 8 and 10 February 1974 where the sisters Marian and Dolours Price had embarked on a hunger strike lasting 205 days. Their demand was for political (rather than 'common criminal') status and the right to serve their sentences in a Northern Ireland prison. The response of the British government was to commence force feeding of the hunger strikers.

The Price sisters, both PIRA members, were part of a twelve-member bombing team that placed car bombs outside an Army recruiting depot, the headquarters of the British Forces Broadcasting Network, New Scotland Yard and the Old Bailey on 8 March 1973. One person died of a heart attack and 265 people were injured.[11] After their conviction and imprisonment, the sisters and fellow team members Gerard Kelly and Hugh Feeney went on hunger strike, a political tool employed in both the suffragette and the Irish nationalist traditions.

The decision by the Collective to call a hunger strike and to link the force feeding of the Price sisters with the suffragettes was meant as a dramatic gesture to raise awareness of and debate on Northern Ireland in the WLM. The reaction, however, was almost wholly negative. In response to a feature article containing details of the plight of the Price sisters, extracts from letters to their family and coverage of the Collective's hunger strike run by the feminist magazine *Spare Rib*,[12] a number of readers' letters were subsequently published indicating that the writers were not convinced by the Collective's action or, indeed, of the nature of the Northern Ireland State and Britain's involvement in sustaining it. One, from Anna Ansraab, was uncompromising. She wrote: 'I object to your [*Spare Rib*] soiling the memory of the Suffragettes by including a 1914 passage about them in the same feature as if it were some kind of direct parallel.'[13] In another, Julie Thompson declared: 'I am writing in the capacity of the Average Woman in the Street who is very hazy as to just what is going on in Ireland and why. Impartial reports are impossible to obtain; those of committed socialists being just as reliable as those of the Army, newspapers, politicians, etc., and I feel your article on the Price Sisters ... only adds to the confusion.'[14]

In response to these, and especially to Julie Thompson's complaint, the *Spare Rib* editorial team of the time gave a detailed response. They argued that they had presented an alternative viewpoint in the light of the welter of information coming from the British media, government and military sources for consumption by the British public on a daily basis; that there was considerable misinformation in the way the conflict was being reported; and that all deaths and injuries were being ascribed to the PIRA, regardless of whether they were perpetrated by the British Army, the police or loyalist paramilitaries. They added, 'the

IRA are always described as terrorists though similar forces operating further away, whether in place or time, are referred to as liberation forces'.[15]

In 1975 the Price sisters came off their hunger strike and were transferred to serve their sentences in Armagh Jail in Northern Ireland. After a year of intense activity the Collective dissolved. The dissolution took place in circumstances where a systematic bombing campaign was conducted by the PIRA in Britain with the aim of putting pressure on the British public to call for the withdrawal of troops from Northern Ireland. The most serious incident was the Birmingham pub bombs in November 1974 in which 21 people were killed and 162 injured (discussed in Laura O'Reilly's chapter 20 in this volume). There were strong differences of opinion about the ethics of bombing civilian targets in some protest organisations in Britain concerned with the Troubles, including the Collective, which often contributed to their demise. Some activists held the view that the bombing campaign in Britain had a significant impact, including Marian Price, who stated: 'I do believe ... they [the British government] protect the mainland ... [T]hey'll sacrifice anything to do that.'[16] Others were of the view that the bombing campaign allowed for the portrayal of republicans as terrorists, that it brought retribution down upon the Irish in Britain and subjected them to the draconian effects of the Prevention of Terrorism Act (PTA) introduced in 1974, and to widespread prejudice or even racism exacerbated by a hostile media.[17] In this climate of tension and fear it was hardly surprising that it was not until 1976 that another activist group on the Irish National Question, anxious to raise feminist issues, came into being in the London area.

The Women and Ireland Group, 1976–80

A tightly policed rally, protected by snipers from the Special Patrol Group in positions on the roofs of Canada House and the National Gallery, was organised for the Northern Ireland Peace Women (later known as the Peace People) in London's Trafalgar Square on a cold Sunday in November 1976. The Trafalgar Square event was part of a worldwide trip made by Mairead Corrigan and Betty Williams, leaders of a movement to generate support for peace in Northern Ireland. Their efforts had been enthusiastically received and the women were everywhere feted and had numerous awards and honours showered upon them, including the Nobel Peace Prize. They joined the Queen Elizabeth Jubilee reception aboard the royal yacht *Britannia* in Belfast Lough, were mentioned in the Queen's Christmas Day address and were granted an audience with the Pope.[18] On the platform in Trafalgar Square, Corrigan and Williams were joined by Joan Baez, the American folk singer and peace activist, and by senior Catholic clerics.

Women and Ireland, a socialist-feminist autonomous collective and successor to the Women and Ireland Collective, participated in the event, but as part of a counter-demonstration to oppose the Peace People. The group had been active for some months before, but the Trafalgar Square event solidified the view that a concerted intervention on the Irish National Question should be initiated once again within the WLM. The mix of women who joined Women and Ireland varied over time as numbers of women passed through at various stages of its existence, but its general profile was of Irish women from both sides of the Irish border. There was also a sprinkling of second-generation Irish, as well as Americans and Australians, and some English women. All espoused feminism and were Left-leaning but were, generally speaking, not members of Left organisations.[19]

The Peace People was launched in Belfast in the summer of 1976 following the deaths of three children and the injuring of their mother when they were hit by a car out of control. The driver, an IRA volunteer, had been shot and badly injured by members of the British Army in hot pursuit. Immediately following the crash a peace movement was launched by the sister of the injured woman, Mairead Corrigan, a witness to the incident, Betty Williams, and a journalist, Ciaran McKeown.[20]

Several hundred women gathered for a silent vigil at the site of the tragedy, followed a few days later by more than ten thousand war-weary people, predominantly women, who turned out for a peace march in Belfast, while double that number marched in Dublin. The marches grew in number and in size, with people from all communities taking part, and there were emotional scenes as women embraced across the sectarian divide. The marches soon extended as far afield as continental Europe and, aided by the media, a local initiative was soon transformed into an international *cause célèbre*. However, within two years of its formation the peace movement was met with accusations of political partiality.

Initially, the Peace People adopted a neutral stance on the conflict, but very quickly they displayed a strong bias against the PIRA and consequently lost the support of the republican population. Notably, Corrigan and Williams failed to criticise the British Army after soldiers had shot twelve-year-old Majella O'Hare and fourteen-year-old Brian Stewart in 1976. Corrigan and Williams issued the following statement:

We do not equate the vicious and determined terrorism of the republican and loyalist paramilitary organizations with the occasional instances when members of the security forces may have stepped beyond the rule of law. And until the Northern Ireland community themselves evolve their own new community institutions and form of government, then the RUC [Royal Ulster Constabulary] and other security forces are the only legitimate upholders of the rule of law.[21]

This stance sealed the fate of the Peace People amongst republicans, for in one fell swoop they had not only shattered any alliances with that section of the population, but broadcast to the world their view that Britain and the local security forces were impartial players in the conflict. By the time Corrigan and Williams became Nobel Peace laureates in 1977, the peace movement had become a spent force.[22]

A recurring theme in the volumes of publicity worldwide that the Peace People received was their association with women's liberation, simply by virtue of being a peace group and being predominantly female. For example, the editorial group of *Women's Report*, a British WLM magazine, declared in 1976 that they perceived 'glimmerings of the existence of a separate women's consciousness about the war in Northern Ireland and the sudden sprouting of a mass movement'.[23] This separate consciousness, it was implied, endowed women with a special vocation for peace based on their common experience as givers of life, carers in the home and frequently carers in the world of work.

The Women and Ireland Group opposed this position and propagated their opposition widely. For instance, in a letter to another British WLM publication, *Scarlet Women*, they wrote: 'Our position is that ... women organizing together should never be viewed as necessarily progressive ... [In fact] there have been a number of situations where women have organized separately as women, and have in the process given support to extremely reactionary and anti-feminist politics'.[24] Women and Ireland cited the example of loyalist women's demonstrations to bring down the Sunningdale Executive in Northern Ireland in 1974, the first attempt to create a power-sharing executive between both communities.[25] Women and Ireland concluded that feminism does not inevitably arise out of women just getting together; it has to be on the basis of a political philosophy.

As campaigning on the Peace People abated in 1977, Women and Ireland were involved in a flurry of activity that consisted of talks to WLM groups, presentations at seminars, workshops and conferences and the production of a collection of conference papers entitled *Irish Women at War*.[26] All had the aim of counteracting the claim made by many feminists that 'Ireland is too complicated and too confusing'.

Another focus of their activism concerned state repression being carried out under the umbrella of the 1974 PTA, and arguing the case for the withdrawal of the British Army. Furthermore, they continued the precedent established by the Women and Ireland Collective in supporting republican working-class women activists in community organisations in Northern Ireland, especially women from the Relatives Action Committees (RACs) which came into being in 1976,[27] and inviting them to meetings in London to talk about their lives.

By 1980, a Manchester Women and Ireland Group had been formed. As the decade progressed such groups developed in eleven other centres ranging from Bristol to Brighton and Dundee and resulted in a Women and Ireland Network being established.[28] By the early 1980s the focus of activists' attention increasingly moved towards women political prisoners as the prison issue assumed centre stage in the Northern Ireland political arena. The Women and Ireland Group dissolved and several of the members joined the London Armagh Co-ordinating Group formed in 1980. Also, several became members of the newly formed Irish Women's Abortion Support Group (IWASG), which provided support for abortion seekers from both sides of the Irish border who were forced to travel to Britain for a safe and legal termination of pregnancy.[29] Northern Irish IWASG members came from both communities, thus providing one of the few opportunities for working together on an issue regarded by feminists as basic to a woman's autonomy, that is, the right to control her fertility.

The London Armagh Co-ordinating Group, 1980–87

Recognition of the plight of republican prisoners gradually seeped into public consciousness in Britain, in particular amongst those active in their trade unions, in the Labour Party and municipal councils, such as the Greater London Council (GLC), in some Irish organisations and in the WLM. The impact of the sponsored visits of the RACs was also felt, as was the campaigning carried out by the Collective and the Women and Ireland groups, amongst many others. One of the first activities of the newly formed London-based Armagh Co-ordinating Group (known as the Armagh Group) in 1980 was to arrange a speaking tour of Britain by Rose McAllister, a Belfast woman who had spent two-and-a-half years on protest in Armagh Jail following the removal of 'special category' (or political prisoner) status in 1976, whereby all prisoners, regardless of the nature of their convictions, were designated 'ordinary criminals'. The protest culminated in the hunger strike of 1980 in which male and female prisoners took part. The female prisoners were not part of the 1981 strike which resulted in the deaths of ten men in the H-Blocks at the Maze Prison.

The prison protests first took the form of a 'no work' strike that escalated into a 'no wash' protest, in which prisoners refused to use the washing and toilet facilities. In the case of the Armagh women prisoners the decision to protest was prompted by a serious assault on prisoners on 7 February 1980 by male warders who also searched and stripped their cells on the pretext of looking for paramilitary uniforms. The wardens locked the women prisoners out of washing facilities and refused them the right to exercise. To highlight the extent of deteriorating conditions in the prison, the women went on a thirteen-month long 'dirty protest'. This involved not only a refusal to wash and 'slop out', but also the smearing of bodily effluent on cell walls and ceilings.[30] The Armagh Group described itself in its occasional bulletin, *Women Behind the Wire*,[31] as a broad women's group whose agenda was to support the six elements of political status which had been removed: the rights to wear one's own clothes (not applicable to women, who always had this right), to refuse prison work, to be granted normal remission on sentence, to access educational facilities, to receive weekly letters and visits and to enjoy free association with other republican prisoners. The group's main emphasis was the republican women political prisoners in Armagh Jail, although it also supported the republican male prisoners' struggle for the reinstatement of political status in the Maze Prison.

In interviews with former members of the group[32] a point was frequently made of the extent of the controversy which occurred in WLM meetings and conferences over whether the plight of the prisoners constituted a feminist issue or not. The nub of the problem came into play with the introduction of menstruation as a marker of sexual difference. The presence of menstrual blood on the walls of Armagh Jail, as well as discarded sanitary towels in the corridors, was a powerful indication of sexualised violence, as body searches, and in particular strip searching, of prisoners were conducted regardless of whether women were menstruating.

Violent scuffles with warders, male and female, often occurred when prisoners refused to remove sanitary pads for inspection, and were the occasion of verbal sexual abuse. By smearing body fluids and faeces on their cell walls, or throwing used sanitary pads into the wing corridors, prisoners were deploying their own blood as an instrument of power against the forces of the State, a point made by the journalist Nell McCafferty[33] and one analysed by Begona Aretxaga in her study of women and nationalism in Northern Ireland.[34] For those who supported the prisoners, Armagh was a feminist issue because of the gender-specific ways in which women were targeted by the prison regime. For those opposed, it was merely an example of women's bodies being colonised, not by the State but by the republican movement.

To those who contended that Armagh was not an issue for feminists, the prisoners gave their interpretation in an open letter which was published in the *Irish Times* in August 1980:

> It is our belief that not only is our plight a feminist issue, but a very fundamental social and human issue. It is a feminist issue in so far as we are women, and the network of this jail is completely geared to male domination. The governor, the assistant governor, and the doctor are all males. We are subject to physical and mental abuse from male guards who patrol our wing daily ... If this is not a feminist issue then we feel that the word 'feminist' needs to be redefined.[35]

On International Women's Day, 8 March 1979, Women Against Imperialism (WAI) mounted a picket of Armagh Jail. The group, in existence from 1978 to 1980, was republican feminist in character, based in West Belfast, and concerned to strengthen the development of women's voices in the republican community. The picket resulted in thirteen people being arrested on charges of assault and obstruction of the public highway, including a London-based Irishwoman, Margaretta D'Arcy, who wrote of her arrest and incarceration in Armagh Jail.[36] Feminists from Bradford, London and Sheffield were present in January 1980 at the court appearance of those arrested. By the time International Women's Day came round on 8 March that year, bolstered by the efforts of WAI, over 400 people attended the picket of the jail, amongst them a large contingent from Britain representing many different organisations, including the Armagh Group.

The practice of the Armagh Group organising and sending an International Women's Day delegation continued for a number of years and became an important feminist marker as attention was increasingly focused on the male prisoners in the H-Blocks and the second hunger strike. The pickets were supported by Sinn Féin's Department on Women's Affairs, inaugurated in 1980,[37] and by the Falls Women's Centre, Belfast, opened in 1982.[38] In 1983 the London Armagh Group set up the Stop the Strip Searches Campaign and contacted feminist groups, Left and humanitarian organisations to help publicise strip searching, which was also being extended to British prisons and police stations. The group made the point consistently that the practice was being regularly inflicted as a form of sexual harassment,[39] a point also made by Di Parkin in chapter 12 in this volume.

The introduction of strip searching in many different types of cus-
todial situations, including of black detainees, political activists and
immigrants, led to the formation of the United Campaign Against
Strip Searching (UCASS) in 1988 following a conference hosted by
the London Strategic Policy Unit and the Association of Labour
Authorities.[40] Funding was made available to the organisation for staff-
ing and the production of publications, a facility never available to
voluntary organisations like the Armagh Group, which inadvertently
contributed to its decline.

A number of factors were responsible for the Armagh Group's decline,
including the duplication of work by UCASS, as well as the effect of
prisoners being allowed to transfer from Britain to serve their sentences
in Northern Ireland. Another reason was the conflict of political priorities adopted by different interest groups, such as those concerned with
the rights of detainees or immigrants. For example, a feminist group,
Women in Prison, promoted the idea of strip searching within defined
limits as a means of preventing women's harbouring of drugs or instru-
ments of self-harm. Writing in *Spare Rib*, Chris Tchaikovsky, founder of
the group, stated that mentally distressed and volatile prisoners should
be prevented from mutilating or killing themselves.[41] There were strong
objections to this position by, amongst others, the Armagh Group[42]
and by Ella O'Dwyer and Martina Anderson, incarcerated in 1986 on
charges of conspiracy to cause explosions in England. From the high
security wing of Durham Jail in the north of England they reported that
they had access to dangerous objects like scissors every day but were still
regularly strip searched.[43]

A high point for the Armagh Group in the struggle against strip
searching came in June 1987 when a demonstration of up to 2,000
participants was organised at Durham Jail by the Women and Ireland
Network, the Newcastle and Leicester Anti-Strip Searching Groups,
Women in Troops Out, the Armagh Group, Southall Black Sisters, the
Newham Monitoring Group and the Irish Prisoners Appeal. The title
and main slogan was: 'End state violence against women' and its target
was the strip searching of Martina Anderson and Ella O'Dwyer being
held at the high-security jail.[44]

Conclusion

How significant were three small feminist groups, so far written out
of history, in their contribution to the Irish anti-imperialist movement
during two decades of the Troubles? First and foremost, they contributed
to the raising of the Irish National Question in the London area (and in

Britain through their connection with the Women and Ireland Network) in one of the most successful social movements of our age, the British WLM. However, they failed to generate an extensive and sustained, rather than intermittent, debate in the WLM, a problem shared in regard to British society generally by other elements of the Irish anti-imperialist movement. Through this they witnessed the limitations of universal sisterhood, and of 'intersectionality' (the recognition of difference and the interlocking of systems of oppression). More positively, they were able to highlight the nature and extent of state violence, particularly where perpetrated on women, and contributed to the 'feminising' of the Troubles by constantly referring to women's agency, emphasising that as actors women were not mere victims 'caught up in the conflict'.

In the second area of interest for the three groups, support for working-class republican women in Northern Ireland, an evaluation of the latter's history and achievements has been in train for some time, including a 2013 study by the Canadian academic Theresa O'Keefe.[45] Recognition is being given to the fact that republican women, primarily working-class, some of them ex-prisoners, have garnered a wide range of achievements within the party structures of Sinn Féin itself, in electoral politics north and south of the Irish border and in the European Union.[46] The community development sector and women's centres are also areas where working-class and ex-prisoner republican women are highly visible, the centres in particular campaigning on feminist and gay issues (excepting reproductive choice, still a 'no go' area for most Irish political parties) as well as providing a wide range of welfare and educational services.[47]

In her study, Theresa O'Keefe emphasises that republican women's participation in the struggle for civil and national rights has provided them with a new identity as political actors and concludes that these developments challenge the essentialist view that nationalism is automatically and intractably hostile to women's interests. Such a transformative process in a deeply conservative and divided society, she argues, 'suggests that women's feminist organising under the rubric of nationalism needs reconsideration to move beyond an account of the ways in which nationalist men and masculinities marginalise and oppress women and instead give due deliberation to the ways in which women challenge patriarchal practices'.[48] Such developments, she says, have, among other things, come about through exchanges with feminists acting in solidarity with republican women, no doubt a point of interest to sisters 'across the water' in Britain, not least, members of the three groups discussed in this chapter. In reflecting on their significance, it can be said that the Women on Ireland Collective, the Women and Ireland Group and the London Armagh

Group played a part in this transformative process and thus have had a bearing on wider constituencies and an importance beyond themselves.

Notes

1 N. Yuval-Davis and F. Anthias (eds), *Woman-Nation-State* (London: Macmillan, 1989).
2 M. Ward, 'National liberation movements and the question of women's liberation: the Irish experience', in C. Midgley (ed.), *Gender and Imperialism* (Manchester: Manchester University Press, 1998), pp. 104–21.
3 A. Rossiter, *Ireland's Hidden Diaspora: The 'Abortion Trail' and the Making of a London-Irish Underground, 1980–2000* (London: Iasc, 2009).
4 A. Rossiter, 'Not Our Cup of Tea: Nation, Empire and the Irish Question in English Feminism in the 1970s and 1980s' (PhD dissertation, London South Bank University, 2006).
5 C. McAuley (ed.), *Women in a War Zone, Twenty Years of Resistance* (Dublin and Belfast: Republican Publications, n.d. [1989]); L. Fitzsimons, *Liberty is Strength, 30 Years of Struggle* (Belfast: Lily Fitzsimons, n.d. [1999]).
6 E. Fairweather, R. McDonough and M. McFadyean, *Only the Rivers Run Free: Northern Ireland, The Women's War* (London: Pluto, 1984); S. Calamati, *The Trouble We've Seen … Women's Stories from the North of Ireland* (Belfast: Beyond the Pale Publications, 2002).
7 B. Aretxaga, *Shattering Silence: Women, Nationalism, and Political Subjectivity in Northern Ireland* (Princeton, NJ: Princeton University Press, 1997).
8 M. Ward, 'The Women's Movement in the north of Ireland twenty years on', in S. Hutton and P. Stewart (eds) *Ireland's Histories: Aspects of State, Society and Ideology* (London: Routledge, 1991), pp. 149–63 (p. 151).
9 L. Edgerton, 'Public protest, domestic acquiescence: Women in Northern Ireland', in R. Ridd and H. Callaway (eds), *Caught up in Conflict: Women's Responses to Political Strife* (London: Macmillan 1986), pp. 61–83 (p. 61).
10 M. Ward and J. McMinn 'Belfast women against all odds', in L. Steiner-Scott (ed.), *Personally Speaking: Women's Thoughts on Women's issues* (Dublin: Attic Press, 1985), pp. 189–200 (p. 192).
11 G. McGladdery, *The Provisional IRA in England: The Bombing Campaign 1973–1997* (Dublin: Irish Academic Press, 2006), p. 236.
12 'News – The Price sisters', *Spare Rib*, 22 (1974), 17–20.
13 A. Ansraab, letter to the Editor, in 'The Price sisters: Some letters', *Spare Rib*, 24 (1974), 26.
14 J. Thompson, letter to the Editor, *Spare Rib*, 24 (1974).
15 Spare Rib Collective, 'The Price sisters: A reply', *Spare Rib*, 24 (1974).
16 McGladdery, *The Provisional IRA in England*, p. 223.
17 See chapters by Finch (10) and Casey (15) in this volume.
18 N. McCafferty, 'The Peace People at war', in N. McCafferty (ed.), *Goodnight Sisters, Selected Writings, Vol. 2* (Dublin: Attic Press, 1987), pp. 104–40.

19 Rossiter, 'Not Our Cup of Tea', pp. 147–8.
20 K. Kelley, *The Longest War, Northern Ireland and the IRA* (Dingle, Co. Kerry: Brandon, 1982), pp. 253–4.
21 Ibid., p. 255
22 Ibid., p. 256.
23 *Women's Report*, 4:6 (September/October 1976).
24 Women and Ireland Group, letter to the Editor, *Scarlet Women*, 4 (July 1977).
25 D. Anderson, *14 May Days: The Inside Story of the Loyalist Strike of 1974* (Dublin: Gill & Macmillan, 1994), p. 84.
26 Women and Ireland Group, *Irish Women at War* (London: Women and Ireland Group, 1977).
27 Aretxaga, *Shattering Silence*, pp. 105–21.
28 A. Rossiter, 'Bringing the margins into the centre', in S. Hutton and P. Stewart (eds), *Ireland's Histories: Aspects of State, Society and Ideology* (London: Routledge, 1991), pp. 223–42.
29 Rossiter, *Ireland's Hidden Diaspora*.
30 S. Darragh, *'John Lennon's Dead': Stories of Protest, Hunger Strikes and Resistance* (Belfast: Beyond the Pale Publications, 2011).
31 London Armagh Group, *Women Behind the Wire* (London: London Armagh Group, 1984).
32 Rossiter, 'Not Our Cup of Tea', pp. 227–38.
33 N. McCafferty, 'It's my belief that Armagh is a feminist issue', *Irish Times* (22 August 1980).
34 Aretxaga, *Shattering Silence*, pp. 135–8.
35 Letter in *Irish Times* (23 August 1980), quoted in C. Loughran, 'Armagh and feminist strategy: Campaigns around republican women prisoners in Armagh Jail', *Feminist Review*, 23 (1986), 64.
36 M. D'Arcy, *Tell Them Everything* (London: Pluto Press, 1981).
37 Aretxaga, *Shattering Silence*, pp. 163–6.
38 Ibid., p. 145.
39 London Armagh Group, *Images from the Armagh Picket* (London: London Armagh Group, 1982).
40 N. Hutchinson, C. Keatinge, J. Kelly, and S. Spurway, *Working Together to End Strip Searching: Report of a Conference 5 December 1987* (London: London Strategic Policy Unit, 1988).
41 C. Tchaikovsky, 'Strip searching – the controversy continues', *Spare Rib*, 180 (1987), 8–9.
42 London Armagh Women's Group, 'No to strip searching – A reply to Chris Tchaikovsky', *Spare Rib*, 181 (1987), 35–6.
43 E. O'Dwyer and M. Anderson, 'O'Dwyer and Anderson reply to Chris Tchaikovsky', letter to the Editor, *Spare Rib*, 182 (1987), 4.
44 J. Hulme, 'Strip search fury', *Morning Star* (15 June 1987).
45 T. O'Keefe, *Feminist Identity Development and Activism in Revolutionary Movements* (Houndmills: Palgrave Macmillan, 2013).
46 *Sinn Féin – Engine for Change. Women in an Ireland of Equals* (June 2004),

Sinn Féin website, www.sinnfein.ie/files/2009/WomensDocument20041.pdf (Accessed 3 August 2014).

47 C. McGing, 'Women candidates and political parties in the 2014 Republic of Ireland local elections', Slugger O'Toole website (posted 23 April 2014), http://sluggerotoole.com/2014/04/23/women-candidates-and-political-parties-in-the-2014-republic-of-ireland-local-elections-by-claire-mcging/ (Accessed 3 August 2014).

48 O'Keefe, *Feminist Identity Development and Activism*, p. 148.

12

Political delegations of women from Britain to the North of Ireland and the campaign against strip searching in the 1980s

Di Parkin

As many argued in the 1980s, the more people who visited Northern Ireland and saw how disastrous the present situation was, the sooner we would bring about the reunification of Ireland and the withdrawal of the British presence. There were many delegations to the North of Ireland from mainland Britain, organised by trade unions and the Troops Out Movement. The practice of delegations to bear witness, return and inform the wider movement was used extensively in the Irish solidarity campaign (as it has been in the campaigns over El Salvador, Cuba and today in Palestine).

This chapter gives an account of delegations of women, primarily organised during the 1980s by Labour Women for Ireland (LWI), the women's section of the Labour Committee on Ireland (LCI), to the North of Ireland. The primary focus of the visits was to raise the profile of the campaign against strip searching of women in Armagh Jail. Whilst the other delegations were important, the LWI was able to take the issues directly back into the Labour Party and have influence on changing party policy. Strip searching was introduced for women remand prisoners in Armagh in November 1982, thirteen years into the British Army occupation. Some 400 women were jailed at Armagh in the 1970s and 1980s for political offences, 32 of whom were imprisoned without trial.[1] The rationale for the searches was that prisoners might have smuggled items back into the jail after their court appearances. This was despite the fact that they were searched to and from court and had never been alone during that time.[2] The psychological torture and intimidation caused by strip searching became the focus for anti-war protest in Britain by women.

In writing this chapter I start with autobiographical reminiscence of my own visit to strip-searched women in Armagh as a member of a LWI

delegation to Belfast and Armagh in 1982. I move on to interviews with
others who also visited, initially women who were with me on my trip,
then, by snowball referral, meeting others who had taken part on other
delegations. I interviewed six other women – Samantha, Anne, Carole,
Angela, Nuala and Rachel – who had also been on LWI delegations.
(They remain anonymous, as activism in support of Irish republicans
is not well regarded, even now, by their employers.) They were either
English or of Irish descent, and in one case an American woman. I interviewed them mainly in their own homes, in one case in the lobby of a
central London hotel, in another at a London railway station, taking
long-hand notes.[3] Oral history gave me direct access to memories of
dramatic moments in their lives.

My own experience, which included having machine guns pointed at
me by representatives of my 'own' State, was a starting point in recaptur-
ing these dramatic memories of the delegations, which also crystallised
an important historic moment. I was aware then, and remember now,
that many activists in England, on the issue of Ireland, faced pressures
that did not exist when campaigning on other issues, further from home.
For example, I was on holiday in November 1987 in Ullapool, with
my family and other Irish activists, in the days when the Soviet fishing
fleet were anchored in the loch. We were followed on three days by the
Special Branch or MI5, first at a tourist salmon-leaping spot, then to
an isolated beach. We saw no other people or cars on the way to the
beach. They also preceded us to a restaurant; we had no telephone in
the cottage, which faced the loch; thus the cottage itself must have been
bugged from across this water. Perhaps they suspected we were making
contact with the Soviet fishermen, who came ashore to buy porn, Levi
jeans and ghetto blasters. It was normal for pro-republican activists in
Britain to be followed by the police and for our phones to be bugged.
Many of us were stopped and questioned by anti-terrorist police officers
at ports of entry; one woman had the contents of her car, including children's nappies, pulled apart and a colleague in Birmingham was raided
by the police. This was the everyday context for us, a context also for
my interviewees.

The LCI had been set up inside the Labour Party in March 1980.[4] By
the end of 1983 its autonomous women's section, LWI, was established.
LWI aimed to build support amongst Labour and trade union women
for British withdrawal from the North of Ireland; it believed that British
women – in particular English women – had a political responsibility
to speak out for British withdrawal. LWI believed that women must
organise as women, to ensure that their interests as women were never
subordinated to other struggles, that women's liberation and national

liberation were inextricably linked. The group worked to develop links with Irish feminists, especially anti-imperialist and republican feminists, and campaigned amongst Labour and trade union women on issues affecting Irish women, especially those issues arising from British involvement in Ireland, such as strip searches.[5]

When I interviewed Samantha, she explained:

> The purpose was to bring feminist ideas into the Labour Party. It was also part of working on anti-imperialism, e.g. SWAPO [the South West Africa People's Organisation]. It focused around things like civil rights abuse. Irish people at the time were vilified and treated as if they weren't really human, in much the same way as Muslim people are today.[6]

Samantha herself had a big influence on others. Angela remembers that she met her and then joined the organisation in 1982: 'I met Samantha and could see the importance of a women's organisation. Everything was so male-dominated, unless you jumped up and down, they would ignore you. So we wrote to all the women members of the LCI; we used to send these monthly mailings.'[7] The mailings (copies of which are now held in the LCI/LWI archive at the Linen Hall Library) gave very thorough, up-to-date accounts of the issues facing women in Ireland. Anne, who was a national officer of the LCI, confirms the male domination of the wider body:

> The LCI was very male-dominated. In the early '80s, the role of women in the Irish struggle was becoming stronger, with the security forces targeting republican women in the strip searching. In order to promote that kind of issue, it was automatic to set up a separate, but linked organisation. We were feminists.[8]

By 1987 the LWI had 200 individual members, and thirteen Labour Party women's sections were affiliated.[9]

LWI wanted to deepen its ability to put the republican point of view in Britain, and for its members to be direct witnesses of the situation in the North:

> There was this idea of delegation and dialogue so that they [republican women] came here, we went there and would use it for publicity here about strip searching and other abuses. It was all part of the other campaigns, for example on the Birmingham Six. It was all to the same end ... Thatcher's strategy was to cut off the oxygen of publicity; the delegations were part of challenging that.[10]

It was shortly after the period of the delegations that the voices of republicans could no longer be heard on British TV or radio, due to the broadcasting ban.[11]

There were some four or five delegations of LWI members, or women's delegations connected with the group. They included one from Sheffield that Anne went on: 'In Sheffield in 1983 there was the idea of sending a women's delegation. I was taken with it and was the only one who knew Belfast. My family is from Fermanagh.'[12] Rachel had already been on a delegation organised by Brent Trades Council and, with two others, had been expelled from it (and from the Greater London Trades Councils) for arranging that they meet the Provisional as well as the Official IRA. This, however, meant that she knew the ropes and could advise on what to do. LWI minutes reported before one of the visits in 1984: 'Six women are about to leave on a delegation to Ireland and we hope to get more women interested in going. We plan to visit the Falls Road Women's Centre and the Defend the Clinics campaign [for contraception and abortion advice].'[13]

On arrival, on my delegation, we all made our way across the city to West Belfast, crossing the war front line. Anne and Carole remember their arrivals similarly:

> The city centre was ringed with tall steel security fences, with soldiers at the narrow turnstiles; there was a woman with a baby in a carrycot and it had to be held vertical going through. We went through the city centre and out through the pedestrian security gate, with the soldiers everywhere.[14]
>
> As soon as you got off the train from Dublin, you came out and saw the saracens. The militarisation of central Belfast was very striking; it was not your obvious city, it was dominated by the British Army. I was very coloured by my sister ... She gave me strict instructions on how to get a black taxi from Castle Street. You get in a taxi and it doesn't leave until it is full; you have to tap on the window when you want to get off and have the right money.[15]

My own memory, as someone who had already been a revolutionary activist for more than fifteen years, was of experiencing a considerable shock at both the militarisation and the poverty. There were adverts for products familiar from England, and yet around the corner came soldiers, squatting and pointing their machine guns (at a time when the State was not routinely street-armed in Britain). Rachel (who was on the same visit as me) put it thus: 'In some ways it was so familiar, yet so different. It is peculiar being part of the same State, having the same post offices, watching the same TV, yet there are the soldiers in the street.'[16] She remembers how, when we decided to walk over to the Protestant Shankill Road, we had to leave behind all the republican ephemera we had just purchased from the Sinn Féin office on the Falls Road. If we had been on the Shankill Road with material identifying ourselves as republican sympathisers, we would have been in danger of attack. I remember that we walked along the pedestrian route through the immense – and to us scary – 'peace wall' separating the Falls and Shankill areas, where the vehicle road had been blocked off by barriers, so that you could not see, shoot or drive straight down it.

> When we walked back through the peace line, we were stopped by soldiers who asked us where we were going and what we were doing. You [Di Parkin] drew yourself up to your full height and berated them in a cut-glass English middle-class accent: what right had they to ask us where we were going, and they backed off.[17]

I remember that it was chilling and strange to be stopped by soldiers, whose guns were for real, and intimidated in our own (or almost our own) London accent. I also now reflect, thirty years later, on my own rashness, assuming that I could use the card of my middle-class Englishness to intimidate armed men!

The contrast between the normal 'at home' of English accents and Coronation Street on the TV, and the wildly 'foreign', oppressive behaviour of the armed forces of our own nation-state, was extremely shocking to me and my interviewees. The other thing that struck most of us was the poverty in Belfast: the terrible housing, just a cold water tap, and inside walls running with wet: 'There were poor facilities, poor design; the housing was soulless, damp';[18] and 'very primitive, small with toilets outside'.[19] Poverty was really evident, hardly anyone had jobs and many were on social security, known as 'the broo'. The benefits offices looked like forts – with barbed wire and boulders outside to prevent bomb attacks – as did the Sinn Féin offices. To an outsider, like Carole, this also was shocking: 'We went to the Sinn Féin offices in the Falls Road; we just rocked up and were welcomed. It was amazing, it looked like something from a war movie; there was no obvious entrance; there was a barricade and boulders.'[20] Anne recalls how:

> We went to the Falls Road Women's Centre, which was above a shop, up the rickety stairs and all piled into the front room. We were given a briefing on what to expect. It was all so well organised like a military operation; I was billeted in Twinbrook [in West Belfast]. It was great to be with a family; they were very poor, but so welcoming. We went to the Republican club; we were very well looked after.[21]

We were made aware of the campaigns on contraceptive rights and abortion (campaigns which are still alive thirty-five years later[22]).

An important part of the work of the LWI and of the delegations was to highlight the conditions of the republican women remand prisoners who were being regularly stripped in Armagh Jail. 'The policy from 9 November 1982 of stripping the women prisoners naked on entering and leaving prison caused them great suffering and aroused sympathy for them both in Ireland and internationally.'[23] A leaflet produced just after the republican women were moved from Armagh to the new prison at Maghaberry explained that since 1982, 3,500 strip searches had been endured by women in Armagh.[24] This degrading treatment also happened to Irish women prisoners in Brixton Prison and, later, Durham Prison in England. Anne remembers this focus on the strip-searched prisoners:

> There was a big thrust on International Women's Day in the demonstration to Armagh. Half of the women on our delegation went into the prison. The demonstration had a great impact. They had big long banners which you held, without banner poles; it had each of the woman prisoner's names on it and we called out each of their names, 'so and so, we support you'. You would see a hand waving out of a cell window.[25]

Rachel and I went into Armagh Jail; we travelled by mini-bus from Belfast. Two of the relatives had given us their visit, because they thought it was politically important for us to experience it.[26] Looking back, I realise how significant our witness must have been, for them to give up seeing a relative.

I personally remember the chill horror of the doors unlocking and locking as we went deeper into the prison, the way the warders blanked us, the vicious way they destroyed gifts of cake and vegetables the relatives had brought. I remember a young, sweet, pretty prisoner, with her make-up and earrings (at a time when British feminists didn't normally dress like that), telling us of her awful experiences. Such experiences are recounted in the LWI's Stop Strip Searching leaflet: 'You are told to strip naked, your body is inspected front and rear. A warder takes hold of your hands and inspects the palms and picks up your feet to inspect the soles ... Menstruating women are ordered to remove their tampons or pads.'[27]

We had been warned that the prisoners might try to pass small letters to us, either in their handshake or under their gums. As Mairead Farrell, a Provisional IRA volunteer and prisoner, later assassinated by the Special Air Service, confirmed in an interview: 'They [women prisoners] exchanged messages by means of small, hidden letters, brought from one jail to another.'[28] Rachel and I have an identical memory of this practice: 'The relatives knew the drill and we followed them. On the way back on the bus a woman opened this tiny letter which she had smuggled out and read it.'[29]

The delegations were a two-way street, as the September 1984 LWI mailing records: 'The idea came up of organising for relatives of women who are being, or have been strip searched to come to London; we have raised £300 and are to ask the London LP [Labour Party] executive for £100 for 4 relatives.'[30] However, in contrast to the superb hospitality we all experienced on our visits to Ireland, it was hard to get the reciprocity in Britain.

> Even on the Left it was hard to get a hearing on Ireland. We had had this wonderful hospitality there, but it was hard to even get accommodation for them here. I thought I had found a place for two delegates, but her partner was scared of having Sinn Féin in the house. So they had to leave and come to my tiny one-bedroom flat, while I went to sleep on someone's sofa.[31]

The tours by prisoners' relatives were mainly organised by local authority women's units.[32] Camden Women's Unit produced a timetable, arrangements about escorts and reminders that 'Security will be very important'.[33] The LWI newsletters show that there were meetings in Sheffield, Birmingham, Derbyshire, Wolverhampton, Mansfield and Manchester, as well as many in London. An LCI newsletter in October notes that: 'Meetings outside London can only be considered if sponsored by a women's committee or a council.'[34] Four of the LWI/LCI activists whom I interviewed, and I myself, were employed by local authority women's units; two of us also worked at the London Strategic Policy Unit (LSPU), child of the Greater London Council. In December 1987, LSPU, with the Association of London Authorities, organised a conference, 'Working Together to End Strip Searching', attended by three hundred people. It passed a resolution saying: 'Strip searching is used to degrade and humiliate. It is a technique of repression used systematically against Irish republican women and is being used increasingly against Black and other ethnic minority women ... and others.'[35]

It was important to LWI activists that we were women organising as women and as anti-imperialists. Carole argues that:

> We had a big influence on women's politics in Britain, we influenced the women's sections in the LP. Women's sections were quite radical; it was a doddle to get women to see what was happening, about strip searching and so on. It was a very positive experience, women embraced the issue. They would talk in very individual, personal terms, telling the story, of what it was like to be strip searched when you were having your period. Women tended to use people's stories to convince people. This had an influence on our ability to bring people to the cause.[36]

According to Nuala, 'Women's organisations were much more prominent in those days; there was a political significance. You could work with a range of women because you were able to identify with them as women.'[37] Both these interviewees are reflecting on the emphasis upon 'the personal is political' in women's politics and how gender was seen as an important starting point for a wider political agenda. But Nuala was also irritated by some British feminists who complained that the republican women wore nail varnish and high heels!

There were also reciprocal tours by Irish women councillors:

> The visits of Irish women councillors were very effective, because there were a lot of women councillors here. We took Lilly, a councillor in Belfast, to NALGO [National Association of Local Government Officers] conference. She slept in a spare bed in our room and one of the other delegates asked, 'Is it safe to have her in our room?'[38]

Nuala is remarking on the prejudicial stereotypes that British trade unionists and even socialists had of republicans.

The delegations gave impetus to resolutions through the Labour Party, for example this model resolution for others to use from Islington North General Committee (GC):

> This GC is totally opposed to the strip searching of women and believes it to be a form of sexual harassment. The GC requests the National Labour Women's Committee and the Trades Union Congress (TUC) to organise a national public event against strip searching with the aim of mobilising the whole labour movement against this degrading practice.[39]

Responding to these resolutions, the National Labour Women's Committee did organise a rally on strip searching in 1987. In 1986 the London Labour Party had agreed to invite republican representatives to its conference. At that time left-wing constituency parties such as Islington North and Hackney North would always choose to put resolutions on Ireland or strip searching to the LP conference, and LWI activists would speak to them. Carole remembers: 'I was on TV, on prime time tele speaking at the conference on strip searching, people would come up and say they had seen me.'[40] Nuala recalls that:

> We got resolutions to LP conference; every year I was a delegate and we always had a resolution on Ireland … The National Labour Women's Conference [in 1986] was on the Isle of Bute. We were unpopular, at this point Kinnock was 'cleansing the party' and they didn't like us because of the Irish stuff. But the conference took a 'Troops Out' resolution.[41]

As Nuala, Rachel and Samantha and I remember, we also put resolutions to National Labour Party conference and, with great attention to security and hostility from the Labour Party leadership, organised fringe meetings, at which Gerry Adams spoke, including in Brighton.

In conclusion, we felt that this activity was important for us as feminists, celebrating the actions of women republicans. As Samantha puts it: 'People were being killed; their families were being killed or locked up. Then there was Bobby Sands' hunger strike and death; it was grim. What struck me most were the women's tenacity and their strength.'[42] Anne argues that 'LWI was a very effective campaign; it did raise awareness among British feminists; it made good connections. A lot of things we did have energised and empowered women making them more confident, having a real impact.'[43] At a political level, Angela is apt: 'Our whole *raison d'être* was to get the Labour Party to change its policy; we got under their skin enough to get them anxious. Kevin McNamara, the party's shadow spokesman on Ireland, would talk to us and listen to us; we were taken seriously. He said "What you say is listened to."'[44] This is reflected in the questions McNamara and other Labour MPs like Clare Short asked in Parliament about the strip searching of republican women prisoners.[45] Looking back, I am impressed with our tenacity and courage, acting inside 'the belly of the beast'[46] to campaign on an unpopular and difficult issue. The work we did in LWI was part of a wider culture of change from the prejudice and stereotyping of republicans as terrorists of the early 1980s to the Good Friday Agreement of 1998. We cannot quantify the exact extent of our impact, but it was part of a whole process of change.

Notes

1 E. Brady, E. Patterson, K. McKinney, R. Hamill and P. Jackson, *In the Footsteps of Anne. Stories of Republican Women Ex-prisoners* (Belfast: Shanway Press, 2011).

2 See Finch, chapter 10 in this volume.

3 The interviews were all conducted in the summer of 2012. Questions asked: What are your main memories of the delegation to the North of Ireland? What did you do and where did you go? What do you remember about the role of the security services? What else struck you? (Probe poverty) What impact did you think we had on the Labour Party?

4 In the course of conducting the interviews I came across the un-indexed archive of the LCI and the LWI, in the home of a former officer of the LCI. This provided my second primary source of material. I indexed this archive and we arranged for it to be moved to the Northern Ireland Political Collection, Linen Hall Library, Belfast. All LCI/LWI reports, minutes, leaflets, newsletters and correspondence referred to below are available in this archive.

5 LWI Newsletter, 1983.

6 Samantha (pseudonym), interviewed by author, summer 2012.

7 Angela (pseudonym), interviewed by author, summer 2012.

8   Anne (pseudonym), interviewed by author, summer 2012.
9   LWI, *Annual Report*, 1988.
10 Samantha, interview.
11 See Pettigrew, chapter 16 in this volume.
12 Anne, interview.
13 Minutes of LWI meeting, March 1984.
14 Anne, interview.
15 Carole (pseudonym), interviewed by author, summer 2012.
16 Rachel (pseudonym), interviewed by author, summer 2012.
17 Rachel, interview.
18 Carole, interview.
19 Rachel, interview.
20 Carole, interview.
21 Anne, interview.
22 A. Rossiter, *Ireland's Hidden Diaspora: The Abortion Trail and the Making of a London-Irish Underground, 1980–2000* (London: IASC, 2009).
23 Raymond Murray quoted in Brady et al., *In the Footsteps of Anne*, p. 11.
24 LWI leaflet, 'Stop strip searching', 1986.
25 Anne, interview.
26 Like all prisons, there were restrictions on the numbers of visitors any one prisoner could have. For us to go into Armagh a relative or loved one of the prisoner had to give up their own visit and give the visitor's pass to us.
27 LWI leaflet, 'Stop strip searching', 1986.
28 Jenny McGeever, 'The story of Mairéad Farrell', *Magill Magazine* (6 October 1986), pp. 8–18 (p. 14).
29 Rachel, interview.
30 LWI Newsletter, September 1984.
31 Samantha, interview.
32 In the mid to late 1980s, radical (Left Labour-controlled) local authorities set up special equalities units on topics such as Race Equality, Disability Equality and Women's Equality. This was way before the law began to require public bodies to positively promote equality, as it did first with the Race Relations Amendment Act in 1992. There were women's equality units in Sheffield, Leicester, and London boroughs such as Lambeth, Camden, Hammersmith, Southwark, Islington, Brent and Ealing where I worked, amongst others.
33 Letter in LWI/LCI archive, 12 November 1985.
34 LCI Newsletter, October 1985.
35 N. Hutchinson, C. Keatinge, J. Kelly and S. Spurway, *Working Together to End Strip Searching: Report of a Conference 5 December 1987* (London: London Strategic Policy Unit, 1988). See Finch, chapter 10 in this volume.
36 Carole, interview.
37 Nuala (pseudonym), interviewed by author, summer 2012.
38 Nuala, interview.
39 LWI Newsletter, 1988.
40 Carole, interview.

41 Nuala interview. The Labour Women's Conference of 1986 is discussed in K. Laybourn and C. F. Collette (eds), *Modern Britain Since 1979: A Reader* (London: IB Tauris, 2003), p. 96.

42 Samantha, interview.

43 Anne, interview.

44 Angela, interview.

45 For the record of Written Questions about strip searching by Kevin McNamara and other Labour MPs to the Secretary of State for Northern Ireland, see http://hansard.millbanksystems.com/search/Armagh+Prison+%28Strip+Searches%29?speaker=mr-kevin-mcnamara (Accessed 17 April 2015).

46 'In the Belly of the Beast. *I mBolg an Bheithígh*' was the title of a talk by the author and others, including other contributors to this book, at St Mary's University College, Falls Road, West Belfast, 6 August 2013, as part of *Féile an Phobail* (the West Belfast Festival): 'In the 1970s and 1980s the conflict in Ireland involving British soldiers, and the cause of the conflict, was often a difficult subject to raise in Britain, especially in the wake of IRA attacks. Yet, throughout, principled activists raised their heads above the parapet, often at personal risk, despite the hostility. In this talk, four of those who worked in solidarity groups – Mary Pearson (Troops Out Movement), Di Parkin (Labour Women for Ireland), Ann Rossiter (Women and Ireland) and Sue O'Halloran (Sinn Féin Britain) – speak of their experiences.' www.feilebelfast.com/wp-content/themes/phobail2013/Feile-2013.pdf, p. 48 (Accessed 17 April 2015).

Part III

Culture and the representation of the Troubles

13

'Every man an emperor': the British press, Bloody Sunday and the image of the British Army[1]

Greg McLaughlin and Stephen Baker

Graham Dawson and Michael Paris have highlighted what they call a 'pleasure culture of war' in Britain that posits the British soldier as a paragon of honest, honourable and courageous manhood, enshrined in the image of the British 'Tommy' and 'our boys'.[2] This figure has long been popularised and celebrated in forms of mass entertainment and has been critical in forging gendered notions of Anglo-British nationhood. As Michael Paris argues, from the mid-nineteenth century the pleasure culture of war was important for imbuing the right values and attitudes to preserve the Empire and ensure national survival during two world wars.[3] To criticise the military would be to strike at the very heart of Anglo-British popular nationalism. As a consequence, nothing less is at stake than the self-image of the British Army, and thus Britain, as paragons of courage and fair play.

This impulse has been at work most recently in the ritual repatriation of the remains of British soldiers killed in Afghanistan, particularly at Wootton Bassett, and in their identikit obituaries – reproduced in media accounts as key elements in the eternal narrative of the 'brave British Tommy'. And it was very evident in British media coverage of the conflict in Northern Ireland, whenever the British Army's role came under scrutiny. Bloody Sunday in Derry, 30 January 1972, was one such case in point. That day, men of the 1st Battalion of the Parachute Regiment (1 Para) opened fire on civil rights marchers, killing thirteen and wounding another thirteen, one of whom, John Johnston, was to die of his wounds five months later. The event was reported worldwide and, with the hindsight of passing years, represented for many observers, historians and journalists a significant turning point in what had become known as 'the Troubles'. This was apparently the moment when a struggle for civil rights died and gave way to a war between the Provisional IRA

and the British State. Yet, the story of Bloody Sunday was based almost
entirely on army lies and propaganda and on the flawed judgment of
Lord Chief Justice Widgery, whose report on 19 April 1972 exonerated
the paratroopers and their officers and cast doubt on the innocence of
the victims.

This was to remain the official version for thirty-eight years until
15 June 2010, when Justice Lord Saville of Newdigate published the
ten-volume report of his public inquiry into what really happened.
Saville found that all of the dead and wounded were innocent, that the
actions of the paratroopers were, as Prime Minister David Cameron
put it in the House of Commons, 'unjustified and unjustifiable'[4] and
that the British Army had lied in the wake of the shootings to cover up
what Jonathan Freedland described as 'the biggest single massacre by
the British military on UK soil since Peterloo'.[5] Even then, however, the
right-wing British press was reluctant to dismiss the evidentially flawed
and prejudicial Widgery Report in favour of the much more credible
evidence contained in the Saville Report. The *Daily Mail* struck a very
defiant note in this regard. Over photographs of two British soldiers
killed in action in Afghanistan the previous day, the front-page strapline
and headline read:

> Both served in Ulster. Both have just died in Afghanistan. After that
> damning Bloody Sunday report, THIS is the...
> TRUE FACE OF OUR SOLDIERS.[6]

For the *Daily Mail* and others, 'The True Face of our Soldiers', an
image of valour and sacrifice deeply rooted in the myths of the Second
World War, was as impervious to the definitive judgment of the Saville
Report as it was to the original events of Bloody Sunday. As we will
show in this analysis, for many in the British press the truth of what 1
Para did that day was – and remains – simply unbelievable.

Our analysis is based on newspaper coverage of three key moments:
Bloody Sunday (31 January and 1 February 1972), publication of
the Widgery Report eleven weeks later (19 and 20 April 1972) and
publication of the Saville Report (16 June 2010). For each of these
sample periods, we selected a cross-section of Britain's leading newspapers comprising the *Daily Telegraph*, *The Times*, the *Daily Mail*, the
Guardian, the *Daily Mirror* and the *Sun*. In our analysis of the coverage of Saville, we also make reference to the *Independent*, which did
not exist in 1972 but whose coverage in 2010 was too significant and
interesting to ignore. We are not concerned with quantitative measure-
ments of balance or objectivity but with a qualitative analysis of the

ideological work going on in the presentation of the story (headlines, structure and language) as well as editorial comment and opinion, and show how this served to project an image of the British soldier according to contemporary context and the ideological predisposition of particular newspapers.

It is important here to set our analysis in the context of our wider study, *The British Media and Bloody Sunday*, which compares and contrasts press coverage in this period with the representations of British TV news and current affairs and film.[7] This is because the problematic press coverage we highlight below was by no means typical of British media representation in the period of study, 1972–2010. For example, the news and current affairs investigations of the BBC and Channel 4 in the 1990s played a positive and decisive role in the growing campaign in Derry for a new public inquiry, while the drama-documentary films *Bloody Sunday* and *Sunday*, both released in 2002, recovered the repressed history of Bloody Sunday as an assault not on Irish republicanism but on a popular movement for civil rights.[8] The liberal or humanist impulses at the heart of such treatments contrast sharply with those conservative sections of the British press unwilling or perhaps unable to see past the official version of what happened and at least question the mythical virtues of the British soldier.

Bloody Sunday

On 31 January 1972, all the newspapers in our sample led with front-page coverage of the killings in Derry, pushing news of strikes, power cuts, unrest in the Commonwealth and inclement weather down the news agenda. Leading the charge to restore national pride and defend the British Army's reputation were the conservative titles, *The Times*, the *Daily Telegraph* and the *Daily Mail*, all of which relied heavily upon the Army's version of what had happened.[9] They insisted that the thirteen dead had lost their lives in a 'battle', a term that suggested some sort of force equivalence between highly trained soldiers and unarmed protestors; and which also served to dignify and legitimise the Army's fatal actions that day.

The *Daily Mail*'s report on page one, 'Derry's Hour of Death', described what happened as 'the bloodiest battle yet between demonstrators and the Army' in Northern Ireland. It quoted the Army's statement that the paratroopers came under a 'fusillade of fire' from several positions and supported this with quotes from their officer in command, Colonel Derek Wilford, and the head of the Army in Northern Ireland, General Robert Ford, both of whom claimed that the soldiers had returned fire only after they had been shot at. The newspaper attributed contradictory accounts to 'bitter civilians', thus bringing their reliability into question.[10] Its editorial readily acknowledged that the soldiers were responsible for the deaths of thirteen people but put the blame firmly on the shoulders of civil rights leaders and the IRA: 'British bullets will be found in most of the bodies,' the *Mail* conceded, 'but the blood is on the consciences of irresponsible political leaders and the fanatical IRA.'[11] The *Daily Telegraph*'s front-page headline was: '13 Shot Dead In Londonderry: IRA fired first says Army.' The item quoted civil rights leaders, John Hume and Bernadette Devlin, as saying, respectively, that the killings were 'another Sharpeville' and an act of 'mass murder', but it was primarily structured around the Army's version of events. It reported that 'IRA gunmen sniped from behind the rioters' and quoted extensively from a statement by General Ford in support of the claim.[12] The *Telegraph* editorial excoriated the civil rights movement and its leaders, accusing them of being as guilty as the IRA for what happened, and exonerated the Army, which, it said, was left with 'no alternative but to fire'.[13] The newspaper's editorial the following day, 1 February, was even more emphatic in its condemnation of the IRA and support for the troops. It rejected the government's decision to establish an inquiry into the shootings on the grounds that it would fail to placate Catholic opinion, demoralise the Army and 'add to the substantial advantages ... which the IRA has already derived from this callously rigged orgy of nationalist martyrdom'.[14] *The Times* also adhered to the Army's version of events. Its front-page story, '3 civilians are killed as soldiers storm the Bogside', reported that the deaths occurred during a 'brief but fierce gun battle'.[15] And while its editorial considered the possibility of 'a breakdown of battle discipline in the Army or a major operational misjudgement', it also asserted that the IRA and the Derry civil rights leaders were ultimately and equally to blame.[16] Common to these conservative newspapers was a determination to seek ideological comfort in the assertion that the demonstrators in Derry had, at least, acted irresponsibly or, worse, facilitated through their actions an attack by republican gunmen on the Army. The fatal consequences were therefore presented as inevitable: the soldiers had been provoked and their violent response was as predictable as it was understandable.

The other newspapers in our sample – the *Guardian*, the *Daily Mirror* and the *Sun* – looked less kindly on the Army's operation and its disastrous outcome; they preferred words such as 'massacre' rather than 'battle' to describe the scene, albeit in attributive quote marks. In the immediate aftermath of the shootings, coverage in the *Mirror* and the *Sun*, both popular tabloids, was striking for the starkness of the reportage and imagery. Their headlines, in large white capital letters against sombre black backgrounds, told a story of gruesome carnage. The *Mirror* led with 'Ulster's Bloody Sunday – 13 shot dead';[17] while the *Sun*'s front-page headline told of 'The Bloody Sunday "Massacre" – "Trigger-happy" paras accused'. It reported that 'An Irish protest march exploded into an orgy of death yesterday … as the paratroopers' advance deep into Londonderry's Bogside turned into a bloody "massacre"'; and that 'British soldiers opened fire on rioters and their blood ran in Derry's gutters'.[18] Both papers carried very striking centre-page photo-features that juxtaposed photos of the troops in action with images of the dead and wounded. The *Sun*'s feature was headed, 'The Paras Charge In – Paratroopers jumped into the Bogside and turned the Sabbath into a Bloody Sunday'.[19] The focus in the *Mirror*'s photo-feature – 'The Derry "Massacre" – Demo that turned into a blood bath' – was very much on the dead and injured.[20]

However, there were also signs even at this early stage of how editorial positions were going to shift over the following few days. In an analysis feature, the *Sun*'s senior correspondent, Brian Woosey, remarked that 'the world will want to know whether the tired, taunted troops over-reacted' or whether the terrorists had asked for it and received a 'martyr's fate'.[21] This was a significant comment because it ran contrary to the rest of the paper's coverage that day, in which there was no inference that any of the dead and injured was involved with the IRA. It also prefigured a more concerted attempt by other newspapers in this sample period to excuse and justify the soldiers' actions. It seems clear that this shift in tone and content came, in part at least, in response to the Army's media campaign to get its version across, as evidenced by the appearance of rather similar features in most newspapers over the next few days on the plight of British soldiers. On 1 February, the *Sun* carried a centre-page feature about the Army in Northern Ireland headlined, 'The Lads With The Worst Job In The World'. It chronicled the abuse the soldiers had suffered daily since their arrival. 'They are on a hiding to nothing', wrote the correspondent. They were spat at and had sewage thrown at them yet somehow remained 'professional', 'tough' and 'hardened to the ice-cold hatred of the mob.'[22] A *Daily Mail* feature – 'My fears, by a soldier' – highlighted the daily travails of a typical infantry soldier serving in Northern Ireland;[23] while the *Daily Telegraph* warned on its front page of a '"Blame Army" drive' and alerted its readers to the threat a putative inquiry might pose to military morale.[24] Although the *Mirror* was the only newspaper in this sample period to question the appropriateness of the British military presence in Northern Ireland and call for the Army to be withdrawn, its columnist John Beavan still sought in the same edition to explain the shootings on Bloody Sunday as somehow understandable in the context of the Army's experience in Northern Ireland up until that point. In an article on 1 February, he reminded readers that 'No troops in the world have ever stood up with such restraint to daily insults and the cowardly snipers and bombers.'[25]

The Widgery Report

The official British response to the shootings on Bloody Sunday was rapid and apparently decisive. On 1 February, Prime Minister Edward Heath appointed Lord Chief Justice John Widgery to conduct a tribunal of inquiry, reminding him in private that 'we [are] in Northern Ireland fighting not only a military war but a propaganda war'.[26] In other words, it was important that his inquiry should manage the controversy of Bloody Sunday and justify the actions of the paratroopers. The Lord Chief Justice did not let him down. He began proceedings on 14 February 1972 and took barely a month to consider the testimonies of most of the soldiers involved, a small selection of over 700 eye-witness statements[27] and flawed forensic evidence. His report, which Derry-born journalist Don Mullan labels 'a convoluted propaganda document',[28] was published on 19 April and, bar some mild criticisms of some of the soldiers and officers involved in the shootings, exonerated the Army from blame and questioned the innocence of some of the victims.[29]

Briefed in advance about the contents of the report, the *Daily Telegraph*, the *Guardian*, the *Daily Mail* and the *Daily Mirror* highlighted on the morning of its publication, 19 April, the essential verdict of the report in short, page-one items:

> Widgery clears paratroops for Bloody Sunday (*Telegraph*).
> 'Army not to blame' – LCJ (*Guardian*).
> Widgery blames IRA and clears the Army (*Mail*).
> Bloody Sunday Paras 'clear' (*Mirror*).[30]

In its edition the next day, 20 April, the *Mail* emphatically bullet-pointed what it saw as the key points of a report that in 'the highest traditions of British justice ... sifts the grey specks of fact from the lurid legend'. Widgery clearly proved for the paper that:

> British troops did NOT fire first.
> The Paras did NOT panic.
> Our men did NOT fire indiscriminately and without provocation into the backs of a fleeing crowd.
> They were NOT sent in to 'give the Bogside a bloody nose'.[31]

However, when it came to the question of ultimate responsibility for the shootings, there was a clear shift of emphasis from the previous day's coverage. Widgery blamed both the IRA for opening fire first and the civil rights movement for organising and leading the banned march in the first place. While this equal apportioning of blame was reflected in previews of the report on 19 April, the overwhelming weight and focus of British press coverage was devoted to the vindication of the paratroopers at the expense of the civil rights movement. The claim that the IRA opened fire first on Bloody Sunday, used by 1 Para to justify the shooting and accepted by Lord Widgery, was suddenly pushed to the background of coverage the following day, 20 April. For example:

[Widgery] points out that there would have been no deaths if the Northern Ireland Civil Rights Association had not organized an illegal march (*Daily Telegraph*).
Illegal march organizers 'made clash inevitable' (*Guardian*).
Widgery blames the organizers of the illegal civil rights march (*Sun*).[32]

The Times was most explicit in its concern for the vindication of the British Army and ultimately for upholding its mythical status in the British public consciousness. Its editorial – 'Widgery's Findings' – referred to the report's dismissal of what it called the 'grosser allegations of misconduct' against the British Army and its operation on Bloody Sunday and added that 'Lord Widgery finds "not a shred of evidence" to support that. Nor will the reader of his report.' This was 'reassuring' because: 'Contrary findings would have been seriously damaging to the morale of the Army in Northern Ireland and to the confidence which its public reposes in it.'[33]

Given the media's coverage of Bloody Sunday, its unquestioning, uncritical treatment of the Widgery Report was somewhat predictable. Yet its coverage went much further than simply amplifying the findings of the Tribunal. It also took to its logical conclusion the ideological spadework of redeeming the British soldier and, by extension, the legitimacy of the Army in the eyes of the British public. It took thirty-eight years before a prolonged, public campaign and compelling new evidence persuaded a reluctant State to establish a public inquiry into what really happened that day. Starting its proceedings in 1998, the Saville (or Bloody Sunday) Inquiry was to be the longest and most expensive in British history, taking twelve years to produce a ten-volume report vindicating the victims and condemning the paratroopers. For the most reactionary sections of the British press, this was tantamount to treachery.

The Saville Report

The Saville Inquiry was a judicial inquiry, not a criminal trial, with a brief to establish the facts of what happened on Bloody Sunday on the basis of previously disregarded eye-witness testimony and new documentary and forensic evidence.[34] Thus its report of 15 June 2010 did not recommend prosecution and carefully avoided legal definitions such as 'murder', 'manslaughter' or 'unlawful killing' to describe the Army's actions. Nevertheless it was welcomed by most of the Bloody Sunday relatives, the majority of people in Derry and all those with an interest in seeing justice done. For its part, the British government accepted the findings of the report as the unequivocal, historical record of what really happened on Bloody Sunday. To a packed House of Commons, Prime Minister David Cameron made a formal statement, which was broadcast live to a packed Guildhall Square in Derry. Responding to Saville's verdict that the dead were innocent and that the shootings were 'unjustified and unjustifiable', the Prime Minister closed with words that were greeted by tumultuous applause at the Guildhall: 'On behalf of our country, I am deeply sorry.' On the surface, the joyous reactions in Derry to the report and to Cameron's apology were newsworthy in themselves and were described positively on the inside pages of all the newspapers we looked at:

> Jubilant families hail the innocent victims (*Telegraph*).
> Hugs, tears and roars on a day of supreme catharsis (*Times*).
> The reaction was instant. An electrifying roar of vindication (*Independent*).
> Roar of relief from heart of Derry (*Sun*).
> Thumbs up for Saville – Crowd cheers as PM apologises for massacre (*Mirror*).[35]

Even the otherwise hostile *Daily Mail* appeared to acknowledge the good-news value of the scene. But its headline, '"They were innocent one and all", says a jubilant Derry', actually worked to downplay the real significance of the moment.[36] It was not the people of Derry who declared the victims' innocence – they always knew that anyway – but a British Law Lord and his Prime Minister. As we go on to show, the positive public response to the Saville Report and its verdict of innocence was, for the conservative press, of secondary importance to its disturbing verdict on 1 Para and, by extension, the British Army. As Max Hastings put it in the *Mail* on the 16 June 2010, the report represented nothing more than 'a grossly misguided excavation of the past'.[37]

In his judgment on the actions of the paratroopers on Bloody Sunday, Saville placed ultimate responsibility for what happened on the Army command, particularly their immediate commanding officer, Colonel Derek Wilford, who was condemned for disobeying orders from Brigade Headquarters. Only two newspapers in our sample, *The Times* and the *Guardian*, led with this judgment on their front pages:

Saville Report condemns 'unjustifiable firing' (*Times*).
Saville report finds Bloody Sunday killings 'unjustified' (*Guardian*).[38]

The *Guardian* followed up on pages 4 and 5 with a detailed summary of the verdict on the Army operation: 'Soldiers fired towards unarmed people who posed no threat'; and on their commanding officers: 'Misjudged deployment, failure to follow orders – and lies'.[39] The other newspapers gave it varying degrees of emphasis on their inside pages. The *Independent* began its substantive coverage on page 2 with 'Saville pins blame for Bloody Sunday on British soldiers'.[40] The other newspapers in our sample also conveyed Saville's judgment in straightforward and unqualified terms, but these appeared at relatively further points in their coverage. The Ulster edition of the *Sun* presented a two-page feature on pages 4 and 5 with block red headlines superimposed on a photograph of the scenes at the Guildhall: 'Finally the Bloody Truth. No Warnings as Soldiers Fired'. On page 5, it recalled the chronology of events that led to the shootings on 30 January 1972 under the heading, 'How army massacre unfolded', without this time rendering the word massacre in attributive quotation marks.[41] However, the *Mail* and the *Telegraph* put a particular spin on events that betrayed their own assumptions about Bloody Sunday rather than conveying the substance of Saville's judgment of what actually happened.

Of all the newspapers, the *Mail* stood out as the most reactionary, hidebound and defiant in its response to the report. In a two-page feature item inside, the paper summarised Saville's account of what happened under the heading: 'The ten minutes of utter madness – How 13 died after Paras defied their orders and went through barriers'.[42] The implication here was that Bloody Sunday marked merely a 'moment of madness' for 1 Para. Yet this confounds common understanding of these soldiers as one of the most disciplined, highly trained regiments in the British Army. The most credible accounts of Bloody Sunday explain that they were deployed in Derry that day to, in the words of General Robert Ford, Commander of Land Forces in Northern Ireland at that time, 'shoot known ringleaders amongst the Derry Young Hooligans after clear warnings have been issued'.[43] However, the *Mail*'s editorial on page 14, 'No excuses, but never forget the context', lent institutional imprimatur to its begrudging, hostile coverage. It opened with reluctant acknowledgement of the report's judgment on the actions of 1 Para on Bloody Sunday: 'Truly, the Saville Report into the events of 38 years ago makes devastating reading for everyone who shares the Mail's fierce admiration of our Armed Forces and our awe of the sacrifices they've made for us, from Northern Ireland to Afghanistan.'[44] The newspaper's appeal to those who shared its 'fierce admiration' determined everything that followed in this editorial. There was no acknowledgement that the victims had been found innocent and that the actions of the paratroopers had been so clearly condemned. The editorial was structured in terms that did in fact excuse what had happened, that disregarded the innocence of those who had died and that, in a rousing conclusion, sought to salvage the reputation of the British Army. Although it admitted that on Bloody Sunday 'our troops fell short of the high standards of discipline and restraint we expect from them, and which they almost always deliver', the *Mail* closed with a tribute to the Army that might well have come scored with the theme tune of the *Dambusters* movie:

> Northern Ireland today is more peaceful than it's been for decades. For this, the overwhelming glory must go to the police and the 250,000 soldiers who served there of whom all but a handful showed almost superhuman restraint … [T]hese men, and their sons and grandsons who are dying now in Afghanistan, are the true face of the British Army. And nothing can diminish the debt we owe them.[45]

Serving in a cavalry role in this editorial rearguard action was the war reporter Max Hastings. In a column entitled 'This grossly misguided excavation of the past', he portrayed the actions of the paratroopers on that 'shocking day for the Army' as somehow anomalous: 'an appalling disciplinary collapse', 'a reckless paroxysm of violence' and a 'spasm of madness [that] overtook a small number of soldiers [and] inflicted devastating damage on the cause of peace in Northern Ireland'.[46]

Those familiar with the political leanings of the *Mail* – a deeply reactionary newspaper and a touchstone of conservative populism in England – will not be surprised to review its very negative response to Saville. Yet, it would be a mistake to assume that its position was somehow atypical of a generally positive media reaction in Britain to the findings of the report. Indeed, only the Northern Ireland editions of the *Sun* and the *Daily Mirror* acknowledged the verdict of innocence without qualification, both in their front-page lead and in their editorials. Their London editions also acknowledged the innocence of the victims, yet, editorially, that was quite beside the point. What concerned them most was the question of whether the paratroopers and their officers would face prosecution; and also the need to consign Bloody Sunday and the Saville Report to history, for the sake either of the peace process or of the reputation of the British Army, or both.

Only Simon Winchester and Jonathan Freedland in the *Guardian* considered the true implications of the Saville Report for the Army and for the British State. In his regular column for the paper, Freedland considered the complaint that the Bloody Sunday victims had been 'elevated to a higher rung in the hierarchy of suffering, their murders scrutinised by a full legal inquiry denied to the others':

> The only answer to that lies in the nature of the killers. For those pulling the trigger in Derry were not volunteers for this or that terrorist faction. They were British soldiers acting in the name of the British state, mowing down their fellow citizens. This is what gives Bloody Sunday its singular quality: it represents the biggest single massacre by the British military on UK soil since Peterloo.[47]

In a lead feature article starting on the front page – 'Amid the tears and cheers, a full stop to Britain's colonial experience' – Simon Winchester, who reported the shootings for the *Guardian*, was one of the very few journalists to spell out the specifics of the Army's actions without then offering justification: 'Men of the support company of the 1st Battalion, the Parachute regiment, had shot without justification. Victims had been shot in the back, or while they were crawling away. Soldiers had lied under oath.'[48] The paper's editorial, 'Derry's moment of truth', was also couched in the kind of blunt language that the Saville Report largely avoided:

> Bloody Sunday was not a premeditated state conspiracy, Saville finds. But the main actors were not brave British soldiers but, too often, trigger-happy paratroopers. The parachute regiment went into Derry's Bogside in response to an order that should not have been given. They fired the first shots at civilians who had been taking part in a civil rights march. The people at whom they fired were unarmed and in some cases fleeing. A few victims were shot on the ground. None of the dead or wounded was doing anything that justified their being shot. The soldiers gave no warnings. They lost their self-control. Then some of them lied about it afterwards.[49]

Notwithstanding the *Guardian's* preference for the 'loss of control' explanation for what 1 Para did that day, which we challenge, its blunt condemnation of their behaviour in Northern Ireland, before and after Bloody Sunday,[50] was exceptional and this is testimony in part to the British Army's public relations expertise.[51] However, as we hinted in our introduction to this chapter, the unquestioning acceptance of the Army version was, for the majority of the British press, as much an ideological imperative as it was a propaganda necessity.

Explaining the coverage

Reflecting on the implications of Bloody Sunday and the Saville Report, Robert Fisk in the *Independent* on 16 June 2010 asked the critical question: had British journalists 'something to answer for in our slavish adherence to the notion of the British Army's integrity?'[52] On the basis of what we have found in our analysis here, the answer to that question is a resounding 'yes'. In the immediate aftermath of the shootings, the Army's version was enough even for journalists who could see that it raised more questions than it provided answers. It was still enough in the wake of the flawed Widgery Report and, remarkably, still held some water even in light of the overwhelming evidence presented in the Saville Report. But was that the result of news processes and production – objectivity, news values and media-source relationships? Or was it the result of an ideological predisposition rooted in a history and tradition of imperialism and colonialism, one that precludes a reflexive, critical understanding among journalists of the military's role and behaviour while serving in Northern Ireland?

The British Army's media response to Saville was the finely nuanced line that 'mistakes were made' but that everyone involved should learn from these and move on. 'Relieved Army has "learnt its lessons"', *The Times* reported on 16 June.[53] On the same day, and under the headline, 'Army chief admits serious failings and declares lessons have been learned', the *Guardian* quoted the reactions to the report of a procession of senior Army officers who might just as well have been regretting 'serious failings' in military catering, such was their lack of specifics. General Sir David Richards assured the paper that 'The way the army is trained, the way it works and the way it operates have all changed significantly.'[54] Critics of the British Army's operations in Basra in the wake of the invasion of Iraq in 2003 would have been surprised to hear that, including those who had read the Aitken Report published in 2008 by the Ministry of Defence, just two years previous to the Saville Report. The report was subtitled, 'An Investigation into Cases of Deliberate Abuse and Unlawful Killing in Iraq in 2003 and 2004'; but it also considered subsequent incidents that were subject to damaging media exposés.[55] For example, on 12 February 2006, *News of the World* online had published leaked video footage of paratroopers arresting a group of young rioters in Basra, taking them to a military base and giving them a severe beating to the delight of the soldier filming it on camera. The Aitken Report records this incident among others and notes that: 'No disciplinary or administrative action was taken' at the time.[56] It found that in other cases involving suspicion of murder or physical abuse, charges were either dismissed at military court or were subject to indeterminate investigation. But what really stands out in the report is not its findings but its public-relations-speak about 'learning lessons from discipline cases'.[57] Indeed, it even referred to the Army's formal 'Lessons Learned Process'.[58]

We raise this case because it might be said to demonstrate in a general sense the effectiveness of state and military propaganda,[59] or at least the success of Army public relations in quashing unwelcome media inquiry into cases of misconduct, abuse or unlawful killing on the part of its soldiers in whatever theatre of operations, including Northern Ireland and on Bloody Sunday in particular.[60] But we suspect there is more to it than that, and while propaganda and public relations depend on the receptiveness of different media and audiences to the intended message or messages, it is clear that in this case the Army's version of events on Bloody Sunday was sown on fertile ideological ground. By that we mean that there were and still are significant sections of the press all too willing to propagate the military's 'good reputation' in whatever circumstances because they share with the military the same ideological and colonialist predisposition to see the killing of the unarmed, subjected 'other' as somehow justified and unproblematic. Indeed, on 30 June 2010, just two weeks after the publication of the Saville Report, the *Nottingham Post* online published a feature article on the Parachute Regiment headed 'Bygones: The Paras', which made no reference whatever to Bloody Sunday but concluded with this tribute: 'Following many famous operations in [the Second World War], the Paras went on to serve everywhere from Palestine to Northern Ireland to the Falklands, playing vital roles and winning numerous awards for gallantry.'[61]

Seamus Deane has argued that 'The killing of Irish people by British troops and the provision of legal justification for it is not just an *ad hoc* policy adopted now and then in particular circumstances; it is not a regrettable accident that arises from the tensions of the situation on random occasions. It as an ideological imperative.'[62] The reporting of Bloody Sunday by the majority of British newspapers we looked at here would appear not only to have underwritten that ideological imperative but also to have naturalised it as unproblematic and indeed inevitable.

Notes

1   This phrase is from Field Marshal Bernard Montgomery's eulogy (circa 1944) to the soldiers of the Paratroop Regiment he founded in 1942 during the Second World War. Cited in the Parachute Regiment Charter: www.army.mod.uk/documents/general/ParachuteRegimentCharter.pdf (Accessed, 30 May 2015).

2 G. Dawson, *Soldier Heroes: British Adventure, Empire and the Imagining of Masculinities* (London: Routledge, 1994), p. 233; M. Paris, *Warrior Nation: Images of War in British Popular Culture, 1850–2000* (London: Reaktion Books, 2000), p. 8.

3 Paris, *Warrior Nation*.

4 Live broadcast, BBC1, 15 June 2010.

5 *Guardian* (16 June 2010). On 16 August 1819, protestors demanding parliamentary reform were charged by cavalry at St Peter's Field, Manchester. Fifteen people were killed and many hundreds more injured.

6 *Daily Mail* (16 June 2010).

7 G. McLaughlin and S. Baker, *The British Media and Bloody Sunday* (London: Intellect Books, 2015).

8 *Bloody Sunday* (dir. Paul Greengrass, 2002); *Sunday* (dir. Charles McDougall, 2002). See our analysis of these films in *The British Media and Bloody Sunday*, pp. 117–42.

9 The *Sunday Times* Insight team was later to produce a report on Bloody Sunday that was much more incisive than anything that had appeared in the British press previously: see 'Insight on Bloody Sunday: the decision to put civilians at risk', *Sunday Times* (23 April 1972), pp. 15–18. See also P. Pringle and P. Jacobson, *Those Are Real Bullets, Aren't They? Bloody Sunday, Derry, 30 January 1972* (New York: Grove Press, 2000). Pringle and Jacobson were two of the Insight reporters involved in the investigation along with Murray Sayle; see M. Sayle, 'Bloody Sunday report', *London Review of Books* (11 July 2002).

10 *Daily Mail* (31 January 1972).

11 *Daily Mail* (31 January 1972). The post mortem reports would show that British Army bullets had been found in the bodies of *all* the victims.

12 *Daily Telegraph* (31 January 1972).

13 Ibid.

14 *Daily Telegraph* (1 February 1972).

15 *The Times* (1 February 1972).

16 *The Times* (31 January 1972).

17 *Daily Mirror* (31 January 1972).

18 *Sun* (31 January 1972).

19 Ibid.

20 *Daily Mirror* (31 January 1972).

21 *Sun* (31 January 1972).

22 *Sun* (1 February 1972).

23 *Daily Mail* (1 February 1972).

24 *Daily Telegraph* (1 February 1972).

25 *Daily Mirror* (1 February 1972).

26 D. Mullan, *Eyewitness Bloody Sunday: The Truth* (Dublin: Wolfhound Press, 1997), p. 27.

27 The eyewitness statements were taken by the Northern Ireland Civil Rights Association and the National Council for Civil Liberties in the days following the shootings. They were retrieved from storage by Don Mullan in 1996 and

eventually submitted to the Saville (Bloody Sunday) Inquiry when it began in 1998. Mullan also published an edited selection in Mullan, *Eyewitness Bloody Sunday*.

28 Mullan, *Eyewitness Bloody Sunday*, p. 43.

29 For a critical, legal analysis of the Widgery Report, see D. P. Walsh, *A Resounding Defeat for Truth, Justice and the Rule of Law*. Commissioned report (Derry: Bloody Sunday Trust, 1997).

30 *Daily Telegraph* (19 April 1972); *Guardian* (19 April 1972); *Daily Mail* (19 April 1972); *Daily Mirror* (19 April 1972).

31 *Daily Mail* (20 April 1972).

32 *Daily Telegraph* (20 April 1972); *Guardian* (20 April 1972); *Sun* (20 April 1972).

33 *The Times* (20 April 1972).

34 Much of this evidence was gathered by the Bloody Sunday Justice Campaign and investigated in a series of reports by Channel 4 News journalists Lena Ferguson and Alex Thomson (1997–98).

35 *Daily Telegraph* (16 June 2010); *The Times* (16 June 2010); *Independent* (16 June 2010); *Sun* (16 June 2010); *Daily Mirror* (16 June 2010).

36 *Daily Mail* (16 June 2010).

37 Ibid.

38 *The Times* (16 June 2010); *Guardian* (16 June 2010).

39 *Guardian* (16 June 2010).

40 *Independent* (16 June 2010).

41 *Sun*, Ulster edition (16 June 2010).

42 *Daily Mail* (16 June 2010).

43 Pringle and Jacobson, *Those Are Real Bullets*, p. 47.

44 *Daily Mail* (16 June 2010).

45 Ibid.

46 Ibid.

47 *Guardian* (16 June 2010).

48 Ibid.

49 Ibid.

50 Pringle and Jacobson, *Those Are Real Bullets*, provides hitherto little-known details of the repressive security operation imposed by 1 Para in Derry in the immediate aftermath of the shootings.

51 L. Curtis, *Ireland: The Propaganda War. The British Media and the 'Battle for Hearts and Minds'* (Belfast: Sásta, 1998); D. Miller, *Don't Mention the War: Northern Ireland, Propaganda and the Media* (London: Pluto Press, 1994).

52 *Independent* (16 June 2010).

53 *The Times* (16 June 2010).

54 *Guardian* (16 June 2010).

55 Ministry of Defence (MoD), *The Aitken Report: An Investigation into Cases of Deliberate Abuse and Unlawful Killing in Iraq in 2003 and 2004* (London: MoD Corporate Publications, 2008).

56 MoD, *Aitken Report*, p. 3.

57 Ibid., p. 22.

58 Ibid.

59 The literature on propaganda and military media strategies is substantial but we are most mindful of work such as that by D. Miller (ed.), *Tell Me Lies: Propaganda and Media Distortion in the Attack on Iraq* (London: Pluto Press, 2004) and H. Tumber and J. Palmer, *Media at War: The Iraq War* (London: Sage, 2004).

60 Of the literature on the British media and the Northern Ireland conflict, Miller, *Don't Mention the War* and Curtis, *Ireland: The Propaganda War* most directly critique military and State propaganda tactics and strategies. G. McLaughlin and S. Baker, *The Propaganda of Peace: The Role of Media and Culture in the Northern Ireland Peace Process* (Bristol: Intellect Books, 2010) looks at a much less organised form of propaganda that arises out of cultural and ideological dispositions, e.g. the drive for conflict resolution and political process and the promotion of a 'peace dividend'.

61 *Nottingham Post* online (30 June 2010), www.nottinghampost.com/Bygones-Paras/story-12210319-detail/story.html (Accessed 15 March 2014).

62 S. Deane, Foreword to E. McCann, *Bloody Sunday in Derry: What Really Happened* (Dingle: Brandon, 1992), p. 11.

14

Suspect stories: William Trevor's portrayals of the Irish in London during the Troubles

Tony Murray

Modern literature in Ireland was born out of conflict. Many of its greatest works have been the result of writers' reflections on the consequences of war and civil strife for the country's people. In the latter part of the twentieth century, the Northern Ireland Troubles (as they were euphemistically called) provided novelists, playwrights and poets with a dramatic backdrop against which to explore the often uneasy interface between public and private allegiances during times of political violence. But while numerous novels were written about the Troubles over their thirty-year history, few looked at how the conflict impacted upon the people of London.

A significant percentage of 'Troubles thrillers', as they became known, were set in London,[1] but, like their parent genre, tended to sensationalise the role of the IRA. While this ensured a certain dramatic purchase, it also tended to obscure the influence of the Troubles on ordinary people's lives. As a consequence, the image that we have inherited of London and its inhabitants from novels such as Shaun Herron's *The Whore Mother* (1973), Max Franklin's *Hennessy* (1975) and *A Prayer for the Dying* (1983) by Jack Higgins, are seriously misleading.[2] The short story rather than the novel has often provided writers with the opportunity to explore the more oblique or occluded dimensions of the Troubles, particularly as they have affected individual lives.[3] This is also the case for those that are set in London.[4] Some of the most sophisticated and nuanced of these have been written by William Trevor, three of which I examine here. Unlike other writers, Trevor's focus on the Irish in London and their interactions with the host community is sustained over a number of such stories. By showing how the conflict impacted personally and differentially upon the everyday lives of individuals, they provide a variety of important insights into the wider ramifications of the Northern Ireland Troubles in Britain and their legacy for British–Irish relations today.

The Provisional IRA's bombing campaign of mainland Britain began in March 1973 and continued intermittently over the next twenty-three years. London was the prime target, with department stores, government buildings and mainline railway stations regularly coming under attack. The bombings resulted in over 100 deaths, more than 2,000 injuries and substantial disruption to the daily life of the city's residents.[5] During this time the Irish community found itself in the spotlight as historical but dormant anti-Irish prejudices within sections of the host population were re-ignited in response to the outrages.[6] This was particularly acute during the days and weeks after a bomb explosion, when the mere possession of an Irish accent became an excuse in some cases for verbal and even physical assault.[7] Irish migrants who had come to the city in the immediate post-war years had put down roots, were building careers and were raising families. As a result, such pressures were all the more profound and many of this generation of Irish migrants kept a low profile for fear of persecution[8] as anti-terror legislation made the Irish in Britain a 'suspect community'.[9] More recently, parallels have been drawn between these experiences and those of the Muslim community in Britain today. In both cases,

> The dominant response to [being identified as a 'suspect community'] was a state of fearfulness, which in turn resulted in behaviour such as lying low, keeping quiet, and avoiding certain places or areas of the city. This provoked diverging reactions ranging from feelings of alienation, with implications for sense of belonging and trust in institutions to various forms of politicisation.[10]

Throughout history, fiction has provided an effective means by which untold or otherwise untellable stories have found a voice. It offers a dialogical space in which both the political tensions and personal ambivalences induced by conflict can be vented and presents, through narrative, a way of elucidating and mediating such matters. The Irish Troubles short story, in particular, appears to have a special facility in this regard. Ronan McDonald has persuasively argued that it 'both reflects the problems of articulation and representation within that fractious political situation and, with its characteristically wry, elliptical point of view, can be a subversive strategy of understatement'.[11]

On the face of it, William Trevor would seem to be an unlikely chronicler of the effects of the Troubles on the Irish in London. Trevor did not live in the city during this time and had no direct connections with the Irish community. Furthermore, his depictions of Irish Londoners prior to the 1970s (which tended to appear in novels rather than short stories) were of marginal and unsympathetic individuals, usually employed as foils against leading English characters or, as one critic described it, as 'narrative "grouting"'.[12] Given such a track record, the stories I examine here, therefore, might be considered somewhat 'suspect' in another sense of the word, that is, in terms of their credibility. Despite this, however, Trevor is well placed to portray the cultural and political nuances in personal relations between the Irish and the English. He was born into a Protestant Anglo-Irish family in County Cork in 1928 and experienced at first hand the social as well as political consequences for his class of Irish independence in the middle decades of the twentieth century. Having lived in England for most of his life and gained a reputation for portraying English and Irish characters with equal verisimilitude, Trevor might be considered an inherently diasporic writer. Furthermore, a distinct change took place in his depictions of the Irish in London as a result of the Troubles. The political and moral dilemmas that Irish Londoners faced during the Troubles provided Trevor, an author who had established a reputation for empathetic portrayals of the vulnerable position of the Anglo-Irish in Ireland (especially during the War of Independence), with similar subject matter, but in a entirely new context.[13] Here was a new location and a new opportunity for him to explore British–Irish relations in what George O'Brien has referred to as 'the private, interpersonal, domestic sphere' where individuals are engaged in 'the trial and error of attempting to overcome malevolence and misfortune, of tolerating difference and bridging divisions'.[14] The three stories by Trevor that I have chosen to examine here provide vivid insights into how such relations within families and between neighbours and co-workers in London were forged in the political and social crucible of the Troubles.

The ambiguous position and complex negotiations of identity that migrant communities experience more generally have been a topic of considerable interest in the social sciences for many years.[15] The work of Avtar Brah and, in particular, her concept of 'diaspora space' has found wide application in recent times.[16] For Brah, diaspora space involves the 'entanglement of genealogies of dispersion with those of "staying put"'.[17] By those who 'stay put', she is referring to the host or receiving community, who, she argues, are as much a part of the diasporic experience as those who migrate. She also points out how identities and allegiances are subject to collision and contestation at certain times and to reassembly and reconfiguration at others. This observation seems particularly pertinent not only to how the relationships and identity positions of Irish people and their hosts in London were profoundly affected by the onset of the Troubles in the 1970s but to how, forty years later, they have been reconfigured by the peace process. Importantly, Brah highlights the key role that narrative plays in the mediation and deployment of various forms of migrant identity under different socio-political circumstances:

> [M]ultiple journeys may configure into one journey via a *confluence of narratives* as it is lived and re-lived, produced, reproduced and transformed through individual as well as collective memory and re-memory. It is within this confluence of narrativity that 'diasporic community' is differently imagined under different historical circumstances. By this I mean that the identity of the diasporic imagined community is far from fixed or pre-given. It is constituted within the crucible of the materiality of everyday life.[18]

Narrative, in other words, is an intrinsic part of how identities are constituted, rather than simply being a vehicle for their expression. It is through narrative, according to Brah, that the concept of diaspora space is best appreciated as a 'site of immanence' where multiple subject positions are 'juxtaposed' and 'proclaimed or disavowed' according to historical circumstances.[19] This 'subject-in-process', as she terms it, 'consciously and unconsciously replays and re-signifies positions in which it is located and invested'.[20] The way in which personal narratives of lived experience are inflected by metanarratives of history and ideology would seem central to such concerns, particularly during times of political conflict. It is at this interface that some of the most telling insights into the deeper social and cultural effects of the Troubles are revealed. In other words, narrative provides a cognitive conduit not only for representing how the specificities of personal experience can be read in the context of historical and political events, but also for how, as readers or listeners, our interpretations of this relationship can change over time.

'Another Christmas' (1978) is familiar territory for William Trevor: how a long-standing personal relationship is challenged by the re-emergence of political enmities from the past. It is a theme more commonly traced in Trevor's work about socially isolated Anglo-Irish Protestants in a predominantly Catholic Ireland. But in this story, set in 1974 (the peak year of the IRA bombing campaign in London), Irish Catholics find themselves in an analogous position. During the Troubles, questions of national allegiance for Irish people in Britain were thrust into the public domain in a way that had not been the case since the Second World War. For the generation of migrants who had settled in London in the post-war period, the IRA's bombing campaign threatened to undermine the efforts made by many of them over previous decades to build mutual respect and understanding with the host population. In this sense, 'Another Christmas' occupies a particularly volatile form of diaspora space, where a conflict between past and present narratives of Irish identity takes place at the domestic interface between migrant and host community and proves to have deleterious consequences for the individuals concerned.

Originally from Waterford, Dermot and Norah are clearly proud of their Irishness and their Catholicism and are typical in many ways of Irish migrants of their generation. Their children have Irish names, Norah is active in community work on behalf of their local parish church, and they are keen to get along with their English neighbours. Over the years, Mr Joyce (their elderly English landlord) has become a close friend of the family who calls for a chat each Friday evening and at Christmas brings 'carefully chosen presents for the children, and chocolates and nuts and cigarettes'.[21] But, like many of their compatriots, the middle-aged couple at the centre of 'Another Christmas' discover that a relationship of mutual respect between themselves and their neighbours, which had been nurtured for over twenty years, can become alarmingly fragile in the wake of an IRA bombing of the capital. One evening, Norah informs her husband that, for the first time in years, Mr Joyce will not be joining them for Christmas dinner. It transpires that the previous August, after a conversation the couple had with Mr Joyce (who refers to the IRA as 'maniacs'), Dermot had argued that 'bombs were a crime but it didn't do to forget that the crime would not be there if generations of Catholics in the North had not been treated like animals' (493). On previous occasions when the subject of the Troubles had come up, Dermot had maintained a diplomatic silence about his political and religious views for the sake of cordial relations with their landlord. But he is a contemplative man who has 'devoted time to thought' and 'balanced everything in his mind' (489, 490). As a consequence, when it comes to Ireland and the Troubles, Dermot is acutely aware of the relationship between historical cause and effect. On the occasion in question, he hopes, by expressing his views, to give Mr Joyce some pause for thought about the reasons for the present conflict in Northern Ireland.[22] As a deeply religious individual, Dermot would, we are told, 'have prayed and considered' before making such remarks (494). Norah, however, considers her husband's comments as nothing more than 'an excuse for murder' (493). Smarting from the embarrassment of what she views as his politically suspect sympathies, she implores her husband to apologise for his behaviour and 'to make it up with Mr Joyce' (492). But Dermot believes Norah is over-reacting and ignores her request. As a result, a profound divergence of opinion opens up between husband and wife.

It becomes apparent that the Troubles and the narratives associated with them have permeated this particular diaspora space in a seriously adverse way. Not only have they undermined the relationship between the couple and their landlord, but they have also destabilised a happy marriage, forcing both parties to take sides on a political issue they had hitherto suppressed for the sake of harmonious relations.

For Dermot, the traditional nationalist narrative to which he is still emotionally attached is something he feels honour-bound to voice. For Norah, on the other hand, such a narrative is anathema, to the point where she disowns any responsibility for what is happening in Northern Ireland. 'Let them fight it out and not bother us', she proclaims, preferring instead to disassociate herself and her compatriots from events across the water (493). From her point of view, consideration of their landlord's sensitivities outweighs any need on the part of Dermot to provide historical context for current events. The IRA's tactics make her feel ashamed of her Irishness and she is unable to tolerate expressions of anything other than revulsion and condemnation of the bombers from her husband. When out shopping, she suddenly begins 'to feel embarrassed because of her Waterford accent' (493) and, reflecting on their original decision to move to London in the first place, she fears that they are 'caught in the trap they'd made for themselves' (492). She wonders whether, due to his political views, Dermot might lose his long-standing job with the gas board and even goes so far as to think that, under 'the present circumstances', objections to him reading people's meters 'would be understandable and fair' (494).

Dermot and Norah are emblematic of a particular generation of Irish migrants who nurtured hopes for a new life in London after the Second World War. But with the onset of the Troubles, they discover that they are not immune from changing political circumstances that prove to severely weaken a partnership sustained by years of mutual tolerance and understanding. Seen within a broader historical context, we witness how an otherwise stable and commendable marriage becomes subject to the conflicted discourses of a long colonial relationship between two countries. Likewise, a similarly long-standing relationship between the couple and their landlord is also undermined. This story, therefore, demonstrates how changing political circumstances during the Troubles caused the diaspora space of Irish London to enter a profound state of flux. As it became radically transformed by the collision between political and personal narratives of identity and allegiance, serious consequences for members of both the migrant and the host community ensued.

The Troubles exert a more oblique yet no less powerful influence on members of both communities in another of Trevor's stories, 'Being

Stolen From' (1981). Bridget Lacy is a shy, middle-aged woman who married a man from the same locality in County Cork and with whom, for over twenty years, she has 'weathered the strangeness of their emigration'.[23] The story is set in the late 1970s in a distinct form of diaspora space, 'a small [London] house in a terrace, with the *Cork Weekly Examiner* to keep them in touch' (746). However, we learn that Bridget's life had changed radically when her husband unexpectedly left her for another woman. This took place shortly after they had adopted Betty, the baby girl of Norma, a teenage English neighbour from across the street. The precise reason why Norma gave up Betty for adoption is not entirely clear. However, according to Norma's current husband, she had suffered from depression and had a tendency to be 'flighty and irresponsible' (746), suggesting that she was too immature and psychologically unstable for the role of motherhood.

The story opens with a plea to Bridget by Norma to return the child (who is now four years old) on the grounds that she has recovered from her mental disorder and is now ready to take up her maternal responsibilities. Having only recently recovered from the shock of losing her husband, the prospect of losing a daughter also is too traumatic a proposition for Bridget and she declines the request. However, Norma's husband, who is a local authority social worker with counselling skills, is more persistent about the matter and makes repeated calls on Bridget, employing gradually more coercive forms of persuasion in the process:

> In what he said, and in the way he looked, there was the implication that this room in a cramped house was an unsuitable habitat for a spirited four-year old. There was also the implication that Bridget at forty-nine, and without a husband, belonged more naturally among the sacred pictures on the walls than she possibly could in a world of toys and children. (747)

Bridget, in the view of Norma's husband, has become clearly unsuitable for the role of an adoptive mother, given her advanced age and her recent separation. Apart from bordering on emotional blackmail, his views also reveal prejudice as regards the Irish woman's overtly religious lifestyle. This, in turn, exposes an instructive cultural disjunction within the diaspora space of the story. Religious iconography was common in the homes of Irish migrants of Bridget's generation but it clearly strikes Norma's husband as suspicious and seems to provoke an unconscious anti-Catholicism. When his initial stratagem fails to persuade Bridget, he refers to the currently problematical position of the Irish in Britain in the wake of the Troubles, arguing that 'the Irish are a different kettle of fish today than they were ten years ago' (757). The clear implication here is that Bridget is no longer a reliable parent, by virtue of her membership of a 'suspect community'. As Michael W. Thomas points out, Bridget's 'rights as an adoptive mother are being erased by reinterpretations of her status, as offered by Norma's husband in the light of current sectarian foment'.[24] Norma's husband goes on to suggest that an Irish family is an inappropriate environment for a child to grow up in under present circumstances. 'That child', he says, 'will have to attend a London school, for instance, where there could easily be hostility ... [N]o mother on earth would care to lie awake at night and worry about that' (757). However, he appears to be unaware that when Bridget first adopted Betty four years before, Norma had raised no such objections. His remarks, instead, seem to be based upon his personal fear that the child will be brought up as part of a 'suspect community' or, as he euphemistically puts it, 'in an atmosphere that isn't always pleasant' (757).

While not directly about the Troubles, the spectre of Irish republican violence is powerfully invoked in this story, reconfiguring, as in 'Another Christmas', the diaspora space within which migrant and host protagonists are positioned. This time, however, rather than present conflict acting as the catalyst for a crisis of relations, it is the anticipation of future hostilities that plays this role. In other words, the 'collision and contestation' that migrant identities are subjected to, in Brah's terms, may not only be historically determined but also imaginatively determined under certain political conditions. Bridget's somewhat passive personality makes her vulnerable to the deployment of such narratives and, in particular, to persuasion by people with ulterior motives. Earlier in the story we learn about how she had allowed a fellow schoolgirl to steal her atlas when she was a youngster. The devotional narratives of her religious upbringing would seem to have played a part in the development of her character, but in her own mind, Bridget believes she simply has an innately fatalistic predisposition. 'It was what you had to accept', she muses, 'what you couldn't kick against: God's will, the Reverend Mother or Father Keogh would have said, but for Bridget it began with the kind of person you were. Out of that, the circumstances of your life emerged' (751). Nevertheless, for the most part, Bridget withstands the emotional coercion placed upon her by Norma's husband, both as a mother and as a Catholic. It is only when the Troubles and the implied untrustworthiness of the Irish in Britain become a lever in negotiations over Betty's custody that we witness her eventual capitulation. The politically adverse nature of the diaspora space in which Bridget finds herself as an Irish migrant in 1970s London undermines her sense of security and ultimately leads to her marginalisation. Norma and her husband, on the other hand, are able to exploit the Troubles for personal advantage but, in terms of wider social relations, only succeed in destabilising an already fragile accord between two communities.

If 'Being Stolen From' demonstrates how the narrative determinants of diaspora space can extend forwards in time, William Trevor's story 'The Mourning' (2000) demonstrates how they can also extend backwards. Liam Pat Brogan, a young man from County Cork, moves to London on the advice of a trusted friend who fixes him up with a job in the construction industry. However, the job does not live up to its promise and Brogan finds himself routinely consigned to the menial task of operating a cement mixer, with little sign of more skilled work in prospect. His digs are less than ideal and he finds himself being bullied by Huxter, the English site foreman, who insists on calling him 'Mick' and disparaging the quality of his work by reference to his Irishness. Before long, Brogan is considering giving up the job and returning to Ireland. He divulges his feelings to Feeny, his point-of-contact when he first arrived in the city. Feeny, an older man, takes Brogan under his wing and tells him that, because of the Troubles, the English look down on 'any man with an Irish accent'.[25] He then lends him money and finds him superior accommodation through a Belfast man called McTighe. But McTighe, it transpires, has 'a mission' planned for Brogan, something Feeny refers to as having 'possessed every Irishman worth his salt'. 'The further from home he was', Feeny adds, 'the more it was there' (79). Aware that Brogan has no police record and, crucially, that he has no previous connections to the paramilitaries, McTighe knows that the mission can be conducted with the minimum risk of detection.[26] In his youth, Brogan had distributed republican magazines in his home village, and subsequent references by Feeny to 'the massacre of the innocents' on 'Bloody Sunday' and to 'the dream of Wolfe Tone' (79) are enough to stir in him latent patriotic sentiments.

The diaspora space of this story is similar to that of 'Another Christmas' but is even more highly charged by discourses of Irish nationalism and anti-Irish prejudice. Brogan's self-esteem is fragile, especially given the prevailing anti-Irish climate of the time. So, when a suitable narrative presents itself, it fortifies him in the face of the daily taunts from his foreman. The following extract reveals how such thoughts begin to take root in his mind:

> Huxter wouldn't know what was going to happen; Huxter would look at him and assume he was the same. The people who did not say hullo when he bought cigarettes or a newspaper would see no difference either. There was strength in the excitement, a vigour Liam Pat had never experienced in his life before. He would carry the secret on to the site every morning. He would walk through the streets with it, a power in him where there'd been nothing. (81)

The allure of a heroic role offers Brogan the means of radically challenging the discursive power relations of the diaspora space within which he is positioned. He becomes aware of 'a vigour [he] had never experienced in his life before' and 'a power in him where there'd been nothing' (81). He is soon seduced into seeing himself as a successor in a long line of Irish patriots. Identifying in particular with a fellow Corkman, Michael Collins, he resolves to carry out McTighe's orders.[27] However, when the night finally arrives for the planting of the bomb in the centre of London, Brogan has a flashback to newspaper reports about a young man from his home town who died while attempting a similar mission in the city. In particular, he recalls how there had been 'the unwanted presence of the lads' at his funeral (a reference to the IRA) and how his father had described the bomber as 'a poor bloody hero' (87, 85). The searing memory of this event is enough to give Brogan pause for thought and, with Big Ben chiming the hour in the background, he drops the explosives he is carrying into the Thames. After fleeing to Ireland, he reflects on how close he came to destroying not only the lives of innocent people but his own. Rather than 'seeing himself in Michael Collins's trenchcoat, with Michael Collins's stride' (83), an alternative take on the grand narrative of republican martyrdom asserts itself. He remembers the horror and sorrow he felt for a person that he now realises he was close to becoming himself, steps back from the brink and renews his religious belief in the sanctity of life.

In a 1983 interview, William Trevor stated: 'Just as the bomber has to avoid looking at the humanity in his victims, we have to seek the humanity in the bomber. We don't have to be sympathetic with the bombers, but unless we find a way to see them as ourselves, the whole thing makes no sense.'[28] The implication here is that literature has a role to play in reaching some kind of understanding of why an individual such as Brogan is driven to such desperate measures. This is a feature, however, which is conspicuous by its absence from most popular novels about the conflict in Northern Ireland. According to Patrick Magee, who conducted an exhaustive study of the genre, in most depictions of Irish republicans 'we encounter again and again the same set of tropes and lurid misrepresentations'.[29] In contrast, 'The Mourning' provides a vivid and sophisticated insight into the mind-set of the ideologically driven bomber. It charts how a respectable but impressionable young man, when confronted by prejudice, is persuaded to carry out an extreme act of violence when under the influence of political ideology and the promise of national immortality. More particularly, the story demonstrates how an Irish migrant in London becomes radicalised as a result of experiences that are not directly related to the conflict in Northern Ireland but stem, rather, from the anti-Irish racism he is subject to at work. This alerts us to the fact that individuals' psychological motivations for involvement in ideologically driven actions, whilst influenced by historical precedent, may not always be solely related to the political circumstances imme-diately associated with them. By setting 'The Mourning' in the highly attenuated diaspora space of Irish London during the Troubles, Trevor provides valuable reflections, therefore, on both the effects of political change on migrant communities and the conflicted narratives by which individual migrants live and act at such times. Equally, the story reveals how, at such times, the workplace, in particular, can become a site for the collisions and contestations of cultural allegiance referred to by Brah and can potentially act as the catalyst for extreme acts of violence.

The impact of the IRA's bombing campaign in London had far-reaching consequences for its citizens. Literary representations of their experiences during the Troubles are rare and, as a result, the texts that do exist provide valuable imaginative perspectives on what Irish people in London and the city's more indigenous inhabitants were experienc-ing and thinking at the time. They also provide insights into the wider historical context of bombings in London. Literary portrayals of the ideologically driven and ruthless young bomber in London can be traced back at least as far as Joseph Conrad's *The Secret Agent* (1907), and the subject became topical again after the events of 7 July 2005 when four young Islamist suicide bombers killed fifty-six people (including themselves) on the London underground and bus network. Each of the three stories I have critiqued here has taken on an additional resonance in the aftermath of '7/7'. They demonstrate how grand narratives of national and religious identity can move to the fore in people's lives at times of major historical change. The precise social and cultural conse-quences of this on individuals vary according to circumstances, but these stories demonstrate how, during the Troubles, the home, neighbourhood or workplace became, to use Mary Louise Pratt's term, a heightened political 'contact zone' between migrant and host community.[30] In a multicultural city such as London in the 1970s and 1980s, this zone was a complex one. Bearing in mind that the Irish were one of the earliest migrant groups to settle in the city, it could be argued that they were part of an already ethnically diverse host community themselves. In some cases, as Norah's experience shows in 'Another Christmas', they displayed responses to the Troubles not that dissimilar to their fellow citizens. In other cases, such as those of her husband and of Brogan in 'The Mourning', they reacted very differently.

By writing about the Irish in London during this period, William Trevor made an important intervention in Troubles fiction by providing a necessary corrective to the more pervasive stereotypes that dominate the genre. His London Irish stories demonstrate how the conflict in Northern Ireland affected the lives of individual Londoners in different ways and to varying degrees according to their sense of attachment and belonging on both sides of the Irish Sea. For members of the Irish migrant community, the Troubles profoundly challenged their sense of attachment to past political and cultural allegiances whilst at the same time necessitating a re-evaluation of their relationships with British friends and acquaintances. For members of the host community, on the other hand, the Troubles provoked dormant anti-Irish attitudes and an inevitable re-acquaintance with the discourses of their country's colonial past. By dramatising these processes, Trevor's stories enrich our understanding of the psychological and emotional impact of historical events on both migrant and host communities. Furthermore, they demonstrate how literary fiction, and the personal and collective narratives contained therein, has a valuable role to play in mediating memories of the Troubles in Britain. This, in turn, can inform the wider discussion of British–Irish relations and contribute to post-conflict understanding.

Notes

1 Approximately 15 per cent.
2 S. Herron, *The Whore Mother* (London: Jonathan Cape, 1973); M. Franklin, *Hennessy* (London: Futura, 1975); J. Higgins, *A Prayer for the Dying* (London: Collins, 1983).
3 H. Ingman, *The History of the Irish Short Story* (Cambridge: Cambridge University Press, 2009), pp. 214–15.
4 For other examples, see: F. Arthur, 'A day at the office', in *Over Here, Over There* (London: Green Ink Writers Group, 1985), pp. 82–8; M. Meehan, 'Hard love', in D. Bolger (ed.), *Ireland in Exile: Irish Writers Abroad* (Dublin: New Island Books, 1993), pp. 152–6; K. Barry, 'Mainland campaign', in *Dark Lies the Land* (London: Jonathan Cape, 2012), pp. 90–101.
5 R. English, *Irish Freedom: A History of Nationalism in Ireland* (London: Pan Macmillan, 2007), p. 375.
6 E. Delaney, *The Irish in Post-War Britain* (Oxford: Oxford University Press, 2007), p. 125.
7 M. J. Hickman and B. Walter, *Discrimination and the Irish Community in Britain* (London: Commission for Racial Equality, 1997), p. 205.
8 S. Sorohan, *Irish London during the Troubles* (Dublin: Irish Academic Press, 2012), pp. 50–4.
9 P. Hillyard, *Suspect Community: People's Experience of the Prevention of Terrorism Acts in Britain* (London: Pluto Press, 1993). See chapters by Casey (15), Finch (10) and O'Reilly (20) in this volume.

10 M. J. Hickman, L. Thomas, S. Silvestri and H. Nickels, *'Suspect Communities'? Counter-terrorism Policy, the Press, and the Impact on Irish and Muslim Communities in Britain* (London: Economic and Social Science Research Council, 2011), p. 4.

11 R. McDonald, 'Strategies of silence: Colonial strains in short stories of the Troubles', in *Yearbook of English Studies* (London: Modern Humanities Research Association, 2005), p. 249.

12 M. W. Thomas, 'William Trevor's other island: The writer and his Irish in England', in *Irish Studies Review*, 6:2 (1998), 153.

13 For an example of how Trevor depicts the impact of the Northern Ireland Troubles on a Protestant family in a predominantly Catholic community south of the border, see W. Trevor, 'The distant past', in *The Stories of William Trevor* (Harmondsworth: Penguin, 1983), pp. 345–51.

14 G. O'Brien, 'In another country: Aspects of Trevor's England', in P. Delaney and M. Parker (eds), *William Trevor: Revaluations* (Manchester: Manchester University Press, 2013), p. 40.

15 See, for instance, A. Feldman, 'Alterity and belonging in diaspora space: Changing Irish identities and "race"-making in the "age of migration"', in N. Yuval-Davis, K. Kannabiran and U. Vieten (eds), *Situating Contemporary Politics of Belonging* (London: Sage, 2006), pp. 100–12; M. J. Hickman, 'Diaspora space and national (re)formations', in *Éire-Ireland*, 47:1 & 2 (2012), 19–44; C. Ní Laoire, 'Discourses of nation among migrants from Northern Ireland: Irishness, Britishness and the spaces in-between', in *Scottish Geographical Journal*, 118:3 (2002), pp. 183–99.

16 A. Brah, *Cartographies of Diaspora: Contesting Identities* (London: Routledge, 1996).

17 Ibid., p. 16.

18 Ibid., p. 183.

19 Ibid., p. 208.

20 Ibid., p. 125.

21 W. Trevor, 'Another Christmas', in *The Stories of William Trevor*, pp. 488–95 (p. 491). Subsequent references to this text are cited in parentheses.

22 This is a common theme in Trevor's work. In a later short story about the Troubles, a middle-aged English woman from Surrey who finds it impossible, like Dermot, not to make connections between Ireland's past travails and its present Troubles is vilified by her peers for doing so. See, W. Trevor, 'Beyond the Pale', in *The Stories of William Trevor*, pp. 691–711.

23 W. Trevor, 'Being stolen from', in *The Stories of William Trevor*, pp. 746–59 (p. 751). Subsequent references to this text are cited in parentheses.

24 Thomas, 'William Trevor's other island', p. 155.

25 W. Trevor, 'The mourning', in *The Hill Bachelors* (London: Viking, 2000), pp. 63–88 (p. 69). Subsequent references to this text are cited in parentheses.

26 One of the reasons that the IRA bombing campaign in London was so effective was because it was mainly carried out by members of the organisation who originated from outside Northern Ireland and were generally unknown to the security forces, most notably the 'Balcombe Street Gang'.

27 Collins joined the Irish Republican Brotherhood (forerunner of the IRA) while living in London. P. Hart, *Mick: The Real Michael Collins* (London: Pan Macmillan, 2006), p. 65.

28 C. Boylan, 'Trevor's troubles', *Sunday Press* (24 April 1983), p. 14.

29 P. Magee, *Gangsters or Guerillas? Representations of Irish Republicans in 'Troubles Fiction'* (Belfast: Beyond the Pale, 2001), p. 2. For less stereotypical portrayals of an Irish bomber or potential bomber in London, see respectively Barry, 'Mainland campaign', and P. McCabe, *Breakfast on Pluto* (London: Picador, 1998). For other studies of the 'Troubles thriller', see B. Rolston, 'Mothers, whores and villains: Images of women in the novels of the Northern Ireland conflict', in *Race and Class* 31:1 (July 1989), 41–57; and A. Kelly, *The Thriller and Northern Ireland since 1969: Utterly Resigned Terror* (Aldershot: Ashgate, 2005).

30 M. L. Pratt, *Imperial Eyes: Travel Writing and Transculturation* (London: Routledge, 1992), p. 7.

15

Writing as survival

Maude Casey

In 1986–87 I wrote a novel, *Over the Water*, in the voice of a fourteen-year-old girl called Mary, whose parents are Irish immigrants.[1] This chapter considers the novel as a response to pressures experienced by Irish people in Britain during the 1980s in the context of Britain's war in the Six Counties. It reflects upon impacts of being Irish in Britain before, and during, the terror imposed by the Prevention of Terrorism Act (PTA), from 1974 onwards. It notes the rise of second-wave feminism in creating opportunities for women writers to be published. It also considers the acts of recounting and writing as processes of survival.

The catalyst for the novel happened one morning in 1986, in my local Post Office in Brighton, where I'd been queuing with my baby to cash our child benefit – in those days given to mothers as a book of vouchers. When it was my turn, I walked over and signed that week's voucher, as you were meant to do, in front of the man behind the counter. I felt his eyes on the top of my bent head. As I passed him the open book, I saw that he'd been having a laugh with his colleagues, and then, as he flicked the book shut, I heard him read out my full names, exaggerating each of the syllables, leaning back in his chair and slapping the book up and down on the counter as he stared straight at my face and said: 'Here's another one of that lot. Coming over here. Taking our money. Breeding like rabbits. Bleeding murdering IRA scum.'

The sense of scorn in the air was tangible and degrading. Everyone in the Post Office – people I'd seen every day in the neighbourhood – stared at me. I was truly alone, in a hostile silence that felt as though at any moment it could flip into violence. Only two years before, the Grand Hotel had been bombed. Twelve years before, in apparent response to pub bombings in Guildford and Birmingham, the PTA had been enacted. Its powers, described at the time by the Home Secretary, Roy Jenkins, as

'Draconian … and unprecedented in peace-time',[2] had not only resulted in the wrongful conviction and imprisonment of seventeen innocent Irish people in Britain, but had also succeeded in rendering suspect anyone with an Irish name or accent. These powers had given people like the man in the Post Office the confidence to say what he'd said.

I was frightened, but I walked out with my head up, talking to my baby to shield her from the abuse directed at us. I clearly felt the presence of my grandmother, and women like her, who had survived dispossession, famine, slaughter and hardship, to produce my daughter and me. In this experience was the seed of the ancestor story I later began to write, a story in which a teenage girl grapples with ideas of identity in her grandmother's kitchen in rural Ireland, and which I wrote to show my daughter that her history was one of courage rather than abjection.

I was lucky: 1986 was also the year that The Women's Press launched the Livewire list of Books for Young Women, whose editor, Carole Spedding, began to commission novels – including one from me, an unknown writer – on the basis of that story. Ros de Lanerolle, founder of The Women's Press, was instrumental in bringing to life the writing of outsider women. In 1983 she'd published Alice Walker's *The Colour Purple*, rejected by every other publisher in London. Later, in 1990, in an article for *Index on Censorship*, De Lanerolle celebrated the recent emergence of The Women's Press, Virago, Sheba, Pandora and others, stating: 'the very existence of women's publishers caused books to be written … [W]omen began to record their experiences … because they now found some prospect of publication.'[3]

In treating women writers with respect, The Women's Press provided space for an emergence from silencing into surviving and thriving. Writing my first sentence – 'We live in England, but.'[4] – I felt the power of that full-stop after the word 'but', halting the completion of the subordinate clause and modifying the modifier, in ways which the novel itself goes on to develop. I also saw that the immediacy of the first-person present tense conveyed the intensity of Mary's experience. It also enabled me to slow down time and speed it up, and to alter the focus from close up to wide angle. However, it was essential for there to be other voices, including those of her father, grandmother, mother and aunt. Recounting histories of Ireland through intimacies of people's lives, these voices draw Mary into a long continuum of resistance, as do the voices of people from Irish myth, upon whom Mary calls for support in her distress.

The anguish, mental and physical, inflicted upon Irish people in Britain during the last century has been difficult to frame and can slip into discourses of victimhood. Memories will sometimes surface, to be shared – or to be fudged in denial. They continue to be discussed in the *Irish Post*, the weekly newspaper self-identified as 'the voice of the Irish in Britain since 1970'. In April 2014, Alex McDonnell wrote in his column: 'If you weren't there, it is hard to imagine how besieged the Irish community felt at the time … under attack from the PTA, the SPG [Special Patrol Group], the media, and politicians from every party.'[5] Today, people feel torn: wishing to remain invisible and to shake off the bad old days, and yet resenting the expectation that they silently swallow something about their sense of self. The many aspects of this complex anguish, and its causes, need space to be aired and analysed.

Frequently, empathy is expressed for Muslim communities, whose targeting under the current PTA has caused them to be referred to as 'the new Irish'.[6] Indeed, Gerry Conlon, one of the Guildford Four, was campaigning for the civil rights of this new, Muslim 'suspect community' until the day he died in June 2014. Gareth Peirce highlighted this in the statement she made announcing Gerry's death on behalf of his family: 'Once a community has been made suspect en masse, every organ of the state will feel entitled, in fact obliged, to discover proof of their suspicions … One of the campaigns that Gerry was most strongly articulating at the time of his death was pointing out what is being done to the Muslim community today.'[7] And in 2014 we have seen this state entitlement acted out in the spiteful arrest and detention of Moazzam Begg, and in his subsequent release, seven months later, without charge.[8]

The scale of the targeting of Irish people by the original PTA – as well as its questionable efficacy – can be seen in Home Office figures published in 1991, which revealed that tens of thousands of people had been detained, of whom 3.1 per cent had been charged with offences under the PTA.[9] The role of the media in inflaming hostility was noted by Harry Disley, the duty solicitor called in October 1974 to defend Pat O'Neill, who had been charged, with Giuseppe Conlon and the Maguire family, with making the Guildford bomb. Six years later, in February 1980, shortly after the death of Giuseppe in prison, in an interview with Gavin Esler for the BBC *Spotlight* programme 'Giuseppe Conlon and the Bomb Factory', Disley described the 'propagandising by the local gendarmerie' which had led him and his fellow lawyers to believe that, in their clients, they would be meeting 'some kind of monsters quite unknown to us'. In no doubt of O'Neill's innocence, Disley expresses disappointment that the justice system, in which he'd had faith all his life, convicted and sentenced O'Neill to prison for twelve years. Asked why this had happened, Disley replies: 'I'm no left-winger … but it's obvious: the almost hysterical anti-Irish feeling at the time – it was constantly being whipped up by the press of this country – much was lost in this wave of feeling.'[10]

Disley's Irish as 'some sort of monster quite unknown to us' had been embedded in people's minds for centuries, laid down by dominant Anglo-Norman and English/British narratives. In 1188, Giraldus Cambrensis (Gerald of Wales) had set the ball rolling in his survey commissioned by FitzGerald and FitzHenry, the Norman nobles who undertook the invasion of Ireland, describing the Irish, who did not live in towns or villages, as 'so barbarous that they cannot be said to have any culture ... They live on beasts only, and live like beasts'.[11] 'This is a filthy people, wallowing in vice.'[12] This view persisted into the early modern period, suiting the colonial project of taking civilisation to the savages.

Shakespeare, in *Henry V*, set during the 1415 siege of Harfleur, presents further signifiers of Irishness in the words of the Irish Captain Macmorris: 'My nation? What ish my nation? Ish a villain, and a basterd, and a knave, and a rascal. What ish my nation? Who talks of my nation?'[13] Here, Shakespeare is writing in April 1599, soon after his patron, the Earl of Southampton, set sail for Ireland to crush the rebellion of Hugh O'Neill, Earl of Tyrone. Shakespeare's script has his Irish captain uttering the aspirations of the Elizabethan State, voicing his own deference to patronage, while playing to his audience's fondness for racial stereotyping. Condemned out of their own mouths, the Irish are firmly fixed in their villainous nature. The implication is that the English are superior to the Irish – just as they were to the French who had surrendered Harfleur – and will defeat them. The foolish 'stage Irishman' used here by Shakespeare was to become a stock figure on the English stage.

This abject depiction of the Irish clashed with another view. For English Literature 'O' and 'A' level courses at school, I read writers, lauded by my teachers, whom I knew to be Irish. The patterns of their syntax, their vocabulary and imagery, were as familiar to me as water. The language of Joyce felt like mine. I'd known Oscar Wilde and his mother, the poet Speranza, since childhood. The Brontë sisters' Irish father had changed his name in order to get on in England. In Heathcliff, Emily created the abused, 'othered', Irish gypsy boy. Yeats was Irish, as were Sterne, Congreve, Sheridan, Lord Dunsany, Oliver Goldsmith, Beckett, Synge, Swift – and so on. Knowing this, and not having it validated, was bewildering. Doubting myself, I asked my (English) English teacher: Aren't these writers Irish? Well no, she said. This is English Literature. Her message was clear: if something has status, it cannot be 'Irish'; instead, we'll appropriate it for ourselves.

Indeed, more acceptable representations of the Irish as barbarous buffoons had flourished for some time. Among a stream of delightful nineteenth-century cartoons in *Punch*, in which the Irish are depicted variously as Caliban, vampires and monsters, is one by Tenniel, who, on 29 October 1881, depicts a human chimpanzee wielding a rock and wearing an 'Anarchy' band on his hat, being kept at bay by the upstanding figure of Britannia, wielding her sword of justice.[14] Tenniel later portrayed the Irish Home Rule movement as the 'Irish Frankenstein' in his cartoon of 20 May 1882, conflating Mary Shelley's scientist, Frankenstein, with the supposed bestiality of the creature he had created.[15]

By the 1950s and 1960s, the Irish were included in the 'No Blacks. No Irish. No Dogs' injunctions displayed in windows in London. I saw that explaining these to me, his child, in response to my curiosity shamed my father. A desire to resist this shame (in Poly Styrene's fabulous words: 'Oh Bondage! Up yours!'[16]) began to shimmer in me, as anti-Irish racism in the 1970s settled into 'good-humoured banter'. Switching on Radio 1 every morning, we were regaled with charming 'jokes' whose punch-line depended on the equation Irish equals 'thick' plus monstrous. In the print media, a Cummings cartoon from the *Daily Express* in August 1971, as delineated by John Kirkaldy, sets the tone for the decade: 'the idiot Irishman ... holds a pistol in each hand to his temples and the caption reads: I'm the last surviving Irishman – but not for long – my left hand won't allow my right hand to have the last word in the argument.'[17] Thus, the war in Ireland, stripped of historical context, dumped in a political vacuum, is explained by the innate violence of the Irish male. This is amplified in the ugliness of Jak's cartoons in the *Evening Standard*, those from Osbert Lancaster and Cummings in the *Daily Express*, Garland in the *Daily Telegraph* and Emmwood in the *Daily Mail*. All hammered home existing tropes of the supposed savagery of the 'Oirish' person in grotesque, simian depictions, critiqued years later by Liz Curtis in her hugely important book.[18]

Irish people had emigrated from colonial under-development to where the work was: urban Britain. White, but identifiable by their voices, when encountering these degrading views of themselves their response was frequently to keep their heads down and their mouths shut. As an observant child, I noticed how, whenever my parents spoke, people tended to mimic their accents, asking them if they had 'the gift of the gab' or whether they'd kissed the Blarney stone. It is a short step from noting these observations, and their effects upon the adults who are your parents, to internalising this disparaging view of who you and your family are.

Moreover, the young second-generation Irish read the cartoons in the papers, heard the Irish jokes and saw the news in contexts – workplaces and social groups – within which we were expected to collude with these representations of who we were. Many of us had English in-laws. So, in the family homes of our boyfriends or girlfriends, wives or husbands, the unspoken demand for collusion entered the most intimate spaces of our lives. The uneasiness and distress we felt occurred silently, invisibly, and many of us internalised it.

Early on in *Over the Water*, I have Mary say of her mother: 'I hate it when she sounds so Irish. ... Mammy knows no one in our road. She is so afraid of ... her Irish voice that she opens her mouth to no one. She says that we should do the same. "Keep your business to yourself", she says.'[19] Referencing *Over the Water* in her discussion of second-generation identity, Moy McCrory suggests that this 'common image of hiding and burying behaviours, of the life lived indoors and the life lived publically being two different arenas, are a constant feature in second-generation experience'.[20]

Indeed, this double vision can work both ways, often with tragi-comic effect. In 2008, Patrick Maguire writes of the confusion of the armed police who came to his parents' house in London in 1974, when he was thirteen, to round up his bewildered (and totally innocent) family under suspicion of making bombs in his mother's kitchen: '"Are you English or Irish?" asked the policewoman. The police had come expecting Northern Irish accents but we talked like Londoners.'[21] And a little later, when another officer was telling his mother, Annie Maguire, that she would have to go to Paddington Green police station with her children, Mrs Maguire's response was: '"Don't touch them! They're English," she cried.'[22]

Deciding whether you were or were not Irish, or English, or British, or any combination of those, felt like a political act, as indeed did not deciding. Increasingly, to be Irish meant being 'othered' as a member of a suspect community. In 1980, asked by Gavin Esler for the aforementioned BBC *Spotlight* programme, 'Giuseppe Conlon and the Bomb Factory', whether he was English or Irish, Patrick Maguire explained that by law he was British, as he'd been born in Belfast and had moved to London when he was four weeks old. He had family in Ireland, and classed himself a Londoner. Esler's subsequent questioning makes it clear that to be from an Irish family per se was held to be synonymous with being 'in the IRA'.[23] It sweeps away notions of identity as being an ongoing process of becoming, in favour of rigid and narrowing definitions.

For second-generation Irish people at that time, a question was: why do you identify yourself as Irish if you've been born and brought up in England? Certainly, many of us identified ourselves as Londoners, or Liverpudlian, Mancunian, Glaswegian and so forth, rather than as British. If we'd been people of colour, perhaps it might have been obvious. We'd have been 'othered' first and British second, grudgingly, if at all. As it was, as soon as our Irishness became evident, we were definitely not included in whatever was the mainstream culture. The very fact of Esler's question to Maguire, 'Were you in the IRA?', speaks of this. Maguire's rueful laughter in his response, 'No, I was in the Scouts', voices the gap between his sense of who he is, and that projected onto him by the mainstream culture, and the either/or-ness which will not allow him to be an Irish Londoner; only a terrorist.[24]

Looking and sounding the same as everybody else, the second generation had grown up imbued with signifiers of Englishness as being superior and somehow safe, as voiced in Annie Maguire's appeal to the police. I have Mary express this when she gazes at idealised holiday adverts on the wall of the railway carriage taking her out of England, through Wales to Holyhead, where her family will embark for Dun Laoghaire, Éire. 'English sounding places ... Stratford-on-Avon and Walton-on-the-Naze ... cosy with the Englishness of crumpets and tea, of evening fires and Agatha Christie, of everything being all right in the end', from which she is excluded, facing 'the icy black water ahead'.[25]

This long, dark train journey from Euston to Holyhead, followed by the gruelling passage on the ferry packed with families hunched over heaps of baggage in the dead of night, was an iconic ritual for Irish people, whether Irish-born 'exiles' or second generation. Calling upon its haunting liminality, I make 'the passage' over the water the place where Mary's father tells her the story of the Famine and its ghosts. This enormous nineteenth-century trauma (for which the word 'event' feels flat and inadequate) became viscerally lived experience for the second generation, in the telling and retelling of family history. Like many other lesser shocks, its effects were managed by the process of an utterance of pain transmitted down the generations. The schism of Partition; the shooting of Michael Collins; the torture and execution of Roger Casement; the violent rampages of the Black and Tans through Ireland in 1919–20; the slaughter of cattle in the bogs during Britain's trade embargo; the haunted silences of the Civil War – all of these became alive in my father's retelling. I felt I'd lived them myself; they entered my own memory.

Diarmaid Ferriter and Colm Tóibín have brought to our attention texts which document the deaths of a few of those people – some say a million between 1846 and 1849; some say twice that number – who died in the Famine. These record the discovery of people's bodies, often huddled together so as to die together. Occasionally, the people are named, recognised by those who found them, with haunting clarity: 'Mary, found dead by a rick of turf; Philip M'Gowan's wife and daughter; Bryan Flanagan, found dead by the roadside.' As Tóibín says: 'the names allow you to imagine them; to think you may have known them'. And Tóibín highlights a difficulty relevant here, which, he says, 'may lie in the relationship between catastrophe and analytic narrative. How do you write about the Famine? What tone do you use?'[26]

The shock waves of a catastrophe on such a scale were so terrible that they prowled down the generations, haunting people – like my own father, for whom it was animated by the lived experience of his grandparents. What kept people going was the recounting of these things to one another, over and over again, in whispered litanies of call and response, sometimes overheard by a child at the corner of a door.

Thus, the Famine came alive for my father – and today, with our growing understanding of post-traumatic stress disorder and vicarious trauma, we know that recounting the unspeakable trauma can bring it to life; can cause time travel to occur; can crack the laws of physics. When recounting details of which he could barely speak, leaving unsaid others whose vast silences resound in my psyche still, my father showed that he, and therefore I, had emerged from a collective grief that had to be passed on: a hunger of the heart and soul, trapped within the memory for generations. These grievous things hang like ghosts lodged within the stones of a house where terrible things were done, terrible choices made.

This was not something his children wanted to hear; we were irritated by reiterated evocations of past torments. For the Irish in Britain, the truth, and the things calling for reparation, were, and are, layered, complicated and still haunted by absence and silence. I convey this additional, second-generational unease, in the irritation and guilt Mary feels at the horrors her father recounts as the boat ploughs through the darkness.

In the 1980s, the litany of repression and shock continued, born of an idea of 'Irishness' which summoned increasingly inhumane responses. The strip searching, force feeding and deaths of young Irish women and men in British jails, and the deaths of the hunger strikers, chillingly expressed the obduracy of the British State in maintaining its interests.

It is hard enough sustaining naked aggression from one person in the street: experiencing it on a daily basis from a state which is targeting you precisely because you are who you are, is very hard. And if you're expected to snigger along with those who belittle 'your lot' as 'a bit Oirish' whenever there is an Irish 'joke' on the radio, and who show their fear and hatred of you for being Irish, the psychological strain is considerable.

Research by Bronwen Walter, presented to the Runnymede Trust's Commission on the Future of Multi-Ethnic Britain, bears this out. Walter collates figures on the size, patterns of settlement, social class, housing conditions and health of the self-identified Irish community in Britain. Figures on illness and causes of death are sobering. Irish-born men are 'the only migrant group whose mortality is higher in Britain than in their country of origin'. In 1981, rates of admission to psychiatric hospitals per 100,000 for Irish-born women from the Republic were 1,167, as compared to 485 for women from England and Wales; 35 per cent of these admissions were for depression.[27] Walter endorses the conclusion reached by Kelleher and Hillier in their investigation into the health of the Irish in England, that 'material and cultural factors interact to create a sense of low self-esteem' in both first and second generations.[28]

As migrants, Irish women often found a crucial sense of community within the parochial activities of the Catholic church in Britain. However, equally, their lives were shadowed by a fear of shame and disgrace. A consequence of the British strategy, after the French Revolution in 1789, of funding and developing as a teaching seminary St Patrick's College of Maynooth, was to create a repressive, parochial Catholicism in Ireland. Henceforth, priests, no longer educated in European seminaries, were given a narrow curriculum based upon rote learning and the catechism, rather than upon the lively debate fostered hitherto by study of the classics and a wide range of theological texts. British Prime Minister Peel's furtherance of this strategy in 1845 appears to have been to snuff out European-influenced republicanism.[29] Certainly, it resulted in extraordinarily cruel and harsh repression of women, for whom the most terrible fate imaginable was to 'get into trouble' by becoming pregnant out of wedlock. The suffering of the unmarried mother and her 'illegitimate' child are now increasingly well documented, as too are the revelations concerning those institutions of the Catholic church tasked with dealing with them. In such an atmosphere, the pressure felt by Irish women in England, in those pre-abortion, pre-contraception days, to bring up their daughters 'modestly', so as to avoid shame and disgrace back home, was considerable. Even today, unwanted pregnancy haunts Irish women. Between January 1980 and December 2013, at least 159,779 women travelled from the Republic of Ireland to access safe abortion services, an estimated twelve a day to England.[30]

I set *Over the Water* in Ireland, during the summer, when many Irish emigrants took their children back to their extended families. Thus, I could speak to Mary's confusion in growing up Irish in London, as well as to that of Bridie, her mother, in bringing up her children in an alien land. I set it in the mid 1960s, when young Londoners were aware of setting new, 'swinging' agendas. So Mary, longing to be stylish like her contemporaries, mortifies her mother with her mini-skirts and Levis, never before seen in Irish lanes.

Both Mary and Bridie endure the strain of the constraints upon them: Mary, in her struggles to resist them and her mother in her attempts to impose them. Her mother has internalised the strictures placed upon women by postcolonial under-development. Blows to her pride and self-esteem in her beleaguered life in London have led her to make few ties there. Instead, she plans all year for the few weeks spent on her parents' farm in Ireland – but once there, she is judged on the behaviour of her children, internalising censorious views of Mary as an object of unease: as a teenage young woman; as alien; as not quite Irish enough. This experience was shared by many women of Bridie's generation.

My wish to assert a young woman's right to autonomy over her own body prompted my account of Mary having her period, which Bridie, projecting the shame imposed on her during her own puberty, calls 'that thing'. In naming Mary, I embody divergent possibilities presented to her as a young Irish woman. Named after the Blessed Virgin, Mary grapples with the constraints upon her sexuality imposed by the church. Her second name, Maeve, is that of Medbh, the multiply wedded pre-Christian ruler of Connaught, who embodies woman as agent of her own life and equal of the men she partnered.

I use retellings of Medbh's conversation with her husband Ailil, of whom she asks that he be 'her equal in bravery, in grace and in generosity' and 'free of envy and meanness',[31] in order to highlight inequalities between men and women, and women's struggle to survive them. As she sits among the women in the segregated benches of the village church, I have Mary transfer her allegiance from the meek Virgin to the Irish triple deity Brighid, whose essence as goddess of poetry, fire, smelting, smithing, healing and whistling in the dark, is syncretised with St Brigit, Catholic patron saint of Ireland, whose statue gazes down on her, and after whom her mother, Bridie, is named.

In England, Irish people like Bridie had kept to themselves, in churches, in Irish clubs and in the pages of the *Irish Post*. Founded in 1970, this created a conduit of communication for Irish people in Britain, whether first or second generation, as the effects of the PTA took hold from 1974 onwards. Its circulation went up from 29,000 to 78,000 by the early 1980s and it was estimated that each copy of the paper was read by 5.5 people.[32] Speaking to Steve Biko's words: 'The most potent weapon in the hand of the oppressor is the mind of the oppressed', it was one part of a process ignited later by Ngugi wa Thiong'o's mind-blowing phrase 'decolonising the mind'.[33] The learning of the Irish language and explorations of Irish mythology were part of this process, as were the wearing of the Tara brooch and Claddagh ring: reminders that, before colonisation, Irish gold and silversmiths were among the most skilful in the world. As a young teenager, my first viewing of the Broichter hoard, with its gorgeously worked golden torc and exquisite miniature boat, from the first century AD, had been a significant milestone in self-definition. It was the first time that I'd experienced something 'Irish' as being not abject; the first time my own mind began an ongoing process of decolonisation.

In 1981, after the deaths of the hunger strikers, anti-Irish hostility intensified. The Irish in Britain Representation Group (IBRG) was founded, at a time when, in the words of Gearoid MacGearailt, IBRG *cathaoirleach* (chair) in the mid 1980s, 'Irish politics were encroaching very emotionally into every household in Britain'.[34] In this climate, the founding of the IBRG was a boost for many first- and second-generation Irish people. Condemning the PTA and British government policy on Northern Ireland, the IBRG was also critical of the stance of the Irish government on divorce, abortion, equal rights for lesbian and gay people and the forced emigration of Irish youth. Its agenda was one of civil rights and social justice; soon branches sprang up all over England.

Also in 1981, a number of inspiring initiatives by Irish people received funding, following the election of Ken Livingstone as Leader of the Greater London Council, and of John McDonnell as Chair of Finance. Policies of multiculturalism, anti-racism and equal rights were translated, in McDonnell's words, into 'concrete realities on the ground'.[35] These included the founding of the London Irish Women's Centre (LIWC) in 1983 and of Green Ink Writers, who went on to found Green Ink Bookshop in 1987, and a range of research and reports on the Irish in Britain commissioned by the London Strategic Policy Unit.[36]

The LIWC gave a space for women to share experiences, which were complex and frequently conflicted. Irish women forced to emigrate from Catholic Ireland in order to claim ownership of their own bodies became targets of the PTA in England. Sometimes they viewed second-generation Irish women, with their London accents, as not being properly Irish, and as being somehow protected by their perceived Englishness. In turn, second-generation women often felt that their self-identification as Irish and their wish to learn the language of their parents and grandparents was ridiculed by first-generation women. Traveller women, supported by the Centre, were occasionally the targets of racism from Irish women – and indeed Ireland today, with its increasingly diverse demography, continues to examine its own racisms, particularly over the sexuality of immigrant women. Running through all of this complexity, there was a mutual sense that Ireland itself had washed its hands of all of us, with particular blind spots for the border, homosexuality and women in general. Michelle Deignan's 2013 film on the LIWC, *Breaking Ground*,[37] documents women's attempts to break taboos – domestic violence; mental illness; abortion; contraception – within a space that was collaborative and supportive. The LIWC did provide a safe space for many women and facilitated a process of thinking of ourselves as survivors, rather than as victims.

Two iconic texts published in 1984 and 1985 contributed to this process of validation for many of us. In *Only the Rivers Run Free: Northern Ireland: The Women's War*,[38] the voices of Irish women maintaining family life and a sense of community in Britain's war reached a wider audience. And Moy McCrory's collection of short stories, *The Water's Edge*,[39] gives utterance to the confident, witty, sometimes hilarious voices of second-generation young women. Self-esteem increases when seeing your experience affirmed in print. Reading these texts was part of my own continuing journey towards self-definition.

Writing fiction is a way of exploring – of having a look, of delving, of treading the precipice, of mapping – at the controls of your own star-ship. The act of writing, painful as it frequently is, is also an exhilarating form of resistance. Those who write are survivors. I re-read Irish forebears: the *Táin Bó Cúailgne*, the Fenian Cycle; as well as calling upon writers from Irish, English, American and African literatures. I recalled the powers of the *seanchaithe* – keepers of word-hoard and lore from the past; transmitters of memory and history – to embody mood, nuance and voice: these performer/storytellers were and are magicians of lighting and vocal sound effect. I channelled their use of repetition, rhyme, rhythm and idiom, weaving a skein of yarns: a psychic layering: a geology and geography of stories; a creation of new space.

As a young writer, I wanted the novel to embody Mary's struggle to be reborn as herself, through harvest, fire, song and sea, and to survive. I wanted it to call to other women and men in exile from themselves. Fear and anguish were transformed as Mary began to channel the strong heartbeat of resistance, in order to imagine a new space into being. Today, almost three decades later, as the 'war on terror' whips up fear of the migrant, 'the other', and engulfs the entire globe in proxy wars, and as climate change hovers around our horizons like the *Bean Sidhe* scratching at the door,[40] the need for us to collaborate in imagining new spaces of hope and resistance is even more urgent.

Notes

1 M. Casey, *Over the Water* (London: Women's Press, 1987).

2 R. Jenkins, House of Commons debate on Terrorism, in *Hansard*, House of Commons Debate, 25 November 1974, vol. 882 col. 35, available at: http://hansard.millbanksystems.com/commons/1974/nov/25/terrorism (Accessed 7 November 2014).

3 R. De Lanerolle, 'Publishing against the other censorship', *Index on Censorship*, 19:9 (1990), 8–9.

4 Casey, *Over the Water*, p. 1.

5 *Irish Post* (12 July 2014).

6 P. Donovan, 'The new Irish', *Guardian* (7 August 2006).

7 H. McDonald and M. Townsend, 'Guildford Four's Gerry Conlon dies of cancer in Belfast', *Observer* (22 June 2014).

8 See 'Moazzam Begg released after terror charges dropped', *BBC News*, 1 October 2014, www.bbc.co.uk/news/uk-29442623 (Accessed 7 November 2014).

9 *Statewatch*, 2 (May/June, 1991), www.radstats.org.uk/no049/statewatch.pdf (Accessed 14 July 2014). See chapter 10 by Finch in this volume.

10 'Giuseppe Conlon and the bomb factory', *BBC Spotlight*, broadcast BBC1 Northern Ireland, 26 February 1980. See the clip of Gavin Esler speaking to Disley and Belfast solicitor Ted Jones: www.bbc.co.uk/programmes/p00hvbwd (Accessed 7 November 2014).

11 Gerald of Wales, *The History and Topography of Ireland*, trans. J. O Meara (Harmondsworth: Penguin, 1982), p. 101.

12 Ibid., p. 106.

13 William Shakespeare, *Henry V*, Act III, scene 2, 123–5.

14 John Tenniel cartoon, 'Two Forces: Irish Land League outlawed. Britannia protects Hibernia (Ireland) with the Force of Law against the Force of Anarchy', *Punch* (29 October 1881); available at www.bridgemanimages.com/en-GB/asset/527702// (Accessed 7 November 2014).

15 John Tenniel cartoon, 'The Irish Frankenstein', *Punch* (20 May 1882); available at www.haverford.edu/engl/faculty/Sherman/Irish/19thc..htm (Accessed 7 November 2014).

16 X-Ray Spex, 'Oh Bondage Up Yours!' (Virgin Records, 1977). Lyric by Poly Styrene (Marianne Elliott-Said), TRO Inc 1977.

17 J. Kirkaldy, 'English cartoonists; Ulster realities', in Y. Alexander and A. O'Day (eds), *Ireland's Terrorist Dilemmas* (Dordrecht: Martinus Nijhoff, 1986), p. 27.

18 L. Curtis, *Nothing but the Same Old Story: The Roots of Anti-Irish Racism* (London: Information on Ireland, 1984).

19 Casey, *Over the Water*, p. 2.

20 M. McCrory, '"This time and now": Identity and belonging in the Irish diaspora', in C. Berberich, N. Campbell and R. Hudson (eds), *Land and Identity. Theory, Memory, and Practice* (Amsterdam and New York: Rodopi, 2012), p. 21.

21 P. Maguire and C. Gebler, *My Father's Watch: The Story of a Child Prisoner in 70s Britain* (London: Fourth Estate, 2008), p. 108.

22 Ibid., p. 109.
23 'Giuseppe Conlon and the Bomb Factory'. See the clip of Gavin Esler inter-
    viewing Patrick Maguire: www.bbc.co.uk/programmes/p00hv7w4/ (Accessed
    7 November 2014).
24 Ibid.
25 Casey, *Over the Water*, p. 15.
26 C. Tóibín and D. Ferriter, *The Irish Famine* (London: Profile Books, 2004), p. 9.
27 B. Walter, 'The Irish community in Britain – diversity, disadvantage and dis-
    crimination', paper presented to the Commission on the Future of Multi-Ethnic
    Britain, 18 June 1999, available at www.runnymedetrust.org/bgIrishCommunity.
    html (no page numbers) (Accessed 7 November 2014).
28 Ibid., quoting D. Kelleher and S. Hillier, 'The health of the Irish in England',
    in D. Kelleher and S. Hillier (eds), *Researching Cultural Differences in Health*
    (London: Routledge, 1996), pp. 103–23 (p. 120).
29 A. Jackson, *Ireland 1798–1998* (Oxford: Blackwell, 1999), pp. 51–4. Here,
    Jackson cites: D. Kerr, *Peel, Priests and Politics: Sir Robert Peel's Administration
    and the Roman Catholic Church in Ireland 1841–46* (Oxford: Clarendon, 1982).
30 Irish Family Planning Association website, www.ifpa.ie/HotTopics/Abortion/
    Statistics (Accessed 7 November 2014).
31 Casey, *Over the Water*, p. 138.
32 B. O hEithir, 'From Clare to here', *Magill*, 9:12 (August 1986), 40.
33 S. Biko, 'White racism and Black Consciousness', in *I Write What I Like: Selected
    Writings* (Chicago: University of Chicago Press, 2002), p. 68; N. wa Thiong'o,
    Decolonising the Mind (London: James Currey, 1986).
34 Quoted in M. Herbert, *The Wearing of the Green* (London: Irish in Britain
    Representation Group, 2001), p. 177. This is an invaluable resource for students
    of the political history of the Irish in Manchester, but also of the IBRG nationally.
35 Quoted in R. Bennett, 'Honest John', *Guardian* (26 September 2006).
36 Publications by the London Strategic Policy Unit (LSPU) include: T. Connor,
    The London Irish (London: LSPU, 1987); B. Walter, *Irish Women in London*
    (London: LSPU, 1988); LSPU Policy Monitoring and Research Group, *Policing
    the Irish Community* (London: LSPU, 1988); *Working Together to End Strip
    Searching: Report of a Conference, 5 December 1987* (London: LSPU, 1988);
    the photo-text exhibition by L. Curtis, J. O'Keeffe, C. Keatinge and J. O'Brien,
    *Hearts and Minds = Anam Agus Intinn: The Cultural Life of London's Irish
    Community* (London: LSPU, 1987); as well as the *Britain and Ireland* teaching
    resources published by the Inner London Education Authority in 1989. See also
    chapters by Rossiter (11) and Finch (10) in this volume.
37 *Breaking Ground: The Story of the London Irish Women's Centre* (dir. Michelle
    Deignan, Toy Factory Films, 2013). See www.breakinggroundfilm.com/.
38 E. Fairweather, M. MacFadyean and R. McDonagh, *Only the Rivers Run Free:
    Northern Ireland: The Women's War* (London: Pluto Press, 1984).
39 M. McCrory, *The Water's Edge* (London: Sheba Feminist Press, 1985).
40 Anglicised as *banshee*, in Irish mythology and folklore the *Bean Sidhe* is the
    spirit whose wailing call or keening is said to herald the imminence of death.

16

The 'oxygen of publicity' and the suffocation of censorship: national newspaper representations of the British broadcasting ban (1988–94)

Max Pettigrew

The Northern Ireland conflict was conducted through a combination of war, words and silence.[1] Besides the obvious physical aspect of the conflict, discursive and censorship battles were inseparable aspects too. This chapter examines a crucial period in which the conflict shifted into the peace process. It was also a period that saw direct censorship over the British broadcast media. Whereas indirect censorship had been operating behind the scenes since Partition and continued throughout the Northern Ireland conflict, the broadcasting ban went further by directly controlling access to the British broadcast media.

The ban made it illegal for broadcasters to give the 'oxygen of publicity' to representatives of eleven republican and loyalist organisations, thus ensuring that the British government's perspective on the conflict dominated the airwaves in England, Wales, Scotland and Northern Ireland.[2] Not only was the broadcasting ban the most severe assault on media freedom during the Northern Ireland conflict, it also amounted to the most stringent control of the broadcast media in Britain since the Second World War.[3] Unsurprisingly, then, a United Nations report on civil and political rights, which gave special attention to freedom of expression, stated that the British broadcasting ban amounted to official censorship and 'reduced knowledge and understanding of the conflict'.[4]

Several studies have analysed how the ban impacted on the British broadcast media.[5] However, very little research has examined how the British newspaper industry reacted to the introduction of the ban on 19 October 1988 and its lifting six years later, on 16 September 1994. This chapter explores how national newspapers, which were not bound by official censorship, represented the broadcasting ban and how support for and resistance to the ban were refracted through the different genres and political allegiances of the British newspaper industry.

Romanticised notions of journalism suggest that the media act as watchdog on the powerful, exposing abuses of the State.[7] However, such a view ignores the economic context to the production of news, the power of newspaper owners over journalistic content, as well as the similar class and ideological positions shared by newspaper owners and those in government.[8] Indeed, far from being champions of media freedom, this study found that several newspapers overtly supported direct censorship against the broadcast media in their editorials. Similarly, these newspapers used their editorials to attack media workers upholding the first principle of the National Union of Journalists' (NUJ) Code of Conduct, which states that a journalist: 'At all times upholds and defends the principle of media freedom, the right of freedom of expression and the right of the public to be informed'.[9]

Media silence, compliance and resistance

In essence, British media reporting of Northern Ireland oscillated between media silence, compliance and resistance. Following Partition, the BBC monopolised broadcasting in Northern Ireland and worked in the interests of Westminster and Stormont, which meant avoiding certain subjects. Ostensibly, the media silence was to prevent disorder, violence and lives being lost, but it also prevented debate on serious issues such as Partition itself and the discrimination faced by the Catholic community.[10] It was only after the civil rights movement in Northern Ireland gained momentum in the mid to late 1960s and was attacked by the Royal Ulster Constabulary (RUC) that the British and international media were compelled to cover the tensions in Northern Ireland.[11]

As Northern Ireland descended into a war zone in the late 1960s and early 1970s, the media became a central tool in the propaganda war.[12] Following an increase in the British government's pressure on the broadcast media, the BBC and ITV (Independent Television) introduced the 'reference upwards' system in 1971. This system was a form of war reporting that operated to restrict what information could be communicated by the broadcasters. Unsurprisingly, it narrowed the parameters of debate, excluded republican voices, encouraged journalists to engage in self-censorship and deterred investigative journalism.[13] 'Anti-terrorist' legislation was also used to control both broadcast and newspaper reporting of Northern Ireland.[14]

In the 1970s and 1980s, censorship battles intensified between the British government and the broadcast media, with the former most often successfully limiting what the latter could say. Despite resistance from organised media workers defending the first principle of their union's

Code of Conduct, more than seventy programmes were cut or delayed before the broadcasting ban was introduced.[15] Furthermore, an increasingly hostile relationship had developed between the British government and the broadcast media following 'major rows over the Falklands [in 1982] and the coverage of the miners' strike in 1984/85'.[16] In addition, in June 1985, as *Real Lives – At the Edge of the Union* (a BBC documentary that interviewed Martin McGuinness of Sinn Féin) was being edited, a Trans World Airlines aircraft was hijacked by members of Hezbollah and held at Beirut for several weeks.[17] The hostage crisis was covered live in the United States and broadcast worldwide on CNN (Cable News Network).[18] After American broadcasters allowed the hijackers to express their political motivations through interviews and press releases, Prime Minister Margaret Thatcher gave a speech at the American Bar Association in London in July 1985 arguing that a symbiotic relationship existed between the media and 'terrorism' and that 'terrorists' should be starved of the 'oxygen of publicity on which they depend'.[19]

Initially, there was no BBC fall-out from Thatcher's speech and *Real Lives* was cleared for broadcast, until one of Rupert Murdoch's newspapers, the *Sunday Times*, alerted British politicians to a documentary 'giving space to terrorists'.[20] What followed was a request from British Home Secretary Leon Brittan urging the governors of the BBC to censor the documentary, echoing Thatcher's words that giving a platform to 'terrorists' would assist their objectives. Although the BBC Board of Governors complied with this government request, *Real Lives* was eventually shown on television two months later, following resistance from organised media workers and protestations from some of the British newspaper industry.[21]

Another major censorship battle between the British government and broadcasters took place in 1988 in the aftermath of the Gibraltar controversy, where three surrendering IRA members were executed by the Special Air Service on 6 March 1988. The discovery of eye-witnesses by the programme-makers of *Death on the Rock* suggested a 'shoot-to-kill' policy was in operation, which infuriated the British government.[22] The failed attempt to censor the ITV documentary revealed the limitations of Westminster's indirect approach of pressuring British broadcasters.

The final series of events that laid the ground for the broadcasting ban related to the IRA's summer offensive of 1988, which involved attacks on a British military base in Germany, as well as attacks against British military personnel in England and Northern Ireland.[23] In May, Thatcher complained that the media were giving the IRA too much publicity and ordered a high-level security review. The broadcasting ban was favoured over internment because the latter had been a disaster for the British government in the 1970s.[24]

The broadcasting ban (1988–94)

The broadcasting ban was introduced in the House of Commons by the British Home Secretary, Douglas Hurd, on 19 October 1988. Firstly, he argued that broadcast statements from, and interviews with, representatives of paramilitary organisations and their political wings had caused offence to the public. Secondly, he claimed that 'terrorists who draw support and sustenance from having access to radio and television' had been given an 'easy platform' by broadcasters to 'propagate terrorism'. Thirdly, he emphasised that the 'restrictions' of the broadcasting ban closely followed those operating in the Irish Republic.[25]

Decades of government pressure had ensured that republican voices were rarely heard in the British broadcast media long before the broadcasting ban was introduced, and if they were interviewed it was often in a hostile manner. The Labour deputy leader, Roy Hattersley, acknowledged this when he stated that the total length of interviews with Sinn Féin and its supporters on ITV in the whole of 1988 was a mere four minutes: 'Three minutes and 59 seconds of that were, he claimed, hostile to Sinn Féin.'[26] In short, the 'easy platform' that Hurd spoke of in his second justification for the ban simply did not exist. IRA members had not been interviewed by the BBC or ITV since 1974 and the Irish National Liberation Army was last interviewed in 1979.[27] A study of Sinn Féin appearances on television news highlighted the limited access given to it before the broadcasting ban was introduced and how the number of interviews with Sinn Féin further decreased afterwards.[28]

The vague language used in Hurd's directive left the interpretation of the ban largely to the broadcasters, which led to an over-cautious application of it.[29] It was far easier for broadcasters to not interview Sinn Féin representatives at all than to risk contravening the new censorship legislation. Consequently, 'the ban played a crucial role in containment by making the possibility of open debate difficult'.[30] The BBC even censored an episode of Star Trek in which Captain Picard and Lieutenant Commander Data discussed the history and meaning of 'terrorism' because it referred to a United Ireland being achieved in 2024 following a successful armed rebellion.[31]

Another outcome of the ban was the difficulty documentary-makers faced in making serious, in-depth, factual programmes on Northern Ireland.[32] That said, there were opportunities for the broadcasters to circumvent the broadcasting ban. One strategy was to dub the broadcast statements of the banned organisations by using actors with similar accents, which were often out of sync.[33] Using subtitles was another strategy.[34] For example, after the Pogues' song about the Birmingham Six and Guildford Four was banned, Independent Television News reported the decision by showing footage of the Pogues in concert whilst rolling the words of the song up on the screen and reciting them.[35] Overall though, the broadcasting ban had a serious impact on media output, further encouraging self-censorship and ensuring that the British government perspective dominated British broadcast media representations of the Northern Ireland conflict.[36]

The third justification Douglas Hurd gave for the broadcasting ban related to censorship in the Irish Republic. It was certainly true that the Irish Republic had used direct censorship against republican voices since the early 1970s.[37] In fact, the Irish broadcasting ban was harsher than the British broadcasting ban in a number of ways: it banned the broadcast of interviews *and* reports of interviews with proscribed organisations as well as party political broadcasts, election coverage and reporting of debates in the Houses of Parliament concerning these organisations, which the British ban did not. That said, one area where the British censorship was stricter than the Irish censorship was the ban on historical footage of proscribed organisations.[38] The Irish broadcasting ban was lifted in early 1994 as part of the peace process. This and the IRA ceasefire on 31 August led to the British government lifting its own broadcasting ban on 16 September.[39]

British newspaper representations of the broadcasting ban

The newspaper industry was not bound by official censorship, but that did not mean that journalists were free from other pressures influencing British newspaper representations of the broadcasting ban and the Northern Ireland conflict more broadly. Newspaper journalists were affected by certain sections of 'anti-terrorist' legislation, which limited their capacity to report the conflict freely and encouraged self-censorship. However, it appears that British newspaper journalists were more restricted by their working conditions rather than by British government interference.

There were important industrial disputes in the years leading up to 1988, which can help to explain the relative weakness of British newspaper workers by the time the British government introduced the broadcasting ban. Ten years before, there had been a major industrial dispute between workers and management at *The Times* and the *Sunday Times*.[40] Both sides stood firm and the newspapers were closed for nearly a year. In 1981, contrary to anti-monopoly provisions, Margaret Thatcher allowed Rupert Murdoch to purchase both newspapers from the Thomson Company.[41] Murdoch's move to Wapping in 1986 was also critical because it shifted the 'power and money away from the trade unionised labour force [to] owners, managers, and editors'.[42] Just two years before the British government introduced the broadcasting ban, the print unions went on strike in Wapping. The subsequent defeat of the strikers broke the strength of the print workers and weakened the power of journalists because the impact of any future strike action they wished to take could be deflected by using news wire copy printed by the weakened print workers.[43] Bearing this in mind, it is apparent that British newspaper workers were in a weak position when the British government introduced the broadcasting ban in 1988. Although the majority of British newspaper owners were supportive of the Conservative Party, sharing similar class and ideological positions, British journalists did not necessarily share this loyalty, but they had little power in their capacity as workers to challenge the ban.

The generic conventions of 'popular', 'mid-market' and 'quality' newspapers, as well as their political allegiances, also structure journalistic content and reflect the attempts of newspaper owners to appeal to different sections of the newspaper audience, which is divided along class lines. Generic conventions within newspapers also structure the discursive practices of journalists depending on whether it is news articles, editorials or op-eds that are being written, impacting on how social events and social actors are framed and represented. The generic conventions of news articles structure what journalists can say, because news articles allow journalists only to amplify what particular social actors have said about the news story being reported, whereas the generic conventions of op-eds and editorials allow the opinions of journalists and editors to be expressed. Although journalists choose which social actors to include and exclude, the generic conventions of news articles do not allow them to overtly support or oppose these social actors. That said, the framing of reported speech through use of quoting verbs and the naming of social actors from which such reported speech originated can shift representations of the same social events.[44]

This author's research analysed six national newspapers, which were representative of the 'popular', 'mid-market' and 'quality' newspaper genres (the *Sun* and *Daily Mirror*, the *Daily Mail* and *Daily Express*, the *Guardian* and *Daily Telegraph*, respectively). These newspapers were also representative of the political allegiances within each of these genres and had the highest circulations at the time.[45] The sampling period in which newspaper articles were collected for analysis ranged from

1 October 1988 to 6 November 1988, and 29 August 1994 to 4 October 1994, eighteen days either side of the dates the British government introduced and lifted the broadcasting ban.

Content analysis was used to quantify British newspaper representations of the Northern Ireland conflict during these periods and ten categories of newspaper coverage were identified based on the most frequently occurring subjects.[46] The content analysis findings revealed that newspaper articles concerning the broadcasting ban accounted for a small amount of British newspaper coverage of the Northern Ireland conflict in the periods when the ban was introduced and lifted. There were 101 broadcasting ban newspaper articles out of the total of 988 relating to the conflict, just 10.2 per cent of the coverage. There were also forty-four mentions of the broadcasting ban in newspaper articles where the main subject of the story was something else relating to the Northern Ireland conflict, 4.7 per cent of the total. Thus it can be said that the broadcasting ban was not considered particularly newsworthy by the British newspaper industry in general.

More specifically, the newsworthiness of the broadcasting ban was dependent on the sampling period and on the newspaper genre. There were considerably more newspaper articles concerning the broadcasting ban when the British government introduced it (seventy-three articles) than when the British government lifted it (twenty-eight articles). This can be attributed to the newspaper articles reflecting the division amongst politicians and other elite social actors over whether to support the broadcasting ban at the beginning. There were also considerably more newspaper articles concerning the broadcasting ban in newspapers representative of the 'quality' press, which accounted for just over half of the 101 broadcasting ban newspaper articles, with 51. This can be explained by the assumed audience demographic of this newspaper genre as editors of the *Guardian* and the *Daily Telegraph* expect their readers to be better educated and more interested in serious news.

The content analysis also revealed that there was a broader range of discourses circulating in the newspaper articles in 1988, as compared to 1994. This is understandable, as there was elite division as to whether media censorship was appropriate for dealing with the Northern Ireland conflict in 1988. By the time the broadcasting ban was lifted in 1994, the elite was united in its opposition to it, which meant a narrower range of discourses. This discursive battle over the legitimacy of the broadcasting ban will now be explored to remember how it was refracted by the British newspaper industry.

Foregrounding and naming the republican movement

During the period when the British government introduced the broadcasting ban, the most frequently expressed discourses in newspaper articles about the ban foregrounded the republican movement as its main targets (fifty-one times) and represented them in pejorative ways (forty-four times). Republican combatants were represented as 'terrorists', 'extremists', 'gangsters', 'godfathers', 'murderers', 'bombers' and 'killers' and Sinn Féin was represented as a 'front', 'mouthpiece' and 'apologist' for the IRA. These interdiscursive constructions were most prominent in newspapers that editorially supported the British government introducing the broadcasting ban, such as the *Sun*, *Daily Mail*, *Daily Express* and *Daily Telegraph*.

That said, the *Guardian*, which was ambivalent towards the ban in its editorials, and the *Daily Mirror*, which was the only newspaper to consistently oppose the ban in its editorials, also represented republicans in this way. Essentially, the violence of republicans was foregrounded, while their political motivations were backgrounded. Several scholars have acknowledged that the British government attempted to depoliticise and de-legitimise the motivations of the republican movement by representing republicans as 'terrorists' and 'criminals'.[47] Therefore, it is hardly surprising that journalists working for British newspapers overwhelmingly amplified this representation.

Starving the 'terrorists' of the 'oxygen of publicity'

Discourses emanating from the British government were frequently expressed in newspaper articles representing the introduction of the broadcasting ban. The discourse arguing that 'terrorists' must be starved of the 'oxygen of publicity' was expressed thirty-four times and can be traced back to the speech Margaret Thatcher made in 1985 at the American Bar Association in London. Although the meaning of this discourse was rarely explained or contextualised in newspaper articles, it was often attributed to her. Arguably, the 'oxygen of publicity' discourse functioned to support the introduction of the broadcasting ban because it perpetuated the British government's contention that the media had given republicans a platform to express their views. As this discourse was dominant in newspaper articles and was mostly repeated without challenge by journalists, it stifled alternative discourses that emphasised the need to understand and alleviate the causes of the conflict. Interestingly, in the same speech Thatcher also said: 'In our societies we do not believe in constraining the media, still less in censorship' and, quoting Benjamin Franklin, '[t]hose who would give up essential liberty to preserve a little temporary safety deserve neither liberty nor safety'.[48] However, none of the journalists chose to acknowledge these points in their newspaper articles, which would have undermined the legitimacy of the British government's introducing direct censorship three years later.

In addition, by excluding the history of the British government's indirect censorship of the British media throughout the Northern Ireland conflict, journalists failed to acknowledge and inform their readers that the direct censorship of the broadcasting ban was merely an extension of this policy. Only one journalist, Richard Norton-Taylor of the *Guardian*, made this connection: 'For 17 years, television executives and editors have censored programmes about the IRA and Sinn Féin. They have been supported by large sections of the British press.'[49] He also acknowledged that when Labour politicians had attempted to build support for government control of the British media earlier in the Northern Ireland conflict, they had not been averse to exaggerating the extent to which the IRA had access to the BBC, like Northern Ireland Secretary, Roy Mason, who in 1976 'accused the BBC of providing a "daily platform" for the IRA'.[50] Interestingly, this journalist critiques the British newspaper industry itself for joining British politicians in claiming that British broadcasters had been 'irresponsible' or that they should censor particular programmes featuring republican voices. Indeed, another discourse, which represented British broadcasters (especially the BBC) as irresponsible, was expressed sixteen times in newspaper articles covering the British government's introduction of the ban, which clearly compounds the discourse arguing that the 'terrorists' must be starved of the 'oxygen of publicity'.

The 'oxygen of publicity' discourse also builds on those foregrounding and naming the republican movement as possessing a monopoly on acts of 'terrorism'. There was a presupposition that the newspaper reader knew and accepted the identity of the 'terrorists', the meaning of the 'oxygen of publicity' and that the former did indeed thrive on the latter. This discourse, therefore, further normalised the discourse of republicans as 'terrorists'. Representing the 'terrorists' as thriving on the 'oxygen of publicity' also operated on the false premise that those trying to maintain Northern Ireland as part of a British United Kingdom did not.

Opposition to the broadcasting ban

Although discourses emanating from the British government were those most often amplified by newspaper journalists, discourses opposed to the ban were also expressed. Opposition to the broadcasting ban was expressed in two main arguments: either that the ban was a 'tactical' mistake or that it limited understanding of the conflict in Ireland and was therefore wrong 'in principle'. Those journalists arguing that the ban was a tactical mistake were opposed to the ban not for its attack on the principle of media freedom, but because the ban prevented them from 'exposing' Sinn Féin.[51] They shared with other social actors such as British politicians the belief that it was in the 'national interest' to maintain Northern Ireland as part of Britain, but differed on which particular policy would best achieve this. In contrast, some journalists, particularly those in the NUJ and the Campaign for Press and Broadcasting Freedom, did not necessarily share the belief that Britain should maintain its presence in Ireland and instead wanted to defend the independence of the British media above all else.

The most prevalent discourse tactically opposing the broadcasting ban argued that the ban was beneficial to the IRA, and featured twenty times in newspaper articles representing the British government introducing the ban. This discourse was expressed by opposition MPs from all parties, including a Tory backbencher. Analysing this discourse reveals not only the differing ways in which the same discourse was expressed by politicians to reinforce their own party-political positions, but also how journalists represented this discourse to reinforce their own newspaper's party-political allegiances and their position on the ban. For example, a journalist in the *Guardian* quoted Roy Hattersley at length and therefore acknowledged that the American dimension of IRA support might increase because of the broadcasting ban:

> The shadow Home Secretary, Mr Roy Hattersley, said the Government had handed the IRA a publicity coup which outweighed the advantage of keeping its representatives off the air. … Mr Hattersley said Labour shared the natural revulsion at the exhibition on television of support for terrorism, but did not believe the effect of the ban would be to help to defeat it. 'Has the Home Secretary not considered the damaging way in which his proposals will be used, particularly in the US, to portray this Government as the enemy of free expression?' he asked. 'Has he weighed that publicity coup for the IRA against the advantage of keeping its representatives off TV?'[52]

In contrast, a *Daily Telegraph* journalist did not quote Roy Hattersley at length and excluded the American dimension from his expression of the discourse representing the ban as beneficial to the IRA: 'Mr Hattersley said the ban would be used as a propaganda weapon to portray the Government as "the enemy of free expression".'[53] As a result, readers of this *Daily Telegraph* article would be unaware as to who would 'use' the ban as a 'propaganda weapon'.

The most prevalent discourse that can be considered opposed in principle to the broadcasting ban during its introduction in 1988 represented the ban as undemocratic and a threat to civil liberties. This discourse was mostly expressed by organised media workers, but left-wing Labour MP Tony Benn was a rare voice in the House of Commons articulating it too. These social actors were more concerned with the democratic foundation of a free media than with maintaining Northern Ireland as part of the United Kingdom. Nearly all manifestations of this discourse occurred in newspapers representative of the 'quality' press. Some expressions illustrated how it was possible to allow non-elite social actors to speak, but most newspaper articles did not feature such voices. In one anomaly, a journalist from the *Daily Telegraph*, which represented the most powerful expressions of this discourse, allowed an unnamed representative of the BBC's NUJ branch and Mike Jempson, a representative of the Campaign for Press and Broadcasting Freedom, to speak:

> The BBC's National Union of Journalists branch said: 'In seeking to cut the oxygen of publicity from terrorists, the Government risks cutting off the oxygen of democracy – the normally free flow of information and views'. … The Campaign for Press and Broadcasting Freedom condemned the Government's decision as a major attack on free speech, which set an alarming precedent. Mr Mike Jempson, Campaign spokesman, said: 'Who will be the next group of people the Government will seek to silence because it doesn't like their opinions and cannot deal in an open and democratic way with the challenge they pose? It is a sad day for media freedom and democracy.'[54]

Organised media workers were rarely allowed to speak in newspaper articles representing the broadcasting ban, but this interesting challenge to dominant discourses illustrates how the broadcasting ban could have been opposed on principled grounds if they had been allowed to do so.

Ban was a farce because of dubbing

The final discourse to be explored in this chapter represented the ban as a farce because of broadcasters' use of Irish actors to dub the words spoken by Sinn Féin representatives. It was the most prevalent discourse supporting the British government's lifting of the broadcasting ban in 1994, with it being expressed twenty-one times. The ban was represented as a farce for failing to silence those voices at which it was aimed, due to actors being used to circumvent it and because the dubbing was often out of sync. Although these were credible criticisms of the ban, such a memory of it avoids acknowledging the seriousness of this direct censorship, the worst in Britain since the Second World War.

As with other discourses explored in this chapter, the extent to which this discourse was altered through selective reported speech depended on the genre of newspaper articles and the political sympathies of individual newspapers, which refracted it in different ways. So, whereas *Daily Mail* and *Daily Express* journalists (incorrectly) fixated on the 'Irish' nationality of the actors and criticised the broadcasters for daring to circumvent the ban, journalists from the *Guardian* chose to criticise the British government for introducing censorship in the first place rather than the broadcasters for resisting it. Either way, the result was that when the British government lifted the broadcasting ban in 1994, the British newspaper industry mostly remembered it for being a farcical mistake rather than a serious erosion of British democracy and media freedom.

Conclusion

Looking back at the history of relations between the British government and media organisations in the Northern Ireland conflict, it is clear that indirect and direct censorship of the media occurred from Partition through to the peace process, when the broadcasting ban was lifted. Although the broadcast media were certainly the main target of pressure from Stormont and Westminster, journalists working in the British newspaper industry were not immune from some of these restrictions such as 'anti-terrorism' legislation, the pressure from their employers and managers to conform to particular representations of the conflict, the structuring influence of the generic conventions between and within the newspaper industry itself, as well as the dominant discourses emanating from the British government and the elite more broadly.

That does not mean that journalists working for these newspapers supported the broadcasting ban; rather, it reflects the power of newspaper owners and the editors they employ to reflect their views, which often involves support for British government policies. Indeed, it is important to acknowledge the antagonism between the professional principles of journalists as workers versus the economic interests of newspaper owners as employers, especially when there is a direct profit motive for newspapers to compete with, and therefore denigrate, the broadcast media, especially the BBC, which was accused of 'irresponsible' coverage contrary to the evidence.

Newspaper support for the broadcasting ban certainly seemed to be motivated by economic competition between the newspaper industry and the broadcast media, with most disdain reserved for the BBC. This was most obviously reflected in Rupert Murdoch's tabloid newspaper, the *Sun*. Aside from the Murdoch-owned Sky television network competing with the BBC for viewers, this media baron also backed

Thatcher's policies through his newspapers in return for her government's circumvention of anti-monopoly laws concerning media ownership. Although workers in both the British broadcast media and the British newspaper industry did attempt to resist the broadcasting ban, they could not match the strength of unity between the British government and the majority of British newspaper owners.

Margaret Thatcher claimed that she did not believe in censorship or talking to 'terrorists', yet her government introduced censorship in the form of the broadcasting ban, whilst having secret talks with those she labelled as 'terrorists'.[55] It is clear that it was the latter, talking, that helped bring the Northern Ireland conflict to an end, with both sides discussing and compromising their long-held positions. We should remember the former, the broadcasting ban, not as being a farcical mistake, but as the serious erosion of democracy and media freedom that it was. When we consider the long history of the British broadcast media being pressured by Stormont and Westminster, it is impossible to isolate this direct censorship as anything other than a culmination in the trajectory of media control established since Northern Ireland was created, which itself leads to questions of how democratic Britain ever was.

Media control and censorship constituted the war of words and silence so inseparable from the physical fighting in the Northern Ireland conflict. As in all wars, truth was the first casualty. In waging the propaganda war against the republican movement, the British government also attacked the British media and, ultimately, the populations of England, Wales, Scotland and Northern Ireland, reducing knowledge and understanding of the conflict. This legacy, which continues to this day, can be overcome only through a wide-ranging re-examination of the conflict, the reasons behind it, including Britain's imperial role in Ireland, and the many absences in the media before, during and after the conflict.

Notes

1 B. Rolston and D. Miller (eds), *War and Words: The Northern Ireland Media Reader* (Belfast: Beyond the Pale, 1996).

2 G. Edgerton, 'Quelling the "oxygen of publicity": British broadcasting and "the Troubles" during the Thatcher years', *Journal of Popular Culture*, 30:1 (1996), 115–31.

3 E. Moloney, 'Closing down the airwaves: The story of the broadcasting ban', in B. Rolston (ed.), *The Media and Northern Ireland* (Basingstoke: Macmillan, 1991).

4 United Nations Economic and Social Council, *Civil and Political Rights, Including the Question of Freedom of Expression*. Report submitted by Mr. Abid Hussain,

Special Rapporteur, in accordance with Commission on Human Rights resolution 1999/36. Addendum: Visit to the United Kingdom of Great Britain and Northern Ireland (Geneva: Office of the United Nations High Commissioner for Human Rights, 11 February 2000), p. 7. Available from: www.unhchr.ch/Huridocda/ Huridoca.nsf/TestFrame/5c111c8bbfc8455d802568b9004ba0fc?Opendocument (Accessed 30 May 2015).

5 L. Henderson, D. Miller and J. Reilly, *Speak No Evil: The British Broadcasting Ban, the Media and the Conflict in Ireland* (Glasgow: Glasgow University Media Group, 1990); Moloney, 'Closing down the airwaves'; R. Lago, 'Interviewing Sinn Féin under the new political environment: A comparative analysis of interviews with Sinn Féin on British television', *Media, Culture and Society*, 20:4 (1998), 677–85.

6 An exception being M. Jempson, 'A shameful anniversary', in L. Curtis and M. Jempson (eds), *Interference on the Airwaves: Ireland, the Media and the Broadcasting Ban* (London: Campaign for Press and Broadcasting Freedom, 1993). Jempson reviewed newspaper coverage of the broadcasting ban the day after and the first Sunday after the British government introduced the ban.

7 J. D. Viera, 'Terrorism at the BBC: The IRA on British television', in A. O. Alali and K. K. Eke (eds), *Media Coverage of Terrorism: Methods of Diffusion* (London: Sage, 1991); D. Miller, *Don't Mention the War: Northern Ireland, Propaganda and the Media* (London: Pluto Press, 1994); J. Curran, 'Mass media and democracy revisited', in J. Curran and M. Gurevitch (eds), *Mass Media and Society* (London: Arnold, 2nd edn, 1996).

8 Miller, *Don't Mention the War*; M. Hayes, 'Political violence, Irish Republicanism and the British media: Semantics, symbiosis and the state', in P. Mason (ed.), *Criminal Visions: Media Representations of Crime and Justice* (Cullompton: Willan Publishing, 2003).

9 S. Adams and W. Hicks, *Interviewing for Journalists* (Abingdon: Routledge, 2nd edn, 2009).

10 A. Smith, 'Television coverage of Northern Ireland', *Index on Censorship*, 1:2 (1972), 15–32; L. Curtis, *Ireland: The Propaganda War. The British Media and the 'Battle for Hearts and Minds'* (London: Pluto Press, 1984); P. Schlesinger, *Putting 'Reality' Together: BBC News* (London: Methuen, 1987); R. Francis, 'Broadcasting to a community in conflict – the experience in Northern Ireland', in B. Rolston and D. Miller (eds) *War and Words: The Northern Ireland Media Reader* (Belfast: Beyond the Pale, 1996).

11 Smith, 'Television coverage of Northern Ireland'.

12 P. Foot, 'Colin Wallace and the propaganda war', in B. Rolston and D. Miller (eds), *War and Words: The Northern Ireland Media Reader* (Belfast: Beyond the Pale, 1996).

13 Curtis, *Ireland: The Propaganda War*; Schlesinger, *Putting 'Reality' Together*; Miller, *Don't Mention the War*.

14 Curtis, *Ireland: The Propaganda War*; Miller, *Don't Mention the War*; Hayes, 'Political violence, Irish Republicanism and the British media'.

15 B. Rolston, 'Resistance and terror: Lessons from Ireland', in P. Scraton (ed.), *Beyond September 11: An Anthology of Dissent* (London: Pluto Press, 2002).
16 Ibid., p. 35.
17 M. Leapman, 'The "Real Lives" controversy', in B. Rolston and D. Miller (eds), *War and Words: The Northern Ireland Media Reader* (Belfast: Beyond the Pale, 1996).
18 Edgerton, 'Quelling the "oxygen of publicity"'.
19 M. Thatcher, 'Speech to American Bar Association', *Margaret Thatcher Foundation* (15 July 1985), www.margaretthatcher.org/document/106096 (Accessed 6 May 2015).
20 Leapman, 'The "Real Lives" controversy', p. 100.
21 Ibid.; Viera, 'Terrorism at the BBC'.
22 Moloney, 'Closing down the airwaves'; Miller, *Don't Mention the War*.
23 Miller, *Don't Mention the War*.
24 Moloney, 'Closing down the airwaves'.
25 Henderson et al., *Speak No Evil*, pp. 10–11.
26 Moloney, 'Closing down the airwaves', pp. 28–9.
27 Ibid.
28 Henderson et al., *Speak No Evil*.
29 Moloney, 'Closing down the airwaves'.
30 Rolston, 'Resistance and terror', pp. 61–2.
31 BBC, *Speak No Evil: The Story of the Broadcasting Ban*. Produced by Francis Welch. Broadcast on BBC4, 4 April 2005.
32 Henderson et al., *Speak No Evil*.
33 J. Eldridge, J. Kitzinger and K. Williams, *The Mass Media and Power in Modern Britain* (Oxford: Oxford University Press, 1997).
34 Lago, 'Interviewing Sinn Féin under the new political environment'.
35 Henderson et al., *Speak No Evil*.
36 Moloney, 'Closing down the airwaves'; Hussain, 'Civil and political rights'.
37 P. Arthur, 'The media and politics in Northern Ireland', in J. Seaton and B. Pimlott (eds), *The Media in British Politics* (Aldershot: Gower, 1987); A. Bairner, 'The media', in A. Aughey and D. Morrow (eds), *Northern Ireland Politics* (Harlow: Longman Group Limited, 1996).
38 D. Miller, 'The history behind a mistake', *British Journalism Review*, 1:2 (1990), 34–43.
39 Eldridge et al., *The Mass Media and Power*; G. McLaughlin and S. Baker, *The Propaganda of Peace: The Role of Media and Culture in the Northern Ireland Peace Process* (Bristol: Intellect Books, 2010).
40 R. Greenslade, *Press Gang: How Newspapers Make Profit from Propaganda* (London: Pan Macmillan, 2004).
41 J. Tunstall, 'The United Kingdom', in M. J. Kelly (ed.), *Media in Europe: The Euromedia Research Group* (London: Sage, 3rd edn, 2004).
42 J. Tunstall, *Newspaper Power: The New National Press in Britain* (Oxford: Clarendon Press, 1996), p. 18.
43 N. Davies, *Flat Earth News* (London: Chatto and Windus, 2008).

44 J. E. Richardson, *Analysing Newspapers: An Approach from Critical Discourse Analysis* (Basingstoke: Palgrave Macmillan, 2007).

45 *Willings Press Guide* (East Grinstead: British Media Publications/Thomas Skinner Directories, Annual Edition 1989; 1990; 1991; 1992; 1993; 1994; 1995).

46 Other subject categories included: the SAS executions of IRA members in Gibraltar and the subsequent inquiry; the attacking or killing of British combatants by the IRA; the attacking or killing of civilians by the IRA, UDA, UFF and UVF; the arrest, imprisonment, release and extradition of IRA suspects/members and associated prisoner controversy; the fourth anniversary of the Brighton bombing and the Conservative Party conference return to the Grand Hotel; and the Peace Process.

47 P. Schlesinger, G. Murdock and P. Elliott, *Televising 'Terrorism': Political Violence in Popular Culture* (London: Comedia, 1983); Curtis, *Ireland: The Propaganda War*; Miller, *Don't Mention the War*; S. Cottle, 'Reporting the Troubles in Northern Ireland: Paradigms and media propaganda', *Critical Studies in Mass Communication*, 14 (1997), 282–96; M. McGovern, '"The IRA are not Al-Qaeda": "New terrorism" discourse and Irish Republicanism', in K. Hayward and C. O'Donnell (eds), *Political Discourse and Conflict Resolution: Debating Peace in Northern Ireland* (Abingdon: Routledge, 2010).

48 Ibid.

49 R. Norton-Taylor, 'Politics confront programme chiefs', *Guardian* (20 October 1988), p. 24.

50 Ibid.

51 Miller, 'The history behind a mistake'.

52 M. Linton, 'Hurd defends ban on terror broadcasts', *Guardian* (20 October 1988), p. 6.

53 A. Looch, 'TV and radio ban on terrorists has mixed Labour reception', *Daily Telegraph* (20 October 1988), p. 20.

54 J. Thynne, 'Damaging precedent says BBC', *Daily Telegraph* (20 October 1988), p. 1.

55 E. Moloney, *A Secret History of the IRA* (London: Penguin Books, 2nd edn, 2007).

17

'The Troubles we've seen': film, television drama and the Northern Irish conflict in Britain

John Hill

In July 2014, the *Mail On Sunday* ran a front-page story entitled 'Fury over Channel 4 insult to MP killed by the IRA'. This was a rather odd piece, involving an attack on the opening episode of the second series of the cult TV programme, *Utopia*. The source of the offence was the programme's inclusion of a fictional scene involving the former Conservative MP (and Shadow Secretary of State for Northern Ireland) Airey Neave along with contemporary news footage referring to his death as a result of an Irish National Liberation Army (INLA) car-bomb in 1979. Neave was widely credited with masterminding the election of Margaret Thatcher as Conservative leader and, due to his secret service connections, his name was also associated with an alleged plot to overthrow Harold Wilson's Labour government (alluded to, for example, in Ken Loach's 1990 film *Hidden Agenda* in which the political conspirator Alec Nevin represents a thinly disguised version of Neave). *Utopia*, however, draws upon rather different conspiracy theories relating to Neave's death by suggesting that he was himself the victim of the British security services which, in this case, are shown to be engaged in an elaborate international plot to engineer population control.[1]

As Channel 4 indicated in response to criticisms of the programme, *Utopia* is a heavily stylised work of fiction which does not suggest that any 'real organisation' was responsible for Neave's death.[2] The programme also appeared at a time when the IRA (and, of course, the INLA) had ceased their paramilitary activities and no longer occupied the prominent place that they once did within the British public imagination (to the extent that the 'dirty tricks' of the secret services might now be regarded as offering a more plausible explanation for the assassination of a right-wing politician than the activities of Irish paramilitaries).

To this extent, the controversy over the programme not only possessed a somewhat manufactured quality but also appeared to hark back to an earlier era when virtually all film and television dramatisations of the 'Troubles', and portraits of republican violence in particular, were met with dismay and expressions of outrage by the British press. This was especially so if the work involved was held to involve the 'exploitation' of real events for entertainment purposes or to mix, in a supposedly mis-leading manner, 'factual' and 'fictional' elements.

Although British media coverage of political events in Northern Ireland during the 1960s initially focused on the justice of the civil rights case and the obstacles to reform represented by unionism/ loyalism, representations of the Troubles changed dramatically fol-lowing the despatch of British troops to Northern Ireland in 1969 and the resurgence of the (Provisional) IRA (PIRA) in 1970. As a consequence of the increased militarisation of the conflict, and the imposition of direct rule from Westminster in 1972, the content of both film and television programmes dealing with the Troubles became the object of increasing scrutiny. In the case of the broadcasters, this led to a growing reluctance to transmit certain kinds of material, the cutting of various programmes and, in some cases, outright bans.[3] While it tended to be current affairs and documentary programmes that attracted the most attention, dramas could also prove contentious, particularly if they were perceived to be employing fictional devices in order to circumvent the rules of 'impartiality' and 'balance' that were held to govern the making of 'factual' programmes. The highly charged political atmosphere that surrounded the Troubles, especially in the wake of the bombings in England from 1973 onwards, also meant that few feature films attempted to draw on Northern Ireland as a source of drama. This was partly on the grounds that the Troubles were unlikely to provide an appropriate source of 'entertainment', but also stemmed from a recognition that almost any film dealing with the conflict might be expected to encounter either production difficulties or critical hostility.

This was particularly so when the material dealt with events in Britain. In comparison to plays and films set in Northern Ireland, that might be said to hold the conflict at a distance for British viewers, dramas located in Britain not only brought the Troubles 'home' but also raised ques-tions, either implicitly or explicitly, about Britain's relationship to, and role in, the continuing conflict. In the following discussion, therefore, I will concentrate on work that is set primarily in Britain rather than in Northern Ireland and examine some of its significant features. This will begin with a consideration of the treatment of the returning British soldier in early TV dramas and how these generated a sense of Northern Ireland's 'otherness' in relation to Britain. This will be followed by a consideration of the representation of the IRA's activities on the British 'mainland' and the ways in which the IRA came to symbolise a horrifying but also apparently unintelligible threat to British institutions. This then leads into an analysis of how the miscarriages of justice that followed in the wake of the IRA's bombing campaigns were turned into dramas that began to subject the British State to criticism. The chapter then concludes with some consideration of the 'peace process' and the relative scarcity of dramas dealing with the divisions and tensions that were a feature of the earlier period.

'A place apart'

Although the United Kingdom government was, of course, responsible for the governance of Northern Ireland, the region was not, in strict terms, a part of Britain and it was common to identify Northern Ireland as 'a place apart', separate and distinct from the rest of the UK.[4] In this way, it also became possible to view the conflict, and the violence it generated, as a problem that was internal to the situation in the North of Ireland and specific to the ethnic and religious divisions that were a feature of it. If this was so, then it also became possible for the British State itself to come to be regarded as 'outside of' or 'above' the conflict, with no direct responsibility for its conduct or continuation. Such a benign view of British involvement in Northern Ireland might be said to have been implicit in a great number of the films and plays dealing with the Northern Ireland Troubles and may be seen, for example, in the genial six-part situation comedy, *So You Think You've Got Troubles*, broadcast by the BBC in 1991. Written by Laurence Marks and Maurice Gran, the plot follows the adventures of a factory manager from London who is relocated to strife-torn Belfast. The comedy's central conceit is that the main character, Ivan Fox, played by Warren Mitchell, is an agnostic of Jewish extraction. As such, he is positioned outside the central political and religious cleavages characteristic of his new home and struggles to make sense of the characters and events that he encounters. In one particularly striking scene in the second episode, he is taken for what appears to be a circuitous drive through the city (crossing from east to west) during the course of which he passes a series of garish unionist murals, followed shortly afterwards by their nationalist counterparts. In this way, the sequence not only evokes a sense of the alien character that the conflict possesses for its visiting English protagonist but also invites an understanding of it in terms of a straightforward battle between Northern Ireland's two warring 'tribes'. At one point Fox refers to Northern Ireland as 'standing fast against logic and reason and good old-fashioned sense' and this invocation of the apparent 'irrationality' of the Northern Irish conflict is commonly linked, in Troubles dramas, to a pessimism about the prospects for political and social change.[5] *So You Think You've Got Troubles* does, nevertheless, demonstrate a degree of departure from the prevailing Troubles paradigm in so far as the relatively sympathetic Fox endeavours to implement a degree of reform through the employment of Catholics in a Protestant-dominated factory. This may be contrasted, however, with the first television dramas to address the role of British soldiers in Northern Ireland – *Letter from a Soldier* (BBC, 1975), *The Vanishing Army* (BBC, 1978), *Chance of a Lifetime* (BBC, 1980) – in which the main characters are confronted with an environment that not only is completely alien to them but which also holds entirely negative consequences for them.

In *Letter from a Soldier*, written by Wilson John Haire, a former soldier is cooped up in his mother's London flat brooding over the letters he sent from Northern Ireland to his now estranged girlfriend. In *The Vanishing Army*, written by a former sergeant-major in the British Army, Robert Holles, a career soldier (played by Bill Patterson) is posted to Northern Ireland where he loses a leg and then, on his return to England, his livelihood. Robert Holman's *Chance of a Lifetime* deals with a young working-class teenager from the north of England who joins the Army with hopes of a better life but ends up dead at the hands of an IRA sniper in Belfast. In all of these television plays, there is little interest in Northern Ireland per se and all or most of the action occurs in England. This, however, is a deliberate strategy that not only draws attention to the men's lack of preparedness for, and understanding of, the situation in which they come to find themselves but also raises questions about the value of the soldiers' presence in Northern Ireland when the reasons for their being there are so unclear and the consequences for them are so damaging. Although all three productions set out to highlight the fate of these ordinary soldiers (whom it is partly implied have been let down by those who sent them to Northern Ireland), the plays' absence of heroics and reluctance to attribute a positive meaning to the men's sacrifices undoubtedly made them unsettling viewing for contemporary audiences. Indeed, Holles accused the BBC of a 'crude and crass piece of censorship' when it dropped the repeat screening of his play from the schedules, following the deaths of Lord Mountbatten (at Mullaghmore) and eighteen soldiers at Warrenpoint in Northern Ireland, on the grounds that its transmission might not help morale.[6] However, if the plays do demonstrate a degree of scepticism about the value of the British Army's presence in Northern Ireland, they also do so by studiously avoiding the political context of the conflict and invoking a view of Northern Ireland as fundamentally 'alien' to both the plays' English characters and, by extension, their viewers in Britain. Although some other dramas – such as *Contact* (1985) and *Bloody Sunday* (2002) – have gone on to investigate the role of the British Army in Northern Ireland in a more searching manner, the continuing potency of this particular dramatic model may be seen in a film such as *'71* (2014), in which a young soldier, fresh from England, discovers himself cast adrift in the alien city environment of Belfast. The novelty of the film is that, within this inhospitable dramatic universe, the British Army, in the form of an undercover outfit, behave no better than the loyalist and republican paramilitaries that they are supposedly combatting. However, as a result of the film's focus upon a central English character caught up in a world that he lacks the means to understand, the film overall simply ends up reproducing a conventional – and primarily British – view of the Troubles as no more than unintelligible chaos.

Bombs in Britain

This sense of the alien and unintelligible may also be found in the first films and TV dramas to deal with the ways in which the violence in Northern Ireland carried over into Britain from the 1970s onwards. Roger MacDougall's play *The Gentle Gunman* – produced (by the BBC) as a television play in 1950 and then as a feature film (by Ealing Studios) in 1952 – established something of a precedent for these. Set during the Second World War, the film focuses on the IRA's bombing campaign of 1939 as a means of highlighting the futility of the IRA's battle for the 'freedom' of Ireland at a time when Britain was already being bombed by the Nazis. What seems to have been the first television play of the modern era of the Troubles, *The Patriot Game* (ITV, 1969), also referred back to this campaign in its treatment of an IRA plot to blow up Battersea Power Station (but inspired by events in Coventry).[7] The play's author, Dominic Behan, argued that the play, in dealing with a 'conflict within a conflict', sought to rescue republicanism from its association with Nazism during this period and to reclaim some of its socialist components.[8] Thames Television, who were evidently nervous about the production, argued that the play's predominant impulse was to show 'how the violence of fanatical patriotism puts innocent people into danger'.[9] Such claims were not enough, however, to convince Ulster Television, who decided that the programme should not be broadcast in Northern Ireland. The fact that the play got made at all probably derived from a perception that its portrayal of historical events possessed only limited relevance for the present. Such a view, however, was destined to be overtaken by events when the PIRA decided to embark upon its bombing campaign in Britain in 1973. The resulting deaths and destruction, however, created such public outrage that hostility towards the IRA and its demands only intensified and made it much more difficult for film and television makers to address the conflict in terms other than a battle against terrorism.

It is not entirely surprising, therefore, that the first allusions to the recent bombings arrived in the form of an Anglo-American thriller, *Hennessy* (1975), produced by American International Pictures, a company with a reputation for injecting contemporary issues into popular genre formats. In this case, the accidental deaths in Belfast of his wife and child, at the hands of a stunned British soldier, prompt the film's main character, Niall Hennessy (Rod Steiger), to head for London where he plans to blow up the Queen at the State Opening of Parliament. This is presented as a personal crusade for justice which, in Hennessy's own words, has 'got nothing to do with politics at all'. Indeed, the IRA leadership try to stop him and go so far as to tip off the Special Branch about his plans, fearing that the political backlash from such an action will only prove detrimental to their cause. Thus, while the IRA are shown to be vicious and ruthless killers, they are also attributed with a degree of political calculation which meant, according to the author of the original story, the actor Richard Johnson, that the film avoided showing the 'terrorists' simply as 'lesser beings'.[10] So, while Johnson also suggests that the film is 'primarily a thriller' that offers no 'political or moral conclusions', its mix of Troubles-related elements and thriller conventions does, nevertheless, render its outlook ambiguous. In line with the film's revenge formula, Hennessy's desire to avenge his family is invested with a clear emotional dynamic. At the same time, his actions are seen to be motivated by the activities of British troops in Belfast that bear more than a passing resemblance to events on Bloody Sunday in Derry in 1972 (and which had themselves acted as a spur to IRA recruitment). His mission, moreover, is shown to come perilously close to success, a situation made all the odder by the mixing of actual footage of the Royal Family and leading British politicians (including the then Prime Minister Edward Heath) with fictional material involving Hennessy/Steiger in the Houses of Parliament. Given these features, it was, perhaps, to be expected that the film should run into difficulties with exhibition. The film was viewed by EMI chairman, John Read, and picture and theatre division head, Bernard Delfont, who decided against showing the film in ABC cinemas on the grounds that the film exploited the Troubles for entertainment.[11] Rank, the owners of the Odeon chain of cinemas, the other main circuit in Britain at the time, decided to follow suit, with the result that the film was, in effect, prevented from obtaining a widespread cinema release.

A similar controversy also beset another thriller, *The Long Good Friday* (1979), originally entitled 'The Paddy Factor', in which a London East End gangster, Harold Shand (Bob Hoskins), becomes increasingly perplexed by the succession of violent attacks upon his 'empire'. Shand's efforts to find out who is 'having a go' at him and why eventually reveal his assailants to be members of the IRA who hold his 'organisation' responsible for the death of some of their members (following a hand-over of cash from a protection racket). Shand initially believes that he can eliminate this threat to his 'manor' but, in the film's famous con-cluding sequence, he is taken prisoner by the IRA, who drive off with him at gunpoint as lengthily held shots observe his changing reactions. Like *Hennessy* before it, the film plays on anxieties concerning the IRA's activities on the British 'mainland', and the threat they pose to British institutions, but is also ideologically ambivalent in the way in which it portrays these. Partly invoking the clashes of ethics to be found in films such as *Performance* (1970) and *The Godfather 2* (1974), the film self-consciously counterposes the economically self-interested, quasi-capitalist gangsterism of Shand to the differently motivated violence of the IRA.[12] As the corrupt policeman Parky (Dave King) explains, the IRA are 'not just gangsters' and it is because of this that Shand ulti-mately proves unable either to understand or defeat them. In a film in which allegory is not far from the surface, the film may be taken to offer a commentary on the British State's own lack of comprehension of the motives of those whom they are fighting, along with a diagnosis of the difficulties involved in seeking to secure a military, rather than a politi-cal, solution to the continuing Northern Ireland crisis. However, in so far as the film's thriller mechanics and generation of suspense depends, for the greater part of the film, upon the withholding of information about the exact nature of Shand's adversaries, it might also be said that the film itself does little to explain the motives (and 'politics') of the IRA beyond 'revenge' for a criminal deal gone sour.[13] In this way, it can be seen to reproduce the very sense of the 'unintelligibility' (and 'otherness') of republican violence that it identifies as a problem for both Shand and, by allegorical extension, the British State, and which has underpinned the prevailing views of the Troubles more generally.

Nevertheless, given the nature of its portrayal of the IRA, it is hardly surprising that the film ran into difficulties following its completion. Lew Grade's Associated Communications Corporation (ACC), the financier of the film, sought to avoid showing the film in cinemas and demanded ten minutes of cuts for the film's transmission on television.[14] Although some of the cuts involved scenes considered to be too violent for television, they also related to the film's representation of the Provisionals. The Managing Director of ITC Film Distributors (a subsidiary of ACC), Alan Kean, for example, commissioned three reports on the film to test the likely performance of the film at the box office. Although all agreed on the film's quality, they were concerned that the portrait of the IRA might prove a deterrent to cinema exhibitors and proposed that references to the IRA be deleted. One of the reports, in particular, was concerned that 'one could be left with the impression that with the IRA turning out triumphant in the end, it gives them free propaganda as a somewhat invincible force that will never be beaten'.[15] In this respect, for all its lack of explanation of the context in which IRA violence occurred, the film's apparent suggestion that the IRA could not be defeated 'militarily' clearly ran against the grain of prevailing discourses within British political culture.

A rather different picture of the IRA, however, had already appeared on television a few years earlier. *Eighteen Months to Balcombe Street* (1977) was an unusual piece produced by London Weekend Television (LWT) to coincide with the sentencing of the IRA active service unit that became known as the Balcombe Street Gang following a six-day siege at the London street of the same name.[16] During 1974 and 1975, the four men in the dock had waged a sustained campaign against 'Establishment' targets such as private clubs, hotels and expensive restaurants and committed a number of murders, including that of the right-wing campaigner Ross McWhirter (who had previously offered a reward for their capture). A reporter for LWT's *The London Programme*, John Shirley, had gained access to the transcripts of the police interrogations of two of the men (Joe O'Connell, Eddie Butler). Rather than incorporating these into a straight piece of current affairs reporting, it was felt that a dramatised documentary would offer the more effective method of revealing 'the way they worked, the problems they faced and the way they lived while they were in London'.[17] The programme was directed by Stephen Frears, whose background was in feature film and television drama rather than in news and current affairs. The resulting film does, however, seek to stick closely to the reported facts, using the transcripts as the basis for extended voice-overs and curtailing the use of dramatic invention and speculative dialogue.

Given that the film's focus is almost exclusively upon the members of the unit, there were fears that the film might glamorise their actions. However, the production maintains an observational distance from the main protagonists and, in the absence of developed narrativisation and characterisation, there is little to encourage our empathy. There was a report, however, that the original co-writer of the programme, Shane Connaughton, had asked for his name to be removed from the credits on the grounds that the film 'showed the Balcombe Street Four as psychopaths without showing the reason why they went to England in the context of Irish history'.[18] It is certainly the case that the film's main focus is the men's preparations for, and implementation of, their plans rather than their political ideas (which feature only cursorily). However, as a result of the film's rather drab observational realism (and lack of licence to depart from documented evidence), what is also striking is how, for all their apparent single-mindedness and lack of conscience about their victims, the men are shown to be really rather 'ordinary' and thus capable of remaining unnoticed in London bedsit-land, despite the 'spectacularly' destructive nature of their activities (and the sustained character of their campaign).

Miscarriages of justice

A noticeable feature of this production, particularly in retrospect, are the references, contained in the men's statements, to the 1974 bombings in Guildford and Woolwich. Indeed, in his speech to the court at his trial, one of the men, Joe O'Connell, publicly admitted his involvement in these bombings in order to draw attention to the injustice of the convictions of those then serving prison sentences for them.[19] Although it took until 1989 for the sentences of those convicted of the Woolwich and Guildford bombings (the Guildford Four) to be overturned, the suspicion that the wrong people had been convicted not only for these offences but also for the Birmingham pub bombings of November 1974 meant that the bombing campaign of 1974–75 came to be associated not just with narratives of the threat of IRA violence (and the difficulties in making sense of it) but also with exposés of miscarriages of justice (see Finch, chapter 10 and O'Reilly, chapter 20 in this volume). The campaign for the release of the Birmingham Six gained added momentum in 1985 when Granada Television's current affairs programme *World in Action* broadcast a one-hour special suggesting that the men had been wrongly convicted. The programme returned to the case in 1987, and once again in 1989 when, following the failure of the men's appeal, it drew parallels with the convictions of the Guildford Four, who had by this time been freed. Although elements of dramatic 'reconstruction' were employed in these programmes, it was decided, in 1990, to go one step further and produce a feature-length drama-documentary, *Who*

Bombed Birmingham?, which it was hoped would not only provide the means of reaching a wider audience but also permit material to be shown (such as interviews with IRA members) that it would not be possible to film in the normal documentary manner.

Made in association with US cable network HBO, the film is identified by Derek Paget as part of a new phase of 'docudrama' revealing the influence of Hollywood.[20] Certainly in comparison to the dramatically understated style of *Eighteen Months to Balcombe Street*, there is considerably more use of techniques associated with fiction: the employment of well-known actors (John Hurt and Martin Shaw) to play the lead characters, the shaping of material according to generic conventions (the detective story, the courtroom drama), the orchestration of events in order to create moments of dramatic suspense and an overtly narrational use of editing and extra-diegetic music. The drama is, nevertheless, still firmly rooted in the research undertaken by the *World in Action* team of Ian McBride, Charles Tremayne and Chris Mullin, the journalist-turned-MP whose book on the case, *Error of Judgement* (1986), partly provided the film's source. Indeed, there was some criticism of the programme for its rather self-regarding positioning of the journalists at the centre of the drama and the resulting aggrandisement of their role in uncovering inadequacies in the forensic and photographic evidence used against the prisoners.[21] More generally, however, the drama's foregrounding of the journalists' investigation played a significant role in shaping how the issues were presented and dramatised. As a result of the production's indebtedness to the detective genre, for example, some of the most atmospheric and dramatically compelling scenes deal with Mullin's attempts to seek out and identify the actual bombers by entering into the murky 'underworld' of the IRA. The film does, at one stage, present an argument between Mullin (John Hurt) and Tremayne (Roger Allam) as to whether it is actually necessary to identify the real bombers in order to establish the innocence of the Birmingham Six. The programme-makers' judgement that it was necessary not only led the film to give over considerable time to this aspect of the investigation but also encouraged them to go ahead and disclose, at the end of the programme, the names of four of the men whom they believed to be guilty. Mullin, who had promised anonymity to the men whom he had interviewed, did not provide these names (which had been given to *World in Action* by the Special Branch) and opposed the decision to reveal them, as did a number of others, including the Labour MP Tony Benn, who referred to it as a 'denial of natural justice'.[22] Relatives and supporters of the Birmingham Six also aired their doubts, expressing the view that the men's case stood on its own merits and that, in naming the alleged bombers, *World in Action* was subjecting them to the same kind of 'trial by media' to which the Birmingham Six had themselves fallen victims prior to their trial.

The other aspect of the film's investigative structure is that the film's conclusion had, of necessity, to remain downbeat, given that innocent men were still in prison (and justice had not yet been seen to be done). *Who Bombed Birmingham?* suggested that, despite the overwhelming evidence of the men's innocence, the British Establishment appeared unable to face up to the wrongs that had been done (with Mullin arguing within the film that 'some mistakes are too big to own up to'). In this respect, the programme appeared to diagnose the failures in the British political system while still holding out the prospect that the exposure of an injustice might yet lead to change. As a result, the programme met with two kinds of responses. More liberal commentators opted for the film's 'preferred reading', maintaining belief in a sense of 'fairness' and asking when the men might finally be free. More conservative opinion, however, found it difficult to accept criticism of the British justice system and claimed that it would only give succour to the IRA. This was expressed most vociferously in the right-wing tabloid the *Sun*, which ran an editorial denouncing the film for discrediting 'the security services, the police and the process of justice' and offering 'propaganda for the IRA'.[23] The Birmingham Six, the paper asserted, were convicted after 'a long painstaking trial' and were 'as guilty as hell'. The Conservative Prime Minister, Margaret Thatcher, did not go quite so far as this but, when asked about the case in the House of Commons the day following the programme's transmission, she declared that a 'television programme alters nothing' and, in an apparent inversion of the concerns expressed by the supporters of the Six, argued that 'trial by television' would not be allowed to substitute for 'the rule of law' (thus rather ignoring how it was the 'rule of law' that the programme had put into question).[24]

These sentiments were expressed before the sentences of the Birmingham Six were finally quashed the following year. However, the hostility towards films and television dramas questioning the role of the 'security services, the police and the process of justice' continued even when clear miscarriages of justice had been proved. This may be seen in the reactions to a number of productions in the early 1990s dealing with the wrongful imprisonment of the Guildford Four (whose convictions were quashed in 1989) and the Maguire Seven (whose convictions for bomb-making were declared unsafe in 1990 and, eventually, overturned by the Court of Appeal in 1991). As in the case of the Birmingham Six, there had been long-standing doubts about the validity of these convictions and the ITV current affairs series *First Tuesday* made a number of programmes between 1984 and 1987 suggesting the innocence of those concerned. The Irish journalist Tom McGurk, who had initially encouraged *First Tuesday* to take up the story, also sought to highlight the damaging personal consequences for those involved in his drama, *Dear Sarah* (1990), based on the letters exchanged between Sarah and Giuseppe Conlon (one of the Maguire Seven, who had by then died in prison). His original script, however, was rejected by the BBC and then dropped by the ITV company Thames as too 'politically sensitive' following the controversy over its programme *Death on the Rock* (questioning the official version of the Gibraltar IRA shootings).[25] The drama was eventually made by the Irish broadcaster, RTÉ (Raidió Telefís Éireann), with pre-sales funding from ITV, but was broadcast only after the British Home Secretary had accepted that the convictions of the Maguire Seven were unsafe. As a result, what might have once served as a 'goad to action' had now become, in the words of one commentator, 'something more elegiac'.[26] This, however, did not prevent complaints in some quarters that, by screening 'another bleeding heart sob story on how British justice gets it wrong', TV chiefs were contributing to 'a barrage of Britain-bashing shows that fire the IRA and weaken our morale'.[27]

This opposition to 'Britain-bashing' gained some added momentum when another documentary drama about the Maguire Seven, *A Safe House*, was broadcast on the BBC the following month. However, it was the big-budget feature film *In the Name of the Father* (1993), dealing with the Guildford Four and Maguire Seven, that was responsible for the greatest controversy, due to its scale of production, emotional power and high public profile. The Ireland–UK–US co-production, *In the Name of the Father*, however, was actually funded by a major US studio, Universal, and demonstrated a clear debt to the conventions of the family melodrama, the bio-pic and the prison film, rather than those of drama-documentary. Starring Daniel Day-Lewis, it was loosely based on Gerry Conlon's autobiography, *Proved Innocent* (1990), and deals with the circumstances leading to his arrest and wrongful imprisonment, subsequent experiences in prison and eventual release in 1989. However, partly in line with the demands for narrative pacing and emotional impact characteristic of Hollywood storytelling, the film offers what its director, Jim Sheridan, referred to as 'a dramatic interpretation of the truth' rather than any attempt at documentary accuracy.[28] This results in a considerable compression of events, the creation of composite characters and the complete invention of some characters and incidents.

Dramatic invention is not, of course, an uncommon feature of the mainstream historical film and bio-pic (and may even be taken to be necessary for an effective dramatisation of some historical events). However, given that it was the facts surrounding the cases of the Guildford Four and Maguire Seven that had been in dispute for so long, it was, perhaps, understandable that some commentators who might have been expected to be sympathetic to the production – including members of the Maguire family and their solicitor Alastair Logan; the historian Robert Kee, who had written an influential book on the subject, *Trial and Error* (1986); and Ronan Bennett, who had collaborated with Paul Hill in the writing of his memoir, *Stolen Years* (1990)[29] – expressed their disquiet at the way in which the film misrepresented events when there did not appear to be a clear need for it to do so (showing, for example, Paul Hill meeting Annie Maguire when, in fact, he had not; turning Conlon's alibi witness into a vagrant he meets in the park; and showing the Guildford Four and Maguire Seven together in court). For Derek Paget, 'made up' scenes in docudrama may play a 'mischievous' role in offering 'alternative truths' to those subscribed to by those in power.[30] However, in the case of *In the Name of the Father*, it was precisely because the official versions of the 'truth' had led to the wrongful imprisonment of those concerned that it became particularly important for the actual evidence of the case to be respected.[31]

Such changes, moreover, may also be seen to have constituted something of an 'own goal', in so far as they provided ammunition to those whose criticism of the film stemmed less from a respect for the facts than from an unwillingness to accept that the police, the judiciary and, indeed, the media themselves had been at fault in the matter. So, while the convictions of the Guildford Four and Maguire Seven may have been overturned, this was insufficient to stop some sections of the British press condemning the film for, as one writer summed it up, 'maligning British justice, romanticising terrorists, boosting support for the IRA and manipulating through factual inaccuracy'.[32] Some of these criticisms did appear to be wide of the mark. As the film's title suggests, the film's interpretation of Gerry Conlon's story involves a clear focus on the changing relationship between Gerry (Daniel Day-Lewis) and his father Giuseppe (Peter Postlethwaite). Thus, despite the claims that the film supported the IRA, the rapprochement between Gerry and Giuseppe that occurs while both men are in prison is clearly shown to involve a rejection of the violence represented by Gerry's surrogate 'father', the ruthless IRA leader, Joe McAndrew (Don Baker) (a representation which, in some quarters, was criticised for simply reproducing the traditional stereotype of the IRA man).[33] However, unlike *Who Bombed Birmingham?* which, as previously noted, was not in a position to offer an affirmative ending, *In the Name of the Father* concludes with the release of the Guildford Four and Gerry Conlon's famous appearance in front of the television cameras outside the Old Bailey. This is not only an emotionally charged moment of personal vindication but also a symbolic triumph over a flawed political and judicial system. While this victory had, of course, depended upon the tenacity of British lawyers, such as Gareth Peirce (Emma Thompson), committed to fair play and justice, the film's (somewhat misleading) portrait of the breakthrough in the case resulting from an official's mistake reinforces a sense of the overall oppressiveness of British institutions.

However, if, as Rosenstone argues, it is a characteristic of mainstream historical films to 'personalise', 'emotionalise' and 'dramatise',[34] then this has implications not only for the way in which Gerry's story of personal redemption unfolds but also for how the workings of the British State come to be represented within the film. For, although the film does point to the mood of anti-Irish sentiment that followed the IRA's bombing campaign (and the licence given to police by the Prevention of Terrorism Act that was rushed through Parliament), Gerry's ordeal is dramatised primarily in terms of a series of encounters with personally unpleasant 'baddies' who conspire against him. This is particularly so of the character of Dixon (Corin Redgrave), the officer initially in charge of Gerry's interrogation. He reappears at various points during the film, doing his best to obstruct the release of the Guildford Four and apparently colluding with an unidentified Home Office official (played by Malcolm Tierney, a character actor with a reputation for parts as villains and rogues). To some extent, this makes a point, recurring across a number of films and television dramas (stretching back to *Hennessy*, in which the police officer Hollis is accused of becoming 'corrupted' by his experiences in Northern Ireland), that British policies and practices in relation to Northern Ireland are compromising normal British standards of justice and democracy (with Dixon, for example, justifying his actions by declaring it's 'a dirty war'). However, in developing this theme through the dramatisation of acts of personal villainy, the film may also be seen to be invoking a somewhat simplified notion of 'conspiracy', rather than attempting to unravel the more complex political and ideological dynamics underpinning Britain's troubled relationship with Ireland (and the Irish in Britain).

As such, the film reveals a tendency shared with many other works that have set out to uncover the operations of political power in Britain. *Some Mother's Son* (1996), written and directed by Terry George (the co-writer of *In the Name of the Father*), also employs an apparently omnipresent Thatcherite politician, Farnsworth (Tom Hollander), to highlight the machinations of the British government during the 1981 hunger strike by Irish republican prisoners in Long Kesh (the Maze

Prison). Ken Loach's *Hidden Agenda* (1990), loosely based on the John Stalker 'shoot-to-kill' inquiry,[35] not only uncovers a conspiracy to pervert the course of justice by the security services in Northern Ireland in the early 1980s but also, as previously noted, a conspiracy on the part of a small group of businessmen, security personnel and politicians to overthrow the Labour government in Britain in the 1970s. While it is certainly true that Loach, and writer Jim Allen, were drawing upon the revelations of former intelligence officers such as Colin Wallace and Fred Holroyd, it is also the case that a gravitation towards conspiracy theory is encouraged by the codes of conventional drama in so far as they allow conspiratorial actions to be shown and dramatised in a way that the more invisible operations of political power cannot be. In this respect, it might be argued that if such works were viewed in some quarters to be 'anti-British' by virtue of their criticisms of British institutions, their actual diagnosis of the 'British Question' was nonetheless constrained by the dramatic strategies that they employed (and the condensing of complex economic, political and ideological forces into personal villainy).

Conclusion

Despite the many criticisms of *In the Name of the Father*, the film's director, Jim Sheridan, suggested, somewhat optimistically, that his film might nonetheless contribute to a process of 'healing'.[36] Indeed, in its desire to give public acknowledgement to past injustices and to offer support for peaceful resistance rather than armed struggle, the film might be said to manifest something of the changing political temper of the period that led to the uneasy paramilitary ceasefires of 1994. These have, in turn, led to a steady flow of films – including *The Boxer* (1997), *Mad about Mambo* (1998), *As the Beast Sleeps* (2001), *The Mighty Celt* (2005), *Five Minutes of Heaven* (2009), *Mo* (2010) – that have sought to represent, and reflect upon, the challenges posed by the peace process within the 'new' Northern Ireland.[37]

By comparison, there have been relatively few works concerned with the legacy of the Troubles in Britain itself. This may be seen to correspond with a more general divergence in attitudes within Northern Ireland and Britain. Thus, whereas the question of how to deal with a divided past has remained a contentious political issue within Northern Ireland, it has largely disappeared from public discourse in Britain (where the conflict is generally regarded as over and done with). This, in turn, may be linked to perceptions that Al-Qaeda, Isis and other radical groups have not only superseded the PIRA as the primary threat to British security but elevated it to a new and even more unsettling level (such that the comedian Stewart Lee has felt able to create dark humour out of the suggestion that the IRA were 'decent British terrorists' by comparison).[38]

One of the few recent productions to look back has been Peter Bowker's three-part television drama, *From There to Here* (2014), dealing with the aftermath of the Manchester bombing of 1996 (one of a number of bombings that occurred following the breakdown of the IRA ceasefire). Focusing on the lives of one particular family, the programme works as a loose 'state-of-the-nation' allegory dealing with the decline of the Conservative government and the rise to power of New Labour. However, by exploring some of the consequences of the bombings upon those who were nearby when it happened, the programme also asks the question whether it is better to remember or to forget what are referred to as 'the cover-ups', 'lies' and 'terrible things' of the past.[39] Although the family saga at the centre of the programme may be too eccentric to carry the full allegorical burden placed upon it (or deal entirely adequately with the experiences of bombing victims), the production's willingness to explore the experiences of the Troubles in Britain and to reflect upon their legacy distinguishes it not only from a programme such as *Utopia*, with its confusing jumble of conspiracy theories, but also from most other film and television dramas of the same period that have preferred to avoid the issues altogether.

Notes

1 See P. Routledge, *Public Servant Secret Agent: The Elusive Life and Violent Death of Airey Neave* (London: Fourth Estate, 2002) for an account of the original theories.

2 See www.channel4.com/info/press/news/channel-4-statement-re-utopia-airey-ne ave (Accessed 29 May 2015).

3 L. Curtis, *Ireland: The Propaganda War* (London: Pluto, 1984); P. Schlesinger, *Putting 'Reality' Together: BBC News* (London: Constable, 1978).

4 According to J. Ruane and J. Todd, while Northern Ireland may be an integral part of the UK, it is in 'the perceptions of the British elite ... "a place apart", differentiated by its geography, history and culture ... where things are done differently, one to which (the more sensible and rational) British way cannot be exported'. See *The Dynamics of Conflict in Northern Ireland: Power, Conflict and Emancipation* (Cambridge: Cambridge University Press, 1996), p. 224.

5 J. Hill, 'Images of violence', in K. Rockett, L. Gibbons and J. Hill, *Cinema and Ireland* (London: Routledge, 1988), pp. 147–93.

6 R. Holles, 'BBC censor strikes again', *Guardian* (31 August 1979).

7 As part of the AHRC-funded research project 'The History of Forgotten Television Drama', based at Royal Holloway, University of London, *The*

Patriot Game has been restored with the help of the British Film Institute and Kaleidoscope. I am also grateful to the AHRC for its assistance with some of the research for this article.

8 TV Times (11–17 October 1969), p. 23.

9 J. Bell, 'The play that's too fiery for Ulster …', Daily Mirror (13 October 1969).

10 Daily Mail (16 July 1975).

11 New Statesman (18 July 1975).

12 J. Hill, 'Allegorising the nation: British gangster films of the 1980s', in S. Chibnall and R. Murphy (eds), British Crime Cinema (London: Routledge, 1999), pp. 160–71; M. McLoone, Irish Film: The Emergence of a Contemporary Cinema (London: BFI, 2000).

13 Hill, 'Images of violence', pp. 174–5.

14 S. Balhetchet, 'The Long Good Friday', A.I.P. & Co., 28, 1980, 3–8.

15 These reports are contained in the personal files of the film's producer, Barry Hanson, to whom I am grateful for access. Hanson ultimately refused to accept the cuts to the film and set about buying back the film from ACC, after which it finally appeared in cinemas.

16 S. P. Moysey, The Road to Balcombe Street: The IRA Reign of Terror in London (Binghamton, NY: Haworth Press, 2008).

17 Daily Mail (19 February 1977).

18 Morning Star (23 February 1977).

19 The Times (8 February 1977).

20 D. Paget, No Other Way to Tell It: Docudrama on Film and Television (Manchester: Manchester University Press, 2nd edn, 2011), pp. 231–2.

21 B. Woffinden, 'What's up Doc?', New Statesman and Society (30 March 1990), pp. 20–1.

22 T. Kirby, 'TV documentary "abuse of power"', Independent (26 March 1990), p. 2.

23 'Who bombed at Granada?', Sun (30 March 1990), p. 6.

24 P. Johnston, 'Thatcher hits at pub bombs trial by television', Daily Telegraph (30 March 1990), p. 4.

25 M. Brown, 'Thames TV withdraws from film on "bombs" case', Independent (25 October 1989), p. 2.

26 T. Sutcliffe, 'Cleared of all charges', Independent (3 July 1990), p. 11.

27 G. Bushell, 'ITV cowards boosting IRA', Sun (3 July 1990), p. 23.

28 Daily Telegraph, (17 December 1993).

29 R. Kee, Trial and Error (London: Hamish Hamilton, 1986); P. Hill with R. Bennett, Stolen Years: Before and After Guildford (London: Doubleday, 1990). The BBC2 film programme, Moving Pictures, considered criticisms of the film in an episode broadcast on 6 February 1994.

30 D. Paget, 'Making mischief: Peter Kosminsky, Stephen Frears, and British television docudrama', Journal of British Cinema and Television, 10:1 (2013), 171–86.

31 For further discussion, see R. Barton, Jim Sheridan: Framing the Nation (Dublin: The Liffey Press, 2002).

32 A. Roberts, '"The spine of the story is true and responsible"', *The Times* (8 February 1994), p. 34.

33 For a discussion of this issue, see M. McLoone, '*In the Name of the Father*', *Cineaste*, 20:4 (1994), 44–7.

34 R. A. Rosenstone (1995), *Visions of the Past: The Challenge of Film to Our Idea of History* (Cambridge, MA: Harvard University Press, 1995), p. 59.

35 See J. Stalker, *Stalker* (London: Harrap, 1988) and P. Taylor, *Stalker: The Search for the Truth* (London: Faber and Faber, 1987).

36 *Sunday Times* (17 October 1993).

37 J. Hill, *Cinema and Northern Ireland: Film, Culture and Politics* (London: BFI, 2006).

38 S. Lee, *How I Escaped My Certain Fate: The Life and Deaths of a Stand-Up Comedian* (London: Faber & Faber, 2011), p. 178.

39 The representation of the victims of bombings in Britain has been largely absent from film and television dramas. This links, in turn, to what has been perceived by the victims as a more general political disinclination within Britain to remember, or enquire further into, such events as the Birmingham bombings. See, for example, the report of the 40th anniversary of the Birmingham bombings in the Birmingham *Express and Star*, www.expressandstar.com/news/2014/11/21/40-years-on-and-no-justice-for-the-birmingham-pub-bombings-victims/imgid7841964/ (Accessed 29 May 2015).

Part IV

Memory, peace building
and 'dealing with the past'

18

Responding to the IRA bombing campaign in mainland Britain: the case of Warrington

Lesley Lelourec

On 20 March 1993, two IRA bombs exploded in the centre of Warrington on a busy Saturday, claiming two young lives and wounding more than fifty others. The attack left the local community shocked and appalled, and provoked a wave of indignation and sympathy nationally, across the water in Ireland and worldwide. The victims' families and members of the local community strove to come to terms with the tragedy by finding ways to foster closer links between Britain and Ireland, in the hope of preventing further acts of violence and hatred. Based mainly on interviews with the key protagonists in Warrington and drawing on local archives, this chapter sets out to place the 1993 Warrington bombing in the context of the IRA's bombing campaign in England. It will highlight the constructive response of the community in the aftermath of the bombing and will explore how this impacted on Anglo-Irish relations, adding new impetus to the fledgling peace process of the 1990s.

The Warrington bombings

Warrington was in fact targeted twice: there had been a previous attack on 25 February 1993 on the Warrington gasworks, which destroyed a gasometer. Three IRA members were apprehended by police constable Mark Toker, who was shot and injured carrying out a routine vehicle check. Two of the attackers were later arrested and sentenced to twenty-five and thirty-five years' imprisonment. The third bomber escaped and was never caught.[1] The second and deadly attack took place on a Saturday lunchtime on Bridge Street, in Warrington town centre, on 20 March 1993, the day before Mother's Day. A warning had been sent to Merseyside Samaritans, indicating that a bomb had been planted outside the Boots store. Police assumed that the warning referred to the Liverpool store and thus evacuated the area. However, two explosive devices, placed in dustbins outside shops, exploded one after the other some seventeen miles away in Warrington, killing three-year-old Johnathan Ball outright and claiming the life of twelve-year-old Tim Parry, who had sustained severe head injuries, five days later.[2] Johnathan had been out buying a Mother's Day card, accompanied by his babysitter. Tim, still recovering from an appendix operation, had gone into town with a friend to buy some Everton football shorts so that he could play in the less strenuous goalkeeping position for his local team. Fifty-six people were injured, including a young mother, Bronwen Vickers, who lost a leg and died from cancer a year later.[3]

The choice of Warrington, a seemingly ordinary small English town situated half-way between Liverpool and Manchester and boasting no major industry, took the local people completely by surprise, as it did not correspond to either a military or economic target. Senior police officers at the time believed that the second bombing may have been a reprisal for the arrest of the two IRA men after the first attack a month earlier.[4] No one was ever convicted for the bombing and the initial investigation ended in 1995.[5]

The number of IRA attacks in England increased considerably from 1990 onwards as the IRA leadership decided to 'take the war to the mainland'[6] (Table 18.1). This strategy was aimed at gaining maximum media attention on the premise that 'one bomb in England is worth 100 in Belfast',[7] so as to make the British public and businesses put pressure on their government to withdraw from Northern Ireland. Indeed, republicans had clearly announced their plan to attack economic targets in 1992: 'The campaign is costing Britain billions of pounds every year and it will only be a matter of time before people say they have had enough.'[8] Gary McGladdery points out that some attacks coincided with specific events such as negotiations from which republicans were excluded, as a way of making themselves heard. For example, the Manchester bombing on 15 June 1996 coincided with the exclusion of Sinn Féin (SF) from official talks. With its ongoing strategy of 'tactical use of armed struggle', the IRA intended to show that it had no alternative but to resort to violence if it was not allowed to participate in the negotiating process.[9]

According to McGladdery, 'There is clear evidence to suggest that the sustained bombing campaign in England during the 1990s arguably shaped the peace process. The City bombings in particular demonstrated the financial cost to the British, while they also drained PIRA [Provisional IRA] resources in Northern Ireland, highlighting the difficulties they faced in sustaining the war in the longer term.'[10]

Table 18.1 Irish terrorist incidents in Great Britain

Year	Bombings	Shootings	Total
1973	86	0	86
1974	127	3	130
1975	21	7	28
1976	8	2	10
1977	14	0	14
1978	4	0	4
1979	3	0	3
1980	2	0	2
1981	8	0	8
1982	2	0	2
1983	3	0	3
1984	1	0	1
1985	1	0	1
1986	0	0	0
1987	60	0	6
1988	1	0	1
1989	3	0	3
1990	15	3	18
1991	36	0	36
1992	57	3	60
1993	48	1	49
1994	31	0	31
1995	0	0	0
1996	7	0	7
1997	7	0	7

Source: London Home Office Organised and International Crime Directorate, 1997, compiled from three tables in Gary McGladdery, *The Provisional IRA in England. The Bombing Campaign 1973–1997* (Dublin: Irish Academic Press, 2006), pp. 227, 229.

Media attention (in terms both of general coverage and particular incidents) was paramount in the battle for hearts and minds during the Troubles.[11] The former editor and journalist, Roy Greenslade, has described a 'hierarchy of death' in the reporting of fatalities during the Troubles.[12] His findings indicated that the British media afforded maximum coverage to British victims of Irish violence, and he listed five distinct levels of coverage. The first rank comprised British people killed in mainland Britain, the second involved members of the security forces, the third was composed of civilian victims of republicans, followed by members of the IRA killed by security forces, and finally victims of loyalist paramilitaries. Greenslade compared the coverage of the Warrington bombing, which was 'front-page news for days and led all the TV and radio news bulletins'[13] to that of the killings of four Catholic men who were shot dead as they arrived for work at Castlerock, County Derry on 25 March, four days after Warrington. The same evening, seventeen-year-old Damien Walsh was shot in the back in West Belfast: 'To say they received scant coverage in the London-based press is to redefine the word scant. The Castlerock murders were covered in five lines in the *Sun*, two paragraphs in *Today*, three paragraphs in the *Express*. [...] The serious papers, the broadsheets, didn't do much better.'[14] However, the pictures of the two young boys from Warrington, which appeared on the front pages and television bulletins – an angelic-looking Johnathan Ball and the school photograph of a smiling Tim Parry – were ones that every family in Britain could instantly identify with. These powerful images reinforced the perception that here were truly innocent victims and confirmed the image of the IRA as barbaric monsters.

The political context

The year 1993 was to be pivotal, with the peace process in its tentative stages; contacts were taking place between various parties who would all ultimately be involved in the Good Friday Agreement (1998). Leader of the Social Democratic and Labour Party, John Hume, and Sinn Féin's (SF) president, Gerry Adams, had first met in secret talks in 1988, resuming discussions in April 1993, with Hume aiming to 'bring the republicans in from the cold', as he was adamant that only an inclusive process involving all the protagonists could bring about a peaceful settlement in Northern Ireland.[15]

When the Warrington bombing occurred, secret communications were underway between British officials and republicans. Despite Prime Minister John Major's denial at the time, news of these communications broke in November 1993, leading Major to tell the House of Commons that it would 'turn his stomach' to speak to Adams.[16] Officially, the British government was refusing to include SF (which it saw as the political wing of the IRA) in what was known as 'talks about talks', until there was a sustained cessation of hostilities. The nature and extent of a series of secret talks between the British government and the republican movement was revealed by the *Observer* in June 1998. The report indicated that a secret channel of communication had existed between the British government and the IRA for three years and the two sides had been in regular contact since February 1993. The fatal Warrington bombing occurred one month after the IRA leadership allegedly sent a message through a secret channel to the British government asking for advice on how to end the conflict.[17] Part of the message allegedly read:

The conflict is over but we need your advice on how to bring it to a close. We wish to have an unannounced ceasefire in order to hold dialogue leading to peace. We cannot announce such a move as it will lead to confusion for the volunteers because the press will misinterpret it as surrender; we cannot meet Secretary of State's public renunciation of violence, but it would be given privately as long as we were sure that we were not being tricked.[18]

In fact, SF refuted the authenticity of this and several other messages.[19] There has been much conjecture as to who actually did send the message. It is thought that an intermediary may have formulated the wording to reflect their own perceptions of what the republican leadership were thinking, in order to spur the British government into action.[20] The following reply from the British government was sent on 26 February 1993 (the day after the attack on the Warrington gasworks): 'We understand and appreciate the seriousness of what has been said: we wish to take it seriously and at face value. That will of course be influenced by events on the ground in the coming days and weeks.' The correspondence continued, with what has become known as 'the 9-paragraph note' sent by the British government on 19 March 1993, the day before the second attack on Warrington.

The importance of what has been said, the wish to take it seriously, and the influence of events on the ground, have been acknowledged. All of those involved share a responsibility to work to end the conflict. No one has a monopoly of suffering. There is a need for a healing process.[21]

According to the UK government version of the contacts, two days after the bombing, on 22 March 1993, the Provisional republican movement responded with the following message: 'It is with total sadness that we have to accept responsibility for the recent action. The last thing we needed at this sensitive time was what has happened. It is the fate of history that we find ourselves in this position, all we can think of at this time is an old Irish proverb: God's hand works in mysterious ways. Our hope is that this hand will lead to peace and friendship.'[22] However, SF also refuted this version in *Setting the Record Straight*: 'The British government version contained a 22 March 1993 message relating to the Warrington bomb. SF did not send this message. It is bogus.'[23] The SF president, Gerry Adams, did, however, make the following statement in the aftermath of the bombing:

Republicans, not least because we have also buried our children, know the agony of the families of Johnathan Ball and Tim Parry. Children are always innocent. None of the rest of us stands guiltless. Those who are now exploiting the understandable emotion and human reaction to the

Warrington explosions know this. Yet they are manipulating the genuine grief and deep sadness of people throughout Ireland to channel public opinion in one direction – against republicans. Republicans have nothing to fear from a genuine peace movement. Sinn Féin has been engaged in developing a peace process for some time now. I welcome any positive approach to building peace but I appeal to those who really wish to end the conflict to beware against letting themselves be cynically used.[24]

Against this backdrop, and just one month after the Warrington bombing, on 24 April, another IRA bomb exploded in Bishopsgate, London, resulting in one death, injuring forty, and causing £1 billion of damage.[25]

In September 2013, during a question-and-answer session following his lecture at the Warrington Foundation for Peace, Martin McGuinness (SF Deputy First Minister in the Northern Ireland Executive) told the audience that he had been preparing to leave for a secret meeting with senior British officials, due to be held on the Monday after the bombing, when he heard news of the explosion. He went on to say that he fully expected those talks to be cancelled. In fact, they went ahead.

The aftermath of the bombing in Warrington

The immediate local reaction to the Warrington bombing, unsurprisingly, was one of anger and bewilderment. Jo Robertshaw, from the local social services helpline reported that: 'The overwhelming difficulty was the question "Why?"'[26] Irish people living in Britain were often victimised during the Troubles, convenient scapegoats in the wake of atrocities,[27] and Warrington's hitherto well-integrated 5,000-strong Irish community initially bore the brunt of anger vented by a small minority. The town's Irish club was targeted by stones and an outhouse was set on fire.[28] However, the attacks ceased quickly after calls for restraint from civic leaders.

The huge media response following the bombing was heightened by the fact that the two fatalities were children. In the Republic of Ireland, the attack sparked an unprecedented peace initiative (which became known as Peace '93), initiated by Susan McHugh, a housewife, who phoned an RTÉ radio *Liveline* programme to voice her indignation as an Irish citizen at what had been committed 'in her name' (i.e. for the goal of Irish unity). She organised a meeting in Trinity College Dublin on 24 March 1993, which was attended by over 1,000 people. The movement gathered momentum and a Rally for Peace was planned for 28 March outside the General Post Office in Dublin. Registers of condolence were opened in over 100 Irish towns, and thousands of bouquets and messages of condolence were laid on St Stephen's Green (these were later flown to Warrington, courtesy of the Irish government, in time for the funeral of Tim Parry).

The Irish head of state, President Mary Robinson, attended both the televised funeral of Tim Parry on 1 April and the memorial service on 7 April. During the service, extracts from a letter from Cardinal Cahal Daly, archbishop of Armagh, were read out by Derek Worlock, the Roman Catholic archbishop of Liverpool:

> Rarely have I experienced such intensity of revulsion and indignation as this atrocity in Warrington has evoked all over Ireland. People here are outraged that such deeds are claimed by the IRA to be done in the name of the people of Ireland. The Irish people reject that claim with vehemence.[29]

In Northern Ireland, several nationalist sources spontaneously condemned the bombing, as exemplified by the nationalist *Irish News* editorial: 'the death of Johnathan Ball advanced the cause of a united Ireland by not one solitary inch; his death, and the death of countless others throughout the present conflict, has cast a shadow over our country'.[30] What caught the public's attention locally, nationally and worldwide was the dignified demeanour of the bereaved parents, Colin and Wendy Parry, and Wilf Ball and Marie Comerford. Their determination that their sons would not be forgotten and that their deaths should have a meaning gave rise to the extraordinary civic response to the bombing that would play a significant part in the peace process.[31]

A victims' appeal fund was set up on 22 March. Both the funeral of Johnathan Ball on 26 March[32] and the high-profile, televised funeral of Tim Parry on 1 April were attended by dignitaries, including President Robinson. Indeed, 1993 would bring together British and Irish heads of state and government on several occasions. A few days later, on 7 April 1993, a memorial service was attended by John Major, Prince Philip representing the Queen and President Robinson.

The parental response

The bereaved parents from the outset adopted an attitude that espoused dialogue and eschewed vengeance. Indeed, Colin and Wendy Parry embarked on a veritable crusade, which has had a two-fold purpose: to perpetuate the memory of their son and to build bridges between Ireland and Britain in the hope of preventing further acts of violence: 'Here was an appealing and, if I may say, a handsome young man, whose life had been snuffed out in an instant. Was he to be just one more statistic in the long line of killings arising out of the Northern Ireland problem? Not if I had anything to do with it he wouldn't.'[33] The actions of the victims' families have focused on striving to contribute in some positive way to further mutual understanding between Britain and Ireland rather than on revenge or simply a demand for bringing the perpetrators to justice. Having never previously set foot on Irish soil, the Parrys, accompanied by Wilf Ball, made their first trip to the Republic of Ireland to attend the Peace concert in Dublin on 24 April 1993 and appear on Gay Byrne's RTÉ programme, the *Late Late Show*. In 1994, the Parrys published their account of events since the bombing, entitled *Tim: An Ordinary Boy*, as a tribute to their son.

The Parrys undertook a series of trips and initiatives in the weeks and months following the death of their son. They embarked on a 'journey of understanding' in July 1993 – a trip to Northern Ireland on a fact-finding mission for a BBC *Panorama* documentary which was broadcast on 6 September 1993, meeting people from both traditions within the region, with the aim of discovering the reasons for the conflict and especially why some people would carry out such an atrocity. This quest for information echoed the bewilderment of so many of the people of Warrington.

Over the years, the families, especially the Parrys, have made countless media appearances and met with the main political leaders, on both sides of the Irish Sea.[34] Colin Parry, in particular, has not shied away from the media. His immense public suffering and dignified reaction has given him huge stature and the moral authority to engage with the other protagonists in the conflict and insist that politicians do the same. According to Marie Smyth:

> It seems that great suffering is perceived as having one of two main social, political and/or moral outcomes: as motivating revenge; or, if the sufferer manages to avoid being driven towards revenge, as morally educating and therefore qualifying the sufferer to act as a 'moral beacon'.[35]

Colin Parry has become a 'moral beacon' in Smyth's sense. The Parrys' insistence on pragmatism and willingness to take risks by engaging directly with those responsible for their son's death, and by supporting the new political arrangements, contrasts to Wilf Ball, who stated: 'I will never forgive the people who did this to me. John Major and Tony Blair have signed the forms for peace, but they have let all the prisoners out of jail and the bloodshed is still going on.'[36] However, Colin Parry, like Wilf Ball, has stopped short of forgiveness. He agreed to meet Martin McGuinness in 2001 at a press conference chaired by Reverend Stephen Kingsnorth, a prominent local Methodist minister, in which the former senior IRA man apologised for the bombing.[37] Wendy Parry campaigned for a lasting response to the death of her son and had the idea of setting up an organisation that would bring young people together from different sides of the divide in the Irish conflict. The Parrys founded a charity in 1995 in memory of the two boys, initially called the Warrington International Youth Centre trust, which became the Tim Parry Johnathan Ball Trust in 1998 and subsequently the Tim Parry Johnathan Ball Foundation for Peace in 2006. The foundation is located in a £3 million Peace Centre in Warrington.

The civic response

Townspeople and key civic and community leaders mobilised to show support for the bereaved families and to strive for peace by building bridges between the people of Britain and Ireland, north and south. Several community groups undertook peace-building initiatives, including members of the local clergy, local councillors and educationalists who created the Warrington Project, Ireland in Schools,[38] Warrington Community Peace Walkers and the Warrington Male Voice Choir (WMVC). Among the prominent participants were the Parrys, who spearheaded a lasting response to the bombing.

The Warrington Project (officially launched on 9 October 1993 in the presence of President Robinson and Prince Charles) was an educational response to the bombing, aiming to bring together schoolchildren from Britain and Ireland. At the inauguration, the Irish President declared: 'It seems to me that the people of Warrington have in this Project the great moral authority which such a community can draw upon when they make a common possession of their suffering and a common purpose of their healing.'[39] The Warrington Project received a £40,000 government grant and its trustees, who included John Dolan, the uncle of Johnathan Ball, were conscious of the need to support projects of a long-term nature. Links were set up between some Warrington schools and schools in the Falls Road, Belfast, in County Down, in Dublin and in County Offaly in the Irish Republic. One particular school in Warrington, the Thomas Boteler High School, was prominent in taking active steps to increase pupils' awareness of Ireland in general, by working on Irish topics:

[S]ince the IRA's bomb attack upon Warrington in 1993, the school has worked hard to develop the Irish dimension within the curriculum. It was felt very necessary to do so in view of the anger, bewilderment, ignorance and misconceptions about Ireland which figured so prominently in pupils' attitudes at the time of the tragedy.[40]

An annual lecture was established by Warrington Project trustees, beginning on 27 May 1999. The inaugural lecture, entitled 'Building bridges: Children's literature and mutual understanding', was given by Robert Dunbar 'to reaffirm the dedication of the people of Warrington to promoting good relations between the peoples of Britain and the island of Ireland through education and to serve as a reminder that the cause of peace requires constant nurturing'.[41]

All the groups and protagonists who had contributed to Warrington's response officially came together in an umbrella organisation, Warrington Ireland Reconciliation Enterprise (WIRE), on 1 September 1995,[42] which coincided with the first anniversary of the IRA ceasefire. WIRE constituted a general forum for exchanging information and sourcing grant aid.[43] For example, the Warrington Peace Walkers began by organising an annual walk to raise money for the victims' fund. On the second anniversary of the bombing, The Bridge organised an Irish festival (*fleadh*) in Warrington which would become an annual event. The WMVC already existed but championed themes of peace and reconciliation after the bombing, becoming hugely involved by touring the island of Ireland and appearing on Irish television. After a benefit concert in aid of the Warrington Victims' Appeal Fund on 16 April 1993, the choir went on to became the first English group ever to participate in a St Patrick's Day parade in South Armagh (1996). An editorial in the *Warrington Guardian* underlines the significant and proactive input of the choir to the peace initiative:

> The WMVC, to its credit, is striving to produce something good out of the evil blot on the town. Peace links have already been established with Dublin and the choir is now to fly out to Canada seeking to influence audiences there – and in particular to reduce North American funding of the IRA terrorists. It is a role they spontaneously adopted. When the politicians are seen to fail us, an initiative of this kind by a Warrington organisation, on behalf of the wider community, must be applauded.[44]

Some members of WIRE did not shy away from courting controversy and came under fire for going too far in reaching out to Irish republicans. For example, WIRE had planned talks for 7 September 1996 and had invited SF chairman Mitchell McLaughlin to Warrington. The IRA ceasefire had broken down on 9 February 1996, with the Canary Wharf bombing, which claimed the lives of two people, injured over forty others and caused over £100 million of damage. Some local residents, including the Reformed Church clergy, pulled out.[45] WIRE was officially wound up on the tenth anniversary of the bombing, although many of the various groups have continued independently; The Bridge continues its work, as do the choir and, of course, the Warrington Peace Centre. There was a feeling among some members of the community that it was time to move on. The Rev. Stephen Kingsnorth, who was at the helm of peace initiatives undertaken by the town centre clergy, commented: 'we have a commitment to carry on the work that has already been done. The Peace Centre is a permanent fixture and we want to give the people of Warrington a chance to lay the bombing to rest.'[46]

The most tangible legacy has undoubtedly been the Peace Centre, a £3 million building providing accommodation, catering facilities, an information technology suite and a sports hall.[47] It is co-owned and co-run by the Foundation for Peace, the National Society for the Prevention of Cruelty to Children and the Warrington Youth Club.[48] The Peace Centre was officially opened on 20 March 2000 by HRH the Duchess of Kent with the former Irish Taoiseach Albert Reynolds and former Prime Minister John Major, who had worked together to initiate the peace process in 1993–94. The foundation is the only organisation located in Great Britain working with the victims and survivors of political violence, including both military and paramilitary ex-combatants. It runs preventative programmes working with children and young people. For Colin Parry, 'this centre is the physical manifestation of our desire for a future without violence. Our aim is to ensure that no other children lose their lives in the way that Tim and Johnathan did. If we invest in children, then we can end the violence.'

A turning point in the peace process

The Warrington bombing and the public response it generated arguably constituted a significant development in the 1990s peace process, on several counts. The attack is seen as being an 'own goal' for republicanism,[49] targeting civilians on a Saturday afternoon in a busy high street in such an ordinary town as Warrington. The scenario of children – innocent victims *par excellence* – being blown up matched the British State's portrayal of the IRA as fanatical murderers and caused outrage within the nationalist community and even within republican ranks. The republican newspaper *An Phoblacht's* editorial a few days after the attack ran: 'Irish Republicans like everyone else were deeply shocked and saddened at the death of a young boy and the injuries caused to many others by the bombs at Warrington. The death of Johnathan Ball is another dreadful milestone in the conflict which republicans wish to see an end to.'[50] But, republicans also reminded their audience that the British security forces had killed children, with plastic bullets, for example, and the editorial went on to blame British authorities for failing to act on the warning.[51]

The wave of popular revulsion expressed in the Irish Republic, championed by President Mary Robinson, took away any justification of a higher cause (i.e. Irish reunification) as citizens on both sides of the Irish Sea reacted by expressing empathy and stressing the common ground in Anglo-Irish relations rather than the 'othering'[52] of either side.

An overarching discourse of mutual understanding and reconciliation emerged which muted the habitual response of simply equating the Irish with the IRA and seeking revenge. Warrington (albeit in a more auspicious context for peace) shifted the focus towards building bridges between Britain and Ireland. The acts of the IRA were set against the dignity of the victims and their families, and the ethos of the civic response was 'talking, not fighting'. (It has to be said that such an approach has not been approved of and shared by all victims of IRA bombings. For instance, the group representing victims of the 1974 Birmingham pub bombings, Justice for the 21,[53] staged a protest outside the Peace Centre in September 2013 to voice its disapproval of Martin McGuinness being invited there to deliver the annual Peace lecture.)[54]

In addition, the tragedy may well have contributed to bringing about a rapprochement between the British and Irish heads of state and governments, who were coming into contact in the public sphere during the funerals and memorial services in a show of sympathy and unity. These public appearances mirrored behind-the-scenes contacts that were certainly taking place between senior civil servants on both sides.

Crucially, the involvement of civic society influenced the debate on whether Britain should engage directly with other key protagonists in the conflict, namely the IRA. It encouraged a move towards an *inclusive* process, with Colin Parry as a moral beacon. Such a discourse would later be encapsulated in the Downing Street Declaration between Prime Minister Major and Taoiseach Reynolds issued on 15 December 1993: 'to foster agreement and reconciliation, leading to a new political framework founded on consent and encompassing arrangements within Northern Ireland, for the whole island, and between these islands'. This wording would become the framework for all subsequent agreements between the two states. Albert Reynolds declared in March 2009 that 'it was a senseless destruction of young life – that's what led us to making the Downing Street Declaration'.[55]

During the course of 1993, several significant meetings and events took place as the peace process gathered momentum. The first meeting between the Queen and President Mary Robinson was held on 27 May 1993. John Hume met the Taoiseach on 7 October 1993 to update him on his talks with Gerry Adams. Mary Robinson symbolically shook Gerry Adams's hand during a visit to West Belfast on 18 June 1993. On

29 October 1993, a joint statement was issued by the Prime Minister and Taoiseach in response to the Hume/Adams talks. However, the Shankill Road bombing of 23 October (10 dead, 57 injured) proved that the conflict was far from over. Finally, on 31 August 1994, the IRA announced a ceasefire on what would have been Tim Parry's thirteenth birthday: 'the most poignant vindication yet of our increasingly strong belief that Tim had not died in vain.'[56]

The small town of Warrington was thrust into the spotlight in tragic circumstances. The town's response, with the bereaved parents at the forefront, was to empower itself to take an active role in the struggle for peace. On 20 March 2003, the tenth anniversary of the bombing, HRH the Duchess of Kent concluded: 'no-one has tried to erase that day's memory but rather there is a feeling of embracing a disaster, a determination to gain from the experience rather than succumb to the evil of violence'.[57] The twentieth anniversary of the bombing, which took place on 16 March 2013, on the site of the explosions, involved the release of twenty doves of peace. Speaking at the ceremony, the Rev. Stephen Kingsnorth declared: 'we commemorate the victims of the terrible atrocity visited upon us but celebrate that good followed from evil as the community of Warrington became a byword for those who work for reconciliation'.[58]

Notes

1 *Warrington Guardian* (26 February 1993) www.warringtonguardian.co.uk/news/news_archive/warrington_bombing/history/4289902.The_first_IRA_attack_on_Warrington/ (Accessed 8 August 2009).

2 Ibid.

3 *Warrington Guardian* (20 March 2013) www.warringtonguardian.co.uk/news/news_archive/warrington_bombing/4274478.Brave_Bronwen_survived_Warrington_Bombing_but_lost_battle_with_cancer_a_year_later/ (Accessed 2 June 2014).

4 Ibid.

5 Statement by ACC Guy Hindle received by author on 1 September 2014: 'Cheshire Police carried out a comprehensive, thorough and professional investigation into the Bridge Street bombings of 1993 – an investigation which saw a dedicated team of detectives follow hundreds of lines of enquiry over a considerable period (the initial investigation ended in 1995). Cheshire Police has not currently got any active lines of enquiry. The case remains unsolved and if any information is received at any time then we would follow the same process as with any other unsolved case and this information would be reviewed.'

6 G. McGladdery, *The Provisional IRA in England: The Bombing Campaign, 1973–1997* (Dublin: Irish Academic Press, 2006), p. 171.

7 Ibid., p. 3.

8 *Belfast Newsletter* (26 November 1992).

9 McGladdery, T*he Provisional IRA in England*, p. 203.

10 Ibid., p. 143.

11 See L. Curtis, *Ireland: The Propaganda War – The British Media and the Battle for Hearts and Minds* (London: Pluto, 1984).

12 Roy Greenslade, the Damien Walsh Memorial Lecture, 4 August 1998. See http://cain.ulst.ac.uk/othelem/media/greenslade.htm (Accessed 24 May 2014).

13 Ibid.

14 Ibid.

15 Hume–Adams joint statements were issued on 24 April 1993; then 25 September, 20 November and 28 August 1994.

16 Hansard House of Commons Debates 6 ser. vol. 231 col. 35 (1 November 1993).

17 See 'Setting the record straight', www.sinnfein.ie/contents/15216, for Sinn Féin's version of communications with the British Government (Accessed 16 May 2016).

18 This quotation comes from the British government version of the message allegedly sent by the leadership of the Provisional Republican Movement, 22 February 1993: http://hansard.millbanksystems.com/lords/1993/nov/29/northern-ireland-iragovernment (Accessed 24 May 2014).

19 The *Observer* carried a report on 28 June 1998 in which it claimed that Denis Bradley, a former Catholic priest, had acted as a means of contact between the Republican movement and the British and Irish governments over a 20-year period. The report also claimed that Bradley was responsible for the message of 22 February 1993, http://cain.ulst.ac.uk/othelem/chron/ch93.htm (Accessed 16 August 2014).

20 J. Powell, *Great Hatred, Little Room: Making Peace in Northern Ireland* (London: Vintage, 2009), p. 72. Also see P. Taylor, 'Disobeyed orders and a dangerous message', *Guardian* (18 March 2008), www.theguardian.com/politics/2008/mar/18/northernireland.past1 (Accessed 30 August 2014).

21 http://hansard.millbanksystems.com/lords/1993/nov/29/northern-ireland-iragovernment (Accessed 30 August 2014).

22 Ibid.

23 www.sinnfein.ie/files/2009/Settingrecordstraight.pdf (Accessed 26 August 2014).

24 Ibid.

25 www.independent.co.uk/news/the-bishopsgate-bomb-one-bomb-pounds-1bn-devastation-man-dead-after-city-blast--two-more-explosions-late-last-night-1457397.html (Accessed 2 June 2014.)

26 G. Dawson, 'Trauma, memory, politics', in K. Rogers, S. Leyersdorff and G. Dawson (eds), *Trauma and Life Stories* (London: Routledge, 1999), p. 193.

27 See M. J. Hickman and B. Walter, *Discrimination and the Irish community in Britain* (London: Commission for Racial Equality, 1997).

28 *Warrington Guardian*, Special Edition: Bridge Street Bombing, 22 March 1993.

29 *Independent* (8 April 1993).

30 Reproduced in *Daily Post* (23 March 1993).

31 Johnathan Ball's parents split up shortly after the bombing. His father died in 2004 and mother in 2009 on the sixteenth anniversary of the bombing.

32 The funeral of Johnathan Ball on 26 March was attended by Gordon Wilson, whose daughter Marie had died in the Enniskillen bombing on Remembrance Day 1987.

33 C. Parry and W. Parry, *Tim: An Ordinary Boy* (London: Hodder and Stoughton, 1994), p. 101.

34 Colin Parry explains that talking to the media was a way for him to continue to nurture the memory of his son and constituted a type of therapy. *Independent* (21 July 1996).

35 M. Smyth, 'The human consequences of armed conflict', in M. Cox, A. Guelke and F. Stephen (eds), *A Farewell to Arms* (Manchester : Manchester University Press, 2000) pp. 133–4.

36 *Liverpool Daily Post* (19 March 2003).

37 *Warrington Guardian* (20 December 2001).

38 See L. Lelourec, 'Promoting mutual understanding and/or enriching the curriculum? The contribution of the Ireland in Schools forum to bringing Ireland into the English classroom', in W. Huber, S. Mayer and J. Noak (eds), *Ireland in/and Europe, Cross-Currents and Exchanges* (Vier: Wissenschaftlicher-Verlag-Trier, 2012).

39 *Liverpool Daily Post* (20 March 2003).

40 'The Irish Dimension', Thomas Boteler High School, available in WIRE archive, Warrington library.

41 R. Dunbar, 'Building bridges: Children's literature and mutual understanding', Inaugural Annual Lecture, Warrington Project, 27 May 1999, available in WIRE archive.

42 Minutes of meeting in WIRE archive, Warrington library.

43 WIRE comprised: Warrington Borough Council (in particular the Leader John Gartside, Deputy leader Mike Hannon and CEO Mike Sanders), the Warrington Project (involving local schools, especially Thomas Boteler High School and its headmaster, John Higgins) and John Donlan (Johnathan Ball's uncle), the Town Centre Clergy (represented by local Methodist minister Rev. Stephen Kingsnorth), the Warrington Peace Walkers, the Warrington International Youth Centre (Colin and Wendy Parry), the Warrington Male Voice Choir (represented by its director Barrie Johnson), The Bridge and Peace '93.

44 *Warrington Guardian* (23 April 1993); *Warrington Guardian* (14 May 1993).

45 *Liverpool Daily Post* (7 August 1996).

46 *Warrington Guardian* (20 March 2002).

47 The Parrys were helped by the then British Secretary of State for Northern Ireland, Mo Mowlam, to raise funds.

48 See www.thepeacecentre.org.uk/.

49 See, for example, Sean O'Callaghan, cited in *Liverpool Daily Post* (20 March 2003).

50 *An Phoblacht* (25 March 1993).

51 Ibid.

52 See M. J. Hickman, 'Binary opposites or unique neighbours: The Irish in multi-ethnic Britain', *Political Quarterly*, January–March 2000.

53 See www.justice4the21.co.uk/ (Accessed 26 August 2014).

54 See www.birminghammail.co.uk/news/local-news/birmingham-pub-bombing-protesters-shout-6066425 (Accessed 26 August 2014).

55 *Liverpool Echo* (31 March 2009).

56 Parry and Parry, *Tim*, p. 357.

57 www.thefreelibrary.com/WARRINGTON+10+YEARS+ON%3A+A+MESSAGE+FROM+THE+DUCHESS+OF+KENT.a098979315 (Accessed 27 March 2016.)

58 www.dailyrecord.co.uk/news/uk-world-news/warrington-bombing-ira-attack-20th-17679 (Accessed 31 August 2014).

19

'There's no way out but through'

Annie Bowman

My name's Annie Bowman.[1] I'm going to talk about the human cost of violent political conflict in terms of the difficulties that the Troubles created for me and the lasting impact it has had on me. Someone once said that there's no way out but through, and this is certainly the case for me, as I was so young when Dad was killed.[2]

I recently met a colleague of my dad's who told me that my dad had done a four-month tour, gone home and had been recalled. He described a man with mood swings and a propensity not to listen. They were being called out thirty to forty times a day, and the enemy was their own people who wore no uniform in an urban environment. Dad was an officer and under pressure to do his job quickly with the minimum of intelligence from his superior officers. This colleague said that he can now see that the traits that Dad had been showing at the time were the traits that we now call PTSD (post-traumatic stress disorder), but at that time and in that job, with the lack of bomb disposal experts in the field, there was no time for his superiors to consider this. At the age of twenty-nine Dad was also under pressure at home to provide for a wife and three kids, and to help his mum and his younger brothers and sisters financially. My dad was not the typical officer from a public school background, as his colleague had assumed, but from a family that had struggled through eviction, and at one point his brother was nearly put into care. And my dad was only twenty-nine when he was killed.

My dad was a bomb disposal officer killed whilst clearing a bomb factory in Derry a few months before my third birthday. I was too young to understand and too young to grieve for my dad at the time. My mum and the extended family found their own grief hard enough to bear, let alone knowing how to deal with the grief of three children under the age of five. My uncle's hair fell out permanently overnight. So they did the terribly British thing of 'keep calm and carry on'.

Apparently we lived in fear for a while that the IRA would kill the rest of us. Mum found it hard to talk to me about Dad, as I would always cry, and I found it hard to listen. As I was growing older I had to keep asking what had happened as my understanding increased, though I could still never listen. So I would keep asking and frustrating my mum. I thought for a long time that he had disappeared and would come back to get me sometime. I had nightmares about fires, but no comfort from Mum because she's not a very demonstrative, huggy sort of mum. The relationship between her and Dad's family was difficult, and her own mother was mentally ill. Growing up, we were very isolated from family and friends, and there was no one for any of us to talk to.

I have no memories of my dad whatsoever. I have only one photo with both of us on it. I have no experience of living in Northern Ireland and I had no real understanding of the Troubles. As a child I couldn't tell the difference between seeing Northern Ireland on the news and a World War Two film, but both of them scared me. At school I was always called a Nazi because I'd been born in Germany and my mum had given me a German name, which I consequently shortened to Annie. I can't remember my dad, and I buried this for thirty years. Over the last ten years or so I have been like Isis looking for the parts of Osiris so that I can bury him and grieve for him. I have asked Dad's brothers and sisters what he was like, I have found one childhood friend and a couple of people who worked with him along the way. But by the time I asked them, it was too long ago for most people to give me the answers I was looking for in any detail, because they'd forgotten. I know more about Dad's death than I do about his life or his personality.

When something as unexpected and catastrophic as this happens to a small child, unless the adults are given help to cope with it, then the trauma persists. No help was available and no help was sought. I cried for my dad all the time as a child. We had no close family or friends growing up and no grave to visit, and no dates were remembered. I didn't know my dad's birthday or the anniversary of his death until I was an adult. As a child, there was no way of talking about what had happened to people outside the family. If anyone asked what my dad's job was, I would say, 'He's dead,' quite bluntly. Northern Ireland was on the news all the time, but no one ever spoke about it, especially not to me. Isolation, silence and fear was what I experienced as a child.

The long-term effect of a violent death on a toddler should not be under-estimated. Although I remember nothing about the days after my dad was killed and I don't remember my dad at all, the traumatised adults around my brothers and me complicated our recovery from this tragedy. As a child I showed many signs of not coping, but no one did anything about it. We lost not only our dad but also the mother our mum would have been and the family we would have been closer to. All three of us, now in our forties, still struggle with depression, and I am now worried that because of my own experiences of being emotionally starved as a child I am not the parent I could have been or want to be, hence extending a legacy of the Troubles to the next generation.

In 2001 I got in touch with Jo Berry, whose father was killed in the 1984 IRA bombing of the Grand Hotel in Brighton and I went to the Glencree Centre for Peace and Reconciliation in Ireland to meet other victims of the Troubles. I had never wanted to go to Ireland, and I was very scared. Because I've never been able to grieve for my dad, when I think of him, the pain is as if he died yesterday. Talking to other victims was very hard. I went a couple of times and cried all the time, but it opened up the idea in me that if I could get better by exposing myself to this unspoken world, then I could maybe help other people. I became involved with the Peace Centre in Warrington and met other people, who have been important to me, and gave me a space where it was safe to talk about Northern Ireland, because people weren't scared of my tears.

Through the Peace Centre I have met ex-soldiers who served in Derry at the same time as my dad, and they helped me to learn what it was like and how scary it must have been, and gave me a context to Dad's death. I've been to Derry and Belfast as a guest of the Army, and met the current bomb disposal teams and talked about their job then and now. They showed me where Dad lived and died in Derry.

My introduction to becoming involved in peace and reconciliation was very slow, and this has been a long journey that may never end. In 2007 Jo Dover at the Peace Centre put my name forward to be part of the Sustainable Peace Network. I remember the first time I met the group; it was the first time I met ex-combatants. I was absolutely terrified, but gradually I talked to individuals one-to-one and found that the ex-IRA members were people who had been hurt too, and needed to tell me about their lives and needed me to listen. Some of them were surprised that their actions to help their own community, and their view that my dad was a legitimate target, had had such a deep, traumatic and long-lasting effect on my life. As a bomb disposal officer, especially once the Troubles had started, his life was at risk. Behind each legitimate target that they killed, the aim of which was to hurt the government and the armed forces, was a whole network of family and friends that had never been considered. Of course, they couldn't consider them, as they had dehumanised their enemy. I know that the many conversations that I had with the many people that I've met on my subsequent visits to Northern Ireland, and especially to Derry, have changed the way people view their own actions.

Although I don't have the opportunity to do public things very often, I've been told that what I have done is having a lasting impact. Some of the people that I have had deep conversations with are still talking publicly about them and, more importantly, they talk to the next generation about the effects that their past actions had on me and my family, in an attempt to stop them from making the same mistakes. I've tried to combat the anger, their anger, with my empathy.

Nowadays we hear about the bomb squad in Afghanistan fairly regularly, and the majority of the public seem to be proud of what our soldiers were doing out there. There is public support for the soldiers when they come back, dead, wounded or alive. There are various charities like Help for Heroes that have become well known; they are remembered on Remembrance Sunday. I am glad we have moved forward, but is this because the enemy in Afghanistan is someone that we can't identify with, that lives far away in a country that looks different to ours and has a culture that most of us don't understand? Northern Ireland wasn't officially a war, our soldiers were fighting in our own country with people who looked like us and spoke the same language. Northern Ireland wasn't remembered until recently on Remembrance Sunday. Were the public ashamed? When I am asked about what I do in Northern Ireland by acquaintances at home I have had people physically turn away from me when I start to explain; not because they disapprove, I don't think, but maybe because it is such a taboo subject, and I have turned a light remark into something ultimately dark that they cannot confront, and so they turn away.

One thing my mum did do for me was to not denigrate Catholics or Irish people for the actions of a minority group. I have heard many anti-Irish sentiments from some of the ex-soldiers I have met, and although I understand why, I have found them very hard to stomach.

I don't know why, but I've always found it hard to believe in evil, in the same way that I find it hard to believe in God. So, because of this, I can't believe that anyone should be vilified when we don't understand things from their point of view. People in my mind always have a positive motivation for everything that they do, even if it is warped in the eyes of others.

I also wonder about whom to blame for the death of my dad. I could blame the youths that were seen leaving the Nissen hut just before the patrol found it; I could blame the adults that were controlling and brainwashing them; I could blame the way the British were failing to understand the human rights of half the society in Northern Ireland. So, if there is no one concrete to blame, whom can I forgive? And for me, forgiveness is a form of communication that needs two people to enter into a discussion. If you take a life for whatever just cause, the punishment is to live with yourself knowing the hurt that you have caused. If you take a life and receive forgiveness, does that make living with what you have done easier? If you forgive someone, isn't that just acting like a God?

Notes

1 This chapter originates in a talk presented at 'The Northern Ireland Troubles in Britain: Impacts, Engagements, Legacies and Memories' conference at Brighton, 11–13 July 2012.
2 Captain Barry Gritten of 321 EOD Unit, Royal Army Ordnance Corps, was a bomb disposal officer and was killed as he tried to defuse a bomb on 21 June 1973.

20

The Birmingham pub bombings, the Irish as a 'suspect community' and the memories of the O'Reilly family

Laura O'Reilly

On 21 November 1974, Birmingham came to a halt after a series of bombs were exploded in two pubs in the city centre. The city had been a regular target for the Provisional Irish Republican Army (PIRA) during the Troubles,[1] and this particular night had severe repercussions for its large Irish community, including the implications surrounding the creation of the Prevention of Terrorism Act (PTA). This chapter will explore these implications in relation to Paddy Hillyard's idea of the Irish in Birmingham as a 'suspect community',[2] with a particular focus on members of the O'Reilly family, from Birmingham, who discussed their memories of the incidents in the years that followed.[3] The chapter sets out to understand why instances such as discrimination towards 'ordinary' people, including my family, occurred as a consequence of the actions of a minority of extremists.

The PIRA campaign in England began in the early 1970s as leading members, such as Sean MacStiofain, felt that 'the British needed a short, sharp shock'.[4] This followed the reintroduction, in August 1971, of the policy of internment without trial of those suspected of belonging to proscribed organisations[5] following its original success in the 1950s. The PIRA carried out its first attack in England on 31 October 1971 at the Post Office Tower in London. Fortunately there were no injuries in this instance.[6] However, the British were now being attacked at home, making the war increasingly personal for many people living in Britain. The importance of this cannot be overstated, as the following years would not only see further political implications, but would also have a great impact on the Irish communities living in England.

Arguably, the Troubles made life both difficult and uncomfortable for many in the large Irish community in England. Irish immigration to England began in the nineteenth century, when poverty forced millions to emigrate to seek better opportunities overseas. As Birmingham was rapidly industrialising there was plenty of work available, and the Irish, who were typically hardworking, were happy to pick up jobs that were often unwanted by English workers, making the city a regular choice for Irish immigrants. The years following the Second World War saw the greatest influx of Irish immigration to Birmingham, as the demand for workers to rebuild the devastated city was at an all-time high.[7] By 1951 there were 58,000 Irish citizens living in the city[8] and their numbers continued to grow, reaching over 70,000 by the 1990s.[9] Carl Chinn, a historian from Birmingham, discusses the relationships between the communities in the city during the twentieth century, mentioning the predominantly good relations that were present prior to 1974.[10] However, relations would get dramatically worse following the tragic events of the Birmingham pub bombings of November that year.

The Birmingham pub bombings

Birmingham was repeatedly targeted by the PIRA during the Troubles, but it is the Birmingham pub bombings that have remained in the city's collective memory. Attacks in the city started in 1973 and, although there were no fatalities, the Irish community within the city were eager to condemn such actions.[11] On 14 November 1974, just days before the Birmingham pub bombings, James McDade, a young volunteer for the PIRA, was killed during a premature explosion whilst he was attempting to plant a bomb in Coventry. This was just three years after his brother had been killed by the British Army in Belfast. However, James was the first member of the PIRA to be killed in England since the organisation began its campaign in March 1973.[12]

Then, on 21 November 1974, Birmingham was shaken by one of the worst attacks to occur during the Troubles. Two bombs exploded in two pubs, killing twenty-one and seriously injuring 183.[13] The first bomb, at The Mulberry Bush, exploded at 8.17 p.m. Police Constable (PC) Rodney Hazlewood witnessed the attack as he responded to a tip-off call made minutes earlier: 'There was the loudest thunderclap and rumbling and the ground shook. Debris was coming down all over the road. It was like a volcano had erupted, people running and screaming.'[14] However, this was not the only bomb planted by the PIRA team in the Midlands that night. Just 300 yards away, the Tavern in the Town, a pub situated below street level and a favourite amongst the city's youth – this night being no exception, with over 100 youngsters crowded into the dimly lit bar – suffered a similar outcome as a second bomb exploded a few minutes later. PC Brian Yates was one of the first to the scene and began clearing the debris and hurried into the pub to try to aid survivors. The scenes he describes are unimaginable: 'The people who were obviously dead were left and the living were dragged clear. I tried to keep count of the dead but gave up after the fifth.'[15] Fortunately a third bomb, set to go off in the Ladywood area of the city, failed to detonate.[16]

The Birmingham pub bombs were more indiscriminate than previous attacks, focusing on two very busy pubs in the city centre. The attacks were a propaganda disaster for the PIRA and condemnation came from both sides of the Irish Sea, including from PIRA leaders. They released a statement saying that 'it has never been and is not the policy of the PIRA to bomb non-military targets without giving adequate warnings to ensure the safety of civilians'.[17] In fact, the PIRA was so unsettled by the number of civilian deaths caused by the Birmingham pub bombings that it would be eleven years before the organisation accepted responsibility for them. In an interview in 1996, Billy McKee, a former member of the Army Council of the PIRA, expressed his shock at the extent of the carnage:

> I never approved of civilian loss of life. I didn't mind our own people and the 'Brits', the security forces going down but I didn't agree with ordinary civilian people losing their lives. At the time there was no report coming in to us about who was responsible and I think it was about a month later that I found out that it was our own people who had carried it out.[18]

The Birmingham pub bombings were arguably a turning point for the conflict in England, and the aftermath was significant, particularly for the Irish communities in England.

The effects of the Birmingham pub bombs

Pre-empting the potential backlash that the Irish communities would face within the city, as there had been previously in 1973, there were strong condemnations of the atrocity from Irish community leaders like Pat McGrath and local Irish councillors such as John O'Keefe. The representatives made it clear that 'we in the Irish community are doing everything in our power to show we do not support violence of this kind'.[19] In some ways, there was also a sense of shame and guilt on the part of the community,[20] as these atrocities were being committed in their name and in many cases for a cause they agreed with, whether they agreed with the methods or not.

Prior to 1974 there were many who understood the root cause of the republican struggle and were often openly sympathetic to the political goals of the PIRA. In the early 1970s there was arguably a distinction between those who were 'for the IRA against British Imperialism', like John Lennon, who famously showed his support during a demonstration in London, and those who could describe their view as 'unconditional but critical support for the IRA', meaning that they supported both the cause and the means by which the PIRA was trying to achieve its goals.[21] Many people, in particular the Irish living in England, could relate to the first definition, as the idea of a united Ireland is a perfectly legitimate political belief to hold. However, by the mid 1970s, and particularly after the pub bombings, in the eyes of many these distinctions were no longer relevant[22] and, understandably, public opinion turned overwhelmingly against the PIRA. An opinion poll of the British public in 1975 showed that 88 per cent of those questioned supported capital punishment for convicted terrorists.[23] This meant that the valid idea of supporting a united Ireland was now interpreted by the British media, public and government as support for the PIRA, a conclusion supported by studies of the representation of the Troubles in the media.

Liz Curtis has examined the methods used by the British media when reporting the conflict. In an attempt to remain objective, they would merely report the 'who, what, where, when', whilst overlooking the context and background, making the violence appear random.[24] This had particular implications for the Irish communities in England. As the background of the violence was ignored, the distinction between the Irish community and the PIRA was blurred, and simplified to one of support for the PIRA's tactics, rather than understanding the wider political sympathy for the republican cause of a united Ireland.[25] Therefore, PIRA bombing in England caused an anti-Irish feeling among the general population, which was encouraged by the media.

There are many examples of this 'anti-Irish feeling' in the aftermath of the bombings. There were 'a wave of attacks on Irish community centres, bars and businesses. Thirty Midlands factories were hit by strikes in protest against the bombings. Attacks on Irish workers were even reported at some factories.'[26] Also, there were more subtle instances, such as the Gaelic Athletic Association having planning permission withheld for over six years, preventing it from developing its Birmingham stadium. But possibly the most common form of discrimination was in the form of jokes about the Irish, who seemed to be fair game for anyone, both in everyday life and on TV or radio.[27] It was often forgotten that some of the victims of the bombings were Irish themselves and one Irish mother even lost both of her sons on that night.[28]

As well as the victims, the Birmingham bombs directly affected the lives of a further six innocent Irishmen, five of whom were arrested on

the evening of the pub bombs as they attempted to board the Heysham–
Belfast ferry on their way to James McDade's funeral. McDade had been
a childhood friend to the men but, unknown to them, was a member of
the PIRA.[29] A sixth man was arrested in Birmingham the following day.
The men were all friends, living in the city after emigrating from Ireland
over the previous decade. None of the men was associated with the IRA
on any terms, but their aim of attending McDade's funeral made them
instant suspects by association – a repercussion of the anti-Irish feeling
that was now prevalent in Britain. The added animosity that evening,
following the attacks, meant that they were in the wrong place at the
wrong time, as five the men had purchased tickets from Birmingham
New Street station and their train had departed just after the bombs
had exploded. There was pressure to secure justice and achieve a 'result
in the fight against terrorism'.[30] As the West Midlands Police sought to
solve one of the biggest cases of mass murder in British criminal history,
the 'Birmingham Six' would become one of a number of similar cases of
miscarriage of justice.[31]

The men were taken to Morecambe police station, where they were
forced to sign confessions after forensic tests indicated that they had
recently handled explosives. Despite errors made in administering
the forensic tests, and the unexplained wounds on the men, which
were overlooked by multiple officers and lawyers, the group of men
were charged, found guilty and sentenced to life imprisonment.[32] The
men had no chance of a fair trial in Birmingham with public pressure to
secure a conviction. Also, the rights of Irish prisoners in English custody
were not the immediate concern of the British, who had supposedly seen
their way of life attacked by these men who seemed intent on killing
innocent civilians.[33] Mr Justice Bridge, the judge in charge of the trial,
told the men, 'you stand convicted on each of twenty-one counts, on the
clearest and most overwhelming evidence I have ever heard, of the crime
of murder'.[34]

After seventeen years in prison and unsuccessful appeals in 1981 and
1987[35] the Birmingham Six were finally released in 1991. The Appeal
Court considered that their convictions were 'no longer satisfactory. It
was judged that neither the confessions nor the forensic scientific evidence upon which the convictions rested were reliable.'[36] It was only
after the organisation in charge of the convictions – the West Midlands
Serious Crime Squad (SCS) – was disbanded in 1989,[37] due to allegations
of corruption, that the appeals of the men were taken seriously. Gareth
Peirce, one of the lawyers involved in the campaign for the freedom of
the Birmingham Six, believes that there were, however, still dozens of
unidentified miscarriages of justice. In 1999 the lawyer called for a new

inquiry into the scale of the corruption committed by the organisation. Peirce said: 'I have no doubt there are dozens of people who have served time in jail but were innocent. The SCS were operating like the Wild West, they were out of control.'[38]

A 'suspect community'?

As predicted by the leaders of the republican movement, there would be political repercussions. The already unpopular policy of internment had been in place since 1971, and since 1973 there had been calls from the Conservative Party to make the PIRA illegal in Great Britain 'whilst it effectively maintains a war against the country'.[39] The Conservatives drew up plans to limit movement between England and Ireland, excluding suspected terrorists completely, but the police had been against this, as it would have been difficult to implement. However, after the extremity of the recent incident they were now in favour:

> The revulsion of ill feeling in the country and parliament following the recent terrorist incidents in Birmingham ... made possible legislation on a package which would provide substantially wider powers for the police and enable the IRA and other terrorist organisations connected with Northern Ireland to be proscribed.[40]

The PTA was introduced just days after the Birmingham bombs in an attempt to 'combat the threat of terrorism'. It 'provided police with extended powers of arrest and detention and gave them new powers to control the movement of persons entering and leaving Great Britain and Ireland'.[41] This intensified the already contested policy of internment, but its quick implementation suggests that it was a panic measure by a beleaguered British government. However, as argued by Hillyard, the implications of this for the Irish communities in England were vast. He argues that the biggest issue with the PTA was that it created a 'suspect community', which the police were very interested in and which took away certain civil liberties for Irish people living in Britain simply because of their ethnicity. However, for Hillyard, one of the most troubling aspects of this was that it created a suspect community not only for the authorities, but also for the public too,[42] and this had a greater, negative impact on regular, innocent Irish people.

The O'Reillys

Ben and Margaret O'Reilly, my grandparents, emigrated in 1963 from Cavan, in the Republic of Ireland, on the border of Northern Ireland, to Sparkhill, Birmingham. Here they raised four children – my father, Barry, and my three aunts, Yvonne, Karen and Dawn. Being the third generation of the family to live in Birmingham, it might be expected that I would have acquired a significant understanding of the Troubles and the effects they had on my own family. However, this was not the case and it was not until this study began and my relatives were formally interviewed that the information that follows came to light. This was the first time in almost half a century that the topic had been discussed within my family and what was interesting, particularly in the second interview, was the understanding that their experiences were 'normal'. First, Ben and Margaret were interviewed together and were asked a series of questions about their experiences of being Irish and living in England during the Troubles and how the introduction of the PTA had affected them. This was followed by a joint interview with Barry, Yvonne, Karen and Dawn. This interview was far less structured than the first, as the O'Reilly children felt more at ease in discussing their experiences growing up as English children of Irish descent living in a large Irish community.

What follows is an attempt to explain some of their experiences, including this normalisation, using Hillyard's research, alongside that of Mary Hickman et al. on community.[43] In addition, the research is used in an attempt to understand, in terms of the bigger picture, how the civil and human rights of ordinary people were affected negatively by the PTA and the creation of the 'suspect community'.

As Ben and Margaret are from the Republic of Ireland and are Catholic, I began by asking for their opinion of the political aspect of the IRA's campaign. Ben's response was:

> The IRA – they were fighting a good cause but doing a lot of wrong things. These things shouldn't have happened, but the IRA was necessary. Ireland had to do something to protect the country. But it's not so much about the country, as the human rights and the civil rights, that's what started the Troubles in Northern Ireland in the 1960s. It wasn't political – it was about civil rights because Catholics weren't allowed to do anything. If you went for a job you were asked what school you went to and that told them who you were – if you went to Catholic school, you didn't get the job. Catholics were third-class citizens in their own country and that's what started the whole trouble.[44]

It is important to note Ben's use of the word 'necessary'. Before the formation of the PIRA there was little in terms of representation and protection for the Catholic community in Northern Ireland, and this is further highlighted by the need for the civil rights marches in 1968.

The denial of civil rights and the perception that Northern Catholics were 'third-class citizens' and unable to defend themselves, which was brought to public attention in Britain during the riots in 1969, is often viewed as an important factor in the re-militarisation of the IRA in the years that followed.

Although not being part of the IRA, or even agreeing with the bombing campaign in England, the family still faced the discrimination that came with being Irish in Britain at the time. Hickman's study on suspect communities supports this; she claims that 'fear and caution were generated by the knowledge of the Terrorism Laws and by what seemed to be the arbitrariness of their implementation'.[45] Throughout the interview Margaret and Ben said they were constantly on their guard. Margaret explained this as follows: 'We say that we weren't but you were very much on your guard that you didn't draw anything on yourself. We know from hearing things, it didn't take a lot to get yourself, well you know ...';[46] and that was where Margaret stopped.

Margaret was referring to the fact that the PTA allowed anyone to be detained for twenty-four hours, even without an actual offence being committed – explaining the feeling of being 'on your guard'. This was perfectly legitimate under the PTA in cases where police had 'reasonable grounds for suspecting that a person was either subject to an exclusion order or guilty of some offence under the PTA'.[47] In theory, this sounds understandable; however, as Hillyard explains, the power to arrest when someone is suspected of being 'concerned in the commission, preparation or instigation of acts of terrorism'[48] does not actually require that a person has committed any offence. Additionally, Hillyard explains that the most worrying aspect of the legislation was that no specific acts were defined under the PTA. This essentially meant that it was the judgement of the officer in the specific situation to decide whether someone was a suspect – making the law appear to be subjective and therefore making any Irish person, including Margaret and Ben, a suspect at all times.

In his study on the influence of internment on the extension of the idea of a suspect community, Chris Davenport explains that people associated with the IRA, as well as some who were merely believed to be sympathetic to the cause, were removed from society and placed in prison. 'This allowed the political authorities to engage in activities such as torture to punish individual challengers as well as figure out what they are engaged in.'[49] Davenport further argues that this was with the intent of isolating and breaking support for the IRA. This led to something as small as Margaret's feeling that she was unable to even carry a copy of the *Irish Post*, because of the risk that someone might misinterpret this.[50] It also had wider implications that I discovered in both interviews, creating an unwillingness to discuss the situation with anyone, particularly those who were not Irish.

Arguably, the PTA may have restricted 'perfectly legitimate political activity and debate around the Northern Ireland question through the creation of a climate of fear, the direct harassment of people and groups involved in Irish politics and by censorship'.[51] This was one of the negative implications of the PTA. It allowed the media, the police and the British public to ignore that there was a difference between simply holding the belief that Ireland should be united and the illegal activity of the IRA in their attempt to achieve this.[52] Margaret and Ben were fully aware of the repercussions of discussing such delicate topics in mixed company, due to the PTA and what the police could do with even the smallest amount of suspicion. As Margaret remembered: 'You were scrutinised going through airports and that ... there were people that were pulled in and questioned for very little reason.'[53] Ben continued: 'The only reason being you were Irish.'[54] Hillyard concludes that the PTA was a discriminatory piece of law, as it was openly directed at one particular section of the public – in this case the Irish. In addition to this, the law meant that if anyone refused to co-operate, they would face prison, a £1,000 fine, or both. The law therefore removed the right to remain silent when questioned, which was enshrined in general law at the time. The implications of this were that if a suspect were to remain silent, the court could make an inference from this, and by remaining silent they would now be committing a new crime, in addition to the one they were previously 'suspected' of. The law could therefore be used legitimately against them in these circumstances. This consequently meant that the civil rights of the people targeted by the PTA were removed, making the Irish community as a whole a suspect one.[55]

I went on to ask what the family understood about the conflict from reporting in the media. Barry responded with:

> What would happen was, you'd see it on the news – an atrocity – okay, and it would be Irish people committing this atrocity and that's all you'd get off the news. It was evil and the people were evil but of course then, my dad [Ben] would pipe up and say hang on a second ... so you'd always get that two sides of the story.[56]

The 'two sides of the story', however, were not represented in the media. It was merely due to the fact that Barry had an Irish father that he learned about the political aspect of the Troubles. Violence dominated British media coverage of the Six Counties. In a survey by Phillip Elliot, he concluded that most stories were about acts of violence or the enforcement of law, referring to the PTA, and that less than a third of stories dealt with the politics surrounding the subject.[57] The British media's lack of coverage in this area therefore adds to the notion of a suspect community, as there was no mainstream explanation for the events or why they were occurring. Consequently, this would have strengthened the idea that the conflict was merely extreme Irish terrorism without a cause.

This silence in discussing the conflict is further highlighted by the conversation that the O'Reilly children had about it. They said, one after another:

> You just wouldn't get into a discussion about it because you'd know for a fact that, unless you were talking to an Irish person, you were not going to meet somebody that was non Irish that was going to be sympathetic towards any of it. (Yvonne)[58]
> Dad was completely against what they were doing but not the cause. (Karen)[59]
> But I'd be happy enough not to enter into a conversation about it. I knew that they wouldn't know what I knew, because I knew the history, and I knew, although unjustifiable, there was a reason that it was happening but they just saw, you know … (Barry)[60]

Dawn finished Barry's comment:

> bloodshed. (Dawn)[61]

Hickman contends that 'when the IRA planted bombs in Britain, their political claims were omitted or downplayed in the establishment's reaction and Northern Ireland featured as something relatively remote'.[62] This media tactic of associating the IRA with irrationality was to discredit and weaken any argument that might be given as to its political agenda.

However, in the case of the O'Reilly children, who were perhaps not fully aware of the extremity of the PTA, there was no one to discuss these topics with. Growing up in a predominantly Irish community meant that everybody already knew the state of affairs, so it was assumed that there was no need for it to be discussed. However, when they left that community, whether by entering the workplace or starting university, this was not the case. Barry elaborates on his experience when he was sixteen and went to work in 1982, and, although not having an Irish accent but having an Irish surname, he was immediately associated with the IRA:

> You see, there were still bombings going on then and if something happened you'd be the first to hear about it off them. You obviously already knew about it but they felt like they had to remind you. It would be 'oh, I see your lot are at it again' or something like that.[63]

This association of 'your lot' is exactly what Hillyard is referring to in the context of a suspect community. Categorising an entire ethnic group based on the actions of a small minority is an example of institutionalised racism. Hickman argues that there are levels of acceptance with regard to Irish racism,[64] in the sense that it occurred so regularly that most British people would not have even deemed it as being racist. This explains why the O'Reilly children felt their experience was 'normal' and, additionally, why they had never discussed it prior to my interview. This was further encouraged by anti-Irish racism in popular culture.

By 1981 there were over one million Irish people living in Britain and by this time the 'notion of the Irish as an inferior race was firmly established in English popular culture and within the state'.[65] Yvonne and Barry expressed their awareness of this in the interview when I enquired about the racism they felt when they entered the workplace:

> As you went to work when you were sixteen you got the trouble, you got all the Paddy comments. (Barry)[66]
> You've got the stigma haven't you; you're not supposed to be bright. I think you were under-estimated as soon as they knew who you were. (Yvonne)[67]

Of course, Yvonne is referring to 'as soon as they knew you were Irish'. This stigma was encouraged by popular culture in Britain and it was reinforced by the media. For example, newspaper cartoonists have often taken up the theme of depicting the Irish as 'bestial or sub-human',[68] while anti-Irish jokes have spread the message that the Irish are less intelligent than the English. This theme has been promoted by actors and comedians and can now be seen to be so pervasive that even the term 'Irish' can often be found being used in everyday conversation to describe behaviour that is confusing or illogical.[69]

A particular aspect of the interviews that stands out is the fact that Ben, Margaret and their children all felt that they stayed within their Irish community for the majority of the time during the period of the Troubles. Margaret worked in Irish-run pubs from 1970 onwards and the children went to Catholic schools, which meant that they socialised with Catholic children of Irish descent. Dawn talked about the time when she moved out of Birmingham in 1995:

> When I went to university in Nottingham, that was the first time, but this was a very different time scale to when they [Barry, Karen and Yvonne] were at school, that's the first time I ever met anybody who wasn't Irish or didn't have Irish family or wasn't of Irish descent. I don't know if you noticed it as a kid but when you moved out of that community, that's when you noticed it – out of that cocoon wasn't it?[70]

Dawn talks about a different time scale to that when her brothers and sisters were at school, having being born over a decade after her oldest sibling, Barry, but this is still quite a shocking statement for somebody who would call herself English and had lived in England her whole life. In her report, *The Irish Community in Britain: Myth or Reality?*, Hickman explains that it is common that a minority population who are displaced, whether by force or voluntarily, search for their roots and may therefore find their sense of belonging, mutuality or identification in the imagined community of the nation to which they feel they belong[71] – explaining the family's sense of being in a 'cocoon'. Additionally, it also explains the community's retreat to that 'cocoon' in an attempt to shield themselves from the effects of the conflict, including the PTA and the racism that followed. Although Ben and Margaret were very careful to make sure that they integrated well in their new society, and were keen to make sure that their children identified with their Englishness too, they still stayed confined to their Irish community. This willingness to blend in, however, wasn't the case for everyone. Dawn explains: 'I went to school with children who were actively encouraged to be anti-English, but we weren't.'[72]

Hickman, explaining the difficulty of migrating from a country that was a former colony of England, argues that as people migrate, they do so with a system of beliefs, understandings, religion and language. Although language may not seem like an important factor for the Irish, this could include accent, which was an issue for many Irish people, as it allowed them to be distinguished as such.[73] These factors have shaped them in a particular way and they are now obliged to come to terms with and make something of the new cultures that are before them. In the case of the Irish in Britain this is a complex situation. People like Ben and Margaret, who disagreed with the British establishment in Ireland, but had chosen to live in England, faced a conflict of ideology that is reflected by Yvonne, asking her dad about the situation:

> I remember saying to dad, we were parked on Court Road, outside the police station funnily enough, waiting for someone to come out of Sparkhill Park and it was around that time that you were talking about. I was about twelve, and he was listening to the news and it was about the IRA as it was every day of the week then and he was getting quite worked up about it, you know saying what he thought and so forth – the unfairness and the unjustness and everything and I remember saying to him, and I didn't mean it in a cheeky way, but I meant it like as a matter of fact. I said, if you felt that strongly about the British establishment, why did you choose to come over here and raise your family over here and he didn't answer me. I think it was the first time he realised the situation he was in, he was now part

of that establishment, even though he had different views about his own
home, he had English children.[74]

This conflicting ideology that was felt by Ben, and most likely by
many Irish people in Birmingham, may be why the majority lived in the
same area, as it is often easier to identify with and understand those
with similar beliefs to your own. Hickman explains this by stating that
Irishness in Britain is different to Irishness generated in Ireland. Often,
'individuals that are prey to racism find themselves constrained as a
community'.[75] This is increased by the sense of confusion that belonging
to a new state, particularly one with which you fundamentally disagree,
would have involved. Essentially, those who feel threatened will often
stick together, and this was shown by the inwardness of the community that was intensified by the Troubles – a community that Ben and
Margaret are still part of today.

Conclusion

The violence in Britain reached its peak in 1974 with the Birmingham
pub bombings, which led to the enacting of the PTA. One of the greatest implications of this legislation was the creation of the Irish living in
Britain as a 'suspect community', with an upsurge in anti-Irish prejudice
in England. This suspect community included my family, who until I
began my research had never fully understood the prejudice they faced
following the anti-terrorism legislation. As the British State has refused
to accept responsibility for any role it may have played in the Troubles,
the British have placed themselves as a disinterested third party who
were attacked by the irrational Irish who are 'innately prone to violence',[76] using the media to reinforce this position.

Arguably, the O'Reilly family, including myself, has been shaped by this
history. Before beginning this study I understood the basic facts about the
conflict in Northern Ireland but had never considered the effects it had
on regular people, people whom I have known growing up. Breaking the
years of silence within the family has now opened up new discussions and
created new understandings of a period that was difficult to live through.

A particular issue within this study was of a more personal nature.
That was the difficulty of discussing such a contentious and perhaps
private topic within my own family and the fact that, while interviewing them, it was often hard to detach myself from the issues raised. The
topic was one that I had previously viewed purely from a historical
perspective, and to now approach it in this way was, at times, tough.
However, the outcome was rewarding and the O'Reillys are now far

more understanding of our own circumstances than we were previously and are now becoming increasingly comfortable with discussing the period among ourselves.

The value of oral history cannot be overstated. It had taken almost half a century for my family to discuss this topic; but over forty years after the events the Birmingham pub bombings, the PTA and the effects they had on an entire community are still not being discussed more generally. It is a travesty that a vital part of the population of a country that prides itself on democracy and equality, was – and arguably still is – made to feel inferior, and guilty of crimes they did not commit and, for the most part, would condemn.

Notes

1 P. Bew and G. Gillespie, *Northern Ireland: A Chronology of the Troubles, 1968–1993* (Dublin: Gill & MacMillan, 1993), p. 7.
2 P. Hillyard, *Suspect Community: People's Experience of the Prevention of Terrorism Acts in Britain* (London: Pluto Press, 1993).
3 This chapter has developed out of research undertaken for my final year dissertation ('The Northern Ireland conflict, 1968–1998, and the impact it had on Irish communities in England') on the BA (Hons) Globalisation: History, Politics, Culture at the University of Brighton, 2014.
4 M. Dillon, *25 Years of Terror: The IRA's War Against the British* (London: Bantam, 1996), p. 163.
5 Bew and Gillespie, *Chronology of the Troubles*, pp. 36–7.
6 G. McGladdery, *The Provisional IRA in England: The Bombing Campaign 1973–1997* (Dublin: Irish Academic Press, 2006), p. 235.
7 C. Chinn, *Birmingham Irish: Making Our Mark* (Birmingham: Birmingham Library Services, 2003), p. 162.
8 Ibid., p. 117.
9 Birmingham City Council, *Irish History in Birmingham* (2014). www.birmingham.gov.uk/birminghamirish (Accessed 21 April 2014).
10 Chinn, *Birmingham Irish*, p. 165.
11 Ibid., p. 162.
12 McGladdery, *The Provisional IRA in England*, p. 89.
13 Dillon, *25 Years of Terror*, p. 188.
14 C. Mullin, *Error of Judgement: The Truth about the Birmingham Bombings* (Dublin: Poolbeg Press, 1990), p. 2.
15 Ibid., p. 4.
16 D. McKittrick, S. Kelter, B. Feeney and C. Thornton, *Lost Lives: The Stories of the Men, Women and Children Who Died as a Result of the Northern Ireland Troubles* (Edinburgh: Mainstream Publishing, 2001), p. 497.
17 PIRA Statement (29 November 1974), quoted in McGladdery, *The Provisional IRA in England*, p. 91.

18 Ibid.
19 Chinn, *Birmingham Irish*, p. 162.
20 Ibid., p. 164.
21 T. McKearney, *The Provisional IRA – from Insurrection to Parliament* (London: Pluto Press, 2011), p. 121.
22 Ibid.
23 McGladdery, *The Provisional IRA in England*, p. 93.
24 L. Curtis, *Ireland: The Propaganda War* (Belfast: Sásta, 1998), p. 107.
25 Ibid., p. 197.
26 McKittrick et al., *Lost Lives*, p. 497.
27 Chinn, *Birmingham Irish*, p. 164.
28 McKittrick et al., *Lost Lives*, p. 500.
29 Mullin, *Error of Judgement*, p. 9.
30 McGladdery, *The Provisional IRA in England*, p. 87.
31 For details of this and other cases, see Finch, chapter 10 in this volume.
32 Mullin, *Error of Judgement*.
33 McGladdery, *The Provisional IRA in England*, p. 68.
34 Ibid., p. 155.
35 Mullin, *Error of Judgement*, pp. 155–220.
36 R. English, *Armed Struggle – History of the IRA* (London: Pan Macmillan, 2008), p. 170.
37 I. Burrel and J. Bennetto, 'West Midlands Serious Crime Squad: Police unit to blame for "dozens more injustices"', *Independent* (1 November 1999). www.independent.co.uk/news/west-midlands-serious-crime-squad-police-unit-to-blame-for-dozens-more-injustices-1120219.html (Accessed 2 March 2014).
38 Ibid.
39 McGladdery, *The Provisional IRA in England*, p. 95.
40 Ibid.
41 Hillyard, *Suspect Community*, p. 4.
42 Ibid., p. 259.
43 M. J. Hickman, *The Irish Community in Britain: Myth or Reality?* (London: University of North London, Irish Studies Centre, 1996); M. J. Hickman, L. Thomas, S. Silvestri and H. Nickels, *'Suspect Communitities'? Counter-Terrorism Policy, the Press, and the Impact on Irish and Muslim Communities in Britain* (London: London Metropolitan University, 2011).
44 Ben O'Reilly, interviewed by the author, Ben and Margaret's house, Birmingham, 2 February 2014.
45 Hickman et al., *'Suspect Communities?'*, p. 20.
46 Margaret O'Reilly, interviewed by the author, Ben and Margaret's house, Birmingham, 2 February 2014.
47 Hillyard, *Suspect Community*, p. 68.
48 Ibid., p. 69
49 C. Davenport, *When Democracies Kill: Reflections from the US, India and Northern Ireland* (Hankuk: Centre for International Area Studies, 2012), p. 15.
50 Margaret O'Reilly, interview.

51 P. Hillyard, *Suspect Community*, p. 238

52 T. McKearney, *The Provisional IRA*, p. 121

53 Margaret O'Reilly, interview.

54 Ben O'Reilly, interview.

55 Hillyard, *Suspect Community*, p. 33.

56 Barry O'Reilly, interviewed by the author, Ben and Margaret's house, Birmingham, 30 March 2014.

57 Curtis, *Ireland: The Propaganda War*, p. 107.

58 Yvonne Button, interviewed by the author, Ben and Margaret's house, Birmingham, 30 March 2014.

59 Karen Bradshaw, interviewed by the author, Ben and Margaret's house, Birmingham, 30 March 2014.

60 Barry O'Reilly, interviewed by the author, Ben and Margaret's house, Birmingham, 30 March 2014.

61 Dawn Cooper, interviewed by the author, Ben and Margaret's house, Birmingham, 30 March 2014.

62 Hickman et al., *Suspect Communities*, p. 7.

63 Barry O'Reilly, interview.

64 Hickman, *The Irish Community in Britain*.

65 Hillyard, *Suspect Community*, p. 3.

66 Barry O'Reilly, interview.

67 Yvonne Button, interview.

68 L. Curtis, *Nothing but the Same Old Story: The Roots of Anti-Irish Racism* (London: Information on Ireland, 1985), p. 4.

69 Ibid.

70 Dawn Cooper, interview.

71 Hickman, *The Irish Community in Britain*.

72 Dawn Cooper, interview.

73 Hickman, *The Irish Community in Britain*.

74 Yvonne Button, interview.

75 Hickman, *The Irish Community in Britain*, p. 13.

76 Curtis, *Nothing but the Same Old Story*, p. 4.

21

'Truth recovery' and the role of the security forces in the Northern Ireland Troubles

Aaron Edwards[1]

> If you stop and think about the dead, who is to build the new world? In three wars we have lost so many husbands, sons and lovers – yet to think of them repels us. They're dead, buried under painted wooden posts – why should they interfere with our lives? For *we* will never die! (Alexander Solzhenitsyn, 'We will never die'[2])

Following in the wake of Prime Minister David Cameron's apology on behalf of the British government for the events on 30 January 1972, during which soldiers from the Parachute Regiment shot dead thirteen unarmed protestors (another man died later), the then Chief of the General Staff, Sir David Richards, issued a public statement on behalf of the Army. 'We must never forget the tragic events of Bloody Sunday,' he said. 'In the thirty-eight years since that tragic day's events, lessons have been learned. The way the Army is trained, the way it works and the way it operates have all changed significantly.'[3] It was a powerful gesture, interpreted by the son of one of the men killed as a way to 'begin to bind ... [those] wounds' opened by the actions of the Parachute Regiment on Bloody Sunday.[4] The publication of the Saville Inquiry's report was the culmination of twelve years of painstaking investigation into the events of that day and concluded with the clearing of the names of the victims, who had been wrongly accused of being 'gunmen and bombers' by the Widgery Tribunal in 1972.[5]

While the Saville Inquiry was seen as a vindication of many years of campaigning for a public inquiry by the Bloody Sunday families, it left several unanswered questions about who should be held account-able for the actions of the military on that day and opened the door to a legal investigation by the Police Service of Northern Ireland (PSNI). Ambivalently, however, Saville did not bind old wounds for everyone and, arguably, re-opened them for those who wished to pursue not only truth but also justice (a point discussed in more detail below). Moreover, the Inquiry pointed up the prospect of the British State and its security forces (comprising the British Army, Royal Ulster Constabulary [RUC, forerunner to the PSNI] and Ulster Defence Regiment) being held accountable for all of the 346 killings (including 145 terrorists) directly attributed to them (the vast majority of Troubles-related killings were perpetrated by non-state armed groupings).[6] In a short analysis of republican attempts to equate security forces actions during the Troubles with those of terrorists,[7] Henry Patterson suggested that this may not be the last time that the actions of the security forces are subjected to such detailed scrutiny by those – principally from the nationalist community – who have continued to campaign for 'truth and justice'. Patterson's conclusion was that Northern Ireland faces 'a decade of commemorations, inquiries and inquests that will focus predominantly on actions of the security forces during the Troubles'.[8]

In light of the controversies that remain about Bloody Sunday and other violent episodes involving the State, this chapter examines three important aspects of the debate around truth recovery and the role of the security forces in the Troubles. First, it asks what role the security forces (defined as including both locally recruited forces and regular British Army units) played in the conflict, according to official state narratives. Second, it examines the apparent obfuscation of security forces' experiences by an anti-state republican agenda. Here the chapter makes the case that republicans do this because of a need to reinforce tropes of meaning that preserve the integrity of the killings carried out by the Provisional IRA (PIRA), while justifying continued hostility to the British State as well as their commitment to a peace process that has locked them into 'a political vice, the handle of which is in the firm grip of the British state'.[9] It is in the immediate context of the peace and political processes established to manage irreconcilable ethno-nationalist identities that we find an attempt to address one of the most destabilising issues in British politics, which culminated in the signing of the Belfast/Good Friday Agreement in 1998.[10] Arguably, as comparative cases elsewhere demonstrate, when progress towards building a new political dispensation is insisted upon by external actors, 'debates about the past are cloaked in socially transformative discourses and symbolism, employed as an adhesive to bind together rival groups in more peaceful relationships'.[11] Third, the chapter asks what consequences these official state and anti-state representations of the past have had on attempts to 'give a voice' to security forces victims (particularly those from Britain) amid the apparent obfuscating of terrorist violence. Often, the personal restraint, courage and professionalism of the vast majority of members of the security forces, in defence of British liberal democracy, are overlooked for a range of political reasons which continue to skew our understanding of the past as it really happened.[12] This chapter aims to rectify that imbalance by outlining how a more inclusive process may be possible so as to maximise the positive move towards truth, justice and reconciliation.

Official state memory and the security forces

In August 1969 the Home Secretary, James Callaghan, approved the deployment of British soldiers onto the streets of Northern Ireland as a preventive measure to quell inter-communal disturbances between Catholic nationalists and Protestant unionists. The troops were initially welcomed by the minority Catholic community after the souring of its relationship with the RUC, despite later attempts by republicans to play down the significance of the Catholic women who offered them tea and sandwiches.[13] While the British State had clear responsibilities upon the outbreak of loyalist and republican violence, London instead chose to continue its support for the embattled unionist-dominated regime in Belfast.[14]

Under the Government of Ireland Act (1920) the Northern Ireland Parliament at Stormont in East Belfast had the 'power to make laws for the peace, order, and good government of Northern Ireland', although it was limited in what it could do in relation to 'matters arising from a state of war'. In effect, the arrangements allowed Westminster to pass the buck for the day-to-day running of all Northern Ireland's affairs (including internal security) to Stormont. From the British government's perspective there was a sense in which the violence produced a 'perfect storm' that left the under-strength RUC operationally incapable of dealing with an increasingly complex security dilemma. Before long the Army found itself assuming responsibility for riot-control measures and became the key agency driving security policy between 1971 and 1976, with the RUC relegated to a supporting role. After 1977 the pendulum swung back in favour of a policing-led response to terrorism, which would last until the termination of Operation Banner, the Military Aid to the Civil Power mission, in 2007.

In British official state memory the actions of the security forces have been regarded as exemplary and a necessary response to the deterioration of the security situation in the province. As one official Ministry of Defence publication later noted, the British Army, in particular, had cause to be 'proud' of its achievement – although it qualified this in light of a more pragmatic reading of the military outcome:

> It should be recognised that the Army did not 'win' in any recognisable way; rather it achieved its desired end-state, which allowed a political process to be established without unacceptable levels of intimidation. Security force operations suppressed the level of violence to a level which the population could live with, and with which the RUC and later the PSNI could cope. The violence was reduced to an extent which made it clear to the PIRA that they would not win through violence. This is a major achievement, and one with which the security forces from all three Services, with the Army in the lead, should be entirely satisfied.[15]

Interestingly, the publication highlighted how little its authors knew about the political context and its effects on the tempo of military operations throughout Operation Banner. Unforgivably, perhaps, it even overlooked how the IRA had altered its own strategy in the late 1970s to take account of British attempts to contain terrorist violence in Northern Ireland.

By the early 1990s the IRA had transformed its strategy to one of an offensive designed to inflict massive damage on the UK economy and, thereby, increase London's appetite for either a military withdrawal or, as it later transpired, a political solution. As part of its new departure in increasing the tempo of terrorist operations the IRA engineered spectacular bomb attacks on the UK mainland, with London and other major cities regarded as prime targets. For John Major's Conservative government the overriding priority was to insulate the City of London (regarded then and since as the engine-room of Britain's economic prowess) from IRA bombs at all costs. The memories of republican atrocities in Belfast and, particularly, bombings in the English cities of Guildford, Warrington, London and Manchester were fresh in the nation's collective psyche,[16] which ultimately spurred the English political class's desire for an end to the 'Irish Troubles' for good (see chapter 18 by Lelourec in this volume). Therefore, by the early 1990s, the watchword in terms of the British state response was containment.[17]

The signing in 1993 of the Downing Street Declaration by John Major and his opposite number in Dublin, Albert Reynolds, signalled the British State's movement towards accommodating Sinn Féin's (SF) electoral growth, after a decade of trying unsuccessfully to halt it on both sides of the border. By the summer of 1994 the PIRA were convinced of the need to allow political negotiations to take their course, and by the end of August they called a ceasefire. 'The IRA are political people. They could read the situation as well as everyone else,' Gerry Adams wrote afterwards. 'There comes a moment in history when one has to take a decision.' Although they had recognised that the Downing Street Declaration was not a solution to the complex problems, the IRA had emerged, argued Adams, as 'a confident, united and unbroken army'.[18]

By the time Tony Blair and his New Labour government came to power in the May 1997 Westminster election, plans to secure a peace deal took on a new urgency. Over the course of Blair's first term as Prime Minister the foundations of a secret deal with the republican leadership – giving assurances that those republican terrorists who had gone 'on the run' during the Troubles could now safely return to their homes in Northern Ireland – were laid. Blair and his coterie of senior advisers were accused of failing to consult Parliament, the ultimate guarantor of British State sovereignty.[19] The existence of this 'administrative arrangement' has since been confirmed by David Cameron, who acknowledged that difficult decisions had been taken by the previous government during peace negotiations in order to secure a deal. Nonetheless, he went on to state, 'we need to be absolutely clear to people that these letters were not, and should not be, any form of amnesty'. It was later confirmed by the Conservative-led Coalition government that these so-called 'comfort letters' (sent to between 187 and 210 terrorist suspects) were little more than a 'terrible mistake'. The Secretary of State for Northern Ireland, Theresa Villiers, subsequently added, when questioned in Parliament, that the 'scheme' had ended in 2012 and the judicial inquiry appointed to look into the letters had cleared the government of any wrongdoing.

There can be no question that when liberal democracies confront terrorists they risk much. In turning to murder by gun and bomb, terrorists are ultimately attempting to remind the citizens of a state that their government cannot protect them. It is, therefore, left to the government to respond to that armed challenge by winning back the trust of the people by taking decisive action to eradicate both the basis of terrorism *and* also the actuality of terrorist violence. In the case of Northern Ireland, though, while New Labour certainly removed the actuality of terrorist violence, it did not fully address the grievances that made small numbers of people resort to what one former senior PIRA volunteer has called the 'argument of force'.[20]

Today, the UK has become increasingly subject to the due process of investigative mechanisms provided under Article 2 of the European Convention on Human Rights (ECHR), which has been incorporated into English domestic law since 2000 and which places an emphasis on the State's responsibilities to its citizens. The wording of the Convention underscores the point well: 'Deprivation of life shall not be regarded as inflicted in contravention of this Article when it results from the use of force which is no more than absolutely necessary.' Under Article 2 provisions, the ECHR found that the British government 'had been in violation of Article 2 (right to life) of the Convention' in the case of McCann and Others v. the United Kingdom. In this incident, the British Army's Special Air Service shot dead three members of an IRA 'active service unit' in Gibraltar before they could detonate a car bomb at a military parade.[21] The case set a precedent in that it opened the door to further legal challenges in respect of active IRA personnel killed by the State.

It is in the context of the State's obligations to its citizens that we find the most contested aspect of the implementation of Article 2, particularly with regard to recent blockages in the legal process. One example that has come to the fore in recent years is the refusal by the British government to appoint an inquiry into the killings of ten people in the Ballymurphy area of West Belfast in August 1971.[22] Naturally, a groundswell of republican opinion has now tended towards calling for an 'independent mechanism' by which to deal with the legacy of past violence, because of its claims that the British government cannot be impartial in the pursuit of justice for nationalists. However, a by-product of republican enthusiasm for exposing wrongdoing by the State has been the creation of a moral equivalence between those who broke the law and those who enforced it – a set of circumstances that has been troubling not only for unionists but for all of those (including constitutional nationalists) who claimed to have been opposed to terrorism during the long years of the Troubles.

Republican narratives on the security forces

That the security forces played a key role in the Troubles is obvious, despite the British State's claims to have acted as an umpire in a sectarian conflict between Protestants and Catholics. Nevertheless, it is in the conduct of that role that much controversy continues to surround security force actions. As Jonathan Tonge has written, in straining 'to defeat the IRA, elements within the British Army, the RUC and the UDR [Ulster Defence Regiment] engaged in illegal activity, which blurred supposed distinctions between legitimate state forces and paramilitary armies'.[23] Although 'collusion' has never been proved to have been systematic or institutionalised within security force ranks (the evidence that is produced is of individual members of the police or army 'going rogue' and taking the law into their own hands), its presence has been highlighted consistently by republicans as 'inescapable fact', with some authors going so far as to claim that it was 'established beyond doubt by these events', thus proving 'that successive British governments and their law enforcement agencies entered into a collusive counter-insurgency campaign with loyalist paramilitaries'.[24] Collusion has been defined by Judge Peter Cory as a synonym of 'connive', which has far-reaching questions for states, including the 'effect of condoning, or even encouraging, state involvement in crimes, thereby shattering all public confidence in important Government agencies'.[25] The import is obvious: the State has a responsibility for safeguarding the rights, liberties and security of its citizens, even when those same citizens may be actively opposed to the constitutional framework and political architecture of the State.

The campaign to highlight 'collusion' between the British State and loyalist 'death squads' has been emphasised by SF, which has spearheaded republican calls for 'truth and justice' in respect of the past and the role of the State and its security forces during the Troubles. Writing about how political republicanism has reappropriated the benign language of peace for political purposes, respected transitional justice scholar Kirk Simpson has concluded that 'Truth and justice are phrases often used interchangeably by such groups without due consideration of the core semantic, taxonomic and conceptual issues at stake.' Citing empirical evidence of a republican 'march for truth' rally in Belfast in August 2007, Simpson continues that the use of these phrases 'represented imitative and divisive politics at its worst, and despairingly it was the same kind of mimetic logic that spawned decades of violence in Northern Ireland'.[26] For anyone attending the event, it was impossible to avoid encountering members of the IRA, who came to Belfast from Crossmaglen in the south-east to Derry/Londonderry in the north-west of Northern Ireland. Curiously, while platform speakers, including former IRA leader Martin Meehan, spoke out about 'collusion' between the State and loyalist terrorists being 'no illusion', there was a general failure to recognise how republican paramilitaries had played a key role in the deaths of 1,800 men, women and children throughout the Troubles.[27] This long litany of atrocities, however, has been explained away by what Simpson has called 'a carefully stylised history' that is 'understandably seductive for republican victims of the conflict' but that 'by its very definition ... appeals only to one side of the community and therefore cannot achieve long-lasting reconciliation'.[28]

In reducing the totality of the Troubles experience to a one-dimensional, ethnicised narrative, pitting the State (and its 'surrogates') against an embattled minority with no other choice than to resort to 'armed struggle', this version of history completely ignores the peaceful alternatives available at the time and elides the suffering inflicted on those who sought to uphold the law as well as the vast majority of Catholics and Protestants who did not resort to violence.[29] Instead, we are treated to calls for the establishment of a 'panel' or 'commission' that is both 'international and independent' and that is 'politically neutral' so as to ensure that the 'search for truth' is unimpeded by the British State, which is portrayed as bearing much of the moral responsibility for the Troubles in Northern Ireland. SF has gone further and articulated the case for the establishment of a 'truth commission' to uncover 'information concealed by the authorities'.[30]

Perhaps the biggest flaw in this argument is the lack of any considera-tion as to how armed non-state actors might be invited to do the same. In classic republican discourse the conflict was reduced to essentially one between the British State and the IRA, with the role of internal republi-can internecine feuds, internal killings of suspected informers (including up to fifteen people who were 'disappeared', tortured, shot and secretly buried by the IRA) and open sectarian warfare between republicans and loyalists airbrushed from the historical record. This is part of an ideological tendency to play up collective suffering while blaming others for violence. Journalist Malachi O'Doherty has written powerfully and convincingly about this tendency towards myth-making within repub-licanism. He makes the pertinent point that 'the flaws are obvious' in this mythology, but that it is not manufactured for those predisposed to applying the rigours of critical thinking in understanding Irish repub-licans; rather, it is 'for the people who see things that way already, to mirror a community's established mythology'.[31]

One of the non-governmental organisations that lobbies on behalf of nationalist victims and survivors of the Troubles is Relatives for Justice (RfJ). In a report into the security forces' killing of four armed IRA men, RfJ outlined how it thought collusion operated in practice:

> The RIR (Royal Irish Regiment) in east Tyrone were working closely with the RUC and Special Branch. Formerly the UDR, the RIR are implicated in numerous acts of collusion and in sectarian killings. It is widely believed that a UVF [Ulster Volunteer Force] gang active in the Mid-Ulster area up until its ceasefire in October 1994 were largely comprised of former and serving UDR/RIR members.[32]

The dearth of credible evidence has not prevented RfJ from making such unsubstantiated claims. However, it is its extrapolation of several incidents into a wider 'relationship that existed between loyalists and the state' that is the most problematic aspect of the skewed analysis advanced by such lobby groups. By hinting towards the existence of a wholesale policy of collusion – without any convincing proof – this nar-rative serves to reinforce the republican agenda of 'blaming the Brits', while completely ignoring the individual choices available to those who took up arms illegally and fed the cycle of endemic sectarianism existing between Catholics and Protestants in Northern Ireland. In his empirical research of republican attitudes to truth recovery, academic Mark McGovern claims:

> If even some of such allegations were found to be true the evidence could point toward a campaign of targeted assassination in this period, many of them known republicans or family members, carried out by loyalist paramilitaries in collusion with the state.[33]

The existence of 'a pattern of policy and practice of the state', argues McGovern, 'is one of the essential issues that any truth recovery process needs to tackle'.[34]

A detailed analysis of individual examples of collusion is beyond the scope of this chapter. However, it is important to reiterate the point that the continued silence on violence perpetrated by republican paramilitaries (especially on their own communities) is inimical to the promotion of positive societal change, respect for human rights and reconciliation. Notwithstanding this truism, of Northern Ireland remaining a deeply divided society, republicans have remained steadfast in their representation of the Troubles as being essentially a tale of the British State's 'oppression' of a minority 'peacefully' pursuing separatism. Although useful for transmitting a message to friendly Irish diaspora communities around the world, this simplistic and morally indefensible narrative overlooks the divisiveness and complexity of the historical record. In Northern Ireland's political present, truth has taken on a one-dimensional form.

'Giving voice' to victims

Debates over the past have had a debilitating impact on the Northern Ireland peace process. Nevertheless, it is generally considered appropriate that the parties to the conflict should confront the legacy of the past in a way that can facilitate moves towards social transformation. As a mechanism for facilitating the articulation of those voices thought to have been marginalised in the wake of the termination of the armed conflict, groups claiming to represent the interests of 'victims' and 'survivors' have moved closer to the centre of the political spotlight. The proliferation of 'victims' groups' in Northern Ireland is not unique: it is seen in many societies that have undergone significant socio-political upheaval due to state and non-state violence.[35] The role of these groups, as Graham Dawson reminds us, is 'to represent the victims of violence, to tell their stories and to promote their interests by lobbying for financial, psychological and other kinds of support'.[36] Inevitably, in a deeply divided society where ethno-nationalism (whether unionist or nationalist in complexion) has become the adhesive binding together communities while pitting them against one another in a zero-sum conflict, there has been a tendency for these competing mechanisms for 'giving voice' to reflect political fault-lines, a mobilisation that has given way to a 'politics of victimhood'.[37]

Kirk Simpson has, however, proposed an innovative model by which it may be possible for victims to be given back their voice in a way that meets Dawson's elucidation of the challenges for the 'psychic work of reparation, and for the political work of building a peace that can be trusted'.[38] In Simpson's view, 'The rediscovery of the voice of the victims of political violence in the transitional context contributes to the political, social and legal rebalancing that is essential to the long-term stability of democratic society.'[39] It is striking how difficult the task of integrating the experiences of the security forces has been in relation to the obstacles highlighted in the pioneering work on truth recovery undertaken by scholars like Dawson and Simpson. One factor highlighted in Simpson's work is the traumatic process of remembering and commemorating victims and the attempts by republican paramilitaries and their supporters to skew the language when referring to their own combatants as 'innocent victims', while claiming that attacks on security forces 'combatants' were legitimate during what they regard as a 'war'. This is problematic, especially since republicans have continually called for inquiries into the deaths of their own 'volunteers' whenever those concerned were armed, dangerous and quite clearly a threat when engaged by security forces.

Dawson has argued that the politicisation of the suffering and trauma experienced by victims and survivors can have a debilitating effect on a nascent peace process. As he makes clear in his influential book *Making Peace with the Past?*, 'when the language of reconciliation demands a forgetting of the past, this amounts to a denial of the psychic and political realities of these communities most affected by the war'.[40] Evidence of this 'denial of the psychic and political realities' can be quite clearly discerned if we examine the circumstances in which security forces personnel lost their lives, particularly since it reveals a silencing of victims who do not 'fit' the narrative of the current victims-centred process in Northern Ireland.

In the case of soldiers serving in Northern Ireland during the Troubles there was a tendency to avoid talking about the effects of the conflict on those from Great Britain (designated in the official roll of honour as 'not from Northern Ireland'). For example, some soldiers found that their families became hostile to Irish people generally whenever their loved ones were deployed to the province (see Dixon, chapter 3 in this volume). As one English soldier from the Coldstream Guards told Max Arthurs in the mid 1980s:

> I've certainly got to the point where I resent going over there, and my wife resents it, and my mother resents it. It's had knock-on effects with my family. My mother won't buy Irish butter, she won't buy Irish linen. She's reacted very strongly: anything with 'Made in Ireland' on it she won't touch. She's not bigoted, she's not a racialist, she's normal, middle-line conservative, but if I bought her a lace tablecloth made in Ireland she would take it as a very gross insult. She hates me going over there.[41]

Not all families reacted in such an antagonistic manner, however, and it is common nowadays to find British Army veterans who recall with enthusiasm their tours of duty in Northern Ireland, despite the dangers that they brought. Yet, beyond the rose-tinted remembrance of military service, there is a tendency to mask the feeling of loss or trauma experienced by the same soldiers (see the chapters by Jenkings and Woodward (7), and Aubertin (2) and McMahon (6) in this volume).

Moreover, one does not have to look far for examples of the trauma that the families of security forces victims have experienced. As a national day of commemoration in the UK, Remembrance Day is typically where one will find the relatives of those killed in action remembered at cenotaphs and services. Speaking after one of these events in 2008, Mrs Hazel Vines, whose husband, Sergeant Major Ron Vines, was killed by the IRA in South Armagh in 1973, described how she found it difficult to recall the circumstances of her husband's death. As she told a BBC journalist in 2008:

> My husband was in the Parachute Regiment 2nd Battalion and we had just got married and had our honeymoon … He was sent to Crossmaglen and blown up in a 400lb bomb. It was just after the honeymoon and I didn't even have a body to bury. I have never got over it. I couldn't do this on Sunday because I am still so emotional about it. We have still so many good people over here though and my husband knew that, he was from Yorkshire.[42]

However, it is also worth mentioning that the loss of a comrade had an effect on those who soldiered alongside Sergeant Major Vines, particularly since he was investigating the source of an explosion that had already killed two soldiers on the same spot. As one soldier recalled, 'one of his abiding memories of the tour was the blood-soaked stretchers being washed down in the shower at Bessbrook'. At the time, official Army sources noted how the people of South Armagh had been 'extremely hostile' to the Army's presence in the area.[43] For soldiers who lost comrades in Northern Ireland there was little assistance afforded by the State in relation to how they dealt with such trauma. It was not until the final stages of the conflict that the symptoms of post-traumatic stress disorder were being correctly diagnosed (see Aubertin, chapter 3 in this volume). As researcher John Lindsay found in a study of British soldiers in the late 1990s:

> For people who were maimed or wounded though, there wasn't any help given. Two soldiers on my patrol were injured in an ambush one night. One of them was seriously hurt, they had to remove a quarter of an inch from his leg and he was discharged from the army on medical grounds. I met him in Paisley a couple of years ago; he's a forgotten man, he had no help or compensation off the army, so he's left living on the dole. Once you're out of the army the army doesn't care, it's the same for the Falklands veterans and the ones with Gulf War syndrome.[44]

Although there are now procedures in place to deal with veterans who suffer trauma, shock and stress in the execution of their military duties (largely as a result of the public exposure of the armed conflicts in Iraq and Afghanistan), charities like Combat Stress have come under increasing pressure to make hospital beds available for returnees from more recent conflicts.[45]

The loss of a loved one in these circumstances is undoubtedly painful. For those who had been married to soldiers for a few years and who had young children, the shock of the news confirming that their loved ones had been killed in action was greeted with understandable emotion. The daughter of Lieutenant-Colonel David Blair, who was killed by the IRA twin bomb attack at Warrenpoint in August 1979 (along with seventeen other soldiers) recalled how she first heard of her father's death:

> 'David's dead.'
> The words were barely audible, but I heard my mother sobbing in the next room. Numb with shock and disbelief, I carried on watching the film with my brother. Then my grandfather came to us. He, too, was in tears and he confirmed what we had already heard through the wall.[46]

The effect of such traumatic deaths is frequently glossed over by the mainstream media and by British official memory when it comes to commemorations for Britain's post-Second World War 'small wars'. This is perhaps best illustrated in official commemorative events, like Remembrance Day, when all of these 'small wars' are lumped together and usually dwarfed by the nation's attention on larger, conventional wars, such as the First World War and Second World War.

Despite the relative silence of Northern Ireland veterans' voices, there have been attempts to highlight the service and sacrifice in more unofficial ways. For example, the oral history work undertaken by former soldier Ken Wharton in several volumes covering the entirety of Operation Banner seeks to collect and preserve for posterity the 'voices from the soldiers who fought in Britain's forgotten war'.[47] As discussed above, the attempts by official state channels to communicate the experience of the security forces in Northern Ireland have been sanitised. While some controversies remain unresolved, the vast majority of security forces personnel performed their duties with courage and forbearance and in accordance with the rule of law. Unfortunately, without a comprehensive mechanism for dealing with the legacy of the violent past, the denial of the 'psychic and political realities of these communities most affected by the war' will continue.

Conclusion

As this chapter has argued, the role played by the security forces in the Northern Ireland Troubles continues to be debated, with some episodes remaining deeply controversial and contested. Arguably, there has been a tendency to reduce what was a three-dimensional conflict fought on many fronts to a simplistic, one-dimensional, ethnicised narrative of the British State's war against the IRA. A more thorough and balanced analysis would ask what the nature of the relationship between the key protagonists actually was, what motivated them, who succeeded and failed in the military arena and whether the State bears sole responsibility for the actions of those who took up arms illegally either in its defence or to oppose it. For as long as people from both communities continue to airbrush the visceral nature of terrorist violence from the story of the Troubles, while attributing every coercive action to the British State and its security forces, the toxicity of the past will continue to bleed into the present and cause further political instability. If we are to avoid the pitfalls outlined by Alexander Solzhenitsyn at the outset of this chapter, then there are clear obligations on all protagonists to actively solidify the gains of the Northern Ireland peace process and work towards a more inclusive form of reconciliation.

Notes

1 The views expressed in this chapter are the author's and not necessarily those of the Royal Military Academy Sandhurst, Ministry of Defence or any other UK government agency.

2 A. Solzhenitsyn, *Stories and Prose Poems* (London: Penguin, 1970), p. 205.

3 HM Government, 'Bloody Sunday Report Published', 15 June 2010. www.gov. uk/government/news/bloody-sunday-report-published. (Accessed 6 July 2014).

4 BBC, 'Relatives' reactions to Bloody Sunday report', 15 June 2010. www.bbc. co.uk/news/10323362 (Accessed 30 June 2014).

5 The Rt. Hon. Lord Widgery, *Report of the Tribunal appointed to inquire into the events on Sunday, 30 January 1972, which led to loss of life in connection with the procession in Londonderry on that day by The Rt. Hon. Lord Widgery,* H.L. 101, H.C. 220 (London: HMSO, April 1972). http://cain.ulst.ac.uk/hmso/ widgery.htm#part3 (Accessed 10 March 2014).

6 The British Army was responsible for 302 deaths (253 Catholics, 32 Protestants and 12 people not from Northern Ireland); the RUC was responsible for a further 56 (45 Catholics, 8 Protestants and 3 people not from Northern Ireland); while the locally recruited UDR was responsible for 8 (5 Catholics, 2 Protestants and 1 person not from Northern Ireland). For a detailed breakdown of deaths see the Sutton Database on the CAIN Web Service. http://cain.ulst.ac.uk/cgi-bin/ tab2.pl (Accessed 6 July 2014).

7 A respected expert on terrorism has identified four key aspects of terrorist activity: a political nature; symbolic use of violence; purposeful targeting of non-combatants; and violence carried out by non-state actors, which, unlike the state use of force, is not restricted by international norms and conventions. See A. K. Cronin, *How Terrorism Ends: Understanding the Decline and Demise of Terrorist Campaigns* (Princeton, NJ: Princeton University Press, 2009), p. 7. See also A. Schmid, 'Frameworks for conceptualising terrorism', *Terrorism and Political Violence,* 16:2 (2004), 197–221, where terrorism is defined as the threat or use of force by non-state military actors to influence a government or place the public – or a section of the public – in fear. Typically, though not exclusively, such groups target non-combatants in a bid to challenge the ability of states to protect their citizens.

8 H. Patterson, 'Equating former terrorists to security forces is a flagrant distortion of history', *Belfast Newsletter* (22 November 2011). See also H. Patterson, 'For many, the Bloody Sunday Saville inquiry has fallen short', *Belfast Telegraph* (16 June 2010).

9 A. McIntyre, 'Modern Irish Republicanism: The product of British State strategies', *Irish Political Studies,* 10:1 (1995), 118.

10 On the conflict-management process in Northern Ireland see B. O'Leary and J. McGarry, *The Politics of Antagonism: Understanding Northern Ireland* (London: Athlone Press, 1996); and J. McGarry and B. O'Leary, *The Northern Ireland Conflict: Consociational Engagements* (Oxford: Oxford University Press, 2004).

11 A. Edwards, 'On the obfuscation of the past', *Peace Review: A Journal of Social Justice,* 27:3 (2015), 354–62.

12 This is evident in reports from non-governmental organisations lobbying on human rights issues and includes Amnesty International, *Northern Ireland: Time to Deal with the Past* (London: Amnesty International, 2013), which reflects

the republican trope of collusion without asking serious questions of terrorist crimes, which account for the lion's share of deaths, injuries, disappearances and continuing violence. It also entertains the fallacy that only states can commit 'human rights abuses', while non-state armed groups are guilty only of 'abuses'.

13 M. O'Doherty, *The Trouble with Guns: Republican Strategy and the Provisional IRA* (Belfast: Blackstaff Press, 1998), p. 64.

14 H. Patterson, *Ireland since 1939: The Persistence of Conflict* (Dublin: Penguin, 2007), pp. 213–14.

15 Ministry of Defence, *Operation Banner: An Analysis of Military Operations in Northern Ireland*, Army Code No. 71842 (London: MoD, July 2006), paragraph 855.

16 R. Needham, *Battling for Peace* (Belfast: Blackstaff, 1998).

17 On the changing nature of the British state response see B. O'Duffy, *British–Irish Relations and Northern Ireland: From Violent Politics to Conflict Regulation* (Dublin: Irish Academic Press, 2007).

18 G. Adams, *Selected Writings* (Dingle: Brandon, 1997), pp. 304–7.

19 See the parliamentary question raised by Kate Hoey MP on this, the Royal Prerogative of Mercy, on 1 May 2014. The Secretary of State for Northern Ireland revealed that this had been 'granted in Northern Ireland 365 times between 1979 and 2002, but this total does not include the period between 1987 and 1997 for which records cannot currently be found'. *Hansard* House of Commons Debates, vol. 579, col. 763W, 1 May 2014.

20 Interview with Tommy Gorman, Belfast, 23 June 2010. Gorman was an operations officer for the Belfast Brigade of the IRA.

21 European Court of Human Rights, *Factsheet – Terrorism and the ECHR*, July 2014, p. 16. www.echr.coe.int/Documents/FS_Terrorism_ENG.pdf (Accessed 24 August 2014).

22 For an in-depth analysis of the events surrounding the shootings see I. Cobain, 'Ballymurphy shootings: 36 hours in Belfast that left 10 dead', *Guardian* (26 June 2014). For more on the British government's rejection of an inquiry see D. Young, 'Ballymurphy massacre: Families furious as Theresa Villiers rules out inquiry', *Belfast Telegraph* (30 April 2014).

23 J. Tonge, *Northern Ireland* (Cambridge: Polity, 2006), p. 85.

24 A. Cadwallader, *Lethal Allies: British Collusion in Ireland* (Cork: Mercier Press, 2013), p. 360.

25 P. Cory, *Cory Collusion Inquiry Report – Billy Wright* (London: HMSO, 1 April 2004), HC 472, pp. 77–8.

26 K. Simpson, *Truth Recovery in Northern Ireland: Critically Interpreting the Past* (Manchester: Manchester University Press, 2009), pp. 26–7.

27 A. Edwards, 'Drawing a line under the past', *Peace Review: A Journal of Social Justice*, 20:2 (April–June 2008), 209–17. Of the 3,700 people who lost their lives in Northern Ireland the vast majority were murdered by terrorists. In raw terms 60 per cent of killings were perpetrated by republicans, 30 per cent by loyalists and 10 per cent by state security forces. For a breakdown on the statistics see D. McKittrick, S. Kelters, B. Feeney and C. Thornton *Lost Lives: The Stories of*

the Men, Women, and Children Who Died as a Result of the Northern Ireland Troubles (Edinburgh: Mainstream, 2004), pp. 1496–7.

28 Simpson, Truth Recovery in Northern Ireland, pp. 27–8.

29 For a critique of how truth recovery can be a 'disruptive presence within settlement processes' see C. McGrattan, 'Spectres of history: Nationalist party politics and truth recovery in Northern Ireland', Political Studies, 60 (2012), 455–73.

30 Sinn Féin, 'Truth: A Sinn Fein Discussion Document' (September 2003).

31 O'Doherty, The Trouble with Guns, p. 37.

32 Relatives for Justice, Ambush, Assassination and Impunity: The Killings of Kevin Barry O'Donnell, Patrick Vincent, Peter Clancy and Sean O'Farrell, Sunday 16 February 1992 (Belfast: Relatives for Justice, February 2012), p. 15.

33 M. McGovern, 'Inquiring into collusion? Collusion, the state and the management of truth recovery in Northern Ireland', State Crime, 2:1 (Spring 2013), 23.

34 Ibid., p. 24

35 Examples include Spain, Chile and Rwanda. See M. Ignatieff, The Warrior's Honour: Ethnic War and the Modern Conscience (London: Vintage, 1999) and A. Rigby, Justice and Reconciliation: After the Violence (London: Lynne Rienner, 2001).

36 G. Dawson, Making Peace with the Past? Memory, Trauma and the Irish Troubles (Manchester: Manchester University Press, 2007), p. 233.

37 Ibid., p. 260.

38 Ibid.

39 Simpson, Truth Recovery in Northern Ireland, p. 76.

40 Dawson, Making Peace with the Past?, p. 61.

41 M. Arthur, Northern Ireland Soldiers Talking (London: Sidgwick and Jackson, 1987), pp. 243–4.

42 R. McKee, 'Poignant memories on Armistice Day', BBC News, 11 November 2008. http://news.bbc.co.uk/1/hi/northern_ireland/7722642.stm (Accessed 24 May 2012).

43 See A. Edwards, The Northern Ireland Troubles: Operation Banner, 1969–2007 (Oxford: Osprey, 2011), p. 45.

44 J. Lindsay, Brits Speak Out: British Soldiers' Impressions of the Northern Ireland Conflict (Derry: Guildhall Press, 1998). Extracts archived at http://cain.ulst.ac.uk/othelem/people/accounts/lindsay.htm (Accessed 1 November 2014).

45 Combat Stress treated 5,000 veterans in 2012. The Chief Executive noted in an annual report that 'we have seen a rapid rise in young men and women who have served in Iraq and Afghanistan seeking our help. This makes up part of the 12 per cent increase in new referrals we receive year-on-year. As a result, waiting times for treatment have increased.'

46 J. Wilsey, The Ulster Tales: A Tribute to Those who Served, 1969–2000 (Barnsley: Pen and Sword, 2011), p. 80.

47 K. Wharton, Bullets, Bombs and Cups of Tea: Further Voices of the British Army in Northern Ireland, 1969–98 (Solihull: Hellion & Company, 2009), p. xxxv. See also his other books A Long Long War: Voices from the British Army in Northern Ireland, 1969–1998 (Solihull: Hellion & Company, 2009) and Bloody Belfast: An Oral History of the British Army's War against the IRA (Stroud: Spellmount, 2010).

22

Commemorating bonds of Union: remembering the Ulster Special Constabulary at the National Memorial Arboretum

L. J. Armstrong

If you pass through the borderlands of Northern Ireland between Fivemiletown and Lisnaskea in County Fermanagh, in an area called Mullaghfad, you will find a church standing isolated in an empty landscape. The countryside here is now forested and largely uninhabited, but this church was once a focal point for the Protestant community who lived here until the 1950s, when the area was cleared for forestation. The church does not appear to be in regular use and has no electricity supply, but has caught the attention of photography enthusiasts and other passers-by who express a curiosity as to its origin.[1] A small graveyard to the side of the church shows evidence of contemporary use. Union flags, poppies and little white crosses mark this place out as a site of memory to those members of the local community who fought for Britain during the First and Second World Wars. Two headstones standing in the graveyard, recently erected, make a more direct political statement (Figure 22.1).

Shining in black marble, these headstones evoke the role memorials play as sites of division as well as sites of memory in Northern Ireland.[2] They have been erected by the Lisnaskea branch of the Ulster Special Constabulary Association (USCA) in memory of two Special Constables, Robert Coulter and James Hall, who were 'Murdered by the IRA'. They serve as a reminder of the local war that was fought so bitterly throughout the 1920s in this area of Northern Ireland close to the border with the Irish Free State. As Graham Dawson states, this area of Northern Ireland holds a sense of 'living at the edge of things'.[3] For the unionist community, living 'on the window ledge of the union', it is necessary to inhabit an imaginative geography made visible through the symbolism of the union: flags, red, white, blue and loyalty to the Crown forces.[4] Struck by the vivid and tangible way in which memory continues to shape the

Figure 22.1 Headstones to Special Constables Robert Coulter and James Hall, erected by the Lisnaskea branch of the USCA, Mullaghfad church, County Fermanagh.

Northern Irish countryside as well as its politics, I wanted to learn more about the stories of Robert Coulter and James Hall, about when the headstones were erected and about the motivations of the USCA, which was apparently still engaged in the act of re-burying its dead.

A relatively quick search put me in touch with the Honorary Secretary of the Lisnaskea branch of the USCA, which sent me further information on the headstones and their histories and put me in touch with local men, also USCA members. By speaking to these people, and reading the literature of the Association, I learned that Robert Coulter and James Hall had been killed in an ambush by the IRA in 1921 during a particularly intense period of 'tit-for-tat' fighting that took place between the unionist and nationalist communities between 1919 and 1925.[5] The story of the deaths of Hall and Coulter has been handed down through the generations in this area. While Special Constable Coulter was said to have been killed instantly, Hall was 'seriously wounded and dragged himself to a nearby house owned by a Sinn Féin member who refused him assistance'.[6] One USCA member told me that the story was 'an important part of their history' which would not be forgotten.[7]

As David Fitzpatrick states, the invocation of the dead provides a 'sharp focus for factional and political conflict' in Ireland.[8] The USCA, which realised that a permanent memorial had not been erected for these men, raised money for the headstones through private means and stood together to remember them at a commemorative ceremony in Mullaghfad in 2006. There was no press coverage of the event, which had the character of a private funeral. 'It was felt by the membership', one USCA member told me, 'that if it had been published in the press, that IRA sympathisers could destroy the memorials and maybe cause damage to the church.'[9] As Jane Leonard suggests in her survey of memorials to the Troubles in Northern Ireland, outdoor police memorials are rare, for this reason.[10]

This quiet but determined effort to establish a permanent memorial to the Ulster Special Constabulary (USC) took place in the context of turbulent change in the political identity of Ulster unionism in Northern Ireland. As Todd et al. argue, the Good Friday Agreement (GFA) set in motion a process of renegotiation of the relationship of Protestants in Northern Ireland to British identity.[11] The sense of Britishness held together by the bonds of union between Northern Ireland and the rest of the UK can be seen to hold multiple meanings and associations, which are fixed according to both local and national boundaries, symbolically and geographically. Many unionists, including the USCA, felt a great betrayal under the terms of the GFA, which they perceived to threaten the bonds of union. These tensions manifested in a significant electoral shift from the Ulster Unionist Party (UUP) to the Democratic Unionist Party (DUP), which gained 50 per cent more seats than the UUP in the 2006 local elections. The UUP, once the majority unionist voice, now held only one seat at Westminster. The DUP declared, 'Let us never forget what it was like when we as a party were forced to sit on the sidelines as our future was being determined, and look on as others squandered the unionist position.'[12]

The determination to 'never forget' also forms a strong component of the USCA identity. Commemorations and memorial services form a major part of its activities, providing an opportunity for this community to perform its Ulster-British identity. It does this three times each year, twice through Orange marches in Northern Ireland and once at the National Memorial Arboretum (NMA) in Lichfield, England. Interestingly, it was the commemoration in Lichfield that it was most keen to speak about. I discovered that in the same summer as the funerary remembrance service at Mullaghfad, the USCA travelled to the NMA to unveil an obelisk to the USC. This apparent pilgrimage to the mainland has become an annual tradition for the Association, funded under the terms of the Victims and Survivors Befriending Grant Scheme, an initiative evolved as a result of the GFA by the Community Relations Council (CRC). The CRC, established in 1990 to promote better community relations between Protestants and Catholics in Northern Ireland, facilitates activities to commemorate the cultural traditions of both communities.

The changing dynamics of Ulster unionist identity in Northern Ireland, readable through public murals, Orange marches and memorials, address the social and cultural history of remembering which continues to inform and shape the evolving peace process and political context in Northern Ireland.[13] However, no established literature has addressed the role Britain plays as an active agent in shaping these cultures of remembrance. In this chapter, the role of Britain will be shown to fulfil both symbolic and geographical functions as a site of memory to the Northern Irish Troubles.

This chapter identifies the USCA memorial at the NMA, first established in 2006, as an effort to commemorate the bonds of union within British identity and as a point of interaction between the church, the State and the local community groups involved in its establishment. It aims to look more closely at how and where this particular memory of the Troubles intersects with broader national commemorative culture in Britain. It asks, what a study of this memorial and its service reveal about the role Britain plays as a site of memory to the Northern Irish Troubles, in both physical and symbolic ways. How might Britain, as a concept and a destination, act as a site of 'respite' for Ulster unionists seeking to make peace with their past? How do these sites of memory compare to the modes of remembrance that take place at home in Northern Ireland?

These questions have been addressed through evidence gathered from interviews with representatives of the USCA and an events organiser at the NMA, in combination with contextual readings of cultural memory.[14] The chapter is structured in three main sections. Firstly, it presents a brief history of the USC and establishes the aims and objectives of the USCA. Secondly, it deals with the memorial established at the NMA in Lichfield. This includes a discussion of the selection of the NMA as a site on which to establish a memorial to the USC and the nature of the commemorative ceremony that took place in 2006. The funding of this ceremony will also be considered. Finally, the chapter presents the USCA memorial at the NMA as a strategic site of negotiation between Ulster and British concepts of unionism, through which the bonds of union are secured.

Unionism has become an increasingly fractured identity in both Northern Ireland and Great Britain. Temporal, geographical and symbolic features of the NMA make it a fascinating site from which to view how these identities coalesce and fragment. Sites of public memory, such as the NMA, provide an important function for unionist groups such as the USCA who seek greater security for their cultural identity. The USC, a deeply divisive force in Northern Irish memory, is valorised by the memorial in this national setting as a peace-keeping body, alongside other UK police units. The chapter suggests that historians should look more closely at the active role Britain plays in commemorating the Northern Irish Troubles.

A history of the Ulster Special Constabulary

Set up in 1920, the USC was established by the British government in response to escalating violence on both sides of the Northern Irish community. The Specials, as they became colloquially known, were divided into three levels: A, B and C. Whereas the As were a full-time police force and the Cs were for emergencies only, Bs were part-time and unpaid volunteers drawn overwhelmingly from the Protestant community, whose main advantage was 'knowing' the political views and activities of their Catholic neighbours.[15] In rural areas particularly, the B Specials set up road checkpoints at will and conducted searches and patrols. They were linked to sectarian murders and collusion with paramilitary organisations, so memories of the Specials are extremely divisive and traumatic, particularly for Catholic communities in Northern Ireland. Sir Basil Brooke, later Viscount Brookeborough and Prime Minister of Northern Ireland, was instrumental in establishing a citizens' defence force in Fivemiletown, Brookeborough, Lisnaskea, Maguiresbridge and

Lisbellaw, surrounding Mullaghfad, some seven months before official permission was given for the establishment of the USC.[16]

Political controversy over the role of the Specials came to a head by the end of the 1960s as Northern Ireland entered a particularly tense period in the history of the Troubles. Partly in response to a growing civil rights movement in Northern Ireland, the British government commissioned Lord Hunt to 'examine the recruitment, organisation and structure of the RUC and the USC and their respective functions and to recommend as necessary what changes are required to provide for the efficient enforcement of law and order in Northern Ireland'. On 3 October 1969, the British government published the Hunt Report, recommending the reform of the RUC in terms of a liberal-democratic model of policing and the complete disbandment of the USC.[17]

The USCA later stated that it was 'betrayed by the mother parliament at Westminster' and blamed a malicious IRA propaganda campaign for its dismissal.[18] One member of the USCA interviewed for this research explained that the Hunt Report made the Specials victims of a 'propaganda campaign' led by the IRA.[19] While the USC was technically disbanded, as Ellison and Smyth state, 'it was replaced by the Ulster Defence Regiment (UDR), which was heavily recruited from members of the Ulster Special Constabulary and soon achieved the same notoriety within the nationalist community'.[20]

The USCA was formed in an effort 'to encourage and promote those activities which conduce to keep the name of the USC in an honoured place in the history of Ulster'.[21] It was established directly after the disbandment of the USC. In 1980, it published a book entitled *Why?*, which stated:

> How often has it been said in Ulster homes, in army messes and even in the corridors of Westminster, that the disbanding of the Ulster Special Constabulary was a mistake? It is little enough to ask that that mistake now be admitted publicly, if only to relieve the hurt and remorse that is felt by the now ageing ex-members of the force, every time a soldier is killed doing a job which was formerly the work of the USC.[22]

As this statement conveys, the USCA quickly identified itself as a victim of the Troubles, before the category of 'victim' became 'the icon' of the peace process.[23] This was exacerbated after the signing of the GFA in 1998, in which the USCA presented itself as a victim of the terms of the Northern Irish peace process, which it felt posed a threat to its Ulster-British identity. The literature of the USCA conveys a great deal of fear, suspicion and anxiety about its place both within the Northern Irish State and within its local communities.[24]

Culturally, the USCA defines itself as a 'large family of loyal subjects' and its identity is founded on a strong sense of Britishness. In a history of the Ulster Specials by Special Constable Arthur Hezlett, he proudly declares, 'I describe my nationality as British first and Irish second in the same way as someone on the other side of the Irish sea could be British and Scottish.'[25] Graham Dawson has described Ulster-British identity as being founded on 'core values grounded in the importance of absolute moral standards and the maintenance of tradition: an attachment to "ethnic" or even explicitly racial purity; and a sense of living history connecting current generations to the "community of ancestors" who fought and died for "King, country and Empire"'.[26] In a commemorative pamphlet published in 2010 at a commemorative ceremony in Lichfield, the Association wrote, 'to the end the B men walked tall as men of Ulster, law abiding subjects of the British realm'.[27]

The USCA sought to memorialise this imagined geography in 2006, through the establishment of the memorial to the USC in the NMA, Lichfield. As the next section explains, this provided the USCA with the opportunity to set the USC's memory within a much broader narrative of the British war effort and to celebrate its contribution as a 'peace-keeping force' in a way that would not be possible at home in Northern Ireland. It shows that the NMA enables the USCA to locate its memory within broader commemorative narratives of heroism and sacrifice, alongside other memorials. This brings into view the agency of Britain as a symbolic and physical site of memory to the Northern Irish Troubles.

The National Memorial Arboretum, Lichfield

The NMA was founded in 1997 as the National Centre of Remembrance in Britain, having been supported by Prime Minister John Major and funded by the National Lottery in the form of the Millennium Commission. It is currently sponsored by the Royal British Legion and the UK Ministry of Defence.[28] While the NMA website describes it as the place 'where our nation remembers', the site has never been the subject of any widespread consultation. Many of its memorials represent personal memories of groups, communities and even individuals, who have raised funds to support acts of commemoration.[29] This includes the military, police, fire and ambulance forces and services, charities, local and overseas organisations as well as marriages, deaths and other personal anniversaries. The financial model of the NMA, which relies upon these private commemorative functions, ceremonies and donations, presents a compelling case of the commercialisation of commemoration in Britain.

The geographical location of the NMA, in the New National Forest between Lichfield and Burton-upon-Trent, is largely inaccessible by foot or public transport. Presented as a passive and neutral space, the NMA has not invited much critical interest from the public or from historians.[30] These qualities of isolation and silence make it an interesting, if troubling, context in which to view the establishment of the first national memorial to the British Armed Forces in the Northern Ireland Troubles. Perhaps for this reason, as Gough states, the NMA has become susceptible to 'strategic' forms of commemoration.[31]

In 2003, the Ulster Ash Grove was planted as a living tribute to the members of the Royal Ulster Constabulary George Cross (RUC GC), the RUC Reserve, the armed forces and other organisations in the service of the Crown who lost their lives as a result of Irish terrorism between 1969 and 2001.[32] This initiative to commemorate the Northern Ireland Troubles at the NMA seems to have been triggered by the *Daily Telegraph*, which published a report in 2000, finding that 719 members of the armed forces had been killed as a result of Irish terrorism between 1969 and 2000.[33] The paper ran a subsequent campaign to 'remember the servicemen and women who died in Northern Ireland'.[34] The timing of this report, two years after the signing of the GFA, suggests that the impetus to memorialise the Troubles in Britain coincided with a feeling of resolution, facilitating a sense of detachment and finality to the Troubles in Britain. The British State was officially represented at the opening of the Ulster Ash Grove, through the attendance of Northern Ireland Secretary Paul Murphy, Security Minister Jane Kennedy and Lieutenant General Philip Trousdell, General Officer Commanding in the province.[35]

The geographical features of Ulster form a major component of the aesthetic arrangement of the Ulster Ash Grove. A three-foot-tall pillar of Mourne granite stands at the centre of the memorial and is surrounded by six boulders taken from the six counties in Northern Ireland, 'arranged in a map of the province'.[36] Seven varieties of ash tree, all common to Northern Ireland, were planted. The accompanying text states:

> The trees planted within this grove represent lives lost in the cause of peace in Northern Ireland and these form an ever changing backdrop to the stone circle and granite pillar. The circle contains one block of stone from each county and [these] are placed to form a symbolic map of Northern Ireland. The stones enclose a simple granite pillar and form a small tranquil place with seats where you are invited to rest and remember those who gave their lives in the service of the people of Northern Ireland.[37]

The instruction here to 'rest and remember' invokes a sense of detachment and tranquility, which is in stark contrast to the politically charged form that commemoration takes in Northern Ireland. The Ulster Ash Grove memorials were all supported through charitable fundraising by their respective commemorative associations in Northern Ireland. Therefore, as well as memorialising the past, they also frame, shape and memorialise the bonds of union that exist between the two geographical locations.

The term 'ever changing' is a recurring motif throughout the NMA and refers partly to the changing geographical shape of the site, as it expands according to the acquisition of new land. However, the term also takes on a wider symbolic meaning in the context of the new memorials, which are continually being added by public and private groups. The Ulster Ash Grove has been 'ever changing' since its opening in 2003, with new memorials established by commemorative associations which represent communities in Northern Ireland. These memorials were supported through charitable fundraising by their respective associations. This includes the Northern Ireland Prison Service, RUC GC and the Widows' Association of the RUC, the Army Dog Unit (Northern Ireland), USC and UDR.[38] All of these memorials function as sites of memory to the bonds of union that were formed through army, police and security forces. Although they vary in size and structure, the memorials frame narratives of sacrifice, duty and honour, bearing the names of individuals who 'gave their lives in service' to the Crown between 1969 and 2001.[39] In this way, the USC memory is slotted into a grander narrative of British citizenship, allegiance and public service.

In 2006, the USCA travelled to the NMA to unveil a black marble and blue limestone memorial inscribed with the names of 246 men of the USC who were killed between 1920 and 1970 (Figure 22.2). The memorial, carved out of black South African granite and blue stone from County Kerry, was of the USCA's own design.[40] The Association commissioned a local memorial company to make the obelisk, which cost it £22,000, all of which was privately raised.[41] The obelisk aesthetic transposes the funerary mode of remembrance in the Mullaghfad church on a grander scale. Significantly, its inscription echoes the Mullaghfad gravestones: 'Dedicated to former members of the Ulster Special Constabulary who were murdered as a result of terrorism'.

The classical form of the obelisk also mimics the golden obelisk, the biggest memorial standing at the centre of the Arboretum, as part of the Armed Forces memorial unveiled by the Queen in 2007. While many of the memorials established here do not reflect wide public consultation or official agreement, their regular, formalised aesthetic presents a unified

Figure 22.2 Obelisk to Ulster Special Constabulary at the Ulster Ash Grove, National Memorial Arboretum, established by the Ulster Special Constabulary Association, 2006.

impression of national commemoration. In this way the NMA, of which the Ulster Ash Grove is one part, takes on the appearance of an official site of national memory. The USC obelisk quietly integrates into the NMA's symbolic landscape.

The unveiling of the obelisk took place on 29 July 2006. Members of the USCA interviewed for this research were present at the ceremony and involved in its organisation. They were especially proud of the attendance of a number of British police officers. Although the service was not widely advertised, an invitation to members of the British police force can be found on the online police forum PUMA, set up to 'remember members of the police services, whether they be full time, part time, reserves or Specials'.[42] It reads, 'On Saturday 29 July, 2006, we will join our comrades from the Ulster Special Constabulary Association at a service of Prayer & Remembrance being held in Lichfield Cathedral at 11.00am'. The forum stated that twenty-five UK Special Constabularies would be in attendance. After the event, a report of the commemoration was posted on the site, stating that the Deputy High Sheriff of Staffordshire, Sir John Giffard, the Mayor and Mayoress of Lichfield, the Deputy Mayor of Birmingham and regular officers from the UK had been in attendance. Constable Richard Stamp from West Midlands Police Drum Corp led the thirty-one standards during the short parade from Lichfield town centre to the cathedral.[43] This display of solidarity between civic leadership in the English Midlands and the USC presents unionism as an active dialogue between England and Northern Ireland at the NMA.

Constable Rob Snow from Humberside police was given the honour of carrying the first candle, lit in memory of all fallen UK police officers, while being led through the cathedral by a lone piper from the Royal Irish Regiment. The USC Historical Platoon, 'immaculately dressed in their 1920s uniforms', provided a guard of honour outside the cathedral. The highlight of the day, for one USCA member interviewed, was the 'dedication service and the unveiling of the obelisk which was carried out by late President and ex-District Commandant, Comrade William John McFarlane, who was ninety years of age, accompanied by the Deputy Lord Lieutenant of Staffordshire, who was an ex-Chief Police Officer'.[44] This USCA member was keen to emphasise that 'also in attendance was the Chairman of Lichfield District Council and his good lady wife along with members of the Northern Ireland Veterans Association which is based in Leicestershire'.[45] He was proud to describe a sense of identification between the British police officers and the USCA. He has continued to attend the services of the USCA at Lichfield, which now take place on an annual basis. In 2012, for example, he said that fifty officers from different police organisations in Britain would be attending the service on 28 July. 'It is very important to me to maintain that connection with GB,' he said.

As Kate Darian-Smith and Paula Hamilton state, 'memories link us to place, to time and to nation: they enable us to inhabit our own country'.[46] The commemorative ceremony at Lichfield enables the USCA to inhabit its imagined geography. When the USCA stands alongside British police forces, it is not only standing to remember the USC, but commemorating the bonds of union between them. Being physically rooted at the NMA allows the USCA to express a sense of certainty about the fixed and unchanging nature of its British identity, in a context of political uncertainty at home.

Travelling from Mullaghfad to the National Memorial Arboretum

The NMA is a place of rich symbolism, patriotism and a strong sense of allegiance and service to the Crown. As such, it is a familiar and comforting place of 'respite' for Ulster unionists who feel isolated culturally. Three coach loads of family and friends of those who served in the USC travelled to attend the service. The funding for this trip was facilitated by the creation of the Victims and Survivors Befriending Grant Scheme, established in 2003 as part of the Northern Ireland CRC's attempt to address the legacy of the past.[47] In 2006, the USCA received 12 per cent of the total funding allocated under this scheme in that year. A grant to the USCA was given for 'a respite weekend to enable USC veterans to attend a memorial service at the National Memorial Arboretum dedicated to those who lost their lives as a result of the troubles' and further grants were given to individual regional branches of the Association. The Omagh branch received an additional £1,050 for twelve of its most isolated members to attend the service.[48]

A wide range of community groups and individuals have been supported under this funding scheme, including Families Acting for Innocent Relatives (FAIR), the RUC GC Association (RUC GC (A)) and UDR Association (UDRA).[49] The RUC GC (A) and the UDRA were, like the USCA, formed to maintain contact and provide support for former members and their families. In so doing, they also work to sustain a historical narrative. Each of these groups promotes a particular interpretation of victimhood in relation to the Northern Irish Troubles. Victimhood has become a contested subject in Northern Ireland and is often defined to fit the perceived needs of local community groups. For instance, the devolved Northern Ireland government defines victims as 'the surviving physically or psychologically injured of violent, conflict-related incidents and those close relatives or partners who care for them, along with those close relatives or partners who mourn their dead'.[50] Other groups, like FAIR, define victims as those who have experienced trauma as a social consequence of the Troubles.[51] Commemorations and memorial services form a significant proportion of activities funded by the CRC to support such victims.

The USCA was not the only group to use the scheme to fund a trip to Britain. In 2006, the RUC GC (A) was also awarded £2,800 to attend 'a remembrance project for members to participate in a National Police Memorial Day in Edinburgh and an additional £1,000 to attend a memorial at the National Police training college at Bramshill, Hampshire'. The Wives Club of the UDR was awarded £2,262 to make a 'respite trip to Blackpool'.[52] England therefore appears to act as a site of pilgrimage for Ulster unionists who see themselves as victims of the Northern Irish Troubles. Politically too, the Ulster Ash Grove at the NMA has been claimed as Ulster unionist territory. In January 2012, DUP representatives made a donation from contributions at their latest party conference to the UDRA, as a contribution to the Northern Ireland section of the NMA. Speaking of this donation, a DUP the Northern Ireland Assembly Member stated, 'As a party the DUP will continue to remember soldiers, members of Her Majesty's Armed Forces and Civilian Services killed during service to their country.'[53]

When I spoke to the events organiser from the NMA who oversees the annual commemorative ceremony of the USCA, she told me that the NMA's role was strictly to facilitate and co-ordinate the event, emphasising that the ceremony was entirely funded by the USCA itself. Keen to distance the NMA from the ideological or political motivations behind commemorative ceremonies, she also acknowledged the sensitivity that surrounded this event, telling me that the 'USCA chooses not to publicise their event on the NMA website and other listings'. Speaking about the role of the NMA, she conveyed a pragmatic attitude, stating 'Our business is remembrance'.[54] By describing the NMA in these terms, as a neutral facilitator, providing a service for 'clients who are in the business of remembering', it is clear that the NMA is keen to absolve any ideological or political role it could be seen as having in the acts of commemorative memory.[55]

At the NMA, within the tranquil site of the Ulster Ash Grove, the USCA's memory of the Troubles takes the appearance of an official one. It is, however, one memory among many. The endorsement of the USC as a 'peace-keeping force', as it is described at the Ulster Ash Grove site, whether it is the intention or not, mutes the voices of contention that would be present in any public memorial at home. As seen in the case of the memorials to Robert Coulter and James Hall described at the beginning of this chapter, the USC is commemorated at the extremes of Northern Ireland, in a very private, isolated place. It is striking, therefore, that the same memories should find such a comfortable space inside the Ulster Ash Grove, a place of tranquility dedicated to peace at the NMA: 'where our nation remembers'.

The inclusivity implied by the NMA's claim to be a national site of memory can, however, also be questioned. The NMA site is a curiously physically isolated and private place for public memory in Britain. Accessibility to the site does not appear to be a priority for its management and the NMA's role as a site of public memory has never been openly addressed; instead it functions largely as a commercial enterprise, reflecting the private interests of institutions, corporations and individuals. This makes the NMA particularly vulnerable to strategic forms of commemoration of which, this chapter has argued, the USCA memorial at the Ulster Ash Grove forms a compelling example.

Conclusion

The NMA is not the only site of memory to the Northern Irish Troubles in Britain. Others offer different perspectives and, in some cases, tell local rather than national stories of remembrance in a British context. However, if historians are now to begin to examine the role of Britain as a site of memory to the Northern Irish Troubles with a more critical eye, the USC memorial at the NMA presents a rewarding place to start. The NMA enables the USCA to claim and enact victimhood status and fulfils its wish to be remembered as a peace-keeping force. In addition, the British State and the devolved Northern Ireland government support these commemorative ceremonies under the terms of the Victims and Survivors Befriending Grant Scheme. Britain therefore plays a very active role in identifying the 'victim' and the 'perpetrator' – both highly contentious terms in Northern Ireland. Through this memorial, the Association realises one of its central aims: 'to keep the name of the USC in an honoured place in the history of Ulster'.[56] With this in mind, the neutral role that the NMA claims to play as a place of remembrance deserves more careful consideration.

From Orange parades to commemorations at the NMA, Britain plays a symbolic role in the public performance of 'bonds of union', but, as with all forms of cultural identity, these are not fixed or immutable, but form a dialogue, the dynamics of which are constantly in motion.[57] As Colin Kidd observes in the *London Review of Books*, the symbolic celebrations of Ulster unionism look, to the contemporary eye, outdated, unfashionable and 'stridently un-British'.[58] This perception of Ulster unionism as something 'other' to British nationalism is increasingly common.[59] However, at the Ulster Ash Grove at the NMA, Ulster unionism is presented in the familiar tropes of British commemorative culture and easily co-exists alongside memorials to the armed forces, under the name of peace-keeping and national sacrifice. Thus, British nationalism works to support and interact with Ulster unionism in very real and tangible ways.

British involvement in commemorating the Northern Irish Troubles is a neglected area for critical commentary. As a result, Britain is often presented as a passive observer of the peace process. The memorial to the USCA at the NMA in Lichfield tells a very different story. That such a contested and bitterly divisive site of memory, identified at Mullaghfad church at the opening of this chapter, could be so easily sited among the trees of the Ulster Ash Grove lends an insight into the seemingly casual, banal ways that Britain plays an active role in commemorating the Northern Ireland Troubles.

Notes

1 Images of the church can be found on photo-sharing websites including Flickr, see dr_urbanus(Martin) (4 April 2009), www.flickr.com/photos/21212853@N08/3415491552/ (Accessed 10 March 2014).
2 See J. Winter, *Sites of Memory, Sites of Mourning, The Great War in European Cultural History* (Cambridge: Cambridge University Press, 1998). Also see J. Leonard, *Memorials to the Casualties of Conflict: Northern Ireland 1969 to 1997* (Belfast: Community Relations Council, 1997). http://cain.ulst.ac.uk/issues/commemoration/leonard/leonard97.htm (Accessed 11 March 2014).
3 G. Dawson, *Making Peace with the Past? Memory, Trauma and the Irish Troubles* (Manchester: Manchester University Press, 2007), p. 217.
4 C. Kidd, 'On the window ledge of the union', *London Review of Books*, 35:3 (7 February 2013).
5 It should be noted that all of these stories survive on anecdotal evidence, passed through generations.
6 For a similar account of the circumstances surrounding the deaths of Special Constables Robert Coulter and James Hall see R. Abbott, *Police Casualties in Ireland, 1919–1922* (Dublin: Mercier Press, 2000), p. 246.
7 Interview with anonymous USCA member (12 April, 2012).
8 D. Fitzpatrick, 'Commemoration in the Irish Free State', in I. MacBride (ed.) *History and Memory in Modern Ireland* (Cambridge: Cambridge University Press, 2001), p. 184.
9 One does not need to go very far to find evidence of how memorials quickly become sites of division in Northern Ireland. Less than a mile from Mullaghfad

church, in a closely bordering nationalist area, a memorial to two IRA men killed by the Royal Irish Constabulary had been vandalised, bearing the words 'No surrender' in paint on the day of my visit (2 January 2011).

10 Leonard, *Memorials to the Casualties of Conflict*.

11 J. Todd et al., 'Does being Protestant matter? Protestants, minorities and the remaking of ethno-religious identity', *National Identities*, 11:1 (2009), pp. 87–99.

12 Peter Robinson, Deputy Leader to DUP Annual Conference in Belfast (4 February 2006), http://cain.ulst.ac.uk/issues/politics/docs/dup/pr040206.htm (Accessed 10 February 2014).

13 A range of approaches to this subject can be found in: R. Foster, *The Irish Story: Telling Lies and Making It Up in Ireland* (London: Allen Lane, 2001); N. Jarman, *Material Conflicts: Parades and Visual Displays in Northern Ireland* (London: Berg, 1997); McBride (ed.), *History and Memory*; E. Bort (ed.), *Commemorating Ireland, History, Politics, Culture* (Dublin: Irish Academic Press, 2004); P. Collins, *Who Fears to Speak of '98? Commemoration and the Continuing Impact of the United Irishmen* (Belfast: Ulster Historical Foundation, 2004); Leonard, *Memorials to the Casualties*.

14 These interviews were conducted by telephone and the names of those interviewed have been anonymised.

15 G. Ellison and J. Smyth, *The Crowned Harp: Policing in Northern Ireland* (London: Pluto, 2000), p. 30.

16 Ibid., p. 25.

17 Report of the Advisory Committee on Police in Northern Ireland, chaired by Baron Hunt (1969), available on CAIN website, http://cain.ulst.ac.uk/hmso/hunt.htm (Accessed 10 February 2014).

18 *Why?* (no place of publication: USCA, 1980), unpaginated. Also available on CAIN, http://cain.ulst.ac.uk/issues/police/docs/usca80.htm (Accessed 10 February 2014).

19 Anonymous USCA member, Interview with Leah Armstrong (10 April 2012).

20 Ellison and Smyth, *The Crowned Harp*, p. 70.

21 *History of the Ulster Specials Constabulary Association* (No place of publication: undated), sent to the author by Honorary Secretary of the USCA, Lisnaskea branch.

22 *Why?*

23 C. Gilligan, 'Constant crisis/permanent process: Diminished agency and weak structures in the Northern Ireland peace process', *The Global Review of Ethnopolitics*, 3:1 (September 2003), 29–34.

24 See, for example, *History of the Ulster Specials* and *Why?*

25 A. Hezlet, *The B Specials: A History of the Ulster Special Constabulary* (London: Pan, 1997; 1st edn, 1972), p. 4.

26 Dawson, *Making Peace with the Past*, p. 212.

27 USCA pamphlet (Undated), sent to the author by Anonymous USCA member.

28 'Our Sponsors', www.thenma.org.uk/about-us/about-us/sponsors/ (Accessed 10 February 2014).

29 www.nma.org.uk (Accessed 19 January 2014).

30 A notable exception is P. Gough, 'Garden of gratitude: The National Memorial Arboretum and strategic remembering', in P. Ashton and H. Kean (eds), *People and Their Pasts, Public History Today* (Basingstoke: Palgrave, 2009).

31 Ibid.

32 The RUC was renamed RUC George Cross in 1999, when it was awarded the George Cross by the Queen.

33 'Why today I will thank those who died in Northern Ireland', *Daily Telegraph* (23 September 2003).

34 Ibid.

35 'Tribute to murdered officers', BBC News, 23 September 2003, http://news.bbc.co.uk/1/hi/northern_ireland/3130566.stm (Accessed 14 October 2014).

36 Ibid.

37 Ulster Ash Grove, National Memorial Arboretum, Lichfield.

38 National Memorial Arboretum, 'All Memorials', www.thenma.org.uk/about-us/memorials/all-memorials/0-d/ (Accessed 12 February 2014).

39 The Northern Ireland Prison Service Memorial (2003) takes the form of a plaque which bears the name of the 'men and women of the Northern Ireland Prison Service who lost their lives as a result of their employment during 1969–2001'. The RUC GC Way Memorial (2003) is an avenue of trees with plaques for each individual Ulster police district marked by an engraved stone at either end. The RUC Widows Association memorial takes the form of two marble benches, which look onto the RUC GC memorial. The Army Dog Unit (Northern Ireland) memorial (2007) was established to 'remember the men and dogs of the Army Dog Unit Northern Ireland, Royal Army Veterinary Corps who have lost their lives in service between 1973 and 2007'. It takes the form of a small stone monument with a red paw badge. The UDR GC (2012) memorial commemorates those who lost their lives between 1970 and 1992. A video of these memorials showing their spatial arrangement within the Ulster Ash Grove at the NMA can be found at www.youtube.com/watch?v=lWYSINRHYdw (Accessed 10 June 2014).

40 Interview, USCA member, Leah Armstrong (30 May 2012).

41 Ibid.

42 PUMA (20 July 2006), www.policespecials.com/forum/index.php?topic/41427-puma/ (Accessed 12 June 2012).

43 Ibid.

44 Anonymous USCA member, Interview with Leah Armstrong (30 May 2012).

45 Ibid.

46 K. Darian-Smith and P. Hamilton (eds), *Memory and History in Twentieth-Century Australia* (Oxford: Oxford University Press, 1994), p. 1.

47 'Victims and Survivors Befriending Grant Scheme, Grants Paid: 2006–7', Community Relations Council Northern Ireland, www.community-relations.org.uk/fs/doc/crc-annual-report-061.pdf (Accessed 14 February 2014).

48 Ibid.

49 Ibid.

50 *Reshape, Rebuild, Achieve: Delivering Practical Help and Services to Victims of*

the Conflict in Northern Ireland (Belfast: Office of the First Minister and Deputy First Minister, 2002), p. 1.

51 FAIR defines itself as a non-political organisation aiming to work in the interests of the 'innocent victims of terrorism in South Armagh'.

52 *Reshape, Rebuild, Achieve*, p. 1.

53 'DUP presents cheque to UDR Association', *Lurgan Mail* (2 January 2012).

54 Interview with Events Organiser NMA, Leah Armstrong (2 July 2012).

55 Ibid.

56 *Why?*

57 See L. Colley, *Acts of Union, Acts of Disunion* (London: Profile, 2014).

58 Kidd, 'On the window ledge'.

59 British artist Grayson Perry's tapestry depicting Orange men marching to commemorate the UVF similarly presents the 'exoticism' of Ulster unionism, which he finds to be 'curiously anti-British'. Grayson Perry, '*Who Are You?*', National Portrait Gallery, London, 25 October–15 March 2014.

23

'I'd find a way to contribute to peace'

Jo Berry

I started this morning[1] by going to the beach and putting my feet in the water, and then looking back at the Grand Hotel. And even though it was in 1984 that my father was killed there,[2] I still have a reaction, a response. And I was just sitting there, just thinking of everything that's happened, and just thinking that, if that hadn't happened, who would I have been, who would I have become? And recognising the choices that I made within two days have completely changed my life.

When my father was killed that day, I was actually about to travel to Africa, and I saw myself as a traveller, a free spirit, and I'd already said goodbye to him. That summer we had become really close, and it was almost like the first bridge I ever built was with him. Because, I had very different politics to him, in fact I didn't really believe in politics, I believed very much in meditation, I saw myself as someone away from the world. But that summer we got very close, and he shared with me why he was a politician and what it meant to him, and it was actually about contributing to peace. He recognised that I was working in my way for peace, so we had a very strong bond.

Within two days of him being killed, I realised I hadn't just lost my father, who I was very close to, but I also felt I was catapulted into a war, into a conflict, and I couldn't go back to being that free spirit any more. Part of me died in that bomb. I felt that I wanted to make a contribution. I started caring about people in Northern Ireland, and every time bombs went off or people were killed, I could feel it. I made a very silent, private vow that I would find a way to bring something positive out of what had happened, and I'd find a way to contribute to peace. I would also try to understand those who had killed him. I didn't know what that meant, I didn't know who to go to, who to speak to. In London in 1984, I couldn't even tell people what had happened to me, because the kind of responses I got were 'Well can't you let go?' I didn't want to let go, it wasn't what it was about at all.

I found myself sharing a taxi with a random person in the street who shared his story in the taxi, and I shared mine, and his brother had been in the IRA, and his brother had been killed by a British soldier. We should have been enemies, we were from different divides, and yet we saw each other as human beings who dreamed of a world where people didn't get killed. And as I left that taxi, the word came to me, I can build a bridge across the divide, and it's something that I can do.

I went to Belfast in 1985 and 1986. I remember arriving in 1985, and even though, living in London, bombs had been going off in my child-hood, I wasn't prepared for arriving to the tanks and the level of fear and the soldiers and the bombs going off. I felt scared and out of my depth, but also, it was important to start meeting people. Through word of mouth, I just met some people who said, 'Come and meet this person'. I found myself sharing my experience to a group in 1985, 800 people at a born-again Christian event, and they were all there, doing their pros-trations to Jesus. I thought they were going to lynch me, because what I was going to say wasn't to do with Jesus at all. But they heard me, they heard what I was trying to say, which was about understanding.

In those days I would use the word 'forgiveness'; these days I find it much harder. But I began to understand the human face, and hearing these stories, got close to a lot of people. I met someone high up in Sinn Féin (SF) in Dublin, and he wasn't allowed to meet me, so we met in hiding, and I remember, I got in one car, and then had to stop and get into another car, and then another car. I felt completely out of my depth. But when I actually got to meet him in a private room in a hotel, and he said to me how sorry he was about my father, but more important than that, he had his son with him, and I saw their relationship, I began to see that somebody is much more than their political beliefs or their belief in using violence.

In 1986 I went to Benburb monastery, near Armagh, and there was a group there, and I was told that if they heard that I had an English accent, they might want to hurt me physically, I'd be so threatening. That was difficult to hear, though I understood it. So I stopped going to Northern Ireland and had a long gap. During this long gap I remember the amount of times I would just be in tears at what was going on, the bombs in England as well as in Northern Ireland.

In 1999 I actually met for the first time someone who had also been affected by the conflict in Northern Ireland, who lived in England, and that was Colin Parry.[3] That completely changed my life, because he invited me to a victims' group at the Glencree Centre for Peace and

Reconciliation in Ireland.[4] It was only in the year 2000 that I really got a chance to deal with the emotional legacy that I had. I had buried so many of the feelings and the trauma, but for many months I got an opportunity to let out some of the anger, some of the pain, some of the grief, and began to meet other people who had similar pains. Nobody there was scared about my own pain, which was such a relief, I had that listening, that witnessing, which is really, really important.

And during that year, I got an opportunity to meet the one person who was responsible, who was caught, who was responsible for the Brighton bomb, who had been released from prison in 1999. I remember turning on the TV in June for the news, and there was Pat Magee being released from prison. We weren't warned or prepared, suddenly there he was. My first thought was, 'is there any remorse in his eyes?' Of course he was met by cameras and he gave absolutely nothing away. I remember being quite angry, 'he's free now, he's free. My life is still being affected, my dad can never come back, and he's free.' But because he was released as part of the peace process, I welcomed that, and the idea of wanting to meet him had been there for a long time, and I knew that now he was out of prison there was going to be this opportunity.

In the year 2000 I met three people who said they could organise the meeting. And I really wanted it, I welcomed it. But each time I heard he didn't want to meet me, which at the time I didn't know why, but I accepted it. Then one day I got a phone call. I was about to get the ferry from North Wales to Glencree, the phone rings to say that he's agreed to meet me that evening. My first thought was, 'I'm not in the mood. I'm not feeling inspired, I'm not caring about peace', I'm just thinking about my little girls and whether they're going to have enough to eat while I'm gone. I was hoovering for some reason, I don't know why I was hoovering. I thought, no, I can trust, this day has been a long day coming, I'm going to trust this is the right day. I was terrified, I was so scared. My whole journey had been about not blaming, giving out blame, but was I going to go there and want to blame him and shout at him and I had no idea how I was going to be. Would he turn up? What would he say?

I remember him walking into the room and straight away he said, 'Thank you for coming. Thank you for inviting me.' And I said, 'Well, thank you for coming.' I asked, 'How come you changed your mind?' He replied, 'Oh I've always said I wanted to meet you.' So how did that yes get translated to a no? I'll never know. We started talking, just the two of us in a room, without anyone else there. Looking back on it, though it was hard, I think it enabled what did happen to happen. He started off by giving me a lot of political justification. I had met men before who had been in the IRA, and I'd met people from SF, and I was quite familiar with it. I was thinking that I probably wouldn't come back for a second round, but at the same time, I could see he had some sensitivity, and I was putting a human face to the enemy, which was helping my own healing.

Something happened about halfway through where he stopped talking, and he said to me, 'I don't know who I am any more, I don't know what to say. When I hear your anger and your grief, and, what can I do to help?' In that moment he had taken off his political hat, he had opened up, and became vulnerable. He shared something very different for the next hour and a half. A new journey started, a journey that I'm still on.

After that first meeting I really wanted to go back for a second one, I didn't feel it was finished, and he felt the same. I discovered that my need to meet him and to see his humanity equalled his need to see me. Although it's been a very challenging journey, it's one that we're still on. If he was here, he would say that he was guilty of demonising the other in the same way that he felt he was demonised. He learned through listening to me and dialoguing and meeting others as well, that he could have sat down with my dad and had a cup of tea. Of course he couldn't have, because the Conservative Party weren't into having cups of tea with the IRA. But, there's a truth in there that they could have just sat down and yes, I could imagine them sitting down together.

I wish that the power of dialogue had been obvious back then. I've learned that, if I'd lived his life and gone through everything he had been through, who knows, I may have made the same choices. I've had that experience also with someone who had been a loyalist paramilitary, and someone who had been in the British Army, and what I've learned about this is the truth, that actually when I really hear people's stories, I could have made the same choices.

For me the idea of 'enemy' and 'other' doesn't exist. I've learned how to choose a non-violent response, how to not blame, how to give up and understand, and what that involves. For the past eleven or twelve years I've been in the public eye. We had a documentary made about us, which went out in 2001.[5] In those days, I was actually quite shy and not as confident as I am now, and it was a huge risk. Was I going to re-traumatise my family? Was I going to make a positive or a negative difference? I didn't know. The deepest thought in me was that if I can help one person by making this documentary, then it's worthwhile. I got a lot of feedback from what I call the *Daily Mail* readers saying that Pat Magee wasn't their idea of a terrorist, and a lot of other people who had been victims and survivors of different conflicts, saying that it had empowered them to make choices for their own journey. When people ask me if I would recommend what I've done, I say, 'No, but I support you in doing what you need to do.' Because, when these appalling things happen to us, a new journey starts, and there's no right or wrong, it's only what's right for us, and this is a very personal response that I have made.

After the documentary was transmitted, there I was in the public eye, and I started getting invited to speak at different events, and that's when I started the organisation Building Bridges for Peace.[6] In the last year, I have done many things: I was in Lebanon with Pat Magee and speaking at a Healing the Wounds of History conference there, sharing a stage with somebody who had been in a Christian militia, a director of intelligence responsible for 10,000 deaths, who is now working in redemption and to create peace in Lebanon. I met someone there from Rwanda who had lost sixty-five members of his family, and at the end of the conference he said to me, 'Jo, will you come to Rwanda in June?' And I went, 'Yes.' Sure enough, the first of June comes and the invitation's there, not much notice, and I went to Rwanda. That was such a privilege. There was a group of us who went there from different parts of the world, different conflicts, linked by an organisation in Brighton called the Guerrand-Hermès Foundation for Peace. When we arrived there, we were told that the conference wasn't going to start, because this government group wanted to talk to us and listen to us. So we had a day where we shared with them, and at the end of it a wonderful bishop said, 'This is the first time anyone's come from the international community, not to teach us what to do, not as experts, not with righteousness, but have come to walk with us and heal together. Therefore we welcome you, you are the right partners.' That's what I feel it's about; it's not that I have any answers for anyone else. I've learned about the importance of support and sharing.

One of my new projects is how we can develop empathy, and how we can change the whole way we resolve violence. I get opportunities I wouldn't have had because of what's happened to me. I was invited to the House of Commons to speak to the All-Party Parliamentary Group on Conflict Issues. To go back to the House of Commons where I'd been as a child, and to speak, in a room where the whole way of communication is, 'while you are speaking I'm going to try and prove you wrong' – that's how I see politics, maybe in a rather naïve way. To go there and talk about win-win solutions, listening, the power of empathy, and to look at the other person in their full humanity. What I have learned more than anything, the reason why my father was killed and many others, is when we don't see people in their full humanity. That doesn't mean that we have to take people being violent sitting down, we can learn to challenge people without actually demonising them.

This 'work' for me, it's how I am as a mother with my three daughters. There were times when they would say to me when they were younger, 'Mum, this is a no-blame house. Do you want to go and sort your anger out? Do you want a cushion?' So, it's very much in my family, and when I go into schools, it's how I am with kids, when I go into prisons, whether it's local or national work. Yes, there are challenges. One of the things that happens is that people project things onto me. I had a prisoner recently get angry with me, and he wasn't really angry with me, but what I was reminding him of. I have that emotional strength to be able to listen to him, to support him and recognise what was going on for him.

There's also the challenge of what happens when I feel like I've gone a bit too far and perhaps upset people. I've still got what I call my 'inner critic', the part of me that sometimes, when I am very vulnerable and take risks, will tell me afterwards, 'Oh you shouldn't have said that.' That's something I work with all the time. There's experiences of when the only person I've been with is Patrick Magee. We're in an aeroplane together, and there's no one else. Sometimes that can be really difficult, because, is he my friend, can I ask him for support when I'm really struggling, or is he the man who killed my father? What, who is he, what's our relationship? It's very unusual. I never know what he's going to say, and there have been times, when for whatever reason, he became very defensive and went back to politically justifying again. That was hard. At the end of one session, about two years ago, I said, 'Actually, I'm not going to do this anymore.' I always have that choice. Within a few weeks I decided that I did want to carry on working with him, because, when I think back to that original impulse of creating something positive, I still feel there's more to learn by working with him, it's still something that I am gaining from.

We were in East Belfast recently, at a cross-community group, and in the audience there were quite a lot of men from a loyalist group, and at the end of the session they all got out their smartphones and had photographs of them with their arms around Pat, laughing with him, wanted to go and have a drink with him. That to me is progress.

I think that one of the most challenging things is that, sometimes after this really emotionally hard work, I don't always have the support that I need, and it's learning to give that to myself. One of the reasons I created Building Bridges for Peace was to create a group around me, so it doesn't all rest on me, and that hasn't quite happened yet. I used to warn my family, my five siblings, my stepmother who was injured in the bomb, if I was going to be on the television, so that they didn't have to watch if they didn't want to. That hasn't happened for a long time. It has been really, really hard, and I think they're just amazing really, the way they've put up with me. Because they've been on a journey, and it's a very different one to mine; for them the context of what had happened wasn't so important, and so they haven't felt the connection that I've been talking about in Northern Ireland.

For the past however many years it is, it feels like I've been transforming my pain into a passion for peace. Whilst before the bomb had gone off I would have been sitting in the Himalayas in a lotus position meditating, now it's about sitting with the people who use violence, sitting with the people who make those orders to use violence, and sitting with people that others aren't communicating with. It's caring about the people who nobody's listening to right now who might use violence. It's understanding the roots of all violence and terrorism and war, and seeing what we can do differently. I really do believe at some point generations will look back and talk about the old days when we believed using violence and bombs was a good way to resolve conflict, and, obviously it's a long way coming. I'm fortunate to be part of an international network of people who have also been affected by genocide, war, terrorism and violence who are also working for peace, and that gives me a lot of support. It gives me a lot of strength. On the days when I feel like it's too difficult, that I want to go and have a 'normal' life, they are the people who support and help me.

I haven't got rid of my blame response yet. When something happens, there's still a part of me that wants to blame someone, make someone wrong and right; I don't think that's ever going to go away. But I believe if we can choose an understanding, non-blame response, we become stronger. I make that choice every single day. Even today when I was sitting outside the Grand Hotel, it feels like I'm always beginning that choice and always need to make that choice. When I look back, nothing's ever going to make me into that person I was or bring back my father, but the opportunities that I have to contribute, I'm really grateful for. I feel like I've just started my work, it's just at the beginning of what I really want to do, and I reaffirm today as I do every day that I will carry on with it.

Notes

1 This chapter originates in a talk presented at 'The Northern Ireland Troubles in Britain: Impacts, Engagements, Legacies and Memories', an interdisciplinary conference co-organised by the University of Brighton, the University of Leicester and the Tim Parry Johnathan Ball Foundation for Peace and held in Brighton, 11–13 July 2012. The talk and the questions and answers that followed were recorded, transcribed and amalgamated to form this written text.

2 Sir Anthony Berry MP was killed in the bombing of the Grand Hotel in Brighton on 12 October 1984.
3 See chapter 18.
4 http://glencree.ie.
5 *Facing the Enemy* (BBC, 2001). Available at: www.dailymotion.com/video/xlsg3m_facing-the-enemy_shortfilms (Accessed 15 November 2015).
6 www.buildingbridgesforpeace.org/who_we_are.html.

24

Performance practices and conflict resolution: Jo Berry and Patrick Magee's *Facing the Enemy*

Verity Combe

It has been said that 'for every one year of conflict we need ten years of reconciliation'.[1] Contemporary conflict resolution differs from the more traditional kinds because it now emphasises post-conflict processes that generate solutions and is much more inter-disciplinary in its scope. Conflict resolution is both an academic and a practical field and a branch of international relations dedicated to alleviating and illuminating sources of conflict. Reconciliation is a process of sustaining conflict resolution that can be developed through dialogue. It will not offer a settlement that is final or fixed and so is regarded as a solution that needs to be continually maintained.

This chapter deals with how performance practice can aid conflict resolution by challenging established histories to create ways for new identities to emerge. Those affected by the Troubles need the space to account for their experiences, and the public in mainland Britain also needs to develop more of an understanding of those affected by the Troubles today, and how they are refiguring their way in British society.

Now that we have moved towards a post-conflict era, we need to learn how to rebuild in the aftermath of the Troubles through a dialogue with the people affected by it. Dialogue is not possible without a willingness to listen, which, in turn, is what facilitates understanding. This dialogical process can help to encapsulate transformation from the negative into the positive by rebuilding from the core of each individual identity, however shifting and heterogeneous these might be.

An excellent way for doing this is through the artistic practice of performance. To perform is to imagine, represent, live and enact present circumstances, past events and future possibilities.[2] It is a platform that can be used to ask important questions about the past in a present-day context. It can accurately account for those who carry the burden of the Troubles while raising awareness for those in the UK who are ill informed and/or indifferent.

This chapter addresses transformation in the form of a performed reconciling dialogue between Jo Berry and Patrick Magee, and I consider the ability of performance to negotiate such transformation by using a demonstration of dialogue as a means of communication with a live audience. This demonstration of dialogue is important because it allows the performers to represent themselves in an unmediated way and control how others perceive their identity. Yet, the performance itself acts as a mediator, the theatrical conventions act as a structural formation to support conflict resolution. There are many examples of theatre and performance that are explicit in their declaration of intent to facilitate understanding.[3] In this case study, it is the formal structure of the staging of the performance itself that helps to create a space for conflict resolution to unfurl.

Berry and Magee's practice is similar to a panel discussion. It is to present a live performance in a formal environment in which the performers retain their own core identities. In other words, they do not take on the story of someone else, but they talk of their own lived and shared experiences. A critical standpoint in much of contemporary performance discourse is where performers are not 'acting' but completing work that informs an audience of the true sense of the performer. This helps the audience to gain new knowledge by facilitating an understanding of integral parts of their personality, and their reasons for using performance as their chosen mode of communication. Performance acts as a means of clear communication that other forms of communication do not satisfy. It should be the case that performance is made because the information performed could not be adequately communicated in any other way.

Performance is defined as a mode of communication, a display that engages the public sphere with the narration of a story that can be communicated visually, textually or orally to an audience of people, enabling them to gain new knowledge. In a more literal sense, meanings of performance can include the following; to accomplish an act, to make public a presentation, to use embodiment as a central instrument of communication and to simulate or represent.[4] Performance engages with how we use our bodies through action and presentation to try to convey meaning. One can perform anywhere at any time, yet there is the possibility for dialogue within the formal structural conventions of theatre and performance that does not exist in everyday life. There is a stage with audience present, and audiences adhere to formal theatrical convention because they are present and silent and they sit and listen to those on stage. As the audience enters into a relationship with those on stage, potentially there is a dialogical aspect to performing that does not exist in normal, everyday exchanges. There is something very important about the space of the stage as a space for conflict resolution in Berry and Magee's performance which exists because of their honesty and attention to detail.

Dialogue is from the Greek word, *dialogos*. *Logos* meaning 'the word' and *dia* meaning 'through'. It refers to a communication that exists through words. By this definition, dialogue is useful to addressing this case study because it is a more considered form of communication than discussion. The British government has sponsored talks on political structures in Northern Ireland, thereby promoting the use of dialogue.[5]

> In a dialogue, each person does not attempt to make common certain ideas or items of information that are already known to him. Rather, it may be said that the two people are making something in common, i.e. creating something new together.[6]

Berry and Magee's process of resolution through dialogue could also be described as a negotiation. Negotiation is defined as conferring to find a way through a difficulty, and to reach mutual agreement through a 'genteel' form of conflict resolution that transforms issues into words. 'Words allow the development of solutions to complex problems, though there is no guarantee of success.'[7] During their performance it is evident that Berry and Magee are sharing their truths and working through their problems with their audience. They do this by keeping their core identity, yet there is a fluidity within both of them, which means that they genuinely communicate and continually create new content that is common to both of them.

Context for the case study

On 12 October 1984 a bomb planted by IRA member Patrick Magee exploded in the Grand Hotel in Brighton during the Conservative Party conference. It was an attempt to kill the Prime Minister, Margaret Thatcher, but instead killed five people attending the conference, including high-profile members of the Conservative party, one of them being Sir Antony Berry, the father of Jo Berry. The bomb's influence helped to produce the Anglo-Irish Agreement during the following year, a London–Dublin accord based partly on counter-insurgency, but which also gave the government of the Irish Republic formal consultative rights over British policy in Northern Ireland.[8] Magee was arrested in 1985 and received eight life sentences, with a recommendation to serve fifty years before being considered for release. He was, in fact, released after fourteen years in 1999, due to the ongoing peace process and the result of the Good Friday Agreement.

Since 2000 he and Jo Berry, one of the daughters of Antony Berry, have been meeting. These meetings were initially instigated as the result of Berry approaching Patrick Magee. Berry has said of this time that it was when all her emotions came to the surface:

> It was just after Patrick Magee had been released from prison that I actually began to feel the anger and rage, and suddenly I was back in the day like it was happening, and it was a very scary experience because the emotions were of the day, not of 1999, and part of that was this incredible anger and rage. How can someone play God? Now he's free, and I'm left with it. No one's need to be heard is so great that they should kill.[9]

Given that they now perform together, it is apparent that Berry's attitude has changed dramatically since her initial response to Magee's release from prison. These meetings have resulted in friendship and an agreement to appear in public and perform a narration of their dialogue, which they have done approximately ninety times,[10] to demonstrate to people where they have arrived at today (2014). This semi-structured conversational performance has been presented, for example, at St James' Church, Piccadilly, London as part of a series of lectures; and at the Duke of York's cinema in Brighton as a post-show talk after a screening of *Soldiers of Peace* (2008), a documentary detailing examples of solutions to conflict, showing that peace can be created from great equity, emancipation, tolerance and understanding. In 2014 it was presented at an event to mark thirty years since the attack on the Grand Hotel, held at The Old Market, Brighton, accompanying a screening of *Beyond Right and Wrong* (2012), a documentary about restorative justice and forgiveness centred on people who have used dialogue, compassion and activism to help heal their broken hearts and repair their broken communities.[11]

The process of reconciliation that has taken place since Magee's release from prison has a long duration that has occurred privately and publicly between the two parties approximately every three months for over a decade. The beginning of the process was very different to where they are now in terms of their reconciliation. 'I think there was a need felt from both of us to meet again, as we'd left the conversation short. There was more to talk about. We must have met up in similar circumstances some fifty times. It doesn't get easier.'[12] Accounting for her reaction to Magee's release in 1999, Berry states that this was when she first started to feel and realise her anger. She confides that she has felt this feeling, but consciously makes a choice to want to change it.

> I wanted to put more attention and energy into the part of me that wanted to find alternatives to blaming, because then I'd stay a victim forever … Yes, I have felt anger. When I felt that kind of pain, absolute rock-bottom pain, I think I have a choice to not go for revenge but end that cycle, it's a choice to see the enemy as a human being, rather than just the enemy.[13]

It is in this moment that a willingness to be part of a process of dialogue and recognition takes hold and brings their humanity into action. They are grappling with very painful issues and facing them in their discomfort. Berry goes on to reveal that Magee showed his vulnerability from their very first meeting and it was this vulnerability that meant they continued to enter and re-enter into a private process of building trust and understanding. In reference to their first meeting, Berry states:

> I was listening and asking questions, telling him about my father and what had happened to me since then, and after about an hour, hour and a half he stopped talking, he wiped his eye and he said, 'I don't know what to say anymore, I don't know who I am.' In that moment I think part of me wanted to run away because I'd realised that this was the beginning of another journey.[14]

This is perhaps the moment where their private experience transmuted into something profound that could be engaged with publicly, to demonstrate a form of resolution. But, equally, there wasn't going to be a precise fixed solution that would appear. They had to work with each other, because Berry could not move forward without Magee's involvement and Magee couldn't move forward without Berry's moral authority. This was a journey that could be carried by performance because it deals with the live moment as its primary mode of communication.

As Berry began the difficult task of listening to Magee, this reinforced a shared sense of humanity. This highlights the constant tension that exists between the fear of facing pain and the difficulty, but necessity, of such a task that runs parallel to the process of reconciliation. It is in this sense that it could be easier to disengage than to build trust. In reality, engaging with what is difficult is exactly what is required to find a way through the problems, because if they disengaged it would mean that they were not staying true to their core identities. So it is not forgiveness that is at stake here, but the courage to face what is difficult and to be honest about it. They have to face it if they are performing it. It is through Berry's desire to listen that Magee realises his momentary crisis of identity. Because she listened and was truthfully present, this then shifted his focus. He no longer had to defend his political agenda because she was giving him the space to be himself in front of her, which in turn meant there was space for him to expose his true vulnerability of being a human. It is not forgiveness (which implies blame and victimhood) that is at stake here, but honesty. So, Berry's act of listening has not only helped her to gain trust from Magee, but it has caused something internal within him to shift and on the basis of these two individuals the restraints and oppression of the wider political context have begun to lift and a transformational approach of humanity is embodied to reach understanding. When this exchange is then represented in the public sphere it is this exact honesty which is shared with audiences. This makes for a genuine experience of a story that must be told by voices that have the moral agency to speak on such matters. It is this agency that accounts for the wider political context in which their identities are situated, and does not deny any aspect of this by placing blame.

Analysis of a *Facing the Enemy* performance

The format of the *Facing the Enemy* talks consists of approximately fifteen minutes of Berry and Magee speaking in turn and afterwards a question-and-answer session lasting approximately forty-five minutes. The talk discussed here was performed and recorded on 22 March 2010 at St James' Church in Piccadilly, London. Magee and Berry sit next to each other on stage, each either sitting on a chair or on a high stool, directly facing the end-on audience. Although there is a host and a roving microphone during the question-and-answer session, there is no convener. The atmosphere on stage is relaxed and the body language of Magee and Berry is open.

The *Facing the Enemy* performances can be seen as art projects in terms of their dialogical practice because they engage with the personal lived experiences of the speakers. This validates the speakers' utterances and the public can relate to their communication. So far, Berry and Magee have been invited to perform to communities in Europe and Africa engaging with conflict and post-conflict issues through various forums that bring together those who are working to alleviate such problems. In each location of their performance, their utterances take on a slightly different context. Although groups of words are repeated, they never constitute the exact same meaning, making a creative tension between repetition and innovation that is deeply involved in modern views of performance.[15] Because their work does not endorse a specific word-for-word repetition, it makes use of its live mode and it is distinctive every time it is performed and the cultural context changes. As Grant Kester says of 'conversation pieces' of this kind:

> In the exchange that follows, both the artist and his or her collabora- tors will have their existing perceptions challenged; the artist may well recognise relationships or connections that the community members have become inured to, while the collaborators will also challenge the artist's preconceptions about his or her own function as an artist. What emerges is a new set of insights, generated at the intersection of both perspectives and catalyzed through the collaborative production of a given project.[16]

It is interesting to note that the audience can resemble a temporary community engaging with conflict resolution, but also, in relation to this they can learn from the performance they are watching, and have the potential to propagate this learning throughout their lives, while interact- ing with other people they meet and future ideas and thoughts they may encounter on an individual level. Sarah Santino further considers that 'the concept of performativity is extended beyond simply that of enact- ment or performance to include a concept of social transformation'.[17]

Berry and Magee's utterances have the particular intention of pro- ducing the performance and the presumed or actual effect upon those who witness it. Merely by using language to tell their story constitutes the performance as a 'propositional act', because they want it to *do* something. They want it to account for their experience accurately and it is through such accuracy that their performance 'records or imparts straightforward information about the facts'.[18] Social transformation evident as a result of Berry and Magee's dialogue is postulated through the perceptions of Berry and Magee as they 'performatively' engage with a new set of perspectives. They want their perspective to facilitate change, while retaining their core identities through their process of communication. This is, in part, demonstrated when Magee explains how things changed for him:

> I went along to that first meeting [with Jo Berry] wearing a political hat through this feeling of obligation to explain. It was only during the course of it that I seen [sic] that there was more to it than that, coming face to face with the pain you've caused, but it was just that need to explain that was a political obligation that later turned into a very personal obligation.[19]

As an audience member, one is not experiencing the initial meeting Magee is discussing, but learning about it through a performative speech- act that can facilitate an observation of how Berry and Magee's personal conflict resolution began. This is evident through Magee's description of his change of attitude, which was prompted by his dialogue with Berry.

Magee has made explicit that each time they perform it is varied and that he and Berry do not repeat the exact same 'script', so that each time it is uttered differently. To highlight this in response to Magee's opening speech, Berry states, 'I have never heard it quite like that before.'[20]

These are performative statements because they are primarily engaging with an action of doing something rather than simply asserting something. Magee's direct response from his first meeting with Berry causes his obligations to transform from the political into the personal and this helps her to refigure a way through her feelings of bereavement and anger. Therefore the performativity of his language has begun to create conflict transformation on a personal level while in a public sphere.

As soon as this transformation is 'live on air' and performed on stage it then shifts into the realm of the observers. In this way, Berry and Magee's performance can be seen as a strategy to create an environment that can contribute to the resolution not only of Berry and Magee's conflict, but also of those of the communities who witness their performance. It is the action of performing itself that carries this information from the private to the public and potentially back to the private again. After Berry and Magee narrate their story they open up the floor so that the audience can question or comment, so their work is not only passively observed, but willingly participated in. All the while Berry and Magee use language as a performative tool to retain their core identities and they use the space of the stage to control how their identities are perceived through their viewers' gaze while telling of their personal lived experience.

Performing their dialogue can re-inform, challenge and rupture pre-existing understanding of the Brighton bombing. This may occur either by educating those who are ignorant or indifferent towards the conflict in Northern Ireland or by facilitating a shift in awareness. The performance helps members of the audience to gain new knowledge of the personal issues that are being grappled with by Berry and Magee. The staging of the performance in such a way creates space for those present to refigure a way through a tough issue by learning from those who have the moral agency to do it.

This notion of staging to create space could be seen as a formula similar to 'pre-negotiation' and 'circum-negotiation' or the 'gentle art of re-perceiving', to use Paul Arthur's description of the role of mediation.[21] So, it is the beginning of a process. In political terms, mediation is seen as a process that happens before a process of negotiation. By this definition, performance has the potential to negotiate conflict resolution because it mediates it by using the space of the stage to intervene.

It provides a literal space and a metaphorical space with a formalised integrity which adds to its sophisticated potential for conflict resolution.

Through the process of dialogue Berry and Magee are working with their conflict and are not expecting to find a final solution to their problems. Privately they establish a common ground as a result of confronting the conflicting issues of the past, while at the same time creating a common dialogue on stage which directly deals with a confrontation and fluidity of such factors. Their dialogue can facilitate this because it is a process of give and take and teasing out possibilities in a multi-faceted approach within the shifting boundaries of live performance. The only thing that is fixed about their performance is that they will be on stage in front of an audience. The personal responses of audience members to these confrontations are in a state of flux as Magee and Berry demonstrate that they accept the reality of no fixed solution. Moreover, it is by this very admission that the performance itself can act as a mode of reconciliation for those on stage and those in the audience.

> The paradox of performance itself, is that it is both old and new, double and singular, a formation and a transformation, a confirmation and a departure, an echoing and a propagation.[22]

The varied repetition of these performances allows them to continually readdress, re-present and resolve in contemporary contexts. It is not fixed and can never be final; Magee states that 'I lapse' and 'OK, I slide' when discussing his process of understanding, and Berry also states:

> If I had lived his [Magee's] life, I may have also decided that violence was the only way to be heard. I don't know ... there's that question mark. And in that knowing that I may have made the same choices ... then I came to thinking, well, there's absolutely nothing to forgive, because I totally understand and empathize. It was a one-off experience and I don't always live that you know, there are times when, I do judge Pat, I find it hard, you know, I don't always reach that point of understanding in me.[23]

Here it is evident that the process of understanding is not always constant, and not always able to be resolved. It is in this admission that performance can access a more valid conception of conflict resolution, because the process is a work in progress and not a single act. The *Facing the Enemy* performances allow conflict resolution to be a grappling, unobtainable process at times, one which does not look for a constant structure of implicit understanding between the two 'actors'. Yet, it is the structure of performance as a temporal phenomenon that facilitates this because it offers the space to allow for this fluidity.

Today, the tone of Magee's political argument is one of active resistance and it is easy to admire the consistency of his opposition to the British establishment. He recognises the establishment as having particular culpability with regard to the repression of the people of Northern Ireland and does not see forgiveness as a necessary prerequisite when it comes to building trust. Here in the live moment of presentation, his opinion is realised and the live mode 'enacts a challenge to established histories and categories of (performance) practice'.[24]

Magee states, 'I don't think I should be forgiven.'[25] Habermas's pragmatic theory of meaning posits that 'all speech acts and utterances are judged on their validity; therefore the meaning of a speech-act depends on its validity claim'.[26] Habermas considers three types of possible validity claims – to truth, to rightness and to truthfulness – that serve as various different ways to account for the verity of a statement, action or belief. Further, in his view, there are four different factors to understanding the meaning of an utterance. Firstly, the recognition of the literal meaning, that Magee does not think his action, as a legitimate 'act of war', requires forgiveness. Secondly, the assessment by the hearer of the speaker's intentions, which is that Magee intends to inform a public in England of his motivations so that they understand him as a person and, in response to this, alter their assumptions about him and understand the reasons for his use of violence. The latter potentially could be seen as retaliation to what he deems as crimes committed by the establishment. Thirdly, knowledge of the reasons which could be adduced to justify the utterance and its content; not that Magee does not feel remorse but that Berry's presence next to him justifies and attests to the fact that Magee's statement has validity. And finally, acceptance of those reasons, and hence the appropriateness of the utterance, is highlighted by the fact that Berry has accepted and continues to accept it, even though Magee's actions have caused her very bereavement. This therefore means that Magee's utterances are validated through his process of reconciliation with Berry. It is her presence on stage that offers him the moral authority to justify his statement. Without him, she would not be there, and without her, he would not be there; in this sense they have begun to work out a shared sense of identity. Berry's comments sit alongside Magee's as they themselves sit side by side on stage.

What is exceptional here, and afforded by the construct of performance, is that no audience member is coerced into accepting his utterance, but they do listen to it. It is the audience's act of listening, and therefore being able to ask difficult questions, which crystallises Berry and Magee's process of reconciliation. The presence of the audience is the lifeblood of this case study for conflict resolution. Additionally, this performance practice encourages the process of reconciliation through dialogue. Berry and Magee do not have to concede to facilitate each other, which is very important because it avoids judgements of right and wrong.

> Communication entails recognition of the other, and 'the awareness of being separate and different from and strange to one another' opens up potentials of creative search for dialogue and understanding of each other. This is also the essence of negotiations. Reaching common ground is not necessarily a product of similar opinions.[27]

Although common ground allows for differences of opinion, what is crucial is that Berry and Magee's performance allows them to negotiate just enough to accommodate the other but also to retain their core identity.

> If I say I forgive Pat then I'm keeping him as the enemy ... Yes on one level it'd be much easier for Pat if he could say, Yes, I was wrong, violence was wrong, but this is real, he's grappling with real issues and that grappling for me, is the fuel for change, showing us the reality.[28]
> [Jo's] not sharing a platform with me because I changed my mind! She's sharing a platform with me, knowing that the core of my views haven't changed. She's demonstrating this willingness to meet and seeing that as a template for the resolution of conflict, broadly, generally, that's the significance.[29]

If Magee had changed his mind, there would not be the opportunity to develop understanding. So, by observing Berry and Magee's relationship during the performance, a deeper understanding of Magee's political motivations is facilitated. Magee's voice is heard and not only that, but it is willingly listened to by Berry and the audience present. Magee and Berry have not coerced each other into agreement or disagreement, and so by participating in a dialogical collaboration with them through being present as an audience member, the listener is not coerced into agreement or disagreement either, and possibly audience members' perceptions are beginning to be challenged because Berry recognises Magee's political motivations by being present with him on stage. It is Berry's presence that attests Magee's morality. He wouldn't be able to make a presentation about his past without her present. The formality of the performance permits the action, of what Berry describes as a 'suspension of judgment'.[30] This means that the formal theatrical convention of being a present yet silent audience member is very important. Nick Crossley writes:

> What makes dialogue so crucial is that it not only precedes a communicative exchange, in the form of turn-taking, but also that it is guided by the mutual expectation of uptake; that its speakers offer reasons to each other

and expect that others will consider their reasons or concerns at least to
the extent that their speech acts contribute to shaping the ongoing course
of the interaction, without anyone exerting control over it or having special
status.[31]

The question-and-answer session creates lateral connections between
performer and audience member within the parameters of performance-
making. For example, when an audience member states:

> I admire your courage at getting up here, but I don't think you're moving
> this thing on very far ... all you're saying is, I understand you, I can listen
> to you, I hear you, but you're not shifting at all.[32]

This example demonstrates that the audience member thinks it is necessary for Magee to attempt to excuse his former political motivations to
create resolution, so in the mind of the audience member, Magee has to
change his core political values for considerable progress to be attained.
If Magee did this he would not be actually shifting anything, despite
admitting that he was wrong and the audience member was right.
Yet, this is exactly what would slow down progress because it would
entrench existing identities, rather than refiguring new ones. The listener's mind would become weighted to their preconceived assumptions,
resulting in a polarisation between their views and Magee's views and
identity, whereas 'the primary feature of the identity change constituting
reconciliation is the removal of the negation of the other as a central
component of one's own identity'.[33] This means that in Magee's case he
should not negate himself and request forgiveness or make an apology
and in the audience member's case he should accept that Magee's motivation is, in part, that of the audience member too.

Public perceptions are directly challenged if the audience are prepared
to listen to performative utterances. The audience have the *ability* to
contest the statements of Berry and Magee. This allows confrontation
without oppression and prejudice and allows for Magee to examine
himself rather than being examined by another as, quite simply, 'if
we defend our own opinions we are not going to be able to have a
dialogue'.[34] It is through open-ended dialogue that a process of reconciliation can essentially take place between Magee and the audience
members. For, 'when a word is uttered it is not merely an individual's
identity that has been invoked, but also a social and historical whole
through which the utterance has been mediated and through which it
has gained a specific evaluation'.[35]

Here, every utterance is deemed to have an origin elsewhere, or some
point of reference that precedes it. The point of dialogue is that it goes

into all the pressures that are behind our assumptions, not just the assumptions themselves, and so dialogue is attempting to get to the root of the social and historical whole described above. If this performance is able to challenge assumptions, and transform opinion, it must cut through preconceived ideas and come to something new, as performer and audience head further into a more considered, more justified, more truthfully informed perception of their experience of the conflict. As Heidegger has suggested, 'It ... might be helpful to us to rid ourselves of the habit of only hearing what we already understand',[36] because 'reconciliation does require admitting the other's truth into one's own narrative'.[37] Magee's political motivations are in part accepted by Berry and he doesn't have to use his political past to justify his actions. They work together on a level of humanity to gain their understanding of each other. It is a process whereby they mutually recognise each other's perspective while retaining their own.

Conclusion

'Forgiveness is done when we no longer care whether or not it is done.'[38] In *Facing The Enemy*, the need for forgiveness as a precursor to conflict resolution is abandoned. In this sense Berry and Magee help to refigure the notion of resolution by negotiating another way through the problems. Through this, the action of listening is advocated to reach an understanding of the issues of the other person. As illustrated by the performance practice of *Facing the Enemy*, if ex-political prisoners apologise to their victims this may hinder the process of conflict resolution in the context of Northern Ireland by encouraging the polarisation of identities. The process that facilitates all reconciliation is dialogue, and by allowing each individual the space to participate in a considered, formal way, adhering to formal conventions of a theatre space, dialogue creates a fluid relationship – in this case between Berry, Magee and their audience – built on willingness, presence and honesty. It is the mediating role of performance that enables this unique connection to exist and creates the space for new identities to unfold.

Notes

1 J. Bercovitch (ed.), *The Sage Handbook of Conflict Resolution* (London: Sage, 2009), p. 558.
2 J. Thompson, *Performance in Place of War* (Calcutta: Seagull Books, 2009), Preface.

3 Derry's Theatre of Witness, for instance, incorporates several drama-based conflict resolution programmes in cross-community contexts.

4 C. M. Cole, 'Performance, transitional justice, and the law: South Africa's Truth and Reconciliation Commission', *Theatre Journal*, 59:2 (2007), 178

5 C. Farrington, *Global Change, Civil Society and the Northern Ireland Peace Process* (London: Palgrave Macmillan, 2008), p. 132.

6 H. H. Saunders, 'Dialogue as a process for transforming relationships', in J. Bercovitch (ed.) *Sage Handbook of Conflict Resolution* (London: Sage, 2009), pp. 376–8.

7 D. G. Pruitt, 'Experimental research on social conflict', in J. Bercovitch (ed.) *Sage Handbook of Conflict Resolution* (London: Sage, 2009), p. 112.

8 J. Tonge, *Northern Ireland* (Cambridge: Polity Press, 2006), p. 53.

9 *Beyond Right and Wrong: Stories of Justice and Forgiveness* (DVD, 2012 Article 19 Films, New York).

10 J. Berry, e-mail correspondence with the author, 25 August 2010.

11 M. Cantacuzino, 'Beyond right and wrong, how film became a peaceful revolution', *Huffington Post* (18 February 2014), www.huffingtonpost.com/marina-cantacuzino/beyond-right-wrong-how-a-_b_4810106.html (Accessed 20 October 2014).

12 Patrick Magee, in *Beyond Right and Wrong*, DVD.

13 Jo Berry, in ibid.

14 Jo Berry, in ibid.

15 M. Carlson, *Performance, A Critical Introduction* (London: Routledge, 1996), p. 58.

16 G. Kester, *Conversation Pieces* (USA: University of California Press, 2004), p. 95.

17 S. Brady, *Crossroads: Performance and Irish Culture* (London: Palgrave Macmillan, 2009), p. 15.

18 J. L. Austin, *How to Do Things with Words* (Cambridge, MA: Harvard University Press, 2nd edition 1975), p. 2.

19 P. Magee, Talk delivered at St James' Church, Piccadilly [audio recording] London, 29 March 2010.

20 J. Berry, Talk delivered at St James' Church, Piccadilly [audio recording] London, 29 March 2010.

21 P. Arthur, '"Quiet diplomacy and personal conversation": Track two diplomacy and the search for a settlement in Northern Ireland', in J. Ruane and J. Todd (eds) *After the Good Friday Agreement: Analysing Political Change in Northern Ireland* (Dublin: University College Dublin Press, 1999), p. 73.

22 S. Gareis, G. Schöllhammer and P. Weibel (eds), *Moments: A History of Performance in 10 Acts* (Cologne: Walther König, 2013), p. 186.

23 J. Berry and P. Magee, Talk delivered at St James' Church, Piccadilly [audio recording] London, 29 March 2010.

24 D. Hedden, *Histories and Practices of Live Art* (London: Palgrave Macmillan, 2012), p. 175.

25 P. Magee, Talk delivered at St James' Church, Piccadilly [audio recording] London, 29 March 2010.

26 J. Finlayson, *Habermas, A Very Short Introduction* (Oxford: Oxford University Press, 2005), p. 39.
27 S. Sofer, cited in P. Arthur, '"Quiet Diplomacy and Personal Conversation"', p. 77.
28 J. Berry, Talk delivered at St James' Church, Piccadilly [audio recording] London, 29 March 2010.
29 P. Magee, Talk delivered at St James' Church, Piccadilly [audio recording] London, 29 March 2010.
30 J. Berry, Talk delivered at St James' Church, Piccadilly [audio recording] London, 29 March 2010.
31 N. Crossley, *After Habermas; New perspectives on the Public Sphere* (Oxford: Blackwell, 2004), p. 133.
32 Audience member, Talk delivered at St James' Church, Piccadilly [audio recording] London, 29 March 2010.
33 Y. Bar-Siman-Tov, *From Conflict Resolution to Reconciliation* (Oxford: Oxford University Press, 2004), p. 119.
34 D. Bohm, *On Dialogue* (London: Routledge, 1996), p. 11.
35 Crossley, *After Habermas*, p. 77.
36 G. Fiumara, *The Other Side of Language* (London: Routledge, 1990), p. 38.
37 Bar-Siman-Tov, *From Conflict Resolution to Reconciliation*, p. 123.
38 T. Swan, www.askteal.com/videos/introverts-and-extroverts (Accessed 22 October 2014).

Index

Full names for abbreviations/acronyms used in subheadings can be found by looking up index entry for that abbreviation/acronym. Names commencing 'Mc' are arranged in the index as if 'Mac'. Page numbers in italics refer to illustrative material in tables, figures and photographs. An 'n' following a page number indicates the number of the note on that page.